# WEST INDIAN FAMILY STRUCTURE

A Monograph from the Research Institute for the
Study of Man

# WEST
# INDIAN
# FAMILY
# STRUCTURE

## By M. G. Smith

UNIVERSITY OF WASHINGTON PRESS
SEATTLE 1962

Published with the cooperation of the
Research Institute for the Study of Man
Vera Rubin, Director

# Acknowledgment

The various field studies on which this monograph is based were undertaken while I was on the staff of the Institute of Social and Economic Research of the University College of the West Indies. To both these bodies, I am greatly indebted for the research opportunities which they provided.

I am also grateful to Dr. Vera Rubin, Director of the Research Institute for the Study of Man in the Tropics, for the support which has enabled the monograph to appear in its present form. Without its battery of tables and diagrams, the text would be seriously weakened; but inclusion of these materials increased the difficulties and costs of printing.

For help in typing the text, I am grateful to my wife, and for typing the numerous tables with great patience to Mrs. Flora Miles of the Institute of Social and Economic Research, University College of the West Indies. Dr. Verne F. Ray, former editor of the American Ethnological Society, has edited the kinship charts with special care, and I wish to thank him for many detailed comments and improvements.

M. G. Smith,
University of California
At Los Angeles

# Contents

▓▓▓▓▓▓▓▓▓▓▓

# WEST
# INDIAN
# FAMILY
# STRUCTURE

⊠⊠⊠⊠⊠⊠⊠⊠⊠⊠

# 1. Introduction

In the following chapters I shall analyze the domestic organization of sample populations in certain West Indian societies. I shall try to extract principles which govern family relations among the populations under study from data on mating and household composition. I call these regulatory principles family structure. From the given facts of domestic grouping and mating practice I shall try to derive the principles of family structure in each sample. I shall then compare the family structure and domestic forms of these different samples in an attempt to establish the quality and degree of their variation, and to determine its bases. In this way I hope to discover whether or not the family organizations of selected West Indian populations are variants of a common system. I also wish to explore the utility of quantitative analyses of household data for the understanding and comparison of family structures.

In this chapter I shall first describe the samples and survey methods on which these studies are based. I shall then consider certain problems which invest studies of family organization based on household composition data. These problems are in part conceptual, but not wholly so. I shall therefore discuss those field conditions which sometimes present difficulties in the study of domestic organization, and I shall try to show how these can be dealt with. Following this, I shall indicate some of the analytic questions which will occupy us in each study, and in conclusion I shall try to define the concept of family structure more explicitly.

The Units of Analysis

The units of analysis and comparison are a series of five samples which I studied in 1953 and 1955. These household samples were drawn from Carriacou, Grenada, and Jamaica. The data on Grenada and Carriacou were collected in 1953. The Carriacou sample

3

contained 224 households; in Grenada I studied an aggregate of 215 households in two quite dissimilar types of community, one urban, the other rural. These two Grenadian samples will therefore be analyzed separately. My Jamaican data were collected in 1955. They also represent samples of two quite different types of community, and they are therefore analyzed separately. During a study of labor conditions in the peasant areas of Jamaica in 1955 I was able to make studies of 1, 015 households in eight rural districts selected by the Director of Statistics, Jamaica. Later that year I studied a systematic sample of 425 households in Kingston, the capital of Jamaica—the Department of Statistics, Jamaica, having kindly supplied me with a sample frame. With the exception of this Kingston sample, all other surveys in this series were censuses of defined localities.

The Carriacou aggregate of 224 households consists of four area samples and contains about one seventh of the island's populations. I began by studying seventy-five households at L'Esterre, where I was living, and then arranged for schoolteachers, whom I had trained carefully, to study fifty households each in three other villages, one lying in each quarter of the island. [1] Owing to an unfortunate oversight, only forty-nine households were studied in one of these villages. Checks revealed no inaccuracies in the information supplied by these assistants.

The two Grenadian communities discussed below were selected for comparison as instances of differing types of Grenadian community. One was a community of peasants, while the other lay in an urban area and contained a population of laborers and tenants. Both sample populations belonged to the lowest socioeconomic level of Grenadian society. The natives of Carriacou occupy a similar position in the colonial social system. Carriacou, a tiny island of thirteen square miles, is administered as a District of the Grenada Government, but it differs profoundly from Grenada in its economy, society, culture, and political organization. As we shall see, these differences include family structure.

The eight areas which I studied in rural Jamaica were selected by the Director of Statistics, Jamaica, who describes the sample as follows:

The eight areas defined for use in connection with the study of rural labour supply constitute a systematic sample of rural areas of which there are some 2, 000 in the island. All main towns including the metropolitan area of Kingston were excluded. The sample was selected so as to give approximately balanced representation of the interior mountain range, the limestone plateau and the coastal plains; to represent conditions of proximity to sugar estates or industrial production, and relative isolation from such influences; and, arising from the above, to represent areas of agricultural labour "shortage," and areas of adequate agricultural labour supply (on small and medium-sized farms).[2]

In other words, these eight areas provide a systematic sample of Jamaican peasants. The great majority of the population in each district consisted of smallholders and their dependents. Of the eight districts studied, six lay above 1,000 feet and two were situated within two miles of sugar estates.

In the survey of these eight districts I was assisted by two men whom I trained for a fortnight in the necessary techniques and methods. These assistants made diagrams of household composition from their notes of household membership at the end of each day. I was thus able to check their work by visits to the households which I had not myself enumerated. A full account of the methods and results of this survey has already been published.[3]

The sample from which my subsample of 425 Kingston households was taken had initially been constructed by the Department of Statistics, Jamaica, for use in their 1953 population survey. This original sample was later stratified and subdivided for the Kingston area so as to exclude middle- and upper-income households, who represented roughly 15 per cent of those in the capital. The remaining sample is therefore representative of lower-income, working-class households. The units of this sample were distributed in different parts of the city in proportions which corresponded to the distribution and density of working-class homes. As the Director of Statistics points out, my subsample is "representative of the working class population of the metropolitan area in all important respects."[4] As in Grenada, the rural and urban population studied in Jamaica belonged to the same socioeconomic level and to the same "social class." They are thus directly comparable with one another and with their Grenadian counterparts.

In the field survey of Kingston households I had three assistants, all of whom had received a week's training solely in the study of household composition. Field work lasted three weeks and field checks covered one in ten of the households studied by each enumerator. This survey was carried out in December, 1955. In March that year the Department of Statistics, Jamaica, had used the subsample which they allocated to me in an inquiry into housing conditions and rents among the urban lower class. By design, the units of this sample were dwelling places and rooms rather than individuals and domestic groups. The frame which was given to me by the Department of Statistics consisted, therefore, of a series of diagrams specifying the rooms in each dwelling place which belonged to the sample, together with their occupants in March, 1955. By checking my list of occupants compiled in December of that year, it is thus possible to calculate the minimum volume of residential mobility among this urban working class; and in the analysis of their household organization it is clearly important to have this knowledge.

These five samples are therefore drawn from the non-East Indian Negroid working- or lower-class folk of Carriacou, Grenada, and Jamaica. They include two urban samples, two peasant samples, and one, the population of which depends heavily on seafaring and emigration. Despite cultural variations among these sample populations, they occupy similar social positions and share a similar folk culture. They are therefore directly comparable with one another, but not with the elite classes of the societies to which they belong. They may also be quite different from the sugar plantation workers in their family organization; recent work by Miss Edith Clarke in Jamaica indicates that there are marked differences in family organization between peasant and plantation populations. [5]

The Use of Household Data in Family Studies

It has been a common practice for writers to generalize about West Indian family organization on the basis of acquaintance with a limited area. [6] Thus far no one has tried to find out whether the family systems of different West Indian populations conform to a single model or not. For this reason it seems premature to generalize about the Caribbean or West Indian family. However, the comparative study of family organization among West Indian populations may be necessary on other grounds also. Perhaps it is only by such comparative work that we can hope to test or develop hypotheses about the structure of family relations in this area.

The pioneer studies of West Indian family organization suffer from certain defects. In place of structural analyses or careful field studies, they tend to offer competing historical explanations of the origin of West Indian family forms. Only recently have detailed quantitative studies of family organization among West Indians been published. [7] With these publications, West Indian family studies have become transformed. They are no longer hypothetical illustrations of African cultural persistence or the aftereffects of slavery; such diachronic speculations have been replaced by emphasis on synchronic analyses of these family systems.

In his study of the Negro family in British Guiana, Dr. Raymond Smith formulated a significant hypothesis which can be tested by comparative materials. Briefly, Dr. Smith says that the variety of domestic forms among the Negro population of British Guiana represents different stages in the development of the domestic elementary family from which all these household groups are derived.[8] He goes on to characterize this system of domestic family relations as a "matrifocal" one in which the males are marginal. He concludes by suggesting that male marginality and matrifocality are common consequences of the low position of these Negro populations in the Guianese status system and socioeconomic structure.[9] In a subsequent paper, he extends this system of hypotheses to the West Indian Negro populations as a whole.[10] Dr. Smith's hypotheses are of great value in that they focus attention on important problems of West Indian society, and do so in a way which permits and calls for empirical tests and investigation. Whether these hypotheses are valid or not, they present a basis and framework for further studies. In this book I shall attempt to test Dr. Raymond Smith's propositions and to carry the analysis further.

In her study of family relations among the Jamaican folk, Miss Edith Clarke does not formulate a set of hypotheses explicitly. However, she does indicate an important set of covariations in family structure and economic context. By comparing a sugar proletariat with two peasant communities, one prosperous and the other impoverished, she shows that domestic organization varies in association with other social and economic conditions. In our five samples there is also a considerable variety of economic and social context; we shall therefore be able to discuss the covariation which Miss Clarke has pointed out, as well as the hypotheses set up by Dr. Smith. However, before we start to analyze the household sample, we should consider its relation to family structure.

Field studies of West Indian family organization are forced to rely heavily on household composition data in view of the lack of reliable explicit rules about family relations. In consequence the household is usually regarded as the fundamental family form and as the unit appropriate for the analysis of family relations. Family relations are then discussed with the individual household as their central unit, and are consequently circumscribed within the frame of domestic organization.

Such an approach combines two basic errors. First, as will be shown, family organization is neither homologous with nor reducible to domestic relations. Second, the appropriate unit for the study of family relations is not the individual household but the total population of sample households. By reference to household composition alone we cannot understand the principles which govern the constitution of domestic groups. To account for the form of any particular household group, or for the frequencies of different domestic forms, we must study their relations with other units and elements in the system represented by the total sample. This is most obvious in households based on conjugal pairs, but it also applies to units the members of which mate with persons living elsewhere and to households which contain half-siblings or the children of noncohabiting parents. Granted incest prohibitions within elementary families, the frequencies of different domestic forms will naturally reflect the mating relations of their past and present members, and in consequence the constitutions of separate domestic groups will be functionally interdependent. Moreover, given a certain set of mating and family patterns, then within clearly defined demographic and socioeconomic limits, the frequency distributions of domestic groups of differing form will tend to be fixed and will express common principles which regulate family relations between the members of different households, as well as within them. These principles are immediately obvious when they redistribute the adult or junior members of domestic groups; but they also operate to preserve or modify unit structures in other ways.

A domestic unit only exists separately when the relations among its members are different from those which they maintain with persons elsewhere, but these differences are not accidents, they are central to the analysis and understanding of the particular unit's structure. The differences may be due to alternative forms of mating or parenthood, or to differences in the relations between collaterals related through men and women. Any changes in the local kinship context of the members of an individual household are therefore liable to modify the household group to which they belong. Clearly, the development of the individual life cycle is a constant source of such change, especially in its kinship aspects.

Apart from such socioeconomic conditions as migration, the interhousehold movement of adults tends to exhibit the influence of conjugal and consanguine ties, and these are also important in governing the residential distribution of children. The simple fact that mating relations may take alternative forms, and that all these alternatives influence the constitution of linked household groups, will show that familial and domestic relations are by no means coterminous, and that the former cannot be reduced to the latter. It follows that the appropriate unit for the analysis of family relations is the total population of a household sample rather than the constituent households themselves.

Some interhousehold relations hold between households as integral units; others are purely dyadic and hold between individuals who live in separate households; yet other relations link one or more members of two or more households. The constitution, boundary, and position of any individual household within this field will accordingly be defined by its interhousehold relations; and in the same way that changes which originate within the household group independently will normally involve changes in its external relations, so too will changes originating in these external relations be often accompanied by changes in the unit's structure. It is easy to see that these external developments may lead to the unit's dissolution and its partial or complete absorption in others nearby. Consequently we cannot adequately explain the form of a domestic group ontogenetically, since its development expresses its interdependence with like units in a common social field. Since family relations precede, envelope, and outlast the individual units of domestic organization, influencing their internal structure and growth alike, households are inadequate as units for the final analysis of family relations, and we cannot therefore describe or explain family structure by means of hypotheses about their growth and development. We may explain the form and development of household groups by the principles of family structure, and since we must derive these principles by the analysis of domestic groups, we can use the data on household composition to verify or illustrate them; but we cannot reduce these principles of family structure entirely to the level of domestic organization. Moreover, in extracting these structural principles from the household composition data presented by our samples, the appropriate units are the total samples rather than their constituent households.

## Family Forms and Structure

It is important to distinguish domestic organization, family types, and family structure before proceeding. In the 1951 edition of *Notes and Queries in Anthropology,* a committee of distinguished anthropologists attempt to define the family and to distinguish the various kinship groups to which this term refers. The writers begin their discussion by acknowledging the imprecision of this term.

The need to define the varieties of family is evident when the use of the word in English is analysed. In common English parlance the word "family" may be used to mean (a) the group composed of parents and children; (b) a patrilineal lineage; (c) a roughly defined cognatic group frequently including affines; (d) a group of relatives and their dependents constituting one household. . . . The first duty of the investigator is to discover by exact methods

the type or types of social group existent in the society which he is inves-
tigating. For this purpose further definitions are necessary. . . . *The elementary or simple family* is a group composed of a father and a mother
and their children, whether they are living together or not. . . *compound
families* are (a) polygynous, a group consisting of a man and two or more
wives and their children; (b) polyandrous, a group consisting of a woman
with two or more husbands and their children: (c) a group formed by the
remarriage of a widow or widower, having children by a former marriage.
. . . The family in this sense is based on marriage, which is defined as a
union between a man and a woman such that children borne by the woman
are recognised as the legitimate offspring of both partners. . . . Enquiries
into the type of family will entail others into the homestead or domicile.
The constitution of the *domestic family*, i. e. the family customarily occupying one homestead, should be ascertained. [11]

The variety of meanings and groups denoted by the word "family"
creates special difficulties for the analysis of family relations.
Following the distinctions made by this Committee of the Royal
Anthropological Institute, we shall have to deal with (1) *the elementary family*, "a group composed of parents and children": (2)
*the bilateral extended family*, "a roughly defined cognatic group,
frequently including affines": (3) *the domestic family*, "a group of
relatives and their dependents constituting one household": and
(4) *compound families*, which arise from successive unions or
marriages of widows, widowers, divorced, or informally separated parents. The interrelations of these several levels and
forms of family relations constitute the family structure in which
we are interested. This family structure is based on the principles
which regulate relations within as well as between the elementary,
compound, domestic, and bilateral extended families of a given
population.

Of these four forms or levels of family relations, only one, the
domestic family, can possibly be equated conceptually with the
household units which provide the main body of our data. It follows
that household composition data alone cannot provide an adequate
account of the family structure. They must be supplemented by
other sorts of information. Moreover, since "the family in this
sense is based on marriage," this supplementary information must
include a detailed account of the mating system.

Household and Family

Before pursuing the relations between family structure and domestic organization further, it is necessary to define the household
and to discuss its relations with other levels of family organization.

In this context, we may also consider some of the problems which confront field studies of household composition.

A household consists of those persons who habitually share a common shelter and food. Thus, the household is not necessarily homologous with any of the family forms just distinguished, not even with the domestic family. In any West Indian community we will find a number of households which consist of one person apiece. In most communities we will also find households consisting of unrelated persons or groups of persons. Both the single-person household and the rarer type which contains unrelated persons are nonfamilial units; but the incidence and characteristics of these nonfamilial units must enter into the analysis of family structure in populations of which they are part, since the isolation or association of these persons are domestic alternatives governed by other factors in the family system.

In addition many households which contain cohabiting couples do not contain elementary families. Some of these households contain no descendants of their mating principals. Many consist of these mates alone; others which include some children of either or both mates by former unions, may be regarded as compound families. In other cases these households may include collateral, affinal, or adopted kin of either or both mating principals, with or without some of their children by former unions. In none of these cases will the household be homologous with an elementary family, and in most of them the household group has not developed from a domestic elementary family.

All households are domestic units, it is true; but not every domestic unit is a domestic family, and domestic families themselves differ quite widely in their kinship structure, some units containing elementary families, while others contain compound families or segments of bilateral extended families, and yet others contain other structurally distinct groups. The relative frequency with which we find these different types of domestic groups within a given population exemplifies the operation of the structural principles which govern family relations among them, and provides us with materials necessary for the definition and analysis of these regulatory principles.

Field and Analytic Problems

The analysis of family structure is thus quite complex and presupposes a comprehensive body of precise data. Unless the field data are sufficiently detailed and comprehensive, several opera-

tions essential for this analysis cannot be undertaken. On the other
hand, an incomplete analysis of the family structure can hardly
explain the domestic organization correctly; nor can it permit us
to see whether these relations do form a system of any type. It
is especially important that we should have comprehensive data
in order that we may be able to assess the degree to which these
relations do form a system, simply because the methods of analysis assume that the materials have the properties and limitations
of a single system of some type.

These cautions are pertinent. Various authorities have simply
written off the West Indian family as chaotic and disorganized. [12]
Others have accepted this disorganization as a fact and sought to
account for it by slavery or by the persistence of Africanisms in
a modified form. [13] I would suggest that the characterization of
West Indian family relations as "chaotic" or "systematic" should
await analyses based on sufficiently comprehensive materials to
provide an accurate model.

In such culturally heterogeneous societies as the West Indies,
we cannot expect informants to provide reliable generalizations
about family forms or relations. Quite apart from variations between "social classes" in this particular, it is difficult to determine
the typical "class" patterns themselves. Individual variability
seems at first glance the rule rather than the exception. Whether
this rule itself reflects some systematic principles of organization,
the layman can hardly tell us, nor can the analyst unless his data
are complete. To be complete, these data must include information
on the age, birth status, marital condition, and history and kinship
interrelations of the members of the household populations studied.
In addition we need sufficient information about the general socioeconomic situation and history of these populations to define their
position within the territorial society. Such socioeconomic information as occupational distribution, household resources, migration
careers, interhousehold kinship and social relations are therefore
necessary. These socioeconomic data serve to define the sample
populations but do not form part of the family analysis. Similarly,
a knowledge of the domestic economy and of the distribution of
domestic roles is necessary in these field studies; but such information has little place in a structural analysis designed to show
how groups of various sorts having particular frequencies arise
and develop. Since all forms of domestic groups must have an
economy, it follows that economic organization alone neither dic-
tates nor qualifies their form.

The numerous variables with which our analysis has to deal

impose certain problems and conditions on the exposition. Analytic complexity enjoins a quantitative treatment, since it is only by trying to relate frequency distributions of various kinds that we can determine the structural principles at work and assess their relative significance for the system as a whole. Moreover, only this type of treatment enables us to see whether the raw materials do or do not reveal a systematic order.

We shall therefore have to isolate various elements or conditions in a number of separate tables, rather than rely on one or two large compilations. Bearing in mind our comparative purpose, we must employ a constant method of analysis for each sample.

## The Boundaries of Household Units

Households are units, the members of which eat and dwell together as a rule. Normally those persons who maintain a common domestic economy and occupy a common dwelling share common productive resources and liabilities, but this need not always be the case.

Problems of household membership and boundary definition arise when an individual sleeps in one place and eats regularly at another; or when a visitor retains membership in a separate domestic unit while entering fully into the life of his host's household. Some domestic employees live on their employer's premises without the status of full household members, and many of these people remain principals of households situated elsewhere. We sometimes find households which do not contain the persons on whose economic contributions these units depend. Some of these absent contributors make their remittances as an obligation of continuing membership; others are clearly not members and may never have lived in the home. This corpus of variation is interesting but manageable. We have to adopt a uniform rule and specify it. In the following studies, I have included as household members all persons who resided for four or more days of the previous week within the units surveyed. I have excluded all who did not.

The circumstances in which the definition of household boundaries becomes formidable are happily rare. A woman may cook for and wash the clothes of a mate or relative who lives elsewhere. These services may be completely noncommercial. If the recipient is the woman's mate, he may also sleep at her home frequently, and will probably take his meals there as a rule. If the man lives by himself and maintains such relations with his mate, it is difficult to decide whether or not they form a common household; but if he lives in a unit with other persons, he must be regarded as belonging to their household despite his marginal position within it. Fortunately that combination of circumstances which is most difficult to handle is extremely rare among the populations studied.

Household Headship

Another feature of household organization which may present important problems in field work and analysis alike is the identification of the household head and the definition of headship roles. In her study of the Jamaican family, Miss Edith Clarke, for instance, has attempted to set up a typology of domestic groups and to analyze their structure without reference to household headship or household heads. [14] In Miss Clarke's view, headship is an imprecise status and household heads are difficult to identify objectively. With this view I cannot agree; and since the analytic problems which arise out of this issue are important to family studies, I shall discuss them in some detail. In my view, the difficulties which definition of headship or the identification of household heads present vary as a function of the different structural positions and forms of household units within as well as between societies; but the systematic analysis of household composition and the comparison of unit samples presupposes the accurate identification of household heads by uniform criteria.

The status, role, and requisite characteristics of the household head vary cross-culturally in many respects, and so does the household unit itself. Among nomadic and seminomadic populations, households are less exclusive and less clearly differentiated units than is usually the case among sedentary populations, but under modern urban conditions, households rarely retain the lifelong allegiance of their core members, and although at any moment they usually have definite boundaries, they remain liable to rapid structural change.

In some societies, such as those of the Muslim Hausa, all households have male heads and these household heads are usually of senior age and status. In such societies the household heads may be directly responsible to the local rulers for the care and conduct of their dependents. Under such circumstances, the status and role of the household head receives explicit political recognition and support. For this reason the definition of requisite characteristics of household heads is uniform and clear, and the transfer or assumption of headship is a matter of public interest.

In other societies, such as those of the British Caribbean, government and the law deal with adults individually, irrespective of their household position. In consequence, the status and role of the household head normally lacks political recognition. The law in such societies defines the individual obligation of adult persons for minors, invalids, or other kin, by reference to such relations as parenthood, filiation, or adoption, without mention of household organization. Nevertheless, even in societies of this type, the status and role of the household head remain important in view of the organizational and familial functions of this unit. At the same time the conditions of headship and the characteristics of household heads are naturally more variable, since they lack uniform and explicit definition. Even so, these roles are not difficult to define, nor are their performers difficult to identify.

We may begin by making a distinction between the principal and dependent members of household groups. Dependents are those members of household groups who do not exercise leadership roles. Most dependents will be junior members, but many are persons of quite senior age. *Principals* are the leaders of the household group, and they may include the head's adult children or resident mate. An absent mate or child whose contributions serve to maintain the group is an absent principal. The household head is *ipso facto* a principal, and in many units the only one. There is no necessary limit to the number of household principals or dependents, although naturally there can be only one head in each household. Principals are distinguished from dependents by their capacity to take independent action which may entail changes in group structure, for example, by their secession.

Among West Indian folk, domestic groups whose principals are conjugal partners usually have male heads. However, this is not always the case, and since the correct analysis and classification of household groups by reference to relations between their members and heads presupposes a correct identification of the heads, it is important to define the conditions under which the normal distribution of this role does or does not hold.

The household head is that person whom the community as well as the household members regard as the head of the domestic group. In addition, the head tends to assert headship whenever necessary. Domestic units based on cohabitation may have female heads if the male partner is ill, incapacitated, or otherwise dependent, socially and economically, on the woman; if for example the woman owns the homestead and the unit's principal resources; or if the man is a recent immigrant to the community and lacks nearby kin, while his partner has kin nearby, and her issue by former unions in the home, often with some of her collaterals as well.

Even these latter circumstances do not automatically entail the woman's headship. However, they undoubtedly represent conditions favorable for her dominance, and in such situations she may be formally recognized as head of the house. Such formal recognition reflects the consensus of community and household members alike, including of course the household principals.

It sometimes happens that a woman who is the dominant member of a household is not formally recognized as its head. Dominance and headship are quite distinct, and this distinction must be carefully observed if our analysis of household organization and conjugal relations is to be useful. Headship is formal leadership and entails formal responsibility. Dominance is actual influence but does not entail corresponding responsibility as a matter of course. The dominant individual, by virtue of dominance, can avoid certain responsibilities. The household head, as head, cannot. The matrifocality which Raymond Smith noticed in Guianese households incorporates strong elements of female dominance. The distinctions which he makes between the marginal and central positions of males and females in the domestic unit are really based on differences between dominance and headship. Edith Clarke, facing the same problem in Jamaica, abandoned the concept of household headship and so avoided the antithesis between male marginality and matrifocality.

In practice there are only two recurrent conditions under which dominance and headship are often separated in domestic units. Both conditions are transitional and mark stages in the development of the household group. One of these is conjugal in character. For example, a childless couple who live in a homestead rented or owned by the woman, and who are economically dependent on her may nonetheless have the man as head. The converse also occurs; we occasionally find a childless couple under a female head although the man is the mainstay of the domestic unit. In both these cases the person formally recognized as the household head is not its dominant member; and in either case if cohabitation continues it is likely that dominance and headship will coincide. In short, the separation of headship and dominance in such units reflects the partners' uncertainty about the future of their conjugal union. Although headship and dominance are analytically distinct, they commonly coincide in units of a stable structure. Clearly, the separation of headship and dominance indicates structural instability, and if this continues for long the unit is likely to dissolve. The divergent distributions of headship and dominance mark transitions in the relations among household principals. These transitions occur between consanguine as well as conjugal kin. As already mentioned, a woman may be dominant economically and socially although her husband or mate remains head of the unit. Such dominant women usually possess independent sources of income, whether from marketing, farming, or gifts, and they may have their children or grandchildren by other unions in the home. Usually the male partner in such a union is in his physical and economic decline, and it is clear that the woman will shortly have formal control of the home and its resources. Contrariwise, widows normally continue as household heads although their resident adult children may dominate and maintain the unit. Occasionally these children may bring their wed or unwed mates to live in the home. This situation is also clearly transitional. Like that in which the woman assumes leadership in her partner's decline, it anticipates the development of the household group which is shortly expected and which will consist in a transfer of headship through the death or departure of the head. Unless bedridden or otherwise incapacitated, widows retain formal headship despite dependence on their resident children, since the alternative is incompatible with the kinship roles of mother and child. Likewise, unless incapacitated or insecurely mated, men retain formal headship, however dependent they are on their mates, since the alternative is incompatible with the principle of male precedence which regulates relations between the sexes at this level of West Indian society.

In most households and for most of their duration, dominance and headship coincide, but the criteria for the determination of headship are simpler than those which indicate dominance. As a formal status, headship has clearly defined rights and responsibilities; but dominance is an interpersonal condition with variable social, economic, affectual, or other foundations. A head who is not the dominant member of his household remains formally responsible for the headship roles; and the dominant members of this household exercise their influence through rather than against him. With households, as with other social groups, formal structure persists despite informal divergence.

The Role of the Household Head

In defining the role of the household head among West Indian folk, we must allow for differences in the sex of the head, in the structure of the household, and in its urban or rural situation. Even with these differences there is a large common element in the roles of household heads.

In rural areas the household head generally owns or controls the homestead and its land. In the towns, tenancy of the home is more common and the head will normally control the dwelling, as its tenant. Besides controlling the homestead, the household head is formally responsible for economic maintenance of the unit, although others may contribute to its upkeep. The head is also ultimately responsible for the socialization and control of junior members of the unit and for the maintenance and care of the aged, although others may actually discharge these tasks routinely. The head is especially responsible for the sexual conduct of childless young women living in his home. The first pregnancies of these girls demonstrate the head's ineffectiveness and accordingly provoke his or her anger. For this reason, a first pregnancy is greeted more harshly by the senior members and especially by the head of the girl's household than subsequent ones, even if the girl remains unmarried.

The head of the house decides who may visit or stay in it; the head is responsible for action to meet such domestic crises as illness or litigation, death, birth, or marriage. He or she is empowered to pledge or alienate the household's capital assets, even when these are not purely private property. The head selects the schools and churches which the household children attend, or agrees to selections made by other members. In certain areas, he is responsible for arranging the apprenticeship or employment of adolescent members of the household. Other members of the unit are free to advocate various courses of action on any matter, and the household head is often expected to solicit external advice; but formal responsibility for appropriate action in the circumstances mentioned above rests with the household head, and it would be quite improper for other members of the unit to take action on behalf of it in such affairs without the head's foreknowledge and consent.

In household and community rituals, the head usually has the most prominent role of the household group. In relations between domestic units or between the unit and official or quasi-official agencies, the household head is often its regulator or sole link. The head is the only member of the unit whose death or departure inevitably initiates an important change in its structure and leadership.

Headship roles vary in their performance with the size, structure, and setting of the units themselves, and even more obviously in relation to the sex and age of the household head and other principals. Even when the head is dominant in the group, these variations are notable. Often such variations are simply concomitants of economic differences between units; but male heads tend to leave routine household activities and organization to their wives or senior womenfolk, whose domestic and kinship roles especially fit them for these functions. Normally these male heads seek to control the household's external relations as fully as they can. In this sense, matrifocality, defined by preoccupation with day-to-day domestic matters, and male marginality, defined by preoccupation with extrahousehold and interhousehold relations, may be accurate descriptive terms; but unfortunately these are not the meanings which Dr. R. T. Smith attaches to this antithesis. Female heads vary in performance of their headship roles according to age, marital condition, and situation, as well as household structure; but on the whole they retain the woman's preoccupation with internal household affairs, and their control of the unit's external relations is generally weaker and less comprehensive than that which men claim and exercise.

To identify household heads in these field studies, we asked, in the community or neighborhood, "Whose house is that over there?" or, pointing, "Who lives over there?" A consensus of replies to these questions generally expressed community identification of the household head. Within the household we would ask "Whose house (home) is this?" or "Who is the head of the home (house)?" The replies we received were generally unanimous and were never contradicted. Finally we would ask the person reported as household head, "Is this your house?" "Are you the head of the home (house)?" Sometimes the senior male in a home would simply assert his authority and headship without any demur, demanding an explanation of our visit before permitting any further discussion. On other occasions the senior woman of the home would refuse to answer any questions until we had received permission from its head. On yet other occasions men would simply deny the headship of the households in which they lived and direct us to their mates or senior kinsfolk as the persons who "rule the home."

In the survey of Kingston, Jamaica, we found ownership or direct tenancy of the dwelling place an extremely useful index of the head's identity. With a scattering of households in this dense urban area, we could not rely on community consensus for the identification of the head, but we found an extremely high correlation between control of the homestead and its headship. Usually also this control was vested in the dominant and senior member of the group. The kinship position of these senior persons provided further evidence on the locus of headship, and apart from the anomalous distributions of dominance and headship already discussed, we found few

cases of indeterminate headship in our Kingston survey, and none
which remained unresolved after further study. On the other hand,
in rural Jamaica where tenancy of the homestead is still quite rare,
despite care in inquiry and candor in response, there were occasional households the headship or boundaries of which remained
indeterminate. Happily these cases were quite rare, and of the
1,015 households studied in rural Jamaica there were only eight of
this sort. Perhaps this is the clearest demonstration of the utility
of the headship concept and the generality of its observance among
these populations. In the analysis of rural Jamaica I have simply
omitted these eight indeterminate households as insignificant.

Among the West Indian "folk" or lower class, the rule is that
males head domestic groups based on their cohabitation, while
females head units based solely on consanguine kinship. The exceptions to these rules have already been discussed. When the
organization of domestic groups does not observe these general
principles, the reversal of expected roles and the conditions which
promote this reversal are immediately obvious and explicit. In
consequence there are very few households among these populations
in which the locus or role of headship is quite obscure.

The Structural Analysis of Domestic Groups

The objective identification of household heads is an essential
field task and first step in the systematic analysis of household
composition. The distribution of headship among persons of differing sex and age is a significant index of social maturity, and
allows inferences to be made about probable variations in household structure. To collate data on the constitution of large numbers
of households, or to analyze and compare them systematically,
some common reference point is clearly essential. For structural
or functional analyses of domestic units alike, headship provides
the natural and the most appropriate reference point. By this means
we can classify populations systematically in terms of their individual relations to the household heads; such systematic classification is essential if we are to develop a uniform morphology
of domestic groups for comparative study. It is also prerequisite
for the analysis of family structure within sample populations,
or for the study of factors which influence the development and
change of domestic units. Either of these analyses presupposes
an exact and systematic breakdown of the kinship composition of
household samples by means of a uniform and economical system
of categories. Such a system may only be possible by reference
to some simple universal feature such as household headship.

Households vary in their size, in the social characteristics of their members, in the bases of their constitution, and in other ways. They differ also in the numbers and proportions of lineal, collateral, or affinal kin within them. Some units arise through conjugal unions, others are groups of consanguine kin. There is no uniformity in their generation structure or kinship span.

The principles which govern the constitution of these differing modes of domestic group will also control their relative incidence. It is therefore necessary to determine the frequency with which groups of different types occur in any population. It is also necessary to determine the frequencies with which particular elements or relations enter into the composition of these differing groups. To this end, a systematic morphology of household units is just as necessary as a systematic study of their dynamics. The former tells us about the relative incidence of different types of groups, while the latter tells us about the ways in which the components of these groups are distributed and related. The morphological distribution provides a necessary check on conclusions suggested by analyses of dynamic elements such as mating history and condition of adults or the distribution of parental roles and the obligations of collateral kinship. We must therefore analyze the adult section of our sample population to determine its mating status, and the junior population to determine the conditions which govern the coresidence or separation of parents and their children, or of collateral kin. To compare household morphology and dynamics among our several samples, we must rely on the distributions of different forms and their components. Naturally any taxonomy which is sufficiently refined and systematic for such comparative work will have to deal with such a wide range of structural variety that no simple derivation of these differing forms from a single source is likely to prove adequate. The probable invalidity of such ontogenetic explanations itself enjoins that attention be given to interhousehold influences or relations which affect the constitution and growth of household units within these samples. These relations and others within the households together constitute the set of regulatory principles which govern the incidence, form, and development of differing types of domestic group; these principles I shall call the family structure.

To define the family structure we must therefore analyze the distribution of mating and parental experience among adults of differing sex and age. Such an analysis will enable us to distinguish alternative mating forms. In addition, we shall have to analyze the junior population by reference to sex, birth status, and coresidence

with or separation from their parents. This analysis will enable us
to define alternative forms of parenthood. We must also analyze
the constitution of household units to determine the relative incidence of the elements which compose them. This analysis will
enable us to define alternative forms of domestic groups and alternative domestic organizations of elementary family units. Since
most of the sample populations above the age of twenty-four may
very well be cohabiting or in charge of their own homes, we shall
set the upper age limit of the group whose coresidence with or
separation from their parents indicates uniformity or difference
of parental roles at twenty-four years. In these analyses we shall
therefore seek to isolate and measure the incidence of alternative
domestic, mating, and parental forms. The first set of alternatives
provides a structural morphology, while the two latter reveal the
structural dynamics. The principles of family structure which we
shall seek to define relate dynamics to morphology, and integrate one with the other. In our view the regularities apparent
in household composition will therefore be due to relations holding
between alternative modes of mating, parenthood, and elementary
family organization. The interdependence of these alternatives may
vary in kind and degree from sample to sample, together with their
systematic organization. High levels of interdependence between
these factors indicate a system which has high degrees of closure.
Low levels indicate the opposite. In systems with high degrees of
closure, we can expect current forms of family structure to persist, given stability in the demographic and socioeconomic context
of the population. This inference does not hold for systems with low
degrees of closure.

We may set up the hypothesis that all the various dimensions and
forms of family relation within a given population form a single
inclusive system. In this event, the domestic family, the elementary or compound family, and the bilateral extended family, to
which the members of these domestic, elementary, and compound
families belong, will all stand in certain systematic relations to one
another. If these relations are circular and interdependent, the
system will be closed; but they may not be circular, and not all
of them may be interdependent, in which case the closure of the
system cannot be complete. However, in either case this totality
will have some internal structure simply because its various components and levels are separately defined by their interrelations
with one another. Thus although the idea of a family system is
hypothetical, the notion of family structure refers to an operational
necessity of the social organization. This does not mean that the

family structure necessarily constitutes or maintains a balanced equilibrium. Available evidence indicates that this may be rarely the case. It does mean, however, that even within narrow limits and in societies with quite irregular or varied familial organization, the totality of family forms and relations will exhibit some internal order and regularity, the conditions of which can be isolated and summarized as the principles of family structure.

These principles are much narrower than the total system of kinship relations. A kinship system includes all relations of consanguinity and affinity observed within a population. The principles of family structure only apply within a clearly delimited sector of the kinship order, that is, to the organization and development of the family forms and relations which they regulate.

The problem of field work is to collect all the data necessary to define the principles of family structure, and to see how they operate. The problem of analysis is to isolate these structural principles from the household data, to define their interrelations, and to determine the degrees and conditions of their common or independent variation.

# 2. Carriacou

Carriacou is one of the many very small Caribbean islands. With an area of thirteen square miles, it is the largest of the Grenadines, and lies twenty-three miles north of Grenada, of which colony it is a district. Its people are mainly Negroid. In 1946 its population was estimated at 6, 700; and another 1, 200 Carriacou folk were then reported to be living in Trinidad.[1]

There were no operating estates on the island in 1953, and sailing in locally built schooners gave more wage employment to the islanders than any other activity. Rainfall averages forty inches a year, and comes irregularly between May and October. Drought is a perennial threat, and domestic water supplies depend on roof catchments. There are no rivers or springs in the island.

Women are mainly responsible for farming. Locally grown food crops include maize, cassava, sweet potatoes, and pigeon peas; cash crops are sea-island cotton and groundnuts. Two of the larger landholders cultivated limes and made lime oil. According to the census of 1946, there were then in Carriacou 1, 366 farms and small plots, most of which were below three acres in size.[2] In short, the Carriacou folk are smallholders whose women care for the gardens, while the men exploit the sea.

Men migrate continuously and in large numbers to Trinidad, Venezuela, Aruba, and Curaçao. There they seek work on the oil fields or in industry. Many settle permanently abroad, others return to marry and establish their homes in Carriacou. Few emigrate to Grenada. Historical records show that male emigration has been a permanent feature of Carriacou society since its large slave population was emancipated in 1838. This emigration is linked with a large excess of adult females among the resident population.

The Anglican and Roman Catholic churches divide the official religious allegiance of the Carriacou folk. Unofficially, the is-

landers maintain a vigorous ancestor cult known as the Big Drum,
the Nation Dance, or simply *Saraca* (sacrifice). A similar duality
is found in kinship. Carriacou folk, who are bilingual and speak
dialects of French and English, employ the bilateral kinship ter-
minology and idioms introduced by the French and British. Nonetheless, they emphasize agnatic kinship, and patrilineages known
as "bloods" are important elements of their society. Blood kinship
within a four-generation range enjoins exogamy; but beyond this
range, also, agnation links units and individuals of common patrilineal origin.

Carriacou political organization consisted in 1953 of a District
Officer and his aides who administered the island under direction
of the Grenada government. Their headquarters were at Hillsborough, the port of entry and capital of Carriacou, a township
with a population of 280 persons, according to the 1946 census.
A magistrate visited the island periodically to hold a court of first
instance; the government also maintained a small hospital under a
resident Medical Officer in the island. The District returned one
elected member to the Grenada House of Assembly, since 1951
on a basis of adult suffrage. The District Officer was assisted
in certain ways by local committees of his own nomination, the
membership of which was confined to a small group of merchants,
officials, and teachers drawn mainly from Hillsborough. For generations the Carriacou folk have been administered from Grenada
and have been dominated by the larger island. It is thus not surprising that they make sharp distinctions between themselves and
the Grenadians. The Grenadians also emphasize that Carriacou
lacks an elite and has no social stratification of Grenadian scale
and type.

Carriacou settlement patterns combine dispersal and compact-
ness. Villages are separated by open land used for pasture or cultivation, or sometimes by forest. Within the villages, homes are
somewhat dispersed, each standing on the householder's land.
Village boundaries follow the historical boundaries of former properties, and each village maintains a separate pond or water hole
for its own use.

Carriacou folk do not rent houses, although they rent land, and
also practice share cropping. They make a distinction between
women's houses, also called dirt houses, which are made of daub-
and-wattle with thatched roofs, and men's houses, which are built
of wood or concrete. Men's houses are sometimes described as
board houses. Men are expected to build their own homes before
marriage. There being no wage employment on the island, they

emigrate in search of the money to build their houses. Carriacou rejection of the idea of house rent forms part of this complex association of housing, marriage, and male maturity. To find quarters to rent, I had to tour the island twice, and although there were many empty houses belonging to emigrants, none was for rent. Finally, the district nurse, whose husband was a well-known shop-keeper, agreed to rent me her empty home at L'Esterre. I remained there for about two months, during which time I made a census of L'Esterre and arranged for fifty adjacent households in each of three villages in the remaining quarters of the island, to be studied. [3]

The Frame of Discussion

   In this and the following sample analyses, I shall employ a uniform procedure. I have accordingly tabulated the survey data in a standard form and order. I shall first discuss the population structure of each sample and then examine the distribution of household headship and the populations of households having heads of different sex. I shall then analyze the distribution of mating and parental conditions among the adult population, and shall follow this with an analysis of the kinship constitution of domestic groups under heads of different sex. In this household composition analysis, I shall isolate lineal, affinal, and collateral elements for special study; and I shall then examine the junior population of each sample, paying special attention to their birth status and sex on the one hand, and their coresidence with or separation from either or both of their parents, on the other. Following this, I shall discuss the residential distribution of those children separated from either or both parents, and shall conclude with a study of the frequency distribution of structurally different types of domestic unit in the sample, paying special attention to variations in generation span or mating relations among the cohabiting principals of these units. For each sample, these analyses are summarized in twenty tables which form an appendix to the discussion. This separation of the quantitative material and the text is unavoidable if the narrative is to be readable and its argument clear. I shall naturally make considerable use of the numerical relations revealed in the tables, but I feel it would be a mistake to overload the text with these frequencies and ratios. However exhilarating they may seem to me, I doubt whether the reader's enthusiasm would bear the strain. Even now the references to ratios and frequencies within the text may seem unduly numerous. However, there is a danger of straying too far from the trees in an effort to see the wood.

In analyzing the kinship constitution of household populations having heads of different sex, I have found the genealogical representation of these relations very useful. Such a presentation enables us to see and examine many features of household structure which would otherwise escape attention. I have accordingly prepared charts of these household populations which are inserted at appropriate points in the text. In each chart the household heads form a single common point of reference. Looking at the charts, we must treat the head as Ego. The differences of mating relation and birth status which are important for our analysis are represented in each diagram, together with the distributions of residents, by their exact kinship ties to the household head.

I shall have to interrupt the following discussion at various points to define and discuss the categories used in some of the tables. This is only necessary when the categorization is unfamiliar; but it is unavoidable on their first appearance in this comparative study, since these categories inform the analysis of all subsequent samples.

Population Structure

The 224 Carriacou households contained a total of 1,040 individuals, 43 per cent of whom were less than fourteen years of age, and 60 per cent of whom were females. Among adults of reproductive age, that is, between the ages of fifteen and fifty-four, there are five women for every three men; among the persons below fourteen years of age the sexes are evenly balanced.

These demographic abnormalities reflect male emigration. This adult emigration artificially inflates the ratio of children in the total population. It also creates this large female surplus. Of 310 adult migrants having claims on a particular land settlement which I studied in 1953, 200 were males. Of the 136 married emigrants, 65 were wives of the absent males; but of the 174 single migrants, only 45 were women. [4]

Adult males above the age of twenty-five represent only 12 per cent of the total sample. Adult females of this age are 27.7 per cent of the sample population. It follows that a large proportion of these homes are likely to have female heads.

Persons above the age of fifty-five represent 14.4 per cent of the sample total, and of these, males account for 3.4 per cent. Thus in the most senior age groups, women outnumber men by three to one. This disparity is partly due to the male emigration already noted, but in part it arises through the high rate of widowhood among females. This widowhood rate cannot be accounted for

solely by the differential hazards which face the sexes. It indicates
that men marry women several years their juniors, and are generally survived by them.

In view of the marked female surplus among the adult population,
the large proportion of children below the age of fifteen is interesting. Assuming strict observance of monogamous sex relations,
it is unlikely that this proportion would be so high, simply because
only three in every five women could be mothers. The implication
is that monogamous sex relations are not strictly observed in this
population. Further, one form of this nonobservance, namely,
that single women bear children for men who do not live with them,
is implicit in the population structure.

The analysis of the distribution of household headship within
this sample is given in Table 2. The majority of senior persons
are heads of households. Approximately three in every five homes
have female heads, but the proportionate incidence of headship
within the sexes is notably higher among men, as shown in Table 3.

All men above seventy years of age in this sample are household
heads, as are all but one of the men above fifty-five years of age.
Of the men aged between forty and fifty-four years 90 per cent are
household heads, but only 40 per cent of those between twenty-five
and thirty-nine have charge of their own homes.

Among the women over seventy, four in every five are household heads; among those between fifty-five and sixty-nine years
of age, the incidence is little lower. However, only 44 per cent
of the women between forty and fifty-four years of age are household heads, a ratio which is less than half that among men of this
age group, and little greater than the ratio among males aged between twenty-five and thirty-nine. Only one woman in nine of this
latter age is a household head. Notably among men and women
below the age of twenty-four the incidence of headship is negli-
gible. From this comparison we conclude that men assume headship more rapidly and more fully than women. By their fortieth
year, most men who remain in the island will be heads of their
own homes, whereas most women will not. But by their fifty-fifth
year most of the female residents will be household heads. Presumably women of this age group obtain headship through the death
of their husbands or senior kin who previously headed the home.
Presumably also these senior kin include a fair number of mothers
of these women. This notion fits well with the low incidence of
headship among women aged twenty-five to thirty-nine. Presumably women of this age group, who are not cohabiting, live with
their senior kin, and normally with their parents. After their fa-

ther's death, when their mother is approximately fifty-five years of age, the mother becomes household head, and if the daughter remains single, she herself is likely to attain headship shortly after her fortieth year, when her mother dies. Such a succession of household heads presumes continuity in the domestic unit, and would mark stages in its development. But this is not necessarily the most frequent way in which people become household heads. Some women under forty may set up their own homes or may become heads of homes through their husbands' migration. Almost all men seek to establish their own homes.

The comparative distribution of headship among adults classified by sex and age shows that female heads above the age of fifty-five outnumber men by approximately five to two. Despite the fact that the relative incidence of headship among males between the ages of forty and fifty-four is twice as great as that among women, there are as many female household heads of this age group as males, owing to the size of the female surplus. Eighty-six per cent of all household heads are above the age of forty, and more than half of the heads are over fifty-five. This means that we are likely to find comparable ratios of household groups with a depth of three generations, and, since most of these senior household heads are women, most of these three-generation units are likely to have female heads. The incidence of two-generation units, such as those consisting of parents and children only, will accordingly be quite low.

We have already suggested that a large number of the surplus females are single mothers. We have also seen that few of these women are heads of their own homes. It follows that they are likely to be living with their parents or senior kin and that their children form the third generation of these households.

The basic assumption which governs these inferences is that the Carriacou population is not formally polygynous. If it were, there would be very little problem, since the surplus females could be accommodated as wives in polygynous households under male heads, and these households would have a larger average size. Demographic structure does not dictate domestic form; it is quite possible for a polygynous population with a demographic structure like that of Carriacou to have quite dissimilar modes of domestic organization. However, demographic facts which are themselves products of kinship relations impose certain conditions on domestic organization within cultural limits. We have seen that a strict observance of monogamy in Carriacou would reduce the ratio of children in the local population sharply, perhaps even to the point at which, granted the continuing emigration, population would decline. That this has not happened indicates that the islanders have modified monogamy in various ways. In consequence of such modification, we can expect to find a high incidence of single motherhood and a fair number of the three-generation households containing segments of elementary families. If the society was polygynous, we would not find such a high incidence of headship among females. This incidence of female headship itself implies that the society is formally monogamous; but a study of the population structure and age-sex distribution of headship indicates that its monogamy is a modified one. In short, the cultural limits on demographic pressures are defined by the distribution of household headship. These limits are set by the form in which monogamy has been modified, and until this form is adequately known and its effects are clearly defined, we cannot validly treat the distribution of headship as a simple succession of transfers within domestic units which develop independently.

Table 4 isolates variations in the number of persons in households having heads of different sex, and Table 5 analyzes the populations of households under male and female heads by age and sex.

Of the ninety-three male household heads, seven live alone. Of 131 female heads, twenty live alone. Thus rather more than one in every ten of these households are single-person units. Another tenth contains two persons each, and the modal household size is three persons. Even so, the average size of households in this sample is 4.6 persons, and if single-person units are excluded, 5.1. As might be expected, households under male heads are considerably larger than those under females, the average population of each category being 5.7 and 3.9 persons respectively. Despite the fact that only 41 per cent of the sample households have male heads, slightly more than half the population live in homes with male heads. There are also a considerable number of large units. A graph of the distribution of households by size is bimodal in form; and this suggests that the sample includes at least two more structurally distinct types of unit. Large units under female heads are more likely to have a depth of three generations than those under males, but undoubtedly several of the male-headed units have this form. Fifty-four per cent of households with female heads contain three persons or less, whereas only 21 per cent of those under males do.

Table 5 shows that nearly one half of the population in households with male heads is below the age of fifty, as against 37 per cent in households with female heads. In these latter households,

females outnumber males by more than two to one, and among the
population above the age of twenty-five, by eight to one. In households with male heads, the sexes are more evenly balanced throughout the entire age span. On the average, each home with a male
head contains three children below the age of fifteen, as against 1.5
in the average home with a female head; but these latter units contain 1.5 times as many persons above the age of fifty-five as do
households with male heads.

Homes with male heads contain fewer women in each adult age
group than do units with female heads. Allowing for a small number
of men who lack resident mates, it is clear that Carriacou men only
have one woman at a time living with them; they adhere to monogamy as far as coresidence is concerned. However, the probable
numbers of single mothers indicate that extraresidential mating is
prevalent, and that it is in this way that monogamy has been modified.

The System of Mating Relations

In order to analyze the mating organization adequately, I have
classified the population by age, sex, and household status on the
one hand, and by marital and parental condition on the other. In
Table 7 all adult members of the sample population are classified
irrespective of these differences of household status; but in Table 8
only those who are not household heads are included, while Table 9
isolates the population of household heads.

Before discussing the distributions presented in these three
tables, I must comment on the categories used to distinguish individuals by mating and parental status. There are six primary
groups of categories, namely, (1) childless single persons, (2)
single persons whose parental status is not known, (3) single parents, (4) those who are or have been consensually wed, (5) married
persons, and, (6) the widowed. The first three groups include all
individuals who are not known to have participated in cohabitation.
The fourth category includes all individuals who have cohabited
consensually but have not married; the fifth category includes all
persons who have married but have not been widowed, irrespective
of their previous mating histories or their present parental status.
Thus no distinction is made among married persons between parents and others. Among the married persons important secondary
distinctions are those between individuals with absent and resident
spouses, and those who have or have not remained single after
informal separation from their spouse. Among those who have
cohabited consensually, the important distinctions are between

persons cohabiting at the time of the survey, those whose unions had been terminated by death, and those separated from their former mates. Although members of this last group are formally single, it seems useful to differentiate them from those single persons who have never taken part in consensual cohabitation. This distinction allows us to gauge the relative incidence and stability of consensual cohabitation within the population concerned. Another distinction is made between childless persons whose consensual unions have come to grief, and parents. This distinction allows us to compare the definition of parental roles which characterizes consensual cohabitation with other definitions characteristic of marriage or extraresidential mating.

Among the single persons, the primary categories are further subdivided. Some of these single persons were known to be mating at the time of survey; others were not mating then, and there was a residue concerning whom we lacked accurate information. These three subdivisions apply equally to the single parents, to childless single persons, and to single persons whose parental status is unknown. In addition, there is a fourth group of childless single persons who have probably never mated and are still in their early or middle teens.

The category just mentioned directs attention to our definition of mating. For purposes of this analysis, mating is defined by public recognition. Single women who become pregnant thereby publicize their mating activities. In the overwhelming majority of cases in Carriacou, the mating relation which leads to pregnancy will already be known to the families and community of the partners. However, in other areas and under other conditions it may happen that a pregnant woman cannot specify her mate, or that the man specified denies paternity. In either of these cases, it is certain that the woman has been mating and she is duly entered in the proper category; but under such circumstances the man cannot be classified as the woman's mate, if he occurs in the sample. In Carriacou this type of ambiguity about mating was happily quite rare. Of more than 200 children in L'Esterre only five were of ambiguous paternity, and this included a pair of twins.

One further comment on this system of categories may be necessary. They combine information on mating and parental status. They also combine information on the past as well as the present mating experience of the adults classified. There is no need to defend these combinations. Obviously a single mother has differing familial responsibilities from a childless single person. Obviously a single parent who has never entered cohabitation occupies a different structural position from one whose cohabitation has broken down. The major difficulty which this system of categories imposes is that of collecting all the information necessary to classify individuals correctly within it. It is true that the unknown categories of these tables contain many individuals; however, the structurally significant category of unknown parental status contains relatively few persons, and the number of people whose current mating status was not known does not affect the analysis of the remainder directly, so long as these people are clearly distinguished.

It is useful to examine the marital condition of the twenty-seven solitary individuals in this sample before proceeding to discuss the adult aggregate. To facilitate this, I have summarized my data on these isolates in Table 6, the categories of which are a simpler version of those already discussed. Of the seven solitary males, five are over forty and two are between twenty-five and thirty-nine years of age. Three of these men are widowers and three have never married. Of the twenty solitary females, seventeen are over forty and the great majority of these are over fifty-five. In short, the ideal transfer of household headship among women in continuing domestic units, outlined above, does not always occur. Of the twenty solitary females, seven are widows and two are women informally separated from their husbands. Another two of junior age have absent husbands, but nine have never wed. It seems that in Carriacou the chances of living alone are approximately equal, whether or not individuals have married and irrespective of sex. On the other hand there are three times as many women living alone as there are men, and whereas five of the seven men in this position are below the age of fifty-four, only six of the twenty women are of this age group. It is still possible for these men to marry, including widowers; but the majority of the women who live alone are unlikely to resume cohabitation although they may take some junior kinsfolk into their homes.

There are 205 adult males in this sample and 393 women. Of the adult males, seventy-seven are below the age of twenty-four and sixty-two of these are childless single persons, while another ten are single but of unknown parental status. Only three of these young men were known to be parents, and only two had entered cohabitation, one of these being married, the other not. It is clear that young men in Carriacou do not usually begin their mating careers before they are twenty-four. Of the fifty-one men aged between twenty-five and thirty-nine, we lack necessary information on fifteen. Another pair were childless single persons; eleven were

single parents, nine of these mating extraresidentially in 1953.
Three were partners in consensual cohabitation and twenty were
married. It is clear that men start mating shortly after their
twenty-fourth year and that many marry then. Those who do not
are more likely to have children by women living elsewhere than
to remain childless. Of the forty-one males aged between forty
and fifty-four in this sample, thirty-five were already married
and one had been widowed. Of the twenty-three males aged between
fifty-five and sixty-nine, nineteen were married and two were
widowers. All thirteen of the men above seventy years old had
married. In short, only six of the seventy-seven men above the
age of forty had not married, and three of these had experience
of consensual cohabitation. Marriage is the rule for Carriacou
men, and it is the statistical norm for mature men, just as lack
of mating experience is the norm for those under twenty-four. The
transitional period occurs between the ages of twenty-five and
thirty-nine, and our data illustrate a strong drive among the men
of this age group to marry, or at the least to mate extraresidentially. Notably, of these 205 men, only seven had participated in
consensual cohabitation which did not mature into marriage. Notably, both men who had separated from their wives were cohabiting consensually in 1952. Apparently, consensual cohabitation
is permissible if marriage has broken down, but not before marriage. Apparently, also, Carriacou marriages rarely break down.
Thus, of the eighty-nine married men in this sample, sixty-eight
of whom are above the age of forty, only two have separated from
their wives.

Among the 393 women in these households, 106 are below the
age of 24. Of these, seven were married and one was cohabiting
consensually in 1953. Eighty-seven were childless single persons
and eleven were single mothers, nine of them currently mating.
Apparently only one in five young women below the age of twenty-
four is likely to mate. Of those who do, two in five will cohabit
and the remainder will mate extraresidentially. Furthermore,
it is extremely rare for these young women to cohabit outside
of marriage. Of the ninety-one women in this sample between the
ages of twenty-five and thirty-nine, we lack adequate information
on the parental status of seven. Of the remainder, thirty-nine are
single, and twenty-three of these are mothers. Of these twenty-
three single mothers, seventeen were known to be mating at the
time of study. All such matings were clearly extraresidential.
Including the seven single persons of unspecified parental status,
forty-six of these ninety-one women between the ages of twenty-five

and thirty-nine are single. Of the remainder, six were cohabiting consensually. Of thirty-nine married women in this age group, ten had husbands overseas and one had separated from her spouse. Such separations are always informal in Carriacou, since religious and legal difficulties prevent divorce.

Among the eighty-two women between forty and fifty-four years of age there are nine whose parental status is obscure. Another nine were childless single persons and there were eighteen single mothers, only one of whom was known to be mating at the time of survey. Of the forty-six women in this age group whose mating career included cohabitation, only one had cohabited consensually and remained unmarried. This woman was separated from her mate in 1953. Of the forty-five married women, nine were widows and eight had absent husbands. The only case of a widow resuming consensual cohabitation occurs in this age group. Apparently women whose marriages have ended in separation or death are not expected to cohabit outside of marriage thereafter. Our sample contains eighty-six women between the ages of fifty-five and sixty-nine, of whom twenty-three are single persons, eight being of unknown parental status, six being childless and the remaining nine single mothers. None of these single women was currently mating. Of the remaining sixty-three, only one had not married. This woman had taken part in a consensual domestic union and been widowed therein. Thirty-four of the other sixty-two women were also widows, and all of these had remained single. Of the twenty-eight wives, five had absent husbands, and seven were separated from their spouses, one of these having resumed consensual cohabitation. Three in every four women above seventy had married, and four fifths of these were widows. Apparently married women have a longer life expectancy in Carriacou than their husbands and also than single women, presumably because they enjoy greater security.

Of these 393 women, 174 had married and another nine had cohabited consensually without marrying later. Of the married women, only nine had left their husbands. In short, less than 5 per cent of the Carriacou marriages dissolved before death. Less than 5 per cent of the Carriacou women whose mating experience includes cohabitation have the status of consensual mates. The importance of marriage and the unimportance of consensual cohabitation are equally marked.

Of almost equal importance is single status among the island women. Of the 393 women in these households, 210 were single persons; even if we exclude the young women under twenty-four,

most of whom have not begun their mating careers, 112 of the
remaining 287 are single persons. Of these 112 single females,
fifty-four were known to be mothers and eighteen were known to
be mating at the time of survey. Even if these proportions are
underestimates, the fact remains that extraresidential mating
represents the statistical and structural alternative to married
cohabitation in Carriacou. Moreover, single persons engaged in
extraresidential mating are mostly women, since very few men
remain unmarried. It follows that the majority of the male partners
of these single women will be found among the married men. This
means that whereas men may marry and mate extraresidentially
with single women simultaneously, for women the alternative to
marriage is extraresidential mating or celibacy. Our figures indicate that single women prefer to mate extraresidentially rather than
to remain celibate.

    We can now account for the surprisingly low incidence of con-
sensual cohabitation and marital breakdown among this population.
Men have exclusive sexual rights to their wives, but the notion of
adultery does not apply to men. In consequence, wives have few
recognized grounds for leaving their husbands. Men, on the other
hand, are loath to cohabit consensually, as much for status reasons
as because of their insecurity in this form of union. The relatively
high rate of dissolution in consensual unions indicates the increased
area for possible dispute therein. One important cause of disputes
among consensually cohabiting couples arises out of the man's
sexual affairs. Men find that marriage is more permissive for them
than consensual cohabitation. In unions of the latter sort, females
assert their sexual rights and refuse to tolerate rivals, perhaps
because of their status insecurity and uncertainty about the future.
Married women, on the other hand, are well aware of their husband's affairs and may even be asked for advice about these from
time to time.

    The Carriacou modification of monogamy emphasizes residential
separation and exclusiveness of cohabiting couples; but whereas
married men may also mate extraresidentially, wives must remain
faithful to their husbands, even in the latter's long absence overseas. Such a system excludes consensual cohabitation as an alternative to marriage or to extraresidential mating. Those consensual
unions which we have been discussing are either anticipations of
marriage or follow on its dissolution. All unmarried women engaged
in consensual cohabitation are below the age of thirty-nine. If they
do not marry by this time, they tend to dissolve their union. The
two women above this age who were currently engaged in consensual

unions had both been married, one being a separated wife, the other a widow.

Notably this system of mating relations offers the large number of surplus females a variety of alternatives. They may remain celibate or mate extraresidentially or attempt a consensual union or marry. To married women it offers a high degree of assurance, a large family, and a longer life expectancy than others. The mating system thus makes the best of both worlds. It also ensures continuing population growth and minimizes the sources of friction liable to arise in a society with these sex ratios.

One point worth some attention is that the majority of the single women of senior years are mothers. This means simply that households of which these women are heads cannot be derived from domestic units which contained their elementary families, since all these women have always been single and have mated extraresidentially. The frequency of these single mothers among the senior female age groups is sufficiently high to show that the hypothetical derivation of three-generation households under female heads from domestic units which initially contained the elementary families of these women does not hold for all groups of this kind. Another point worth noting is the high incidence of single parenthood among women. This incidence illustrates the strength of the female preference for nondomiciliary unions with married or single men rather than consensual cohabitation with single ones. The woman's position within the nondomiciliary union is superior to that which she has in consensual cohabitation, at any rate in Carriacou. The consensual cohabitation may break down at any time, and it will be dissolved if it does not develop into marriage before the woman reaches middle age. In these unions, the woman depends economically on her mate to a greater degree than in the extraresidential union. In unions of the latter sort, women can draw on their kin for assistance, and they are also free to consider proposals from other men, including offers of marriage. Moreover, the dissolution of a nondomiciliary union does not create a public stir. Finally, the great majority of the males are already married, and cannot entertain ideas of cohabitation, although they are able to mate extraresidentially.

Tables 8 and 9 are significant primarily because they describe the relation between household status on the one hand and marital condition and parental status on the other. Differences of age and sex are incorporated in this analysis. In sum these tables show that eighty-four of the ninety-three male household heads have been married, whereas only seven of the 112 males who are not household heads have done so. Among males, marriage and household headship go together. The chances that an unmarried man will be a household head are slight indeed, but no slighter than the chance that a male household head will be unmarried. Notably, two of the seven unmarried males engaged in consensual cohabitation lacked the status of household heads. In other words, the definition of relations between partners in consensual unions is imprecise; and for this reason also, such unions are more likely to break up than marriages. The fact that only seven of the 112 males who were not household heads were married also indicates that married couples live separately in the man's home. Only very rarely do we find couples living together in homes which include their parents. Extended families may be common, but they do not include intact elementary families whose principals belong to the intermediate generation.

The fact that most household heads are married men implies that most wives are not household heads. In fact, only one of the eighty-two women whose spouses were present have this status, whereas fourteen women with absent spouses do. All fifty-nine widows are household heads, and of the eight women separated from their husbands five have this status. The two women who have entered consensual cohabitation after marriage are also household heads. In short, whereas married women have little chance of becoming household heads so long as their husbands remain with them, they always enjoy this status as widows, and also when their husbands are absent.

Of the 210 single women, ninety-eight are below the age of twenty-four and consequently include no household heads; but forty-nine of the remainder, that is, nearly one half, are heads of their own homes, and the great majority of these forty-nine women for whom our information is adequate are mothers. It follows that a large portion of the mature single women will live in their own homes with their children. Such units cannot be derived from domestic elementary families directly. They represent the necessary consequences of, and adjustments to, a system of extraresidential mating; and they reveal significant differences in the definitions and allocations of parental roles in this type of union and in marriage. Bearing these points in mind, we may summarize the principal facts and implications of the foregoing discussion as follows: (1) The local population contains a large female surplus. (2) There are a large number of households with female heads. (3) The majority of the female household heads belong to the senior age groups and have previously married. (4) There are a large number of

single women, many of whom are household heads and mothers.
(5) A significant portion of the household sample consists of single-person units. (6) The overwhelming majority of middle-aged and senior males are married and head their own homes. (7) Consensual cohabitation is anomalous and rare. (8) The statistical and approved alternative to marriage for Carriacou women is the extraresidential union. (9) Men may maintain extraresidential relations after marriage, but they are expected to marry, and do so. (10) Three fourths of the household heads are over forty years old and most of them are likely to have grandchildren alive. (11) Women predominate among the senior household heads and consequently units containing members of three or more generations are likely to have female heads. (12) A large proportion of these households differ in form and origin from units based on the elementary family.

The Composition of Domestic Groups
   To compare and analyze the structure of households having heads of different sex, I have enumerated all dependents in these homes by reference to kinship with their household head. These data are tabulated summarily in Table 10 and represented on the kinship charts of these two household categories. To avoid overloading the table with categories, I have had to omit reference to differences of birth status and age among the population classified. Likewise, the table does not distinguish siblings by their mode of siblingship, nor does it analyze the issue of siblings or children as fully as we should like. Category 25 of Table 10 includes all resident kin of the household head's mate or spouse, without further distinction. The details of these categories are represented in the chart and will be discussed below. Before proceeding to these details, it is useful to examine Table 10 for the outline of structure which it presents.
   Of the eighty-five resident mates or spouses of these household heads, only three are to be found in homes with female heads. Of the 437 dependents of male household heads, 290 or 66 per cent are the issue of these men, and of these 248 are the head's children; of the 379 resident dependents of female household heads, 288 or 75 per cent are issue of these heads, but of these only 146 are the head's children, the remaining 142 being their grandchildren or great-grandchildren. Clearly, there are many more grandchildren of the head in homes with female heads than in units under males. Conversely, there are many more children living in their fathers' homes than living with their mothers only.
   One in twenty resident dependents of male household heads is

descended from the head's mate by a former union; dependents of this category are almost entirely absent from homes with female heads. Approximately one in every six resident dependents of female household heads is a sibling or descendant of a sibling of the head; but kin of these categories are almost entirely absent from homes with male heads. We find no siblings of these male household heads living with them; nor do such units include the issue of the head's sisters; but sisters' issue account for two in every three resident collaterals of female household heads.

Neither category of households includes patrilateral kin of the heads, other than paternal half siblings and their issue; remote matrilateral kin occur in both categories of households, but are commoner in those with female heads.

Of the thirty-nine miscellaneous members of homes with male heads who are classified in categories 22-27 inclusive, thirty-five are kin of the head's mate or spouse but not descended from her. No home with a male head includes the head's parent; nor do such homes include resident mates or spouses of the mate's children, or boarders. Of the seventeen miscellaneous members of units with female heads, only one is the mother of the head, and nine are resident mates or spouses of the head's children, most of these being the daughters' mates. The only boarder present in this sample lives in a home with a female head. The eight adopted persons in these households are divided equally between the two categories. Clearly Carriacou domestic groups are exclusively based on kinship; for this reason, the significant number of single-person units is of special interest. Such units indicate the selective operation of kinship factors in domestic placement. These factors do not operate randomly, as our comparison of the structure of households with male and female heads has just shown.

The most striking differences between these two categories of households consist in the exclusion of collateral kin of male household heads, and the substantial numbers of these collaterals included in homes with female heads. The large complements of affinal kin living in homes with male heads and their exclusion from units under females are clearly part of the same general pattern. Men do not accommodate their collaterals in their homes. Women do; and, after marriage, they will bring these collateral kin, as well as some of their children by former unions, into their husbands' homes. However, even women do not take their brothers into their homes; we find no case in which men live in homes of which their siblings are head, and very few cases in which they live with their mates in homes of which these women or their parents are heads. In short, men have no alternative to establishing their own homes, other than staying in their parents' homes. If they cannot afford to marry, or if their marriages are unsuccessful, they may have to live alone, since their collaterals will not accommodate them. Women also are never found living in their brothers' homes; and only rarely will they be found living with their sisters, though their children will readily be taken into their sisters' homes.

We can compare the distribution of collateral and lineal kin summarily, by examining the composition of the groups of resident grandchildren in homes of either type. Of the forty-one resident grandchildren in homes with male heads, ten are sons' sons and three are sons' daughters. Daughters' children outnumber sons' by two to one; but the resident grandchildren of these men are hardly more than the number of resident affinal kin not descended from their spouses. Of 137 resident grandchildren of female household heads, only forty-one are sons' issue, and most of these are sons' daughters. Notably there are more than three times as many grandchildren living in homes with female heads as in those with male heads.

Homes with female heads contain sixty-eight collaterals. Collateral kin living with female principals in homes with male heads number thirty-five. There are in all 107 collaterals living with kin who are the principals of these households; and in only four cases are these principals males. Set beside the consistent preference for daughters' issue in both types of home, this peculiar distribution of collaterals requires attention; and in Tables 11 and 12, I have isolated this collateral component for analysis at two levels. However first we must distinguish various types of matrikin.

Categories 19 to 21 of Table 10 include the mother's sister, the mother's sister's issue, and the mother's mother's sister's issue; category 18 isolates the sister's issue. All four categories, and others of like kinship constitution, denote materterine kin. Categories 6, 7, 9 and 22, which include daughters' issue, and mothers, isolate uterine kin. Materterine kin are persons whose mothers or maternal grandmothers were sisters or the children of sisters, This term was recently introduced by Professor Schapera, who defined it as follows: "I use this term (from Latin *matertera,* maternal aunt) for cousins whose mothers are sisters. "[5] It will be noticed that I have extended Professor Schapera's usage to distinguish uterine and materterine kin from one another and from other categories of cognatic kin. This distinction is essential in the present analysis, since the collateral component consists almost

entirely of women's kin, and the resident grandchildren are mainly
daughters' issue. In short, we have to compare the operation of
uterine and materterine kinship principles.

Of the resident kin of female principals living in mens' homes,
twenty-four are collaterals of the same generation as their linked
principal, or are of junior generation. All sixty-eight resident
collaterals of female household heads belong to these generations.
I have therefore isolated these groups for analysis, ignoring the
four resident collaterals of male household heads, owing to their
numerical insignificance. Table 11 shows that whereas only five
of these ninety-two collaterals are siblings of the principals with
whom they live, sixty-four are the issue of these principals' siblings. Seven are patrilateral kin and sixteen are matrilateral kin.
We have adequate information on the birth status of seventy-four
of these ninety-two collaterals; eighteen are legitimate, fifty-six
are not. All but one of these legitimates are the issue of full siblings. Apparently patrilateral and matrilateral kin are unlikely to
be living with their collaterals if their parents are married. Moreover, three fourths of the collateral kin of female principals are
likely to be illegitimate. Given this incidence of illegitimacy among
the resident collaterals of female principals, it is obviously necessary to examine more carefully the nature of the kinship tie which
links them to these women. Table 12 accordingly classifies the
resident collaterals of these female principals by their sex, birth
status, generation remove from the linked principal, and especially
by the sex of the parent through whom kinship is traced to this
principal. For obvious reasons, full siblings are excluded from
Table 12.

Of the twenty-two collaterals living with female principals in
homes with male heads, nineteen are connected to these principals
through their mothers; and of these nineteen, only one is known to
be legitimate; sixteen are known to be otherwise. Of the sixty-five
collaterals living with female household heads, sixteen trace kinship to these women through their fathers, and of these five are
known to be legitimate, seven are known to be otherwise. Of the
forty-nine whose kinship is traced through their mothers, eleven
are known to be legitimate, thirty-two are known to be otherwise.
In sum, only nineteen of these eighty-seven resident collaterals
of female principals trace kinship through their fathers. Three in
every four are linked to these principals through their mothers,
and of these materterine kin four in every five are known to be
illegitimate. In short, the collateral component of these households
consists largely of the illegitimate issue of the materterine kins-

women of female principals. Significantly enough, the proportions
of these illegitimate offspring of materterine kin among collaterals
of women living with their husbands is higher than in homes with
female heads. This difference indicates that women can accommodate such kin more easily in their husbands' homes than can
women who live alone. This in turn demonstrates the extent to
which men accommodate the illegitimate offspring of their wives'
kinswomen, as well as those of their wives themselves; and this
contrasts sharply with the exclusion of their own kin and illegitimate issue from the homes of these men.

We have isolated a basic structural principle of the Carriacou
family system. Illegitimate offspring remain in the care of their
mothers and mothers' kin. Legitimate offspring apparently remain
in their fathers' care. Many illegitimate children are accommodated
by their materterine kinswomen in the latter's homes. Others are
accommodated by their mothers or uterine kinswomen in the latter's homes. In providing accommodation for their wives' illegitimate offspring and illegitimate collaterals, while excluding their
own unlawful issue and relatives from their homes, men are im-
plicitly taking some care of one another's children, but not of all
of them; there are apparently three alternatives for the domestic
accommodation of illegitimate children; they may live with their
mothers, separately; or they may live with or apart from their
mothers in homes of which their mothers' kinswomen, materterine
or uterine, are the heads; or they may live in the homes of their
uterine or materterine kinswomen's husbands. They are not likely
to live with their fathers or fathers' brothers or fathers' fathers;
and although many live with their fathers' mothers, this proportion
is small, relative to the total population of illegitimate children.

If we look at Table 12 once more, we shall see that the relative
incidence of kinship traced through the mother increases steadily
with each generation remove among these resident collaterals,
at the same time that aggregates in each generation decline. These
data indicate that while we are not dealing with a matrilineal system, there are strong materterine kinship bonds within a three-
generation range, especially between women. These bonds provide an important alternative source of accommodation for single
women as well as their children; and the generality of their recognition in this society is shown by the incidence of such kinship
in homes with male heads.

It is clear that female responsibilities for illegitimate children
are important. These responsibilities are sometimes channeled
along collateral lines; more often they are not. In either event,

fathers have different parental roles and relations with their lawful
and unlawful children, as well as with their lawful and unlawful
mates. Clearly these relational differences in mating and parenthood form a single system. On marriage, a man assumes responsibility not only for his wife and their joint offspring, but for her
offspring by previous unions as well as for some of her less for-
tunate kin. His wife does not assume any comparable obligations
for his kin or other issue. In contrast, women who mate extraresidentially assume the primary domestic responsibilities for
the offspring of their unions, while retaining their own personal
independence to a high degree. The paternal obligations of their
mates are defined by ritual as well as by custom and folk mores.
These men are expected to contribute as fully as they can to the
upkeep of their extraresidential family, but within this framework
the mother has primary authority and responsibility for the child.
In short, the definitions of parenthood which are linked with the
mating alternatives practiced in Carriacou are mutually exclusive
and consistent. Together they form a single system. In this system
consensual cohabitation has little place, since the definitions of
mating and parental roles within it are incompatible with the exclusive dichotomy on which the system of marriage and extraresidential mating is based.

## The Distribution of Children

Our analysis has defined the Carriacou family structure as one
which is based on a systematic duality. This duality consists of two
alternative modes of mating and two alternative definitions of parenthood. Linked with this duality we find two clearly distinguished
sets of kinship roles for men and women. Men are expected to be
independent. They are bound to one another by strong patrilineal
ties nonetheless. Women may utilize affinal, uterine, or materterine kinship to adjust to their various situations. On the whole,
there is greater diversity of kinship situation among women than
among men. An important element in this diversity is the primary
female responsibility for illegitimate offspring of extraresidential
matings. We have seen that the women are expected to take care of
these illegitimate children, just as men are expected to marry and
take care of their lawful families in their own homes. To test and
complete our analysis of Carriacou parenthood, we must examine
the distribution of children in these homes, giving special attention
to differences associated with lawful and unlawful birth status. The
relevant information on this subject is presented in Tables 13 to 17
inclusive.

Table 13 isolates and classifies the resident lineal issue of these household heads. Distinctions of age are included at the foot of the table, only those offspring below the age of twenty-four being enumerated in the last line. For convenience, great-grandchildren are included with other issue of the head's sons or daughters. A glance at the charts will give the details necessary for any adjustment.

Of the 290 resident issue of male household heads, only seventeen are above the age of twenty-four, and only thirty are known to be illegitimate. Of the 288 resident issue of female household heads, fifty-nine are above the age of twenty-four and more than half of those whose birth status is known are illegitimate. Of the eighty-nine children of these female heads whose birth status is reported, thirty-three are illegitimate. Individuals whose birth status is not reported are all above twenty-four years of age. Of the 232 resident children of male household heads who are below the age of twenty-four, only thirteen are illegitimate. Half of the daughters' issue living in homes with male heads are legitimate and three in four of the sons' issue in these homes are also lawful. In homes with female heads, three in seven of the sons' resident issue are lawful, but less than one in three of the daughters' resident issue. Clearly women accommodate illegitimate grandchildren and children in their own homes with far greater frequency than men; and clearly they accommodate their daughers' unlawful issue more readily than their daughters' lawful issue or their sons' issue of any kind. These patterns agree with the preceding analysis; but do not describe the distribution of children completely, since collaterals and their issue are omitted.

In Table 14 I have classified the resident dependents of these households by sex, birth status, and age, and by reference to the presence of either parent in the same household. Of the 711 dependents analyzed here, 244 live with both parents and 230 of these are in their fathers' homes. Two hundred and twelve live apart from both parents and 128 of these live in homes with female heads. A further 165 live with their mothers apart from their fathers, and of these 148 live in homes with female heads. Only eighteen live with unwidowed fathers apart from their mothers. Only six live with their widowed fathers, as against sixty-six, all of whom are lawful, living with widowed mothers. Excluding these seventy-two children of widowed parents, there remain 639, of whom 38.2 per cent live with both parents, 33.2 per cent live apart from both parents, 25.8 per cent live with their mothers only, and only 1.8 per cent live with their fathers apart from their mothers. Of the 212 children who live apart from both parents, 134 or 63 per cent are known to be illegitimate. Of the 165 children who live with their mothers apart from their fathers, 118 or 71 per cent are also illegitimate; but of the 244 children who live with both parents, 234 or 96 per cent are legitimate and 221 of these live in homes with male heads. These distributions validate the preceding analysis fully, and they cannot be explained in any other way.

Tables 15 to 17 analyze the distribution of those children who live apart from one or both of their parents by reference to their birth status and the kin with whom they live. Only those dependents below the age of twenty-four are included in these tables. Of the children separated from both parents, only six live with nonkin. Sixty-two per cent of the remainder live with their matrilateral kin or with some kinswoman. The remaining 32.5 per cent live with their patrilateral kin or with some kinsman. The totals living with their mothers' and fathers' parents are approximately equal; but those who live with their mother's mother or mother's sister outnumber others living with their father's mother or father's sister by two to one. The handful of children who live with their fathers apart from their mothers merit attention for two reasons. First, very few of these children are found living with their fathers in homes which do not include other adult kin or mates of their fathers. Second, the number of children who live apart from their mothers and with their fathers is only one tenth of those who live with their mothers apart from their fathers.

Of 170 children below the age of twenty-four who live with their mothers apart from their fathers in these households, 109 or 64 per cent are unlawful. Of the sixty-one lawful children in this position, twenty-three have widowed mothers and twenty-five are the children of men who are absent overseas. These forty-eight all live in homes which lack adult kin other than their mothers. The overwhelming majority of the illegitimate offspring who live with their mothers apart from their fathers do so in homes which contain adult kin or mates of these mothers; and the majority of these adult kin are women linked to the children by uterine or materterine ties. Of these 170 children, seventy-seven are males, but there is no observable difference in the incidence of illegitimacy between the sexes. This means that illegitimate children of either sex are treated alike as regards parental responsibilities and household accommodation. Conversely, all legitimate children are treated alike; but the difference between legitimate and illegitimate children which expresses the different parental obligations associated with the alternative mating patterns is marked and consistent. Although the details of Tables 13 to 17 are undoubtedly of interest, we need

not linger further with them, since their details merely confirm
our analysis but contribute nothing new.

The Variety of Domestic Forms
An analysis of the total population resident in homes with heads of
different sex enables us to isolate broad differences in the composition of these categories of units; but it does not indicate their
morphological range or the incidence of differing types of group
within it. These dimensions of the domestic organization are obviously important, and are accordingly isolated in Tables 18 and
19.

Table 18 presents the frequency distribution of domestic units of
differing structural types within the sample. Its basis is a morphology of domestic forms which needs a brief introduction. This
morphology distinguishes eleven types of unit, and for each type
there is an additional distinction between pure cases and those
which contain accretions. Pure cases are those households all the
members of which are included in the category label. Accretions
are all persons other than mates and issue of the household head,
with the sole exception of siblings living with heads who lack resident mates.

The primary basis of this morphology is the distinction between
units having a lineal core and all others. Another important distinction is that between units the principals of which are mates or
spouses, and others. The third important element in this morphology is the generation depth of the structural core. Single-
person units and those which contain siblings or childless couples
only, include only one generation. Household heads or couples who
live with their children form two-generation units. Heads or couples
living with their grandchildren form three-generation units, even if
the intermediate generation is absent; but the important structural
differences which center about the presence or absence of this
intermediate generation are formally noticed in the classification.
Finally, the last two categories isolate units having a depth of four
or more generations, distinguishing those in which the principals
are resident couples from others whose heads lack a resident mate.

Two further points call for comment. Category 2 isolates siblings
who live together, with or without issue, but without any coresident
mates. Siblings with coresident mates are classified in categories
which are based on couples. In fact, we do not find any cases in
which a person with a resident mate lives as a dependent in the
home of a sibling. The sibling with a resident mate will always
head a unit of this constitution. I have accordingly isolated those

households based on siblingship which do not include resident mates
because they represent an important structural alternative to coresident mating, and one which allows the siblings to mate extraresidentially.

Category 4 isolates units the principals of which are childless
couples. In this classification, a couple is regarded as childless
when there are no resident issue of the couple in the home. Such
couples may very well have children or grandchildren of either
partner living with them; or they may have had children who are
no longer in the home. From the morphological point of view, these
facts are irrelevant to their classification. By definition, units
having childless couples as their principals cannot contain the
elementary or extended families of these persons, and are therefore
structurally distinct.

Of the 224 households in this sample, 67 per cent are pure types
in this morphology. The incidence of pure structural types in homes
with heads of different sex is almost identical. Of these 224 homes,
twenty-seven contain single persons and another seventeen contain
individuals living with people who are neither their mates, siblings,
nor offspring. Together, these forty-four units represent nearly one
fifth of the total sample. There are only four homes based on siblingship and all of these have female heads. In twenty-seven cases,
representing 12 per cent of the sample, the household consists of a
single parent and children, and all but one of these have female
heads. In fifteen cases, representing 6 per cent of the sample, the
principals are childless couples; and in all but one of these cases
the head is a man.

Excluding units based on siblingship, which may be residues of
previous household groups, it is clear that at least 38. 4 per cent
of the households in this sample neither contain elementary families
nor can be derived from them. It is also likely that some of the
remaining units have neither contained nor developed from elementary families.

Categories 6 and 8, which isolate single household heads and
their grandchildren, with or without the intermediate generation,
together account for just over a quarter of the sample households,
and in almost all cases these units have female heads. We have
already seen that the grandchildren resident in such units are for
the most part the illegitimate offspring of extraresidential associations; and in many cases the grandmothers who head these homes
have borne their children in the same way. The number of households consisting of mothers and children only or with accretions
may thus be set against the number consisting of an old woman and

her grandchildren. This gives some idea of the probable incidence of units which have never contained a resident male mate of the head, among the total containing three generations lineally descended from female heads presently living without mates. The relevant ratios of the total sample are 12 per cent and 25.9 per cent, respectively.

It is easy to see how units consisting of a woman and her children may grow to include a third generation. We cannot therefore assume that all three-generation units under female heads have developed from households which contained the elementary families of these heads; and even if some of the mothers who live with their children have absent husbands, or if some of the childless couples have absent children, there remains a sufficient proportion of such units which have never at any time incorporated an elementary family for the hypothetical derivation of these household forms from elementary family units to be inadequate and unacceptable.

Given the invalidity of this basic hypothesis, the others put forward by Dr. R. T. Smith to account for this developmental order become unnecessary. [6] In place of this developmental hypothesis, we must recognize that the divergent constitutions of these household groups are necessary effects of the duality in the forms of mating and parenthood. These alternatives are the dynamic elements which govern the constitution and development of domestic units. The morphological classification of household groups simply describes their distribution and effects.

We need not delay much longer over Table 19. The only important point to be noted is the difference in the incidence of three-generation units with or without the intermediate generation. Units containing members of three successive generations are over three times as frequent as those which contain alternate generations only. However, the generation structure of these households is not defined entirely by their structural cores. Siblings, for example, may have their children or grandchildren with them. A household, the principals of which are a childless couple, may have a depth of three generations through the inclusion of collaterals or the grandchildren of one of the principals. The large number of resident collaterals of female principals has been shown to include several members of the second descending generation. I have accordingly presented an exact analysis of the generation structure of the sample households in Table 19, based on the morphological categories just discussed. From this we see that over one half of the households under female heads have a depth of three or more generations, whereas less than one third of those with

male heads do. Over one half of the homes with male heads are
two-generation units but less than one third of those with female
heads. Fourteen per cent of all households contain one generation
only. Roughly half of the units based on childless couples have
a three-generation depth; and of the thirty-seven households based
on single women with or without accretions, ten have a depth of
two and seven of three generations. The greater generation depth
of households with female heads confirms our initial inferences
based on the age-sex distribution of headship.

Table 20 completes our analysis. It isolates all domestic units
based on mating principals and classifies them by reference to
the type of mating relation as well as their structure. Eighty-
three of the eighty-six units isolated there have male heads and
in seventy-nine of these units the principals are married. Of the
fifteen childless couples, four are unwed; of the fifty-five couples
who have children, only three are unwed. Of the fifteen childless
couples, only three live by themselves. Of the fifty-five with children, thirty-eight live by themselves. Couples who have their
grandchildren but not their children with them have no accretions
in their homes. Table 20 shows how rare it is for cohabitation to
occur in Carriacou without marriage. It also shows the strength
of the marriage bond over the years.

Conclusion

Carriacou domestic organization is governed by principles which
regulate mating and parenthood and integrate their dual forms into
a single system. This system assumes that each man honors his
mating and parental obligations independently, and requires that
he marry. It discourages males from taking their collateral kin
or their own grandchildren into their homes. Nor may they take
their illegitimate children by extraresidential unions to live with
them, since these children remain under their mother's authority.
Women who mate extraresidentially are thus responsible for the
accommodation of their offspring, and have a number of kinship
alternatives open to them. They may live alone with their children;
or they may live with their parents or collateral kin; or they may
place the children separately with their kinsfolk, including the
father's kin; or they may take these children into their husband's
home on marriage. These alternative modes of child placement
are necessary correlates of the extraresidential mating pattern,
with its definition of parental responsibilities, in a society where
men are heads of homes containing their lawful families. This
extraresidential mating system has obvious values in a society

with as many surplus females as Carriacou; however, it is not the only alternative to marriage, and there are many childless single women in the island. Extraresidential mating may also be prevalent in societies with a more equal sex ratio than Carriacou. The structurally decisive feature of the Carriacou system is the integration of extraresidential unions and marriage. In order that these may be integrated with one another, consensual cohabitation must be excluded, since the parental and mating obligations of coresident couples must be lasting and clearly defined. This means that cohabitation must be based on lifelong marriage, and that married women will not be able to resume extraresidential mating.

## TABLE 1

### POPULATION OF THE SAMPLE HOUSEHOLDS, CLASSIFIED BY SEX AND AGE

| Age | Number | | | Percentage | | | Females |
| | Male | Female | Total | Male | Female | Total | per Male |
|---|---|---|---|---|---|---|---|
| 0- 4 | 69 | 81 | 150 | 6.7 | 7.8 | 14.5 | 1.29 |
| 5-14 | 147 | 145 | 292 | 14.1 | 14.0 | 28.1 | 0.98 |
| 15-24 | 77 | 106 | 183 | 7.4 | 10.1 | 17.5 | 1.40 |
| 25-39 | 51 | 91 | 142 | 4.9 | 8.8 | 13.7 | 1.78 |
| 40-54 | 41 | 82 | 123 | 3.9 | 7.9 | 11.8 | 2.00 |
| 55-69 | 23 | 86 | 109 | 2.2 | 8.3 | 10.5 | 3.60 |
| 70 and Over | 13 | 28 | 41 | 1.2 | 2.7 | 3.9 | 2.15 |
| TOTAL | 421 | 619 | 1,040 | 40.4 | 59.6 | 100.0 | 1.47 |

## TABLE 2

### HEADS OF THE SAMPLE HOUSEHOLDS, CLASSIFIED BY SEX AND AGE

| Age | Number | | | Percentage | | |
| | Male | Female | Total | Male | Female | Total |
|---|---|---|---|---|---|---|
| 15-24 | 1 | 1 | 2 | 0.45 | 0.45 | 0.9 |
| 25-39 | 20 | 10 | 30 | 8.95 | 4.45 | 13.4 |
| 40-54 | 37 | 36 | 73 | 16.4 | 16.2 | 32.6 |
| 55-69 | 22 | 62 | 84 | 9.8 | 27.7 | 37.5 |
| 70 and Over | 13 | 22 | 35 | 5.8 | 9.8 | 15.6 |
| TOTAL | 93 | 131 | 224 | 41.4 | 58.6 | 100.0 |

## TABLE 3

### DISTRIBUTION OF HOUSEHOLD HEADSHIP AMONG ADULT MEMBERS OF THE SAMPLE POPULATION, CLASSIFIED BY SEX AND AGE

| Age | Total | Male HHs* | %HHs | Total | Female HHs* | %HHs | % HHs in Both Sexes |
|---|---|---|---|---|---|---|---|
| 15-24 | 77 | 1 | 1.3 | 106 | 1 | 0.94 | 1.1 |
| 25-39 | 51 | 20 | 39.2 | 91 | 10 | 11.0 | 21.0 |
| 40-54 | 41 | 37 | 90.5 | 82 | 36 | 44.0 | 59.4 |
| 55-69 | 23 | 22 | 96.0 | 86 | 62 | 72.0 | 77.0 |
| 70 and Over | 13 | 13 | 100.0 | 28 | 22 | 78.5 | 85.5 |
| TOTAL | 205 | 93 | 45.5 | 393 | 131 | 33.3 | 37.6 |

*HHs = Household heads.

## TABLE 4

### HOUSEHOLDS OF THE SAMPLE, CLASSIFIED BY SEX OF HEAD AND NUMBER OF PERSONS

| Number of Persons | Sex of Head Male | Female | Total | Male HHs* | Total Female HHs | Total |
|---|---|---|---|---|---|---|
| 1 | 7 | 20 | 27 | 7 | 20 | 27 |
| 2 | 2 | 22 | 24 | 4 | 44 | 48 |
| 3 | 11 | 29 | 40 | 33 | 87 | 120 |
| 4 | 14 | 17 | 31 | 56 | 68 | 124 |
| 5 | 13 | 11 | 24 | 65 | 55 | 120 |
| 6 | 10 | 10 | 20 | 60 | 60 | 120 |
| 7 | 13 | 12 | 25 | 91 | 84 | 175 |
| 8 | 8 | 5 | 13 | 64 | 40 | 104 |
| 9 | 7 | 1 | 8 | 63 | 9 | 72 |
| 10 | 5 | 2 | 7 | 50 | 20 | 70 |
| 11 | 0 | 1 | 1 | 0 | 11 | 11 |
| 12 | 2 | 1 | 3 | 24 | 12 | 36 |
| 13 | 1 | 0 | 1 | 13 | 0 | 13 |
| TOTAL | 93 | 131 | 224 | 530 | 510 | 1,040 |
| Excluding persons living alone | 86 | 111 | 197 | 523 | 490 | 1,013 |

| Averages: | | | | | | |
|---|---|---|---|---|---|---|
| including solitary persons | | | | 5.7% | 3.9% | 4.60% |
| excluding solitary persons | | | | 6.1% | 4.4% | 5.15% |

*HHs = Household heads.

## TABLE 5

### AGE AND SEX DISTRIBUTION OF HOUSEHOLD POPULATION, CLASSIFIED ACCORDING TO THE SEX OF THE HEAD

| Age | Male Head Male | Female | Total | Per cent | Female Head Male | Female | Total | Per cent | Total Male %HHs* | Female %HHs |
|---|---|---|---|---|---|---|---|---|---|---|
| 0- 4 | 38 | 50 | 88 | 16.6 | 31 | 31 | 62 | 12.2 | 8.5 | 6.0 |
| 5-14 | 81 | 84 | 165 | 31.2 | 64 | 64 | 128 | 24.9 | 15.9 | 12.2 |
| 15-24 | 34 | 47 | 81 | 15.3 | 42 | 59 | 101 | 19.9 | 7.8 | 9.7 |
| 25-39 | 29 | 41 | 70 | 13.2 | 22 | 50 | 72 | 14.1 | 6.8 | 6.9 |
| 40-54 | 37 | 29 | 66 | 12.4 | 4 | 53 | 57 | 11.2 | 6.3 | 5.5 |
| 55-69 | 23 | 20 | 43 | 8.1 | 0 | 66 | 66 | 13.0 | 4.2 | 6.3 |
| 70 + | 13 | 4 | 17 | 3.2 | 0 | 24 | 24 | 4.7 | 1.6 | 2.3 |
| TOTAL | 255 | 275 | 530 | 100.0 | 163 | 347 | 510 | 100.0 | 51.1 | 48.9 |

*HHs = Household heads.

## TABLE 6

### HOUSEHOLDERS LIVING ALONE, CLASSIFIED BY AGE, SEX, AND MARITAL STATUS

| | Male -24 | -39 | -54 | -69 | 70+ | Total | Female -24 | -39 | -54 | -69 | 70+ | Total |
|---|---|---|---|---|---|---|---|---|---|---|---|---|
| Never married | 0 | 2 | 1 | 0 | 0 | 3 | 0 | 1 | 2 | 3 | 3 | 9 |
| Marital status n/k* | 0 | 0 | 1 | 0 | 0 | 1 | 0 | 0 | 0 | 0 | 0 | 0 |
| Married, spouse absent | 0 | 0 | 0 | 0 | 0 | 0 | 1 | 1 | 0 | 0 | 0 | 2 |
| Married, separated | 0 | 0 | 0 | 0 | 0 | 0 | 0 | 0 | 1 | 1 | 0 | 2 |
| Married, widowed | 0 | 0 | 1 | 1 | 1 | 3 | 0 | 0 | 0 | 4 | 3 | 7 |
| TOTAL | 0 | 2 | 3 | 1 | 1 | 7 | 1 | 2 | 3 | 8 | 6 | 20 |

*n/k = Not known.

## TABLE 7

ALL ADULT MEMBERS OF THE SAMPLE POPULATION, CLASSIFIED BY SEX, AGE, MARITAL CONDITION, AND PARENTAL STATUS

| Mating and Parental Status | Male | | | | | | Female | | | | | |
|---|---|---|---|---|---|---|---|---|---|---|---|---|
| | -24 | -39 | -54 | -69 | 70+ | Total | -24 | -39 | -54 | -69 | 70+ | Total |
| **1. Childless single persons** | | | | | | | | | | | | |
| a. Mating now n/k* | 12 | 1 | 1 | 0 | 0 | 14 | 40 | 16 | 3 | 1 | 0 | 60 |
| b. Probably never mated | 47 | 0 | 0 | 0 | 0 | 47 | 42 | 0 | 0 | 0 | 0 | 42 |
| c. Not mating in 1953 | 2 | 1 | 0 | 0 | 0 | 3 | 4 | 0 | 6 | 5 | 0 | 15 |
| d. Mating in 1953 | 1 | 0 | 0 | 0 | 0 | 1 | 1 | 0 | 0 | 0 | 0 | 1 |
| Total childless single persons | 62 | 2 | 1 | 0 | 0 | 65 | 87 | 16 | 9 | 6 | 0 | 118 |
| **2. Single persons, parental status n/k** | | | | | | | | | | | | |
| a. Mating now n/k | 10 | 15 | 1 | 1 | 0 | 27 | 0 | 7 | 7 | 2 | 0 | 16 |
| b. Not mating now | 0 | 0 | 0 | 0 | 0 | 0 | 0 | 0 | 2 | 6 | 3 | 11 |
| c. Mating now | 0 | 0 | 0 | 0 | 0 | 0 | 0 | 0 | 0 | 0 | 0 | 0 |
| Total single persons, parental status n/k | 10 | 15 | 1 | 1 | 0 | 27 | 0 | 7 | 9 | 8 | 3 | 27 |
| **3. Single parents** | | | | | | | | | | | | |
| a. Mating now n/k | 0 | 2 | 0 | 0 | 0 | 2 | 2 | 3 | 10 | 0 | 0 | 15 |
| b. Not mating now | 0 | 0 | 0 | 0 | 0 | 0 | 0 | 3 | 7 | 9 | 4 | 23 |
| c. Mating now | 3 | 9 | 1 | 0 | 0 | 13 | 9 | 17 | 1 | 0 | 0 | 27 |
| Total single parents | 3 | 11 | 1 | 0 | 0 | 15 | 11 | 23 | 18 | 9 | 4 | 65 |
| **4. Consensually wed** | | | | | | | | | | | | |
| a. In 1953 | 1 | 3 | 1 | 1 | 0 | 6 | 1 | 6 | 0 | 0 | 0 | 7 |
| b. Separated, childless | 0 | 0 | 0 | 0 | 0 | 0 | 0 | 0 | 0 | 0 | 0 | 0 |
| c. Separated, with children | 0 | 0 | 0 | 0 | 0 | 0 | 0 | 0 | 1 | 0 | 0 | 1 |
| d. Widowed, single | 0 | 0 | 1 | 0 | 0 | 1 | 0 | 0 | 0 | 1 | 0 | 1 |
| Total consensually wed | 1 | 3 | 2 | 1 | 0 | 7 | 1 | 6 | 1 | 1 | 0 | 9 |
| **5. Married persons** | | | | | | | | | | | | |
| a. Spouse present | 1 | 20 | 34 | 18 | 9 | 82 | 6 | 28 | 28 | 16 | 4 | 82 |
| b. Spouse absent | 0 | 0 | 0 | 0 | 0 | 0 | 1 | 10 | 8 | 5 | 0 | 24 |
| c. Separated, single | 0 | 0 | 0 | 0 | 0 | 0 | 0 | 1 | 0 | 6 | 1 | 8 |
| d. Separated, not single | 0 | 0 | 1 | 1 | 0 | 2 | 0 | 0 | 0 | 1 | 0 | 1 |
| Total married person | 1 | 20 | 35 | 19 | 9 | 84 | 7 | 39 | 36 | 28 | 5 | 115 |
| **6. Widowed persons** | | | | | | | | | | | | |
| a. Widowed, single | 0 | 0 | 1 | 2 | 4 | 7 | 0 | 0 | 8 | 34 | 16 | 58 |
| b. Widowed, not single | 0 | 0 | 0 | 0 | 0 | 0 | 0 | 0 | 1 | 0 | 0 | 1 |
| Total widowed persons | 0 | 0 | 1 | 2 | 4 | 7 | 0 | 0 | 9 | 34 | 16 | 59 |
| GRAND TOTAL | 77 | 51 | 41 | 23 | 13 | 205 | 106 | 91 | 82 | 86 | 28 | 393 |

*n/k = Not known.

## TABLE 8

### ADULT MEMBERS OF THE SAMPLE POPULATION OTHER THAN HOUSEHOLD HEADS, CLASSIFIED BY SEX, AGE, MARITAL CONDITION, AND PARENTAL STATUS

| Mating and Parental Status | Male | | | | | | Female | | | | | |
|---|---|---|---|---|---|---|---|---|---|---|---|---|
| | -24 | -39 | -54 | -69 | 70+ | Total | -24 | -39 | -54 | -69 | 70+ | Total |
| 1. Childless single persons | | | | | | | | | | | | |
| a. Mating now n/k* | 12 | 1 | 1 | 0 | 0 | 14 | 40 | 15 | 3 | 1 | 0 | 59 |
| b. Probably never mated | 47 | 0 | 0 | 0 | 0 | 47 | 42 | 0 | 0 | 0 | 0 | 42 |
| c. Not mating in 1953 | 2 | 1 | 0 | 0 | 0 | 3 | 4 | 0 | 2 | 2 | 0 | 8 |
| d. Mating in 1953 | 1 | 0 | 0 | 0 | 0 | 1 | 1 | 0 | 0 | 0 | 0 | 1 |
| Total childless single persons | 62 | 2 | 1 | 0 | 0 | 65 | 87 | 15 | 5 | 3 | 0 | 110 |
| 2. Single persons, parental status n/k | | | | | | | | | | | | |
| a. Mating now n/k | 10 | 15 | 0 | 0 | 0 | 25 | 0 | 5 | 3 | 1 | 0 | 9 |
| b. Not mating now | 0 | 0 | 0 | 0 | 0 | 0 | 0 | 0 | 1 | 0 | 1 | 2 |
| c. Mating now | 0 | 0 | 0 | 0 | 0 | 0 | 0 | 0 | 0 | 0 | 0 | 0 |
| Total single persons, parental status n/k | 10 | 15 | 0 | 0 | 0 | 25 | 0 | 5 | 4 | 1 | 1 | 11 |
| 3. Single parents | | | | | | | | | | | | |
| a. Mating now n/k | 0 | 2 | 0 | 0 | 0 | 2 | 2 | 2 | 5 | 0 | 0 | 9 |
| b. Not mating now | 0 | 0 | 0 | 0 | 0 | 0 | 0 | 2 | 2 | 1 | 1 | 6 |
| c. Mating now | 3 | 7 | 1 | 0 | 0 | 11 | 9 | 15 | 1 | 0 | 0 | 25 |
| Total single parents | 3 | 9 | 1 | 0 | 0 | 13 | 11 | 19 | 8 | 1 | 1 | 40 |
| 4. Consensually wed | | | | | | | | | | | | |
| a. In 1953 | 1 | 0 | 0 | 1 | 0 | 2 | 1 | 6 | 0 | 0 | 0 | 7 |
| b. Separated, childless | 0 | 0 | 0 | 0 | 0 | 0 | 0 | 0 | 0 | 0 | 0 | 0 |
| c. Separated, with children | 0 | 0 | 0 | 0 | 0 | 0 | 0 | 0 | 0 | 0 | 0 | 0 |
| d. Widowed, single | 0 | 0 | 0 | 0 | 0 | 0 | 0 | 0 | 0 | 0 | 0 | 0 |
| Total consensually wed | 1 | 0 | 0 | 1 | 0 | 2 | 1 | 6 | 0 | 0 | 0 | 7 |
| 5. Married persons | | | | | | | | | | | | |
| a. Spouse present | 0 | 5 | 2 | 0 | 0 | 7 | 6 | 28 | 27 | 16 | 4 | 81 |
| b. Spouse absent | 0 | 0 | 0 | 0 | 0 | 0 | 0 | 8 | 2 | 0 | 0 | 10 |
| c. Separated, single | 0 | 0 | 0 | 0 | 0 | 0 | 0 | 0 | 0 | 3 | 0 | 3 |
| d. Separated, not single | 0 | 0 | 0 | 0 | 0 | 0 | 0 | 0 | 0 | 0 | 0 | 0 |
| Total married persons | 0 | 5 | 2 | 0 | 0 | 7 | 6 | 36 | 29 | 19 | 4 | 94 |
| 6. Widowed persons | | | | | | | | | | | | |
| a. Widowed, single | 0 | 0 | 0 | 0 | 0 | 0 | 0 | 0 | 0 | 0 | 0 | 0 |
| b. Widowed, not single | 0 | 0 | 0 | 0 | 0 | 0 | 0 | 0 | 0 | 0 | 0 | 0 |
| Total widowed persons | 0 | 0 | 0 | 0 | 0 | 0 | 0 | 0 | 0 | 0 | 0 | 0 |
| GRAND TOTAL | 76 | 31 | 4 | 1 | 0 | 112 | 105 | 81 | 46 | 24 | 6 | 262 |

*n/k = Not known.

## TABLE 9

### HOUSEHOLD HEADS, CLASSIFIED BY SEX, AGE, MARITAL CONDITION, AND PARENTAL STATUS

| Mating and Parental Status | Male | | | | | | Female | | | | | |
|---|---|---|---|---|---|---|---|---|---|---|---|---|
| | -24 | -39 | -54 | -69 | 70+ | Total | -24 | -39 | -54 | -69 | 70+ | Total |
| **1. Childless single persons** | | | | | | | | | | | | |
| a. Mating now n/k* | 0 | 0 | 0 | 0 | 0 | 0 | 0 | 1 | 0 | 0 | 0 | 1 |
| b. Probably never mated | 0 | 0 | 0 | 0 | 0 | 0 | 0 | 0 | 0 | 0 | 0 | 0 |
| c. Not mating in 1953 | 0 | 0 | 0 | 0 | 0 | 0 | 0 | 0 | 4 | 3 | 0 | 7 |
| d. Mating in 1953 | 0 | 0 | 0 | 0 | 0 | 0 | 0 | 0 | 0 | 0 | 0 | 0 |
| Total childless single persons | 0 | 0 | 0 | 0 | 0 | 0 | 0 | 1 | 4 | 3 | 0 | 8 |
| **2. Single persons, parental status n/k** | | | | | | | | | | | | |
| a. Mating now n/k | 0 | 0 | 1 | 1 | 0 | 2 | 0 | 2 | 4 | 1 | 0 | 7 |
| b. Not mating now | 0 | 0 | 0 | 0 | 0 | 0 | 0 | 0 | 1 | 6 | 2 | 9 |
| c. Mating now | 0 | 0 | 0 | 0 | 0 | 0 | 0 | 0 | 0 | 0 | 0 | 0 |
| Total single persons, parental status n/k | 0 | 0 | 1 | 1 | 0 | 2 | 0 | 2 | 5 | 7 | 2 | 16 |
| **3. Single parents** | | | | | | | | | | | | |
| a. Mating now n/k | 0 | 0 | 0 | 0 | 0 | 0 | 0 | 1 | 5 | 0 | 0 | 6 |
| b. Not mating now | 0 | 0 | 0 | 0 | 0 | 0 | 0 | 1 | 5 | 8 | 3 | 17 |
| c. Mating now | 0 | 2 | 0 | 0 | 0 | 2 | 0 | 2 | 0 | 0 | 0 | 2 |
| Total single parents | 0 | 2 | 0 | 0 | 0 | 2 | 0 | 4 | 10 | 8 | 3 | 25 |
| **4. Consensually wed** | | | | | | | | | | | | |
| a. In 1953 | 0 | 3 | 1 | 0 | 0 | 4 | 0 | 0 | 0 | 0 | 0 | 0 |
| b. Separated, childless | 0 | 0 | 0 | 0 | 0 | 0 | 0 | 0 | 0 | 0 | 0 | 0 |
| c. Separated, with children | 0 | 0 | 0 | 0 | 0 | 0 | 0 | 0 | 0 | 1 | 0 | 1 |
| d. Widowed, single | 0 | 0 | 1 | 0 | 0 | 1 | 0 | 0 | 1 | 0 | 0 | 1 |
| Total consensually wed | 0 | 3 | 2 | 0 | 0 | 5 | 0 | 0 | 1 | 1 | 0 | 2 |
| **5. Married persons** | | | | | | | | | | | | |
| a. Spouse present | 1 | 15 | 32 | 18 | 9 | 75 | 1 | 0 | 0 | 0 | 0 | 1 |
| b. Spouse absent | 0 | 0 | 0 | 0 | 0 | 0 | 0 | 3 | 6 | 5 | 1 | 15 |
| c. Separated, single | 0 | 0 | 0 | 0 | 0 | 0 | 0 | 0 | 1 | 3 | 0 | 4 |
| d. Separated, not single | 0 | 0 | 1 | 1 | 0 | 2 | 0 | 0 | 0 | 1 | 0 | 1 |
| Total married persons | 1 | 15 | 33 | 19 | 9 | 77 | 1 | 3 | 7 | 9 | 1 | 21 |
| **6. Widowed persons** | | | | | | | | | | | | |
| a. Widowed, single | 0 | 0 | 1 | 2 | 4 | 7 | 0 | 0 | 8 | 34 | 16 | 58 |
| b. Widowed, not single | 0 | 0 | 0 | 0 | 0 | 0 | 0 | 0 | 1 | 0 | 0 | 1 |
| Total widowed persons | 0 | 0 | 1 | 2 | 4 | 7 | 0 | 0 | 9 | 34 | 16 | 59 |
| **GRAND TOTAL** | 1 | 20 | 37 | 22 | 13 | 93 | 1 | 10 | 36 | 62 | 22 | 131 |

*n/k = Not known.

## TABLE 10

### POPULATION OF THE SAMPLE HOUSEHOLDS, CLASSIFIED BY RELATIONSHIP TO THE HOUSEHOLD HEAD AND SEX OF HEAD

| Categories of Kin | Male Head Number | Male Head Per cent | Female Head Number | Female Head Per cent | Total Number | Total Per cent |
|---|---|---|---|---|---|---|
| 1. Spouses and mates | 82 | 18.8 | 3 | 0.8 | 85 | 10.4 |
| 2. HH's* sons | 116 | 26.6 | 58 | 15.3 | 174 | 21.4 |
| 3. HH's daughters | 132 | 30.2 | 88 | 23.2 | 220 | 27.0 |
| 4. HH's children | 248 | 56.8 | 146 | 38.5 | 394 | 48.4 |
| 5. HH's sons' sons | 10 | 2.3 | 17 | 4.5 | 27 | 3.3 |
| 6. HH's sons' daughters | 3 | 0.7 | 24 | 6.3 | 27 | 3.3 |
| 7. HH's daughters' sons | 15 | 3.4 | 39 | 10.3 | 54 | 6.6 |
| HH's daughters' daughters | 13 | 3.0 | 57 | 15.0 | 70 | 8.5 |
| HH's grandchildren | 41 | 9.4 | 137 | 36.1 | 178 | 21.7 |
| 8. HH's sons' grandchildren | 0 | 0.0 | 1 | 0.3 | 1 | 0.1 |
| 9. HH's daughter's grandchildren | 1 | 0.2 | 4 | 1.0 | 5 | 0.6 |
| Total lineal issue of HH | 290 | 66.4 | 288 | 75.9 | 578 | 70.8 |
| 10. HH's mates' sons by others | 3 | 0.7 | 2 | 0.5 | 5 | 0.6 |
| 11. HH's mates' daughters by others | 11 | 2.5 | 1 | 0.3 | 12 | 1.5 |
| 12. HH's mates' sons' sons | 1 | 0.2 | 0 | 0.0 | 1 | 0.1 |
| 13. HH's mates' daughters' sons | 3 | 0.7 | 0 | 0.0 | 3 | 0.4 |
| 14. HH's mates' daughters' daughters | 4 | 0.9 | 0 | 0.0 | 4 | 0.5 |
| Issue of HH's mates by others | 22 | 5.0 | 3 | 0.8 | 25 | 3.1 |
| 15. HH's brothers | 0 | 0.0 | 0 | 0.0 | 0 | 0.0 |
| 16. HH's sisters | 0 | 0.0 | 5 | 1.3 | 5 | 0.6 |
| 17. HH's brothers' issue | 3 | 0.7 | 16 | 4.2 | 19 | 2.4 |
| 18. HH's sisters' issue | 0 | 0.0 | 39 | 10.3 | 39 | 4.7 |
| HH's siblings and their issue | 3 | 0.7 | 60 | 15.8 | 63 | 7.7 |
| 19. HH's mother's sister | 0 | 0.0 | 1 | 0.3 | 1 | 0.1 |
| 20. HH's mother's sister's issue | 1 | 0.2 | 6 | 1.6 | 7 | 0.9 |
| 21. HH's mother's mother's sister's issue | 0 | 0.0 | 1 | 0.3 | 1 | 0.1 |
| Categories 19 to 21 | 1 | 0.2 | 8 | 2.2 | 9 | 1.1 |
| 22. HH's mother | 0 | 0.0 | 1 | 0.3 | 1 | 0.1 |
| 23. HH's children's mate or spouse | 0 | 0.0 | 9 | 2.3 | 9 | 1.1 |
| 24. Kin of HH's children's mates | 0 | 0.0 | 1 | 0.2 | 1 | 0.1 |
| 25. Other kin of HH's mate or spouse | 35 | 8.0 | 1 | 0.3 | 36 | 4.5 |
| 26. HH's adopted children | 4 | 0.9 | 4 | 1.2 | 8 | 1.0 |
| Categories 22 to 26 | 39 | 8.9 | 16 | 4.3 | 55 | 6.8 |
| 27. Boarders | 0 | 0.0 | 1 | 0.2 | 1 | 0.1 |
| TOTAL | 437 | 100.0 | 379 | 100.0 | 816 | 100.0 |

*HH = Household head.

TABLE 11

RESIDENT COLLATERALS OF FEMALE PRINCIPALS, CLASSIFIED BY KINSHIP CATEGORY, BIRTH STATUS, AND SEX OF HOUSEHOLD HEAD

| Kinship Category | Male Head | | | | Female Head | | | | Total |
|---|---|---|---|---|---|---|---|---|---|
| | L* | U* | N/K* | All | L | U | N/K | All | |
| Full siblings | 0 | 0 | 2 | 2 | 0 | 0 | 3 | 3 | 5 |
| Issue of full siblings | 2 | 9 | 1 | 12 | 16 | 28 | 7 | 51 | 63 |
| Patrilateral kin | 0 | 3 | 0 | 3 | 0 | 3 | 2 | 5 | 8 |
| Matrilateral kin | 1 | 5 | 1 | 7 | 0 | 8 | 1 | 9 | 16 |
| TOTAL | 3 | 17 | 4 | 24 | 16 | 39 | 13 | 68 | 92 |

*L = Lawful, i.e., legitimate; U = Unlawful, i.e., illegitimate; N/K = Birth status not known.

TABLE 12

RESIDENT COLLATERALS OF FEMALE PRINCIPALS, CLASSIFIED BY SEX, BIRTH STATUS, GENERATION, SEX OF PARENT THROUGH WHOM KINSHIP IS TRACED, AND SEX OF HOUSEHOLD HEAD

| Generation | Sex of Linking Parent | Households with Male Head | | | | | | | Households with Female Head | | | | | | | Total | | | | | | |
|---|---|---|---|---|---|---|---|---|---|---|---|---|---|---|---|---|---|---|---|---|---|---|
| | | L* M* | L* F* | U* M | U* F | N/K* M | N/K* F | Total | L M | L F | U M | U F | N/K M | N/K F | Total | L M | L F | U M | U F | N/K M | N/K F | Total |
| 0 | Male | 0 | 0 | 0 | 0 | 0 | 0 | 0 | 0 | 0 | 0 | 2 | 0 | 0 | 2 | 0 | 0 | 0 | 2 | 0 | 0 | 2 |
| | Female | 0 | 0 | 1 | 1 | 1 | 0 | 2 | 0 | 0 | 1 | 1 | 0 | 0 | 2 | 0 | 0 | 2 | 2 | 1 | 0 | 5 |
| | Total | 0 | 0 | 1 | 1 | 1 | 0 | 2 | 0 | 0 | 1 | 3 | 0 | 0 | 4 | 0 | 0 | 2 | 4 | 1 | 0 | 7 |
| -1 | Male | 0 | 2 | 0 | 1 | 0 | 0 | 3 | 0 | 5 | 2 | 1 | 0 | 1 | 10 | 0 | 5 | 2 | 7 | 0 | 1 | 13 |
| | Female | 0 | 1 | 3 | 2 | 13 | 1 | 10 | 2 | 6 | 2 | 9 | 5 | 0 | 28 | 2 | 7 | 5 | 18 | 6 | 1 | 38 |
| | Total | 0 | 3 | 3 | 3 | 13 | 1 | 13 | 2 | 11 | 4 | 16 | 5 | 1 | 38 | 2 | 12 | 7 | 18 | 7 | 22 | 51 |
| -2 | Male | 0 | 0 | 0 | 0 | 0 | 0 | 0 | 0 | 1 | 1 | 0 | 0 | 1 | 3 | 0 | 1 | 1 | 0 | 0 | 1 | 3 |
| | Female | 0 | 0 | 3 | 6 | 5 | 0 | 6 | 0 | 2 | 6 | 8 | 9 | 3 | 15 | 2 | 3 | 7 | 10 | 8 | 0 | 21 |
| | Total | 0 | 0 | 3 | 6 | 5 | 1 | 6 | 1 | 2 | 9 | 8 | 3 | 10 | 18 | 2 | 3 | 9 | 10 | 8 | 1 | 24 |
| -3 | Male | 0 | 0 | 0 | 0 | 0 | 0 | 0 | 0 | 0 | 0 | 0 | 0 | 1 | 1 | 0 | 0 | 0 | 1 | 0 | 0 | 1 |
| | Female | 0 | 0 | 0 | 0 | 0 | 0 | 0 | 0 | 0 | 0 | 2 | 0 | 0 | 4 | 0 | 0 | 2 | 2 | 0 | 0 | 4 |
| | Total | 0 | 0 | 0 | 0 | 0 | 0 | 0 | 0 | 0 | 0 | 3 | 2 | 0 | 5 | 0 | 0 | 3 | 2 | 0 | 0 | 5 |
| All generations | Male | 0 | 2 | 0 | 1 | 0 | 0 | 3 | 1 | 4 | 4 | 3 | 1 | 3 | 16 | 1 | 6 | 4 | 4 | 1 | 3 | 19 |
| | Female | 0 | 1 | 7 | 9 | 1 | 1 | 19 | 3 | 8 | 11 | 21 | 0 | 6 | 49 | 3 | 9 | 18 | 30 | 1 | 7 | 68 |
| | TOTAL | 0 | 3 | 7 | 10 | 1 | 1 | 22 | 4 | 12 | 15 | 24 | 1 | 9 | 65 | 4 | 15 | 22 | 34 | 2 | 10 | 87 |

*L = Lawful, i.e., legitimate; U = Unlawful, i.e., illegitimate; N/K = Birth status not known; M = Male; F = Female.

## TABLE 13

RESIDENT LINEAL ISSUE OF THE HOUSEHOLD HEAD, CLASSIFIED BY SEX, BIRTH STATUS, GENERATION, SEX OF PARENT THROUGH WHOM DESCENT IS TRACED, AND SEX OF THE HOUSEHOLD HEAD

| Sex and Birth Status | Households with Male Head | | | | Households with Female Head | | | | Total | | | |
|---|---|---|---|---|---|---|---|---|---|---|---|---|
| | Own Issue | Sons' Issue | Daughters' Issue | Total | Own Issue | Sons' Issue | Daughters' Issue | Total | Own Issue | Sons' Issue | Daughters' Issue | Total |
| Males | | | | | | | | | | | | |
| L* | 104 | 9 | 8 | 121 | 25 | 7 | 16 | 48 | 129 | 16 | 24 | 169 |
| U* | 5 | 1 | 5 | 11 | 17 | 16 | 33 | 66 | 22 | 17 | 38 | 77 |
| N/K* | 8 | 0 | 0 | 8 | 16 | 0 | 1 | 17 | 24 | 0 | 1 | 25 |
| All males | 117 | 10 | 13 | 140 | 58 | 23 | 50 | 131 | 175 | 33 | 63 | 271 |
| Females | | | | | | | | | | | | |
| L | 115 | 1 | 6 | 122 | 31 | 11 | 14 | 56 | 146 | 12 | 20 | 178 |
| U | 8 | 2 | 9 | 19 | 16 | 8 | 35 | 59 | 24 | 10 | 44 | 78 |
| N/K | 9 | 0 | 0 | 9 | 41 | 0 | 1 | 42 | 50 | 0 | 1 | 51 |
| All females | 132 | 3 | 15 | 150 | 88 | 19 | 50 | 157 | 220 | 22 | 65 | 307 |
| Total | | | | | | | | | | | | |
| L | 219 | 10 | 14 | 243 | 56 | 18 | 30 | 104 | 275 | 28 | 44 | 347 |
| U | 13 | 3 | 14 | 30 | 33 | 24 | 68 | 125 | 46 | 27 | 82 | 155 |
| N/K | 17 | 0 | 0 | 17 | 57 | 0 | 2 | 59 | 74 | 0 | 2 | 76 |
| GRAND TOTAL | 249 | 13 | 28 | 290 | 146 | 42 | 100 | 288 | 395 | 55 | 128 | 578 |

*L = Lawful, i.e., legitimate; U = Unlawful, i.e., illegitimate; N/K = Birth status not known.

## TABLE 14

DISTRIBUTION OF CHILDREN WITHIN THE SAMPLE HOUSEHOLDS, CLASSIFIED BY SEX OF HEAD, WITH SPECIAL REFERENCE TO THE PRESENCE OF EITHER PARENT IN THE HOUSEHOLD, AND TO THE AGE AND BIRTH STATUS OF THE CHILDREN OF EITHER SEX

| Age | Households with Male Head | | | | | | | Households with Female Head | | | | | | Total | | | | | | |
|---|---|---|---|---|---|---|---|---|---|---|---|---|---|---|---|---|---|---|---|---|
| | LS* | LD* | US* | UD* | N/KS* | N/KD* | Total | LS | LD | US | UD | N/KD | Total | LS | LD | US | UD | N/KS | N/KD | Total |
| **a. Both parents present** | | | | | | | | | | | | | | | | | | | | |
| 0- 4 | 27 | 34 | 1 | 3 | 0 | 0 | 65 | 5 | 2 | 0 | 1 | 0 | 8 | 32 | 36 | 1 | 4 | 0 | 0 | 73 |
| 5-14 | 56 | 51 | 1 | 3 | 0 | 0 | 111 | 0 | 3 | 0 | 0 | 0 | 3 | 56 | 54 | 1 | 3 | 0 | 0 | 114 |
| 15-24 | 19 | 23 | 0 | 1 | 0 | 0 | 43 | 0 | 3 | 0 | 0 | 0 | 3 | 19 | 26 | 0 | 1 | 0 | 0 | 46 |
| 25-39 | 5 | 5 | 0 | 0 | 0 | 0 | 10 | 0 | 0 | 0 | 0 | 0 | 0 | 5 | 5 | 0 | 0 | 0 | 0 | 10 |
| 40 + | 0 | 1 | 0 | 0 | 0 | 0 | 1 | 0 | 0 | 0 | 0 | 0 | 0 | 0 | 1 | 0 | 0 | 0 | 0 | 1 |
| Total | 107 | 114 | 2 | 7 | 0 | 0 | 230 | 5 | 8 | 0 | 1 | 0 | 14 | 112 | 122 | 2 | 8 | 0 | 0 | 244 |
| **b. Both parents absent** | | | | | | | | | | | | | | | | | | | | |
| 0- 4 | 5 | 5 | 2 | 5 | 0 | 0 | 17 | 0 | 2 | 5 | 5 | 0 | 12 | 5 | 7 | 7 | 10 | 0 | 0 | 29 |
| 5-14 | 11 | 6 | 9 | 11 | 0 | 1 | 38 | 10 | 8 | 21 | 20 | 1 | 59 | 21 | 14 | 30 | 31 | 1 | 3 | 97 |
| 15-24 | 2 | 4 | 5 | 9 | 1 | 2 | 23 | 6 | 10 | 13 | 17 | 1 | 47 | 8 | 14 | 18 | 26 | 1 | 3 | 70 |
| 25-39 | 0 | 0 | 1 | 2 | 0 | 2 | 5 | 0 | 1 | 3 | 5 | 1 | 10 | 0 | 1 | 4 | 7 | 0 | 3 | 15 |
| 40 + | 0 | 0 | 0 | 1 | 0 | 0 | 1 | 0 | 0 | 0 | 0 | 0 | 0 | 0 | 0 | 0 | 1 | 0 | 0 | 1 |
| Total | 18 | 15 | 17 | 28 | 1 | 5 | 84 | 16 | 21 | 42 | 47 | 2 | 128 | 34 | 36 | 59 | 75 | 1 | 7 | 212 |
| **c. Mothers only present** | | | | | | | | | | | | | | | | | | | | |
| 0- 4 | 0 | 1 | 3 | 2 | 0 | 0 | 6 | 3 | 5 | 17 | 15 | 0 | 40 | 3 | 6 | 20 | 17 | 0 | 0 | 46 |
| 5-14 | 0 | 1 | 0 | 5 | 0 | 0 | 6 | 11 | 10 | 19 | 16 | 0 | 56 | 11 | 11 | 19 | 21 | 0 | 1 | 62 |
| 15-24 | 0 | 0 | 2 | 2 | 0 | 0 | 4 | 6 | 5 | 8 | 13 | 1 | 33 | 6 | 5 | 10 | 15 | 1 | 1 | 37 |
| 25-39 | 0 | 0 | 0 | 0 | 0 | 0 | 0 | 1 | 2 | 2 | 9 | 0 | 14 | 1 | 2 | 2 | 9 | 0 | 0 | 14 |
| 40 + | 0 | 0 | 0 | 1 | 0 | 0 | 1 | 0 | 1 | 0 | 4 | 0 | 5 | 0 | 1 | 0 | 5 | 0 | 0 | 6 |
| Total | 0 | 2 | 5 | 10 | 0 | 0 | 17 | 21 | 23 | 46 | 57 | 1 | 148 | 21 | 25 | 51 | 67 | 1 | 1 | 165 |
| **d. Fathers only present** | | | | | | | | | | | | | | | | | | | | |
| 0- 4 | 0 | 0 | 0 | 0 | 0 | 0 | 0 | 0 | 0 | 1 | 0 | 0 | 1 | 0 | 0 | 1 | 0 | 0 | 0 | 1 |
| 5-14 | 1 | 2 | 2 | 3 | 0 | 0 | 8 | 0 | 0 | 1 | 1 | 0 | 2 | 1 | 2 | 3 | 4 | 0 | 0 | 10 |
| 15-24 | 0 | 0 | 2 | 2 | 0 | 0 | 4 | 0 | 0 | 0 | 0 | 0 | 0 | 0 | 0 | 2 | 2 | 0 | 0 | 4 |
| 25-39 | 0 | 0 | 2 | 1 | 0 | 0 | 3 | 0 | 0 | 0 | 0 | 0 | 0 | 0 | 0 | 2 | 1 | 0 | 0 | 3 |
| 40 + | 0 | 0 | 0 | 0 | 0 | 0 | 0 | 0 | 0 | 0 | 0 | 0 | 0 | 0 | 0 | 0 | 0 | 0 | 0 | 0 |
| Total | 1 | 2 | 6 | 6 | 0 | 0 | 15 | 0 | 0 | 2 | 1 | 0 | 3 | 1 | 2 | 8 | 7 | 0 | 0 | 18 |

TABLE 14 (continued)

DISTRIBUTION OF CHILDREN WITHIN THE SAMPLE HOUSEHOLDS, CLASSIFIED BY SEX OF HEAD, WITH SPECIAL REFERENCE TO THE PRESENCE OF EITHER PARENT IN THE HOUSEHOLD, AND TO THE AGE AND BIRTH STATUS OF THE CHILDREN OF EITHER SEX

| Age | Households with Male Head | | | | | | | Households with Female Head | | | | | | Total | | | | | | |
|---|---|---|---|---|---|---|---|---|---|---|---|---|---|---|---|---|---|---|---|---|
| | LS* | LD* | US* | UD* | N/KS* | N/KD* | Total | LS | LD | US | UD | N/KD | Total | LS | LD | US | UD | N/KS | N/KD | Total |
| **e. With fathers, mothers dead** | | | | | | | | | | | | | | | | | | | | |
| 0- 4 | 0 | 0 | 0 | 0 | 0 | 0 | 0 | | | | | | | 0 | 0 | 0 | 0 | 0 | 0 | 0 |
| 5-14 | 1 | 1 | 0 | 0 | 0 | 0 | 2 | | | | | | | 1 | 1 | 0 | 0 | 0 | 0 | 2 |
| 15-24 | 1 | 1 | 0 | 0 | 0 | 0 | 2 | | | | | | | 1 | 1 | 0 | 0 | 0 | 0 | 2 |
| 25-39 | 0 | 2 | 0 | 0 | 0 | 0 | 2 | | | | | | | 0 | 2 | 0 | 0 | 0 | 0 | 2 |
| 40 + | 0 | 0 | 0 | 0 | 0 | 0 | 0 | | | | | | | 0 | 0 | 0 | 0 | 0 | 0 | 0 |
| Total | 2 | 4 | 0 | 0 | 0 | 0 | 6 | | | | | | | 2 | 4 | 0 | 0 | 0 | 0 | 6 |
| **f. With mothers, fathers dead** | | | | | | | | | | | | | | | | | | | | |
| 0- 4 | | | | | | | | 0 | 1 | 0 | 0 | 0 | 1 | 0 | 1 | 0 | 0 | 0 | 0 | 1 |
| 5-14 | | | | | | | | 2 | 6 | 0 | 0 | 0 | 8 | 2 | 6 | 0 | 0 | 0 | 0 | 8 |
| 15-24 | | | | | | | | 9 | 9 | 0 | 0 | 0 | 18 | 9 | 9 | 0 | 0 | 0 | 0 | 18 |
| 25-39 | | | | | | | | 13 | 14 | 0 | 0 | 0 | 27 | 13 | 14 | 0 | 0 | 0 | 0 | 27 |
| 40 + | | | | | | | | 2 | 10 | 0 | 0 | 0 | 12 | 2 | 10 | 0 | 0 | 0 | 0 | 12 |
| Total | | | | | | | | 26 | 40 | 0 | 0 | 0 | 66 | 26 | 40 | 0 | 0 | 0 | 0 | 66 |
| **Totals by sex of household head** | | | | | | | | | | | | | | | | | | | | |
| 0- 4 | 32 | 40 | 6 | 10 | 0 | 0 | 88 | 8 | 10 | 23 | 21 | 0 | 62 | 40 | 50 | 29 | 31 | 0 | 0 | 150 |
| 5-14 | 69 | 61 | 12 | 22 | 0 | 1 | 165 | 23 | 27 | 41 | 37 | 0 | 128 | 92 | 88 | 53 | 59 | 1 | 1 | 293 |
| 15-24 | 22 | 28 | 9 | 14 | 1 | 2 | 76 | 21 | 27 | 21 | 30 | 2 | 101 | 43 | 55 | 30 | 44 | 4 | 177 | |
| 25-39 | 5 | 7 | 3 | 3 | 0 | 2 | 20 | 14 | 17 | 5 | 14 | 1 | 51 | 19 | 24 | 8 | 12 | 3 | 71 | |
| 40 + | 0 | 1 | 0 | 2 | 0 | 0 | 3 | 2 | 11 | 0 | 4 | 0 | 17 | 2 | 12 | 0 | 6 | 0 | 20 | |
| TOTAL | 128 | 137 | 30 | 51 | 1 | 5 | 352 | 68 | 92 | 90 | 106 | 3 | 359 | 196 | 229 | 120 | 157 | 8 | 711 | |

*LS = Lawful son; LD = Lawful daughter; US = Unlawful son; UD = Unlawful daughter; N/KS = Son, birth status not known; N/KD = Daughter, birth status not known.

## TABLE 15

CHILDREN SEPARATED FROM BOTH PARENTS, CLASSIFIED BY KINSHIP TO PRINCIPAL IN WHOSE HOMES THEY LIVE

### Matrilateral Kin

| Guardians | Wards Number | Per cent |
|---|---|---|
| 1. Mother's mother | 55 | 26.7 |
| 2. Mother's mother and father | 19 | 9.1 |
| 3. Mother's sister | 27 | 13.0 |
| 4. Mother's father | 3 | 1.6 |
| 5. Matrilateral kinswoman | 17 | 8.2 |
| 6. Cognatic kinswoman* | 13 | 6.4 |
| TOTAL | 134 | 65.0 |

### Patrilateral Kin

| Guardians | Wards Number | Per cent |
|---|---|---|
| 1. Father's mother | 30 | 14.3 |
| 2. Father's mother and father | 16 | 7.8 |
| 3. Father's sister | 12 | 6.0 |
| 4. Father's wife | 4 | 2.0 |
| 5. Agnatic kinsman | 4 | 2.0 |
| 6. Cognatic kinsman | 1 | 0.4 |
| TOTAL | 67 | 32.5 |

With nonkin in homes with female heads, 6 juniors = 2.5%

*Cognatic kin: shorthand term for kin of the specified sex connected to the ward through individuals of both sexes.

## TABLE 16

CHILDREN LESS THAN 24 YEARS OF AGE, LIVING WITH THEIR FATHERS APART FROM THEIR MOTHERS, CLASSIFIED BY SEX, BIRTH STATUS, AND STATUS OF FATHER OR KIN WITH WHOM THEY LIVE

| | Male | | | Female | | | | | |
|---|---|---|---|---|---|---|---|---|---|
| | L* | U* | Total | L | U | Total | L | U | Total |
| 1. Father widowed | 1 | 0 | 1 | 1 | 1 | 2 | 2 | 1 | 3 |
| 2. Father and father's mother | 0 | 1 | 1 | 0 | 0 | 0 | 0 | 1 | 1 |
| 3. Father and F's father and mother | 0 | 0 | 0 | 0 | 1 | 1 | 0 | 1 | 1 |
| 4. Father and F's unwed mate | 1 | 1 | 2 | 2 | 0 | 2 | 3 | 1 | 4 |
| 5. Father and father's wife | 0 | 2 | 2 | 0 | 0 | 0 | 0 | 2 | 2 |
| 6. Father and F's mother and brother | 0 | 1 | 1 | 0 | 0 | . | 0 | 1 | 1 |
| 7. Father and father's father | 0 | 0 | 0 | 0 | 1 | 1 | 0 | 1 | 1 |
| TOTAL | 2 | 5 | 7 | 3 | 3 | 6 | 5 | 8 | 13 |

*L = Lawful, i.e., legitimate; U = Unlawful, i.e., illegitimate.

## TABLE 17

CHILDREN LESS THAN 24 YEARS OF AGE, LIVING WITH THEIR MOTHERS APART FROM THEIR FATHERS, CLASSIFIED BY SEX, BIRTH STATUS, AND STATUS OF MOTHER OR KIN WITH WHOM THEY LIVE

| | Male | | | Female | | | | | |
|---|---|---|---|---|---|---|---|---|---|
| | L* | U* | Total | L | U | Total | L | U | Total |
| 1. Mother wed | 13 | 0 | 13 | 12 | 1 | 13 | 25 | 1 | 26 |
| 2. Mother unwed | 0 | 12 | 12 | 0 | 15 | 15 | 0 | 27 | 27 |
| 3. Mother widowed | 10 | 0 | 10 | 13 | 2 | 15 | 23 | 2 | 25 |
| 4. Mother wed, separated | 0 | 0 | 0 | 0 | 0 | 0 | 0 | 0 | 0 |
| Total with mother only | 23 | 12 | 35 | 25 | 18 | 43 | 48 | 30 | 78 |
| 5. Mother and M's mother | 4 | 19 | 23 | 3 | 12 | 15 | 7 | 31 | 38 |
| 6. Mother and M's father and mother | 0 | 0 | 0 | 1 | 0 | 1 | 1 | 0 | 1 |
| 7. Mother and mother's unwed mate | 0 | 3 | 3 | 0 | 4 | 4 | 0 | 7 | 7 |
| 8. Mother and mother's husband | 0 | 2 | 2 | 0 | 6 | 6 | 0 | 8 | 8 |
| 9. Mother and mother's sister | 0 | 2 | 2 | 0 | 6 | 6 | 0 | 8 | 8 |
| 10. Mother and M's M's mother | 0 | 0 | 0 | 0 | 3 | 3 | 0 | 3 | 3 |
| 11. Mother and M's M's father and mother | 0 | 1 | 1 | 0 | 0 | 0 | 0 | 1 | 1 |
| 12. Mother and M's mother and sister | 0 | 1 | 1 | 0 | 5 | 5 | 0 | 6 | 6 |
| 13. Mother and M's M and M's husband | 0 | 2 | 2 | 0 | 0 | 0 | 0 | 2 | 2 |
| 14. Mother and M's F's mother | 0 | 1 | 1 | 0 | 0 | 0 | 0 | 1 | 1 |
| 15. Mother and M's M and M's brother | 0 | 2 | 2 | 0 | 4 | 4 | 0 | 6 | 6 |
| 16. Mother and F's mother and brother | 1 | 0 | 1 | 1 | 0 | 1 | 2 | 0 | 2 |
| 17. Mother and M's M's sister | 1 | 2 | 3 | 2 | 1 | 3 | 3 | 3 | 6 |
| 18. Mother and M's M's B's daughter | 0 | 0 | 0 | 0 | 1 | 1 | 0 | 1 | 1 |
| 19. Mother and M's F's sister | 0 | 1 | 1 | 0 | 1 | 1 | 0 | 2 | 2 |
| Total with mother and M's kin | 6 | 36 | 42 | 7 | 43 | 50 | 13 | 79 | 92 |
| TOTAL | 29 | 48 | 77 | 32 | 61 | 93 | 61 | 109 | 170 |

*L = Lawful, i.e., legitimate; U = Unlawful, i.e., illegitimate.

## TABLE 18

### FREQUENCY DISTRIBUTION OF DIFFERING TYPES OF DOMESTIC UNIT WITHIN THE SAMPLE

| | Households with Male Head | | | Households with Female Head | | | Total | | | |
|---|---|---|---|---|---|---|---|---|---|---|
| | No Plus Others | Others | Total | No Plus Others | Others | Total | No Plus Others | Others | Total | Per cent |
| 1. Single persons | 7 | 0 | 7 | 20 | 17 | 37 | 27 | 17 | 44 | 19.7 |
| 2. Siblings | 0 | 0 | 0 | 1 | 3 | 4 | 1 | 3 | 4 | 1.8 |
| 3. Household head and children | 1 | 0 | 1 | 21 | 5 | 26 | 22 | 5 | 27 | 12.0 |
| 4. Childless couples | 3 | 11 | 14 | 0 | 1 | 1 | 3 | 12 | 15 | 6.7 |
| 5. Couples and children | 38 | 16 | 54 | 0 | 1 | 1 | 38 | 17 | 55 | 24.6 |
| 6. Household head and grandchildren | 0 | 0 | 0 | 11 | 3 | 14 | 11 | 3 | 14 | 6.2 |
| 7. Couples and grandchildren | 5 | 2 | 7 | 0 | 0 | 0 | 5 | 2 | 7 | 3.1 |
| 8. Household head, children, and grandchildren | 1 | 1 | 2 | 32 | 10 | 42 | 33 | 11 | 44 | 19.7 |
| 9. Couples, children, and grandchildren | 5 | 2 | 7 | 0 | 1 | 1 | 5 | 3 | 8 | 3.6 |
| 10. Household head and issue to 4th generation | 0 | 0 | 0 | 4 | 1 | 5 | 4 | 1 | 5 | 2.2 |
| 11. Couples and issue to 4th generation | 1 | 0 | 1 | 0 | 0 | 0 | 1 | 0 | 1 | 0.4 |
| TOTAL | 61 | 32 | 93 | 89 | 42 | 131 | 150 | 74 | 224 | 100.0 |
| PERCENTAGE | 65.5 | 34.5 | 100.0 | 68.0 | 32.0 | 100.0 | 67.0 | 33.0 | 100.0 | |

## TABLE 19

### DOMESTIC UNITS OF STRUCTURALLY DIFFERING TYPES, CLASSIFIED BY SEX OF HEAD AND GENERATION RANGE

| | Households with Male Head | | | | | Households with Female Head | | | | | Total | | | | |
|---|---|---|---|---|---|---|---|---|---|---|---|---|---|---|---|
| | Generation Range | | | | | Generation Range | | | | | Generation Range | | | | |
| | 1 | 2 | 3 | 4 | Total | 1 | 2 | 3 | 4 | Total | 1 | 2 | 3 | 4 | Total |
| 1. Single persons | 7 | 0 | 0 | 0 | 7 | 20 | 10 | 7 | 0 | 37 | 27 | 10 | 7 | 0 | 44 |
| 2. Siblings | 0 | 0 | 0 | 0 | 0 | 1 | 3 | 0 | 0 | 4 | 1 | 3 | 0 | 0 | 4 |
| 3. Household head and children | 0 | 1 | 0 | 0 | 1 | 0 | 24 | 2 | 0 | 26 | 0 | 25 | 2 | 0 | 27 |
| 4. Childless couples | 3 | 4 | 7 | 0 | 14 | 0 | 1 | 0 | 0 | 1 | 3 | 5 | 7 | 0 | 15 |
| 5. Couples and children | 0 | 49 | 5 | 0 | 54 | 0 | 1 | 0 | 0 | 1 | 0 | 50 | 5 | 0 | 55 |
| 6. Household head and grandchildren | 0 | 0 | 0 | 0 | 0 | 0 | 0 | 14 | 0 | 14 | 0 | 0 | 14 | 0 | 14 |
| 7. Couples and grandchildren | 0 | 0 | 7 | 0 | 7 | 0 | 0 | 0 | 0 | 0 | 0 | 0 | 7 | 0 | 7 |
| 8. Household head, children, and grandchildren | 0 | 0 | 2 | 0 | 2 | 0 | 0 | 42 | 0 | 42 | 0 | 0 | 44 | 0 | 44 |
| 9. Couples, children, and grandchildren | 0 | 0 | 7 | 0 | 7 | 0 | 0 | 1 | 0 | 1 | 0 | 0 | 8 | 0 | 8 |
| 10. Household head and issue to 4th generation | 0 | 0 | 0 | 0 | 0 | 0 | 0 | 0 | 5 | 5 | 0 | 0 | 0 | 5 | 5 |
| 11. Couples and issue to 4th generation | 0 | 0 | 0 | 1 | 1 | 0 | 0 | 0 | 0 | 0 | 0 | 0 | 0 | 1 | 1 |
| TOTAL | 10 | 54 | 28 | 1 | 93 | 21 | 39 | 66 | 5 | 131 | 31 | 93 | 94 | 6 | 224 |
| PERCENTAGE | 11.0 | 58.0 | 30.0 | 1.0 | 100.0 | 16.0 | 30.0 | 50.0 | 4.0 | 100.0 | 14.0 | 42.0 | 42.0 | 2.0 | 100.0 |

## TABLE 20

CONJUGAL UNIONS IN THE SAMPLE HOUSEHOLDS, CLASSIFIED BY THEIR BASIS, THE TYPE OF DOMESTIC UNIT IN WHICH THEY OCCUR, AND THE SEX OF THE HOUSEHOLD HEAD

| Morphological Types | Male Head | | | Female Head | | | Total | | |
|---|---|---|---|---|---|---|---|---|---|
| | Wed | Unwed | Total | Wed | Unwed | Total | Wed | Unwed | Total |
| 1a. Childless couples only | 2 | 1 | 3 | 0 | 0 | 0 | 2 | 1 | 3 |
| b. Childless couples plus others | 9 | 2 | 11 | 0 | 1 | 1 | 9 | 3 | 12 |
| Total childless couples | 11 | 3 | 14 | 0 | 1 | 1 | 11 | 4 | 15 |
| 2a. Couples and children only | 37 | 1 | 38 | 0 | 0 | 0 | 37 | 1 | 38 |
| b. Couples, children plus others | 14 | 2 | 16 | 1 | 0 | 1 | 15 | 2 | 17 |
| Total couples and children | 51 | 3 | 54 | 1 | 0 | 1 | 52 | 3 | 55 |
| 3a. Couples and grandchildren only | 5 | 0 | 5 | 0 | 0 | 0 | 5 | 0 | 5 |
| b. Couples, grandchildren plus others | 2 | 0 | 2 | 0 | 0 | 0 | 2 | 0 | 2 |
| Total couples and grandchildren | 7 | 0 | 7 | 0 | 0 | 0 | 7 | 0 | 7 |
| 4a. Couples, children, and grandchildren only | 5 | 0 | 5 | 0 | 0 | 0 | 5 | 0 | 5 |
| b. Couples, children, grandchildren plus others | 2 | 0 | 2 | 1 | 0 | 1 | 3 | 0 | 3 |
| Total couples, children, and grandchildren | 7 | 0 | 7 | 1 | 0 | 1 | 8 | 0 | 8 |
| 5a. Couples and issue to 4th generation | 1 | 0 | 1 | 0 | 0 | 0 | 1 | 0 | 1 |
| TOTAL | 77 | 6 | 83 | 2 | 1 | 3 | 79 | 7 | 86 |

# 3. Latante

Grenada, the "isle of spices," has an area of about 120 square miles and lies ninety miles northeast of Trinidad at latitude 12 degrees and longitude sixty-one degrees. It was originally colonized by the French, ceded to the British in 1763, recaptured by the French in 1779 and returned to the British permanently in 1784. French influence persists in the peasant *patois* or dialect and in Roman Catholicism. Until 1838 the great majority of the Negro population were slaves, and sugar was the main export crop. Since then the exslaves and their descendants have developed into a peasantry, and cocoa and nutmeg cultivation have displaced sugar.

The beauty of Grenada lies in its rugged broken surfaces. Most of the island is over 1,000 feet in height and a large portion is 2,000. Rainfall is high, and the easterly trade winds produce an equable climate. The food staples, such as the bluggo (a variety of plantain), breadfruit, and avocado pears, and export staples such as cloves, cinnamon, cocoa, nutmeg, or copra are tree crops; but in addition the peasants grow maize, yam, coco, dasheen and tannia, sweet potatoes, pigeon peas, and the like.

During the transition from sugar to cocoa and spices, estates changed hands frequently and were often broken up into small parcels for sale to exslaves. During this process the exslaves and their offspring became a peasantry. According to the census of 1946, Grenada then contained 4,562 plots of less than an acre each and 5,053 parcels varying from one to fifteen acres in size. There were also 373 holdings of more than 15 acres.[1] However, despite this wide distribution of land, the 109 holdings over 100 acres in size were together listed as containing 38,000 of the estimated 63,000 acres in the island; so that estates still dominate the colonial economy and society alike.[2]

In the 1946 census the population of Grenada Island was estimated

66

at about 66,000, giving an over-all density of approximately 550 persons per square mile. Of this population, approximately 11,300 or 17 per cent live in the four townships in the island. The great majority of the remainder are peasants and agricultural laborers. Often the Grenadian peasant is also an agricultural laborer.

I visited Grenada in 1952 as a member of the Institute of Social and Economic Research of the University College of the West Indies. My assignment was a study of Grenadian society and culture. The information already given directed my attention to the rural and urban lower class. Accordingly, I selected two communities for detailed study. One of these, Latante, provides the material discussed in this chapter; the other, Grenville, will be analyzed next. The people of Latante were smallholders, growing cocoa and nutmeg, corn, peas, and roots, and rearing cattle as well as small stock. In addition many of them worked on nearby estates, and a few were small shopkeepers or craftsmen. The people of Grenville were for the most part landless tenants and laborers living just inside the town. No one at Latante employed domestic help. The people there describe themselves as "one royal family" and emphasize their kinship connections. In the Grenville sample, there were a few households which drew domestic labor from the immediate neighborhood; and interhousehold kinship ties were few. Latante and Grenville may be taken to represent the rural and urban lower classes in Grenada, respectively. In both places I made a census of a defined area, mapping the distribution of households within it. I lived for some months in each of these communities, and my data on them are consequently more complete than on the other samples of this series. These two samples will be compared, along with the others, later.

Population, and the Distribution of Headship

There is a total of 490 persons in the 102 contiguous households studied at Latante. The distribution of this population by sex and age is presented in Table 1. Forty per cent of the total sample are below the age of fifteen; only 10 per cent are above fifty-five. Thus half the sample population is between the ages of fifteen and fifty-five; and within this age range, women outnumber men by 1.2 to 1.0. This sex ratio is fairly equal but less so than that for the total sample, which is almost exactly par. It seems that some men leave the community before or during middle age. A few others were still serving prison sentences for offenses committed during the labor disturbances of 1951. The most important features of this population distribution are its nearly equal sex ratio and large ratio of adults in the reproductive age groups.

The distribution of household headship by sex and age is summarized in Table 2, and its incidence among persons of the same sex and age group is isolated in the following table. Of the 102 households, sixty had male heads. All resident males above the age of fifty-four were heads of their own homes, but only one of fifty-three men below the age of twenty-four was a household head. Rather more than half the men aged twenty-five to thirty-nine were heads of their own homes, and nineteen of the twenty-two men between forty and fifty-four years of age were also household heads.

Women attain household headship more slowly and less fully than men. There is only one female household head below the age of twenty-four, which supports the decision to regard this age as the turning point between young and mature adulthood. Less than one in five of the women between twenty-five and thirty-nine years of age are household heads, and only 40 per cent of those between forty and fifty-four. Two thirds of the women between fifty-five and sixty-nine are household heads, and four fifths of those above this age. Four in every nine adult men at Latante are heads of their own homes, as against one in every four women. These data illustrate the normalcy of male household headship in Latante. Soon after their twenty-fourth year, most men will establish their own homes. By their fifty-fifth year, all men will be household heads. Nonetheless, 40 per cent of these households have female heads; and there is a rough equality in the number of men and women over fifty-five years of age. In short, the large ratio of female household heads cannot be explained fully by widowhood. Exactly one half of these female household heads are between the ages of twenty-five and fifty-four. Despite approximate sex parity in this population, there are a sizable number of young or middle-aged women living in homes of which they are head. Little more than one third of all household heads are above fifty-four years of age. This also limits the possible incidence of households containing two generations of the head's descendants.

The average number of persons per household in this sample is 4.8. Units under male heads average 5.36, while those under females average 3.76 persons each. The modal size of household is one with four persons. Households vary in their size from single-person units, of which there are twelve, eight of these containing women, to groups containing ten or more persons. If we exclude the twelve single-person units, the remaining households have an average size of 5.45 persons. The households of this sample are thus relatively large.

Table 5 analyzes the population living in households with heads of differing sex, by age and sex. The sixty units with male heads contain 332 persons, or just over two thirds of the total population. Children below the age of fifteen represent 40 per cent of this population; males represent 54 per cent. Less than one twelfth of the folk who live in homes with male heads are over fifty-five years of age. In these units, the sex ratios are almost equal for persons aged between fifteen and fifty-four; this suggests that most of these men are cohabiting.

Of the 158 persons living in units with female heads, children below the age of fifteen represent 38 per cent and females represent 64 per cent. Only five men above twenty-four years of age live in homes with female heads. All members of these households above fifty-five years of age are women, and this group represents roughly one in every seven of the total. In short, units containing three lineal generations inclusive of the head are more likely to have female heads than otherwise; but units whose principals are engaged in cohabitation rarely have female heads.

The twelve solitary individuals in this sample are analyzed by sex, age, and marital status in Table 6. Two of the four solitary males and four of the eight solitary females have never married; three of these twelve people have separated from their spouses. Nine of them are over fifty-five years of age; none is below twenty-four, and only two, one of each sex, are below thirty-nine. Apparently younger people seldom live alone, old men and women may have to do so.

The Mating Organization

In Table 7, all adults in this sample are classified by reference to marital and parental status on the one hand, and sex and age on the other. Table 8 isolates those adults who are not household heads for identical analysis, and Table 9 reports the distribution of these conditions among the household heads themselves. The classification which informs these tables contains no category of single persons of unknown parental status, since I had complete information about this population. For only three of the males above the age of twenty-five do we lack knowledge about current mating. All childless single persons below the age of twenty-four who are listed as of unknown mating status are unlikely to have had a regular mate. All were young persons in the early experimental period.

Of the fifty-three young men under twenty-four in this sample, fourteen were mating extraresidentially at the time of survey, and two were partners in consensual unions. None was married, but thirty-seven had not yet begun their mating career. Of the thirty-seven men aged between twenty-five and thirty-nine, only seven were childless. Of the twelve single men in this group, ten were mating extraresidentially. Another eleven were partners in consensual cohabitation; an equal number were living with their wives; two had already separated from their wives, and one had resumed consensual cohabitation after being widowed. Apparently marriage, consensual cohabitation, and extraresidential mating have almost equal appeal to the men of this age group. Significantly, two of the fourteen married men in this group were already separated.

Of the twenty-two men in these homes aged between forty and fifty-four, only two were single, and only three were cohabiting consensually. The remaining seventeen were living with their wives. All but two of the fifteen men between fifty-five and sixty-nine had married, and ten had resident spouses. One was a widower, another was separated from his spouse, and the third had an absent wife. All five men over seventy had married. One of these was a widower, one had an absent wife, and one was separated from his wife. There were no men over fifty-four years of age living in consensual domestic unions.

These data reveal a single coherent pattern. Men may mate extraresidentially before their twenty-fourth year, but very few establish domestic unions, and none of those who do so marry at this time. However, before they are thirty-nine most men will be living in domestic unions, and the numbers who do so within and without marriage will be approximately equal. Moreover, the number of single men of this age group engaged in extraresidential unions will be much the same as of those living in marriage or in consensual domestic unions. By the time they are fifty-four, four in every five men are married, and most of the remainder live in consensual domestic unions. Beyond this age point we find no men participating in consensual cohabitation, and only one in ten who remain single. In other words, men begin by mating extraresidentially; in the next phase they establish domestic unions, but at this point only about a third of the age group will marry, and consensual cohabitation is evidently the forerunner of marriage. By the time they are middle-aged, very few men remain single or in consensual cohabitation.

There are thus three recognized mating alternatives in this system, and these are arranged in serial order, the one succeeding the other as the individual matures. Men who fail to convert their extraresidential unions into domestic ones before their thirty-ninth year may find it difficult to maintain the mating relation thereafter. Likewise, men who fail to convert their consensual domestic unions into marriage before they are fifty-four will lose their mate. In this system the extraresidential relation, consensual cohabitation, and marriage each have their proper time and place in the individual life cycle. Young men who fail to perceive this and marry too soon risk an early separation from their wives. Old men who do not realize that marriage is the only form of mating open to them will probably not mate at all; but within the period approaching middle age, consensual cohabitation, marriage, and the extraresidential relation are equally open to males. We can check this analysis by examining the mating patterns of females.

Our sample households contain 164 women, fifty-nine of whom are below the age of twenty-four. Of these young women, thirty-one had not yet begun their mating careers. Of the remaining twenty-eight, one had married, four were cohabiting consensually, and twenty-three were mating extraresidentially. Clearly the extra-residential union is the norm for young women of this age group as well as for young men. Of the forty-four women between the ages of twenty-five and thirty-nine living in these households, eleven were single, and seven of these were mating extraresidentially at the time of survey. Of the remaining thirty-three, twelve were cohabiting consensually, and twenty-one had married. One of these married women had an absent spouse, another was a widow; there were fifteen living with their husbands, and four already separated from them. For women of this age group therefore, cohabitation is the norm and marriage is the usual as well as the preferred form. However, a significant proportion of these women cohabit consensually. Of the thirty-two women aged between forty and fifty-four, twenty-four had already married and nineteen of these were living with their husbands. Four were widows and one had an absent spouse. Of the seven single women in this age group, four were childless and only one was mating extraresidentially. Only one of these thirty-two women between the ages of forty and fifty-four was cohabiting consensually. Clearly, marriage is the requisite form of mating for women between the ages of forty and fifty-four. The extraresidential and consensual unions are both equally avoided by women of this age. Of the nineteen women aged between fifty-five and sixty-nine, five had not married. Three of these were single mothers, but only one continued to mate. No woman in this age group was cohabiting consensually. Half of the fourteen married women were widows; one had an absent spouse, four lived with their husbands, and two were separated. Eight of the ten women over seventy had married and six of them were widows. Another woman had been widowed from a consensual union, and the tenth person was a childless single woman.

Clearly the succession of mating forms appropriate to women of different ages has the same order as that for men, the only difference being that women enter the different phases shortly before men. The mating form appropriate at one stage of an individual's life cycle is inappropriate and disapproved at another. Self-respecting individuals will therefore withdraw from mating rather than maintain an inappropriate relation. This mating system contains three alternatives, the extraresidential union, consensual cohabitation, and marriage; it integrates them by placing them at different points in the individual life cycle. Presumably an extraresidential relation may develop through the stage of consensual cohabitation into marriage; and presumably this ideal development does sometimes occur; but irrespective of the development of particular relations, the system enjoins individual development and defines this as an orderly progression from extraresidential mating into consensual domestic union and so to marriage. In consequence, most of the married people belong to the senior age groups, and most of the senior people are married. Most of the unmarried people belong to the junior age groups and most of the junior people are unmarried. Strikingly, most members of either sex engaged in consensual cohabitation are between twenty-five and thirty-nine years of age. It is within this age range that consensual cohabitation is most likely to occur.

The reality and strength of this orderly succession is evident from the history of nonconformists, as well as from the distribution of characteristics among those who conform. Nonconformists in this system may belong to one of two groups: those who marry too young, or those who do not marry when they should. Our data indicate that those who marry too young often come to grief, and that those who do not marry at the appropriate time lose the chance of mating and may have to live by themselves. Both unmarried men above the age of fifty-five were in this position; as were two of the six single women of this age. Of the twenty married women between the ages of twenty-five and thirty-nine, one quarter lived apart from their husbands; and it is at least likely that the two separated wives of senior age may have parted from their husbands soon after an early marriage. Couples already accustomed to one another through consensual cohabitation are less likely to separate after marriage than are those who proceed directly from the extraresidential relation into marriage—at any rate in this community.

Most of the women whose spouses were absent were also unlikely to live with their husbands again; nonetheless, there is sufficient obscurity about the state of these unions to merit separate classification. Certainly, these marriages were unstable, and significantly two of these cases involved women who had married at an earlier age than usual. The rate of marital breakdown at Latante is fairly high, ten of the sixty-eight married women in these households having separated from their husbands finally or otherwise, while another two had left their husbands in the community and gone away. When a marriage breaks down at Latante, either party may migrate, but men do so more frequently. In consequence, women provide a better basis for estimating the rate of marriage breakdown.

One anomaly which does not occur is the resumption of consensual cohabitation by widows, whatever their age. If widows were freely to do this, the serial order of mating forms would be thrown into confusion. Apparently widowers might cohabit consensually if they are young, but the expectation is that they will shortly remarry; their consensual cohabitation at this stage accordingly reflects the preference at Latante for this mating form to precede marriage. Widows may remarry but they may not cohabit consensually. Marriage represents a status achievement appropriate to maturity; the married person who resumes cohabitation consensually is repudiating his own status. Conversely, the extraresidential mating form expresses immaturity and is appropriate to young persons, while the consensual domestic union is the appropriate prelude to marriage.

Excluding young men and women under twenty-four years of age, there are sixteen single men and twenty-four single women in this sample. In short, four in every five men and women over twenty-four years of age have engaged in one form of cohabitation or another. Several of the mature single women and men are also childless.

Tables 8 and 9 are of special interest in that they define the association between household headship and mating status among people of different age and sex. One of the two young men under twenty-four who are cohabiting consensually is a household head, the other is not. Eight of the eleven males between twenty-five and thirty-nine who mate in this way are household heads. So are two of the three men between forty and fifty-four who cohabit consensually. In short, males tend to be heads of households based on their consensual cohabitation, but in one third of these cases they are not. The contrast with marriage is clear. Of the forty men whose wives lived with them, only one was not a household head. Presumably males engaged in consensual cohabitation are often motivated to marry by the desire to stabilize their union through the assertion of defined authority and responsibilities within it. Notably our sample includes no persons whose consensual unions had broken down, apart from one woman widowed in this context. Consensual unions at Latante have binding implications; they are necessary preludes to marriage, rather than experiments. The experimental phase and situation ends with extraresidential mating; but because of its structural position, male leadership in consensual unions varies more widely than in other forms; and in consequence of this variability, at the individual as well as the structural level, motivation for marriage develops among consensual mates.

All widowers in our sample, and all but one of the men with absent or separated wives, were heads of their own homes. Only two of the sixteen single men over twenty-five years of age were household heads; marriage and male household headship go together. The converse holds true. None of the forty women who lived with their husbands in these homes was a household head; all but one of the eighteen widows, and seven of the ten women with absent or separated husbands were heads of their own homes. So were two of the fifteen women engaged in consensual cohabitation. In two other cases the consensual partners lived with parents of one of them. Of the remaining sixteen female household heads, ten were single mothers of lower average age than the other six childless women. Fifteen of the twenty-four single women above the age of twenty-five were household heads. Whereas marriage delays headship among women, and consensual cohabitation tends to do the same, single status, especially single motherhood, seems to imply or presume household headship.

The status implications of alternative mating forms are further illustrated by Tables 8 and 9. Few of the young people engaged in extraresidential mating are household heads, and none of these is a man. At the other extreme, all but one of the widowed persons are heads of their own homes, and after marriage only two out of forty-six men are not household heads. Thus the succession of mating forms corresponds with the normal increase of individual status through maturity. Minors mate extraresidentially, unestablished adults do so in consensual domestic unions, but marriage marks maturity. The integration of these mating forms is based on associations between male household headship, marriage, and maturity by age. This mating system will obviously influence the form and growth of domestic groups, under heads of either sex.

The Composition of Domestic Groups

Table 10 is a summary analysis of the dependent population of households with heads of different sex, by their relationship to the head. The exact composition of these two categories of households is depicted in the charts. The total dependent population of these households is 388 persons, 272 of whom live in units with male heads. Three in every five dependents living in homes with male heads are children of the head, grandchildren and great-grandchildren bringing the lineal issue up to 68 per cent of the total. The heads' mates form another 18 per cent of these dependents, so that 86 per cent of the dependent population of these homes consist of the head's mate and issue. In addition, collateral kin and issue of the head's mate by other unions account for 4.4 per cent and 3 per cent of the resident dependents. Junior affines (isolated in categories 25 and 26) represent 1.2 per cent. There are no siblings of male heads living in these homes; but there are some children of siblings, and two thirds of these are sisters' issue. There are no parents of male heads living in these homes, nor any patrilateral kin; but there are as many matrilateral kin as there are resident issue of sisters. In all, only ten resident members representing 3.7 per cent are collaterals of these male heads. Moreover, membership in these units is almost exclusively confined to kin, only one adopted and one unrelated person being present in them.

Of the 116 dependents living in homes with female heads, only two are mates of the heads, and in both cases these are unwed. As the chart shows, only two of the fifty-six resident children of these household heads are also the issue of the two resident mates. Grandchildren living in these homes form a quarter of the dependent population, being exactly half of the number of resident children. Including the four great-grandchildren present, the lineal issue of the heads represent three quarters of the dependent population. Kin and issue of the heads' resident mates number three and two persons, respectively, and together form less than one twentieth of the dependent population; but the heads' collaterals are one seventh of the total, most of these being sisters or sisters' issue. In only one case each do we find a resident brother or mother of a female household head; no brothers' issue live in these homes, but patrilateral kin outnumber matrilateral kin in the remoter

ranges (see diagram, pp. 274-75). Two households contain resident
mates of the heads' daughters, and one contains a child of the head's
son's mate as well. With this exception, there are no unrelated
residents in these homes.

Clearly, the major differences in composition between units
with male and female heads are represented by the distribution of
resident mates, children, grandchildren, affines, and collaterals.
Given male household headship of units based on cohabiting couples,
and the prevalence of widowhood among females, the differential
distribution of mates, children, and grandchildren need not sur-
prise us. Nonetheless, it is important to note that 163, or 75 per
cent of the 219 children of these household heads are to be found
in their fathers' homes; also that of the fifty-one resident grandchildren of these household heads, twenty-three, or 45 per cent
live in homes of which their grandfather is head. Despite the fact
that lineal issue represent three fourths of the dependent population of female household heads, and little more than two thirds
of those in male homes, sixty-eight per cent of the 275 resident
issue of these household heads are to be found in the homes of
their fathers, grandfathers, or great-grandfathers. True, lineal
descendants form a larger proportion of the dependent population
living in homes with female heads than in those with male heads;
but in absolute numbers, those living in their fathers' homes are
by far the majority.

As the charts show, these households contain neither half siblings
of the head nor their issue. On the other hand, they include remoter
patrilateral and matrilateral kin. The absence of these half siblings
and especially of maternal half siblings confirms the preceding
analysis of mating indirectly. It does so by indicating the strength
and durability of fertile mating relations. However, heads of homes
may have children by their successive mates with them. The domestic separation of these children as adults arises largely through
the stress on cohabitation in a separate household.

Of the 163 children living in their fathers' homes, twelve are
the offspring of these men's former unions. There are also in these
homes six children of the resident mates of these men by former
unions. Men have more children by other unions living with them
than do their mates. Of the twenty-six single mothers in this
sample, thirteen are less than twenty-four years of age, and nine of
the remainder are household heads. Apparently women whose mating behavior does not conform to the rules of this serial system
will be domestically isolated. Those who do may take some of their
children into the homes of their husbands or mates, but the fathers

of these children are also likely to care for them in their own homes.

There are thus three distinct definitions of parenthood. Women keep their offspring by extraresidential unions with them while these unions last. If they break up, the men may ask that the children be placed with them or with their materterine kin or parents. Alternatively, the extraresidential relation may develop into consensual or legal cohabitation. Under such circumstances, the man is fully responsible for the offspring; but if these domestic unions break down, the distribution of these children and of responsibilities for them tends to vary according to the circumstances of the breakdown and the individual situation. Legally, the female partner in a consensual domestic union is the recognized guardian of the child; socially, the father is responsible; in marriage legal and social definitions of paternal responsibility coincide; and in the extraresidential relation, the legal and social definitions of maternal responsibility also cohere.

Men's responsibilities for accommodation of the issue of their own broken unions, as well as for some issue of their mates' broken unions, serves to limit the number of collaterals whom they can accommodate. Since these responsibilities are common to all males alike, their resident collaterals are mainly matrilateral and materterine kin. Reciprocally, households with female heads will include some patrilateral dependents. The number of these collaterals is limited by the strength of parental responsibilities among men as well as women. There are eleven resident collaterals of mates of male household heads, and ten collaterals of the heads, in these homes. There are three resident collaterals of the two resident mates of female household heads, and twenty collateral dependents of these female heads themselves living in their homes. Tables 11 and 12 analyze the constitution and recruitment of the resident collaterals of female principals.

Of these twenty-seven resident collaterals of female principals, two thirds are siblings or their children, and siblings' children represent one half of the total. Only five of these twenty-seven individuals are known to be legitimate. About 50 per cent live in homes of which their kinswomen are heads. Excluding one male collateral whose parental link remained obscure, and the five full siblings of these women, the remaining twenty-one are analyzed in Table 12 by sex, birth status, generation remove from the linked principal, and the sex of the parent through whom kinship is traced. Of these twenty-one collaterals, eighteen traced kinship to these female principals through their mothers, and of these eighteen,

thirteen were illegitimate. All three persons connected with these
female principals through their fathers were illegitimate. Men
rarely place their illegitimate offspring with their collateral kin,
and never their lawful issue. Essentially, this leaves only materterine kin to be cared for by female principals.

Table 13 analyzes the resident lineal issue of these household
heads. All individuals of unspecified birth status in this table are
above the age of twenty-four. For convenience, great-grandchildren
have been included among sons' and daughters' issue. The kinship
charts specify their exact connections.

Of the 155 resident children of male household heads who are
below the age of twenty-four, twenty-four or 15.5 per cent are
unlawful. Of the forty-four children of similar age living in their
mothers' homes, twenty-seven or 61 per cent are unlawful. All
twenty-three resident grandchildren of male household heads below
the age of twenty-four are unlawful, and nineteen of these are
daughters' children. Of the thirty-two grandchildren of similar age,
living with their grandmothers, only three are lawful, and twenty-
five are daughters' issue. Among the resident grandchildren in
either category of these homes, daughters' issue outnumber sons'
by more than four to one; in homes with male heads, this ratio
is five to one. Clearly either men leave the offspring of extraresidential unions with the mother and mother's kin or they take
them into their own homes, with or without the mother. Only rarely
do they place them with their own fathers; and not very often with
their own mothers.

Eighty-eight per cent of the 187 resident issue of male heads
are these men's children. In homes with female heads, sixty-four
per cent of these descendants are children of the heads. The correspondence between these latter ratios and the incidence of differing birth statuses in homes of either category is impressive.
Eighty-five per cent of the resident issue of male heads are legitimate, 61 per cent of those of female heads are not. Modally, units
under male heads contain the lawful children of the head, those
under female heads contain the unlawful children and grandchildren
of the head. It is true that units with male heads also include many
unlawful offspring of the heads' daughters; but these remain a small
portion of the total lineal issue within them. The significant thing
is the scarcity of sons' children, lawful or other, in their grandparents' homes.

The Distribution of Children
Table 14 carries the analysis further by isolating all dependents

with one or more parents alive for detailed study. These children are classified by sex, age, and birth status, as well as by coresidence with or separation from either or both parents in homes under heads of different sex. Our sample contains 330 individuals to whom this analysis applies. Of them, 220 live in homes with male heads, and 144 or 65 per cent are legitimate. Only thirty-five of the 110 children in homes with female heads are lawful. Of these 330 children, 147 or 44.5 per cent live with both parents, 39 per cent being legitimate, and all of them living in homes with male heads. Of the 22 per cent who live apart from both parents, less than one in five is legitimate; and this group is fairly evenly divided among units with male and female heads. Only 4.8 per cent of these children live apart from their mothers and with their fathers. Another 2.3 per cent live with their widowed fathers. One in five live with their mothers apart from their fathers, and of these less than one in five is legitimate; however, one third of this category live in homes with male heads. Thirty of these 330 children are over twenty-four years of age and eleven of these are males.

One half of these children live with their fathers in homes with male heads, and in 90 per cent of these cases the child's mother is also present. In 80 per cent of these cases family relations are based on marriage. Excluding children of widowed mothers, only one fifth of the total live with their mothers apart from their fathers, and the aggregate living apart from their fathers, with or without their mothers, is no greater than that living with both their parents in homes with male heads.

These data show that the majority of the Latante children live in elementary families, of which their fathers are the recognized heads and of which marriage is the recognized basis. Many live apart from their fathers, and even more live apart from both parents; but neither of these two groups includes more than half the number living with both parents; and both of these groups are unavoidable concomitants of the system of mating and parenthood already discussed. Notably, homes with male heads include over 40 per cent of those children who live apart from their fathers, with or without their mothers.

Tables 15 to 17 describe the kinship distribution of those children below the age of twenty-four who live apart from both parents or either of them. Of the sixty-seven children living apart from both parents whose kinship connections are adequately known, forty-five live with their matrilateral kin, eighteen with their patrilateral kin, and four live with unrelated persons. Thirteen of these sixty-

seven individuals are legitimate. Fourteen live with their mother's
mother, seven with their mother's parents, nine with their father's
mother and one with both his parents. Thus nearly one half live with
their grandmothers, and two thirds of these with their maternal
grandmothers. Another eight live with their mother's sister and two
with their father's sister. Only one lives with the mother's father
and one with the father's father. This distribution illustrates the
primacy of matrikinship in the accommodation of children separated
from both parents. Even more clearly it shows how these roles are
undertaken by kinswomen rather than men.

Of the nineteen children below the age of twenty-four who are
living with their fathers apart from their mothers, only one lived
in a home which also contained adult consanguine kin of the father;
twelve lived with their fathers and fathers' mates or spouses. The
six lawful children of widowed or separated fathers lived with these
men alone. With the exception of these, the remainder are all unlawful.

Of the seventy-two children who live with their mothers apart
from their fathers, forty-six live in homes which contain no other
adult consanguine kin. Fifty-four of these seventy-two children
are unlawful; but only one of the twenty-six children living with
their mothers and mothers' adult kin is legitimate; clearly young
women who have children by extraresidential unions are often found
living with their senior kin; however, single women living alone
have nineteen unlawful children with them.

We have seen the variety of residential alternatives for the placement of illegitimate children at Latante. These alternatives are
necessary features of the familial system. Given three alternative
mating forms, each with its own definition of parental roles, a
multiplicity of alternatives for the domestic placement of children
is well-nigh unavoidable. The multiplicity of mating forms itself
rules out the possibility that all the children not living with both
their parents will be found within one alternative type of domestic
group.

The Variety of Domestic Forms

The remaining three tables in the Appendix enumerate the incidence of structurally distinct types of domestic groups. Table 18
is a morphological classification of these units and gives their
frequencies. Table 19 analyzes units of differing form by their
generation depth. Table 20 isolates households based on the cohabitation of their principals, and examines the basis of the conjugal union.

Of the 102 homes in this sample, over 70 per cent consist of structural cores without accretions. Single persons and units based on the siblingship of the principals represent 13.7 per cent and 1.9 per cent of the total, respectively. Units whose cores are a single parent and offspring, form another 13.7 per cent of the sample; and those having childless couples as their principals represent 16.6 per cent. Excluding units based on siblingship, 44 per cent of the households in this sample deviate from the ideal of coresidential elementary families; most of these deviant households cannot be derived from domestic elementary families. They represent significant alternatives to this domestic form, and these alternatives are governed by the system of mating and parenthood which regulates family relations at Latante.

Of the total sample, 28.5 per cent are households based on co-resident elementary families of the principals. All but one of these have male heads, and two thirds are exclusively elementary family units. There are no homes based on males and their grandchildren, and none which contain couples and their grandchildren, without the intermediate generation. Units consisting of women and their grandchildren, with or without the intermediate generation, are 16.8 per cent of the total. Two thirds of these include the intermediate generation. There are eight households under male heads which contain three lineally successive generations, including the head, six of these having couples as principals. In all, more than one fifth of the sample contain the grandchildren of the heads, two thirds of these having female heads. In addition there are three units with a depth of four lineal generations. Clearly the domestic organization includes three major alternatives: adults may live alone, with their siblings or childless mates, or as single parents in generationally shallow units; or they may live in elementary families; or with their grandchildren, with or without resident mates and children. The first group of alternatives is not reducible to residues of the other two, nor is the third group wholly derivable from the second, since single women may have the issue of their single children living in their homes, and such homes will never have contained a complete elementary family. There is a necessary coexistence of these three major domestic alternatives in a system which integrates three alternative forms of mating and parenthood. Moreover, since these mating and parental forms are serially organized, there is a tendency for the frequencies of these domestic alternatives to remain constant. Despite a tendency for the individual to move through this series of domestic alternatives over the years, this is not always the case. Many persons,

especially women, remain single throughout their lives. The development of individuals and that of household groups are quite distinct. Although the elementary family is the basic mode of domestic
grouping at Latante, it cannot be the only one, so long as the present mating system persists.

Of these households 34 per cent have a depth of three or more
generations. Among units with male heads, 27 per cent and among
those with female heads, 41 per cent have this depth. One fifth of the
households contain one generation only; one third of those with female heads and half of those under males have a two-generation
depth. Only three of the twenty-nine households based on couples
and their children have a depth of three generations. Only seven
of the seventeen households based on childless couples contain one
generation only. Only one of the fourteen households based on single
parents and their children have a depth of three generations. There
is a marked tendency for structural cores to exclude accretions
in these units. Given the multiplicity of domestic alternatives already discussed, and their relative frequencies, the number of
probable accretions will not be large.

Of the seventeen childless couples who are principals in these
homes, nine are unwed. Of the twenty-nine couples with children
who are principals in these homes, twenty-four are married. Adults
may cohabit before having children, in which case they do so consensually; but most couples with children will be married. Women
who have had children by extraresidential mates may take these
with them into a consensual domestic union which lacks its own
offspring. If the union endures, these children remain with the
couple when they marry. Alternatively, the single mother may
leave her offspring with her parents when she enters a domestic
union; however, we have seen that persons will more often accommodate their grandchildren when their children also live with them.

Conclusion

The division of parental roles at Latante corresponds with differences in the alternative forms of mating, but this correspondence does not preclude men from having their children with them
or in the homes of their kin. Almost, one may say, the mating system enjoins this assistance for some of the single mothers. In consequence, although most of the offspring of extraresidential mates
remain with their mothers or mothers' kin, many are taken care of
by the father or his relatives; and this duality in parental roles
for the children of extraresidential unions reinforces the bilateral organization of kinship which it assumes. In short, the com-

plex of mating and parental forms is well integrated with the wider framework of kinship as well as with the domestic organization.

## TABLE 1

### POPULATION OF THE SAMPLE HOUSEHOLDS, CLASSIFIED BY SEX AND AGE

| Age | Number | | | Percentage | | | Females |
|-----|--------|--------|-------|--------|--------|-------|---------|
| | Male | Female | Total | Male | Female | Total | per Male |
| 0 -4 | 31 | 38 | 69 | 6.3 | 7.8 | 14.1 | 1.22 |
| 5-14 | 74 | 51 | 125 | 16.1 | 10.4 | 26.5 | 0.69 |
| 15-24 | 53 | 59 | 112 | 10.8 | 12.1 | 22.9 | 1.11 |
| 25-39 | 37 | 44 | 81 | 7.5 | 9.0 | 16.5 | 1.19 |
| 40-54 | 22 | 32 | 54 | 4.5 | 6.5 | 11.0 | 1.46 |
| 55-69 | 15 | 19 | 34 | 3.0 | 4.0 | 7.0 | 1.26 |
| 70 and Over | 5 | 10 | 15 | 1.0 | 2.0 | 3.0 | 2.00 |
| TOTAL | 237 | 253 | 490 | 49.2 | 51.8 | 100.0 | 1.07 |

## TABLE 2

### HEADS OF THE SAMPLE HOUSEHOLDS, CLASSIFIED BY SEX AND AGE

| Age | Number | | | Percentage | | |
|-----|--------|--------|-------|--------|--------|-------|
| | Male | Female | Total | Male | Female | Total |
| 15-24 | 1 | 1 | 2 | 1.0 | 1.0 | 2.0 |
| 25-39 | 20 | 8 | 28 | 19.5 | 7.9 | 27.4 |
| 40-54 | 19 | 13 | 32 | 18.6 | 12.8 | 31.4 |
| 55-69 | 15 | 12 | 27 | 14.6 | 11.8 | 26.4 |
| 70 and Over | 5 | 8 | 13 | 4.9 | 7.9 | 12.8 |
| TOTAL | 60 | 42 | 102 | 58.6 | 41.4 | 100.0 |

## TABLE 3

### DISTRIBUTION OF HOUSEHOLD HEADSHIP AMONG ADULT MEMBERS OF THE SAMPLE POPULATION, CLASSIFIED BY SEX AND AGE

| Age | Male | | | Female | | | % HHs in |
|-----|-------|------|------|-------|------|------|----------|
| | Total | HHs* | %HHs | Total | HHs* | %HHs | Both Sexes |
| 15-24 | 53 | 1 | 1.9 | 59 | 1 | 1.7 | 1.8 |
| 25-39 | 37 | 20 | 54.0 | 44 | 8 | 18.2 | 34.2 |
| 40-54 | 22 | 19 | 86.5 | 32 | 13 | 40.4 | 59.4 |
| 55-69 | 15 | 15 | 100.0 | 19 | 12 | 63.3 | 79.3 |
| 70 and Over | 5 | 5 | 100.0 | 10 | 8 | 80.0 | 86.5 |
| TOTAL | 132 | 60 | 45.5 | 164 | 42 | 25.5 | 34.4 |

*HHs = Household heads.

TABLE 4

HOUSEHOLDS OF THE SAMPLE, CLASSIFIED BY SEX OF HEAD AND NUMBER OF PERSONS

| Number of Persons | Sex of Head | | | Total | | |
|---|---|---|---|---|---|---|
| | Male | Female | Total | Male HHs* | Female HHs | Total |
| 1 | 4 | 8 | 12 | 4 | 8 | 12 |
| 2 | 8 | 4 | 12 | 16 | 8 | 24 |
| 3 | 3 | 9 | 12 | 9 | 27 | 36 |
| 4 | 10 | 7 | 17 | 40 | 28 | 68 |
| 5 | 7 | 4 | 11 | 35 | 20 | 55 |
| 6 | 8 | 6 | 14 | 48 | 36 | 84 |
| 7 | 4 | 3 | 7 | 28 | 21 | 49 |
| 8 | 6 | 0 | 6 | 48 | 0 | 48 |
| 9 | 2 | 0 | 2 | 18 | 0 | 18 |
| 10 | 5 | 1 | 6 | 50 | 10 | 60 |
| 11 | 1 | 0 | 1 | 11 | 0 | 11 |
| 12 | 1 | 0 | 1 | 12 | 0 | 12 |
| 13 | 1 | 0 | 1 | 13 | 0 | 13 |
| TOTAL | 60 | 42 | 102 | 332 | 158 | 490 |

| Averages: including solitary persons | 5.36% | 3.76% | 4.80% |
|---|---|---|---|
| excluding solitary persons | 5.75% | 4.63% | 5.45% |

*HHs = Household heads.

TABLE 5

AGE AND SEX DISTRIBUTION OF HOUSEHOLD POPULATION, CLASSIFIED
ACCORDING TO THE SEX OF THE HEAD

| | Male Head | | | | Female Head | | | | Total | |
|---|---|---|---|---|---|---|---|---|---|---|
| Age | Male | Female | Total | Per cent | Male | Female | Total | Per cent | Male %HHs* | Female %HHs |
| 0- 4 | 22 | 28 | 50 | 15.1 | 9 | 10 | 19 | 12.0 | 10.2 | 3.9 |
| 5-14 | 51 | 33 | 84 | 25.2 | 23 | 18 | 41 | 26.0 | 17.1 | 8.4 |
| 15-24 | 41 | 37 | 78 | 23.5 | 12 | 22 | 34 | 21.5 | 15.9 | 6.9 |
| 25-39 | 28 | 28 | 56 | 16.9 | 9 | 16 | 25 | 15.8 | 11.4 | 5.1 |
| 40-54 | 19 | 19 | 38 | 11.4 | 3 | 13 | 16 | 10.1 | 7.8 | 3.3 |
| 55-69 | 15 | 5 | 20 | 6.1 | 0 | 14 | 14 | 8.9 | 4.1 | 2.9 |
| 70 + | 5 | 1 | 6 | 1.8 | 0 | 9 | 9 | 5.7 | 1.2 | 1.8 |
| TOTAL | 181 | 151 | 332 | 100.0 | 56 | 102 | 158 | 100.0 | 67.7 | 32.3 |

*HHs = Household heads.

TABLE 6

HOUSEHOLDERS LIVING ALONE, CLASSIFIED BY AGE, SEX, AND MARITAL STATUS

| | Male | | | | | | Female | | | | | |
|---|---|---|---|---|---|---|---|---|---|---|---|---|
| | -24 | -39 | -54 | -69 | 70+ | Total | -24 | -39 | -54 | -69 | 70+ | Total |
| Never married | 0 | 0 | 0 | 2 | 0 | 2 | 0 | 1 | 1 | 1 | 1 | 4 |
| Married, spouse absent | 0 | 0 | 0 | 0 | 1 | 1 | 0 | 0 | 0 | 0 | 1 | 1 |
| Married, separated | 0 | 1 | 0 | 0 | 0 | 1 | 0 | 0 | 0 | 1 | 0 | 1 |
| Married, widowed | 0 | 0 | 0 | 0 | 0 | 0 | 0 | 0 | 0 | 0 | 2 | 2 |
| TOTAL | 0 | 1 | 0 | 2 | 1 | 4 | 0 | 1 | 1 | 2 | 4 | 8 |

TABLE 7

ALL ADULT MEMBERS OF THE SAMPLE POPULATION, CLASSIFIED BY SEX, AGE, MARITAL CONDITION, AND PARENTAL STATUS

| Mating and Parental Status | Male | | | | | | Female | | | | | |
|---|---|---|---|---|---|---|---|---|---|---|---|---|
| | -24 | -39 | -54 | -69 | 70+ | Total | -24 | -39 | -54 | -69 | 70+ | Total |
| **1. Childless single persons** | | | | | | | | | | | | |
| a. Mating now n/k* | 29 | 1 | 2 | 0 | 0 | 32 | 27 | 2 | 2 | 0 | 0 | 31 |
| b. Never mated | 8 | 0 | 0 | 0 | 0 | 8 | 4 | 1 | 0 | 0 | 0 | 5 |
| c. Not mating in 1953 | 0 | 1 | 0 | 0 | 0 | 1 | 0 | 0 | 2 | 2 | 1 | 5 |
| d. Mating in 1953 | 12 | 5 | 0 | 0 | 0 | 17 | 10 | 1 | 0 | 0 | 0 | 11 |
| Total childless single persons | 49 | 7 | 2 | 0 | 0 | 58 | 41 | 4 | 4 | 2 | 1 | 52 |
| **2. Single parents** | | | | | | | | | | | | |
| a. Mating now n/k | 0 | 0 | 0 | 0 | 0 | 0 | 0 | 1 | 2 | 0 | 0 | 3 |
| b. Not mating now | 0 | 0 | 0 | 2 | 0 | 2 | 0 | 0 | 0 | 2 | 0 | 2 |
| c. Mating in 1953 | 2 | 5 | 0 | 0 | 0 | 7 | 13 | 6 | 1 | 1 | 0 | 21 |
| Total single parents | 2 | 5 | 0 | 2 | 0 | 9 | 13 | 7 | 3 | 3 | 0 | 26 |
| **3. Consensually wed** | | | | | | | | | | | | |
| a. In 1953 | 2 | 11 | 3 | 0 | 0 | 16 | 4 | 12 | 1 | 0 | 0 | 17 |
| b. Separated, childless | 0 | 0 | 0 | 0 | 0 | 0 | 0 | 0 | 0 | 0 | 0 | 0 |
| c. Separated, with children | 0 | 0 | 0 | 0 | 0 | 0 | 0 | 0 | 0 | 0 | 0 | 0 |
| d. Widowed, single | 0 | 0 | 0 | 0 | 0 | 0 | 0 | 0 | 0 | 0 | 1 | 1 |
| Total consensually wed | 2 | 11 | 3 | 0 | 0 | 16 | 4 | 12 | 1 | 0 | 1 | 18 |
| **4. Married persons** | | | | | | | | | | | | |
| a. Spouse present | 0 | 11 | 17 | 10 | 2 | 40 | 1 | 15 | 19 | 4 | 1 | 40 |
| b. Spouse absent | 0 | 0 | 0 | 1 | 1 | 2 | 0 | 1 | 1 | 1 | 1 | 4 |
| c. Separated, single | 0 | 2 | 0 | 1 | 1 | 4 | 0 | 4 | 0 | 2 | 0 | 6 |
| d. Separated, not single | 0 | 0 | 0 | 0 | 0 | 0 | 0 | 0 | 0 | 0 | 0 | 0 |
| Total married persons | 0 | 13 | 17 | 12 | 4 | 46 | 1 | 20 | 20 | 7 | 2 | 50 |
| **5. Widowed persons** | | | | | | | | | | | | |
| a. Widowed, single | 0 | 0 | 0 | 1 | 1 | 2 | 0 | 1 | 4 | 7 | 6 | 18 |
| b. Widowed, not single | 0 | 1 | 0 | 0 | 0 | 1 | 0 | 0 | 0 | 0 | 0 | 0 |
| Total widowed persons | 0 | 1 | 0 | 1 | 1 | 3 | 0 | 1 | 4 | 7 | 6 | 18 |
| GRAND TOTAL | 53 | 37 | 22 | 15 | 5 | 132 | 59 | 44 | 32 | 19 | 10 | 164 |

*n/k = Not known.

# TABLE 8

## ADULT MEMBERS OF THE SAMPLE POPULATION OTHER THAN HOUSEHOLD HEADS, CLASSIFIED BY SEX, AGE, MARITAL CONDITION, AND PARENTAL STATUS

| Mating and Parental Status | Male | | | | | | Female | | | | | |
|---|---|---|---|---|---|---|---|---|---|---|---|---|
| | -24 | -39 | -54 | -69 | 70+ | Total | -24 | -39 | -54 | -69 | 70+ | Total |
| **1. Childless single persons** | | | | | | | | | | | | |
| a. Mating now n/k* | 29 | 1 | 2 | 0 | 0 | 32 | 27 | 1 | 0 | 0 | 0 | 28 |
| b. Never mated | 8 | 0 | 0 | 0 | 0 | 8 | 4 | 1 | 0 | 0 | 0 | 5 |
| c. Not mating in 1953 | 0 | 1 | 0 | 0 | 0 | 1 | 0 | 0 | 2 | 0 | 0 | 2 |
| d. Mating in 1953 | 12 | 5 | 0 | 0 | 0 | 17 | 10 | 1 | 0 | 0 | 0 | 11 |
| Total childless single persons | 49 | 7 | 2 | 0 | 0 | 58 | 41 | 3 | 0 | 2 | 0 | 46 |
| **2. Single parents** | | | | | | | | | | | | |
| a. Mating now n/k | 0 | 0 | 0 | 0 | 0 | 0 | 0 | 0 | 0 | 0 | 0 | 0 |
| b. Not mating now | 0 | 0 | 0 | 0 | 0 | 0 | 0 | 0 | 0 | 0 | 0 | 0 |
| c. Mating now | 2 | 5 | 0 | 0 | 0 | 7 | 12 | 4 | 0 | 0 | 0 | 16 |
| Total single parents | 2 | 5 | 0 | 0 | 0 | 7 | 12 | 4 | 0 | 0 | 0 | 16 |
| **3. Consensually wed** | | | | | | | | | | | | |
| a. In 1953 | 1 | 3 | 1 | 0 | 0 | 5 | 4 | 11 | 0 | 0 | 0 | 15 |
| b. Separated, childless | 0 | 0 | 0 | 0 | 0 | 0 | 0 | 0 | 0 | 0 | 0 | 0 |
| c. Separated, with children | 0 | 0 | 0 | 0 | 0 | 0 | 0 | 0 | 0 | 0 | 0 | 0 |
| d. Widowed, single | 0 | 0 | 0 | 0 | 0 | 0 | 0 | 0 | 0 | 0 | 1 | 1 |
| Total consensually wed | 1 | 3 | 1 | 0 | 0 | 5 | 4 | 11 | 0 | 0 | 1 | 16 |
| **4. Married persons** | | | | | | | | | | | | |
| a. Spouse present | 0 | 1 | 0 | 0 | 0 | 1 | 1 | 15 | 19 | 4 | 1 | 40 |
| b. Spouse absent | 0 | 0 | 0 | 0 | 0 | 0 | 0 | 0 | 0 | 0 | 0 | 0 |
| c. Separated, single | 0 | 1 | 0 | 0 | 0 | 1 | 0 | 3 | 0 | 0 | 0 | 3 |
| d. Separated, not single | 0 | 0 | 0 | 0 | 0 | 0 | 0 | 0 | 0 | 0 | 0 | 0 |
| Total married persons | 0 | 2 | 0 | 0 | 0 | 2 | 1 | 18 | 19 | 4 | 1 | 43 |
| **5. Widowed persons** | | | | | | | | | | | | |
| a. Widowed, single | 0 | 0 | 0 | 0 | 0 | 0 | 0 | 0 | 0 | 1 | 0 | 1 |
| b. Widowed, not single | 0 | 0 | 0 | 0 | 0 | 0 | 0 | 0 | 0 | 0 | 0 | 0 |
| Total widowed persons | 0 | 0 | 0 | 0 | 0 | 0 | 0 | 0 | 0 | 1 | 0 | 1 |
| GRAND TOTAL | 52 | 17 | 3 | 0 | 0 | 72 | 58 | 36 | 19 | 7 | 2 | 122 |

*n/k = Not known.

## TABLE 9

### HOUSEHOLD HEADS, CLASSIFIED BY SEX, AGE, MARITAL CONDITION, AND PARENTAL STATUS

| Mating and Parental Status | Male | | | | | | Female | | | | | |
|---|---|---|---|---|---|---|---|---|---|---|---|---|
| | -24 | -39 | -54 | -69 | 70+ | Total | -24 | -39 | -54 | -69 | 70+ | Total |
| **1. Childless single persons** | | | | | | | | | | | | |
| a. Mating now n/k* | 0 | 0 | 0 | 0 | 0 | 0 | 0 | 1 | 2 | 0 | 0 | 3 |
| b. Never mated | 0 | 0 | 0 | 0 | 0 | 0 | 0 | 0 | 0 | 0 | 0 | 0 |
| c. Not mating in 1953 | 0 | 0 | 0 | 0 | 0 | 0 | 0 | 0 | 2 | 0 | 1 | 3 |
| d. Mating in 1953 | 0 | 0 | 0 | 0 | 0 | 0 | 0 | 0 | 0 | 0 | 0 | 0 |
| Total childless single persons | 0 | 0 | 0 | 0 | 0 | 0 | 0 | 1 | 4 | 0 | 1 | 6 |
| **2. Single parents** | | | | | | | | | | | | |
| a. Mating now n/k | 0 | 0 | 0 | 0 | 0 | 0 | 0 | 1 | 2 | 0 | 0 | 3 |
| b. Not mating now | 0 | 0 | 0 | 2 | 0 | 2 | 0 | 0 | 0 | 2 | 0 | 2 |
| c. Mating now | 0 | 0 | 0 | 0 | 0 | 0 | 1 | 2 | 1 | 1 | 0 | 5 |
| Total single parents | 0 | 0 | 0 | 2 | 0 | 2 | 1 | 3 | 3 | 3 | 0 | 10 |
| **3. Consensually wed** | | | | | | | | | | | | |
| a. In 1953 | 1 | 8 | 2 | 0 | 0 | 11 | 0 | 1 | 1 | 0 | 0 | 2 |
| b. Separated, childless | 0 | 0 | 0 | 0 | 0 | 0 | 0 | 0 | 0 | 0 | 0 | 0 |
| c. Separated, with children | 0 | 0 | 0 | 0 | 0 | 0 | 0 | 0 | 0 | 0 | 0 | 0 |
| d. Widowed, single | 0 | 0 | 0 | 0 | 0 | 0 | 0 | 0 | 0 | 0 | 0 | 0 |
| Total consensually wed | 1 | 8 | 2 | 0 | 0 | 11 | 0 | 1 | 1 | 0 | 0 | 2 |
| **4. Married persons** | | | | | | | | | | | | |
| a. Spouse present | 0 | 10 | 17 | 10 | 2 | 39 | 0 | 0 | 0 | 0 | 0 | 0 |
| b. Spouse absent | 0 | 0 | 0 | 1 | 1 | 2 | 0 | 1 | 1 | 1 | 1 | 4 |
| c. Separated, single | 0 | 1 | 0 | 1 | 1 | 3 | 0 | 1 | 0 | 2 | 0 | 3 |
| d. Separated, not single | 0 | 0 | 0 | 0 | 0 | 0 | 0 | 0 | 0 | 0 | 0 | 0 |
| Total married persons | 0 | 11 | 17 | 12 | 4 | 44 | 0 | 2 | 1 | 3 | 1 | 7 |
| **5. Widowed persons** | | | | | | | | | | | | |
| a. Widowed, single | 0 | 0 | 0 | 1 | 1 | 2 | 0 | 1 | 4 | 6 | 6 | 17 |
| b. Widowed, not single | 0 | 1 | 0 | 0 | 0 | 1 | 0 | 0 | 0 | 0 | 0 | 0 |
| Total widowed persons | 0 | 1 | 0 | 1 | 1 | 3 | 0 | 1 | 4 | 6 | 6 | 17 |
| **GRAND TOTAL** | 1 | 20 | 19 | 15 | 5 | 60 | 1 | 8 | 13 | 12 | 8 | 42 |

*n/k = Not known.

# TABLE 10

## POPULATION OF THE SAMPLE HOUSEHOLDS, CLASSIFIED BY RELATIONSHIP TO THE HOUSEHOLD HEAD AND SEX OF HEAD

| Categories of Kin | Male Head Number | Male Head Per cent† | Female Head Number | Female Head Per cent† | Total Number | Total Per cent† |
|---|---|---|---|---|---|---|
| 1. Spouses and mates | 51 | 18.2 | 2 | 1.7 | 53 | 14.0 |
| 2. HH's* sons | 90 | 33.1 | 28 | 24.1 | 118 | 30.5 |
| 3. HH's daughters | 73 | 26.8 | 28 | 24.1 | 101 | 26.1 |
| 4. HH's children | 163 | 59.9 | 56 | 48.2 | 219 | 56.6 |
| 5. HH's sons' sons | 2 | 0.8 | 2 | 1.7 | 4 | 1.0 |
| 6. HH's sons' daughters | 1 | 0.4 | 5 | 4.3 | 6 | 1.5 |
| 7. HH's daughters' sons | 8 | 3.0 | 11 | 9.5 | 19 | 4.9 |
| 8. HH's daughters' daughters | 12 | 4.2 | 10 | 8.6 | 22 | 5.75 |
| 9. HH's grandchildren | 23 | 8.4 | 28 | 24.1 | 51 | 13.15 |
| 8. HH's sons' grandchildren | 1 | 0.4 | 0 | 0.0 | 1 | 0.25 |
| 9. HH's daughters' grandchildren | 0 | 0.0 | 4 | 3.5 | 4 | 1.0 |
| Total lineal issue of HH | 187 | 68.7 | 88 | 75.8 | 275 | 71.0 |
| 10. HH's mates' sons by others | 3 | 1.1 | 0 | 0.0 | 3 | 0.75 |
| 11. HH's mates' daughters by others | 3 | 1.1 | 1 | 0.8 | 4 | 1.0 |
| 12. HH's mates' sons' sons | 2 | 0.8 | 0 | 0.0 | 1 | 0.5 |
| 13. HH's mates' daughters' sons | 0 | 0.0 | 1 | 0.9 | 1 | 0.25 |
| Issue of HH's mates by others | 8 | 3.0 | 2 | 1.7 | 10 | 2.5 |
| 14. HH's brothers | 0 | 0.0 | 1 | 1.5 | 1 | 0.25 |
| 15. HH's sisters | 0 | 0.0 | 3 | 2.6 | 3 | 0.75 |
| 16. HH's brothers' issue | 2 | 0.8 | 0 | 0.0 | 2 | 0.5 |
| 17. HH's sisters' issue | 4 | 1.4 | 8 | 6.9 | 12 | 3.0 |
| HH's siblings and their issue | 6 | 2.2 | 12 | 10.4 | 18 | 4.5 |
| 18. HH's mother | 0 | 0.0 | 1 | 0.9 | 1 | 0.25 |
| 19. HH's matrilateral kin | 4 | 1.5 | 1 | 0.9 | 5 | 1.25 |
| 20. HH's patrilateral kin | 0 | 0.0 | 3 | 2.6 | 3 | 0.75 |
| 21. Mate of HH's patrilateral kin | 0 | 0.0 | 1 | 0.8 | 1 | 0.25 |
| Other kin of HH | 4 | 1.4 | 6 | 5.2 | 10 | 2.5 |
| 22. HH's mates' siblings and their issue | 7 | 2.8 | 1 | 0.9 | 8 | 2.0 |
| 23. HH's mates' matrilateral kin | 1 | 0.4 | 2 | 1.7 | 3 | 0.75 |
| 24. HH's mates' patrilateral kin | 3 | 1.2 | 0 | 0.0 | 3 | 0.75 |
| HH's mates' resident kin | 11 | 4.4 | 3 | 2.6 | 14 | 3.5 |
| 25. HH's daughters' mates and spouses | 1 | 0.4 | 2 | 1.7 | 3 | 0.75 |
| 26. Issue of HH's sons' mates by others | 2 | 0.8 | 1 | 0.9 | 1 | 0.75 |
| Junior affinal kin | 3 | 1.2 | 3 | 2.6 | 6 | 1.5 |
| 27. Adoptions | 1 | 0.4 | 0 | 0.0 | 1 | 0.25 |
| 28. Unrelated persons | 1 | 0.4 | 0 | 0.0 | 1 | 0.25 |
| 29. Boarders, servants, etc. | 0 | 0.0 | 0 | 0.0 | 0 | 0.0 |
| Adoptions and nonkin | 2 | 0.8 | 0 | 0.0 | 2 | 0.5 |
| TOTAL | 272 | 100.0 | 116 | 100.0 | 388 | 100.00 |

*HH = Household head.

To reduce the number of the percentage decimals, I have simplified these ratios, and made other alterations where necessary. Though not exact, these percentages correspond closely.

## TABLE 11

RESIDENT COLLATERALS OF FEMALE PRINCIPALS, CLASSIFIED BY KINSHIP CATEGORY, BIRTH STATUS, AND SEX OF HOUSEHOLD HEAD

| Kinship Category | Male Head L* | Male Head U* | Male Head N/K* | Male Head All | Female Head L | Female Head U | Female Head N/K | Female Head All | Total |
|---|---|---|---|---|---|---|---|---|---|
| Full siblings | 0 | 0 | 1 | 1 | 0 | 2 | 2 | 4 | 5 |
| Issue of full siblings | 1 | 5 | 0 | 6 | 3 | 4 | 1 | 8 | 14 |
| Patrilateral kin | 0 | 3 | 0 | 3 | 1 | 2 | 0 | 3 | 6 |
| Matrilateral kin | 0 | 1 | 0 | 1 | 0 | 1 | 0 | 1 | 2 |
| TOTAL | 1 | 9 | 1 | 11 | 4 | 9 | 3 | 16 | 27 |

*L = Lawful, i.e., legitimate; U = Unlawful, i.e., illegitimate; N/K = Birth status not known.

## TABLE 12

RESIDENT COLLATERALS OF FEMALE PRINCIPALS, CLASSIFIED BY SEX, BIRTH STATUS, GENERATION, SEX OF PARENT THROUGH WHOM KINSHIP IS TRACED, AND SEX OF HOUSEHOLD HEAD†

| Generation | Sex of Linking Parent | MH L* M* | MH L* F* | MH U* M | MH U* F | MH N/K* M | MH N/K* F | MH Total | FH L M | FH L F | FH U M | FH U F | FH N/K M | FH N/K F | FH Total | T L M | T L F | T U M | T U F | T N/K M | T N/K F | Total | Total |
|---|---|---|---|---|---|---|---|---|---|---|---|---|---|---|---|---|---|---|---|---|---|---|---|
| 0 | Male | 0 | 0 | 0 | 0 | 0 | 0 | 0 | 0 | 0 | 0 | 0 | 0 | 0 | 0 | 0 | 0 | 0 | 0 | 0 | 0 | 0 | 0 |
| | Female | 0 | 0 | 0 | 0 | 0 | 0 | 0 | 0 | 0 | 0 | 1 | 0 | 0 | 1 | 0 | 0 | 0 | 1 | 0 | 0 | 1 | 1 |
| | Total | 0 | 0 | 0 | 0 | 0 | 0 | 0 | 0 | 0 | 0 | 1 | 0 | 0 | 1 | 0 | 0 | 0 | 1 | 0 | 0 | 1 | 1 |
| -1 | Male | 0 | 0 | 3 | 0 | 0 | 0 | 3 | 0 | 0 | 0 | 0 | 0 | 0 | 0 | 0 | 0 | 3 | 0 | 0 | 0 | 3 | 3 |
| | Female | 0 | 0 | 0 | 5 | 0 | 0 | 5 | 0 | 4 | 0 | 2 | 0 | 0 | 6 | 0 | 4 | 0 | 7 | 0 | 0 | 11 | 11 |
| | Total | 0 | 0 | 3 | 5 | 0 | 0 | 8 | 0 | 4 | 0 | 2 | 0 | 0 | 6 | 0 | 4 | 3 | 7 | 0 | 0 | 14 | 14 |
| -2 | Male | 0 | 0 | 0 | 0 | 0 | 0 | 0 | 0 | 0 | 0 | 0 | 0 | 0 | 0 | 0 | 0 | 0 | 0 | 0 | 0 | 0 | 0 |
| | Female | 1 | 0 | 0 | 0 | 0 | 0 | 1 | 0 | 0 | 2 | 2 | 1 | 0 | 5 | 1 | 0 | 2 | 2 | 1 | 0 | 6 | 6 |
| | Total | 1 | 0 | 0 | 0 | 0 | 0 | 1 | 0 | 0 | 2 | 2 | 1 | 0 | 5 | 1 | 0 | 2 | 2 | 1 | 0 | 6 | 6 |
| GRAND TOTAL | | 1 | 0 | 3 | 5 | 0 | 0 | 9 | 0 | 4 | 2 | 5 | 1 | 0 | 12 | 1 | 4 | 5 | 10 | 1 | 0 | 21 | 21 |

*L = Lawful, i.e., legitimate; U = Unlawful, i.e., illegitimate; N/K = Birth status not known; M = Male; F = Female.

†One resident collateral male of the first descending generation whose parental link with the female principal of the home remained unspecified is excluded.

## TABLE 13

RESIDENT LINEAL ISSUE OF THE HOUSEHOLD HEAD, CLASSIFIED BY SEX, BIRTH STATUS, GENERATION, SEX OF PARENT THROUGH WHOM DESCENT IS TRACED, AND SEX OF THE HOUSEHOLD HEAD

| Sex and Birth Status | | Households with Male Head | | | | Households with Female Head | | | | Own Issue | Sons' Issue | Total Daughters' Issue | Total |
|---|---|---|---|---|---|---|---|---|---|---|---|---|---|
| | | Own Issue | Sons' Issue† | Daughters' Issue | Total | Own Issue | Sons' Issue | Daughters' Issue‡ | Total | | | | |
| Males | L* | 69 | 0 | 0 | 69 | 11 | 0 | 2 | 13 | 80 | 0 | 2 | 82 |
| | U* | 16 | 2 | 8 | 26 | 12 | 2 | 11 | 25 | 28 | 4 | 19 | 51 |
| | N/K* | 5 | 0 | 0 | 5 | 5 | 0 | 0 | 5 | 10 | 0 | 0 | 10 |
| All males | | 90 | 2 | 8 | 100 | 28 | 2 | 13 | 43 | 118 | 4 | 21 | 143 |
| Females | L | 62 | 0 | 0 | 62 | 6 | 0 | 1 | 7 | 68 | 0 | 1 | 69 |
| | U | 8 | 2 | 11 | 21 | 15 | 5 | 11 | 31 | 23 | 7 | 22 | 52 |
| | N/K | 3 | 0 | 1 | 4 | 7 | 0 | 0 | 7 | 10 | 0 | 1 | 11 |
| All females | | 73 | 2 | 12 | 87 | 28 | 5 | 12 | 45 | 101 | 7 | 24 | 132 |
| Total | L | 131 | 0 | 0 | 131 | 17 | 0 | 3 | 20 | 148 | 0 | 3 | 151 |
| | U | 24 | 4 | 19 | 47 | 27 | 7 | 22 | 56 | 51 | 11 | 41 | 103 |
| | N/K | 8 | 0 | 1 | 9 | 12 | 0 | 0 | 12 | 20 | 0 | 1 | 21 |
| GRAND TOTAL | | 163 | 4 | 20 | 187 | 56 | 7 | 25 | 88 | 219 | 11 | 45 | 275 |

*L = Lawful, i.e., legitimate; U = Unlawful, i.e., illegitimate; N/K = Birth status not known.

†Includes one unlawful daughter of the household head's lawful son's unlawful daughter.

‡Includes 4 daughters' grandchildren, 2 male and 2 female (see Chart) all unlawful.

## TABLE 14

DISTRIBUTION OF CHILDREN WITHIN THE SAMPLE HOUSEHOLDS, CLASSIFIED BY SEX OF HEAD, WITH SPECIAL REFERENCE TO THE PRESENCE OF EITHER PARENT IN THE HOUSEHOLD, AND TO THE AGE AND BIRTH STATUS OF THE CHILDREN OF EITHER SEX

| Age | Households with Male Head | | | | | | Households with Female Head | | | | | | Total | | | | | |
|---|---|---|---|---|---|---|---|---|---|---|---|---|---|---|---|---|---|---|
| | LS* | LD* | US* | UD* | N/KS* | Total | LS | LD | US | UD | N/KS | Total | LS | LD | US | UD | N/KS | Total |
| **a. Both parents present** | | | | | | | | | | | | | | | | | | |
| 0- 4 | 9 | 16 | 4 | 4 | 0 | 33 | 0 | 0 | 1 | 2 | 0 | 3 | 9 | 16 | 5 | 6 | 0 | 36 |
| 5-14 | 29 | 23 | 4 | 1 | 0 | 57 | 0 | 0 | 2 | 0 | 0 | 2 | 29 | 23 | 6 | 1 | 0 | 59 |
| 15-24 | 28 | 20 | 0 | 0 | 0 | 48 | 0 | 0 | 0 | 0 | 0 | 0 | 28 | 20 | 0 | 0 | 0 | 48 |
| 25-39 | 2 | 2 | 0 | 0 | 0 | 4 | 0 | 0 | 0 | 0 | 0 | 0 | 2 | 2 | 0 | 0 | 0 | 4 |
| 40 + | 0 | 0 | 0 | 0 | 0 | 0 | 0 | 0 | 0 | 0 | 0 | 0 | 0 | 0 | 0 | 0 | 0 | 0 |
| Total | 68 | 61 | 8 | 5 | 0 | 142 | 0 | 0 | 3 | 2 | 0 | 5 | 68 | 61 | 11 | 7 | 0 | 147 |
| **b. Both parents absent** | | | | | | | | | | | | | | | | | | |
| 0- 4 | 0 | 0 | 3 | 1 | 0 | 4 | 1 | 1 | 1 | 2 | 0 | 5 | 1 | 1 | 4 | 3 | 0 | 9 |
| 5-14 | 2 | 0 | 8 | 5 | 0 | 15 | 1 | 1 | 8 | 8 | 0 | 18 | 3 | 1 | 16 | 13 | 0 | 33 |
| 15-24 | 1 | 3 | 4 | 4 | 0 | 12 | 0 | 3 | 2 | 8 | 0 | 13 | 1 | 6 | 6 | 12 | 0 | 25 |
| 25-39 | 0 | 0 | 1 | 1 | 1 | 3 | 0 | 0 | 1 | 1 | 1 | 3 | 0 | 0 | 2 | 2 | 2 | 6 |
| 40 + | 0 | 0 | 0 | 0 | 0 | 0 | 0 | 0 | 0 | 2 | 0 | 2 | 0 | 0 | 0 | 2 | 0 | 2 |
| Total | 3 | 3 | 16 | 11 | 1 | 34 | 2 | 5 | 12 | 21 | 1 | 41 | 5 | 8 | 28 | 32 | 2 | 75 |
| **c. Mothers only present** | | | | | | | | | | | | | | | | | | |
| 0- 4 | 0 | 0 | 6 | 7 | 0 | 13 | 0 | 1 | 6 | 4 | 0 | 11 | 0 | 1 | 12 | 11 | 0 | 24 |
| 5-14 | 0 | 0 | 2 | 4 | 0 | 6 | 2 | 1 | 5 | 7 | 0 | 15 | 2 | 1 | 7 | 11 | 0 | 21 |
| 15-24 | 0 | 0 | 0 | 0 | 0 | 0 | 2 | 2 | 3 | 7 | 0 | 14 | 2 | 2 | 3 | 7 | 0 | 14 |
| 25-39 | 0 | 0 | 1 | 1 | 0 | 2 | 2 | 3 | 0 | 1 | 0 | 6 | 2 | 3 | 1 | 2 | 0 | 8 |
| 40 + | 0 | 0 | 0 | 0 | 0 | 0 | 0 | 0 | 0 | 0 | 0 | 0 | 0 | 0 | 0 | 0 | 0 | 0 |
| Total | 0 | 0 | 9 | 12 | 0 | 21 | 6 | 7 | 14 | 19 | 0 | 46 | 6 | 7 | 23 | 31 | 0 | 67 |
| **d. Fathers only present** | | | | | | | | | | | | | | | | | | |
| 0- 4 | 0 | 0 | 0 | 0 | 0 | 0 | 0 | 0 | 0 | 0 | 0 | 0 | 0 | 0 | 0 | 0 | 0 | 0 |
| 5-14 | 0 | 0 | 6 | 0 | 0 | 6 | 0 | 0 | 0 | 0 | 0 | 0 | 0 | 0 | 6 | 0 | 0 | 6 |
| 15-24 | 2 | 1 | 1 | 3 | 0 | 7 | 0 | 0 | 0 | 0 | 0 | 0 | 2 | 1 | 1 | 3 | 0 | 7 |
| 25-39 | 1 | 0 | 1 | 0 | 0 | 2 | 0 | 0 | 0 | 0 | 0 | 0 | 1 | 0 | 1 | 0 | 0 | 2 |
| 40 + | 0 | 1 | 0 | 0 | 0 | 1 | 0 | 0 | 0 | 0 | 0 | 0 | 0 | 1 | 0 | 0 | 0 | 1 |
| Total | 3 | 2 | 8 | 3 | 0 | 16 | 0 | 0 | 0 | 0 | 0 | 0 | 3 | 2 | 8 | 3 | 0 | 16 |

## TABLE 14 (continued)

DISTRIBUTION OF CHILDREN WITHIN THE SAMPLE HOUSEHOLDS, CLASSIFIED BY SEX OF HEAD, WITH SPECIAL REFERENCE TO THE PRESENCE OF EITHER PARENT IN THE HOUSEHOLD, AND TO THE AGE AND BIRTH STATUS OF THE CHILDREN OF EITHER SEX

| Age | Households with Male Head | | | | | | Households with Female Head | | | | | | Total | | | | | |
|---|---|---|---|---|---|---|---|---|---|---|---|---|---|---|---|---|---|---|
| | LS* | LD* | US* | UD* | N/KS* | Total | LS | LD | US | UD | N/KS | Total | LS | LD | US | UD | N/KS | Total |
| **e. With fathers, mothers dead** | | | | | | | | | | | | | | | | | | |
| 0– 4 | 0 | 0 | 0 | 0 | 0 | 0 | | | | | | | 0 | 0 | 0 | 0 | 0 | 0 |
| 5–14 | 0 | 0 | 0 | 0 | 0 | 0 | | | | | | | 0 | 0 | 0 | 0 | 0 | 0 |
| 15–24 | 1 | 2 | 2 | 1 | 0 | 6 | | | | | | | 1 | 2 | 2 | 1 | 0 | 6 |
| 25–39 | 1 | 0 | 0 | 0 | 0 | 1 | | | | | | | 1 | 0 | 0 | 0 | 0 | 1 |
| 40 + | 0 | 0 | 0 | 0 | 0 | 0 | | | | | | | 0 | 0 | 0 | 0 | 0 | 0 |
| Total | 2 | 2 | 2 | 1 | 0 | 7 | | | | | | | 2 | 2 | 2 | 1 | 0 | 7 |
| **f. With mothers, fathers dead** | | | | | | | | | | | | | | | | | | |
| 0– 4 | | | | | | | 0 | 0 | 0 | 0 | 0 | 0 | 0 | 0 | 0 | 0 | 0 | 0 |
| 5–14 | | | | | | | 3 | 1 | 2 | 0 | 0 | 6 | 3 | 1 | 2 | 0 | 0 | 6 |
| 15–24 | | | | | | | 5 | 1 | 0 | 0 | 0 | 6 | 5 | 1 | 0 | 0 | 0 | 6 |
| 25–39 | | | | | | | 1 | 2 | 0 | 1 | 0 | 4 | 1 | 2 | 0 | 1 | 0 | 4 |
| 40 + | | | | | | | 2 | 0 | 0 | 0 | 0 | 2 | 2 | 0 | 0 | 0 | 0 | 2 |
| Total | | | | | | | 11 | 4 | 2 | 1 | 0 | 18 | 11 | 4 | 2 | 1 | 0 | 18 |
| **Totals by sex of household head** | | | | | | | | | | | | | | | | | | |
| 0– 4 | 9 | 16 | 13 | 12 | 0 | 50 | 1 | 2 | 8 | 8 | 0 | 19 | 10 | 18 | 21 | 20 | 0 | 69 |
| 5–14 | 31 | 23 | 20 | 10 | 0 | 84 | 6 | 3 | 17 | 15 | 0 | 41 | 37 | 26 | 37 | 25 | 0 | 125 |
| 15–24 | 32 | 26 | 7 | 8 | 0 | 73 | 7 | 6 | 5 | 15 | 0 | 33 | 39 | 32 | 12 | 23 | 0 | 106 |
| 25–39 | 4 | 2 | 3 | 2 | 1 | 12 | 3 | 5 | 1 | 3 | 1 | 13 | 7 | 7 | 4 | 5 | 2 | 25 |
| 40 + | 0 | 1 | 0 | 0 | 0 | 1 | 2 | 0 | 0 | 2 | 0 | 4 | 2 | 1 | 0 | 2 | 0 | 5 |
| TOTAL | 76 | 68 | 43 | 32 | 1 | 220 | 19 | 16 | 31 | 43 | 1 | 110 | 95 | 84 | 74 | 75 | 2 | 330 |

*LS = Lawful son; LD = Lawful daughter; US = Unlawful son; UD = Unlawful daughter; N/KS = Son, birth status not known.

# TABLE 15

DEPENDENTS BELOW THE AGE OF 24 WHO LIVE APART FROM BOTH PARENTS IN THE SAMPLE HOUSEHOLDS, CLASSIFIED BY SEX, BIRTH STATUS, AND RELATION TO THE HOUSEHOLD PRINCIPALS WHO ARE THEIR KIN

| Matrilateral Kin | Male L* | Male U* | Female L | Female U | All |
|---|---|---|---|---|---|
| 1. Mother's mother | 1 | 7 | 1 | 5 | 15 |
| 2. Mother's mother and father | 0 | 4 | 0 | 3 | 7 |
| 3. Mother's sister | 1 | 1 | 3 | 3 | 8 |
| 4. Mother's brother | 1 | 0 | 1 | 0 | 2 |
| 5. Mother's brother's spouse | 1 | 0 | 0 | 0 | 1 |
| 6. Mother's husband's parents | 0 | 1 | 0 | 0 | 1 |
| 7. Mother's absent kinsman's spouse | 0 | 1 | 0 | 0 | 1 |
| 8. Mother's father | 0 | 1 | 0 | 0 | 1 |
| 9. Mother's mother's mother | 0 | 0 | 0 | 1 | 1 |
| 10. Mother's mother's sister | 0 | 1 | 0 | 1 | 2 |
| 11. Mother's mother's brother | 1 | 0 | 1 | 0 | 2 |
| 12. Mother's father's sister's daughter | 0 | 0 | 0 | 1 | 1 |
| 13. Mother's F's brother's spouse | 0 | 0 | 0 | 1 | 1 |
| 14. Cognatic kinsman | 0 | 0 | 0 | 1 | 1 |
| 15. Own full sister | 0 | 0 | 0 | 2 | 2 |

| Patrilateral Kin | Male L | Male U | Female L | Female U | All |
|---|---|---|---|---|---|
| 1. Father's mother | 0 | 4 | 0 | 5 | 9 |
| 2. Father's mother and father | 0 | 0 | 0 | 1 | 1 |
| 3. Father's father | 0 | 1 | 0 | 0 | 1 |
| 4. Father's brother | 0 | 0 | 0 | 1 | 1 |
| 5. Father's sister | 0 | 1 | 0 | 1 | 2 |
| 6. Father's spouse | 0 | 0 | 0 | 1 | 1 |
| 7. F's F's brother's daughter | 0 | 0 | 0 | 1 | 1 |
| 8. F's M's B's son's daughter | 0 | 1 | 0 | 0 | 1 |
| 9. F's sister's son | 0 | 1 | 0 | 0 | 1 |
| Total father's kin | 0 | 8 | 0 | 10 | 18 |
| Total mother's kin | 5 | 16 | 6 | 18 | 45 |
| Total unrelated persons | 0 | 2 | 2 | 0 | 4 |
| GRAND TOTAL | 5 | 26 | 8 | 28 | 67 |

*L = Lawful, i.e., legitimate; U = Unlawful, i.e., illegitimate.

## TABLE 16

### CHILDREN LESS THAN 24 YEARS OF AGE, LIVING WITH THEIR FATHERS APART FROM THEIR MOTHERS, CLASSIFIED BY SEX, BIRTH STATUS, AND STATUS OF FATHER OR KIN WITH WHOM THEY LIVE

|  | Male | | Female | | |
|---|---|---|---|---|---|
|  | L* | U* | L | U | Total |
| 1. Father widowed | 0 | 0 | 2 | 0 | 2 |
| 2. Father wed | 0 | 3 | 0 | 3 | 6 |
| 3. Father unwed, not single | 0 | 2 | 0 | 0 | 2 |
| 4. Father wed, mother dead | 0 | 3 | 0 | 1 | 4 |
| 5. Father wed, spouse absent | 3 | 0 | 1 | 0 | 4 |
| 6. Father and father's father and mother | 0 | 1 | 0 | 0 | 1 |
| TOTAL | 3 | 9 | 3 | 4 | 19 |

*L = Lawful, i.e., legitimate; U = Unlawful, i.e., illegitimate.

## TABLE 17

### CHILDREN LESS THAN 24 YEARS OF AGE, LIVING WITH THEIR MOTHERS APART FROM THEIR FATHERS, CLASSIFIED BY SEX, BIRTH STATUS, AND STATUS OF MOTHER OR KIN WITH WHOM THEY LIVE

|  | Male | | Female | | |
|---|---|---|---|---|---|
|  | L* | U* | L | U | Total |
| 1. Mother widowed | 6 | 0 | 1 | 0 | 7 |
| 2. Mother wed | 0 | 1 | 1 | 0 | 2 |
| 3. Mother wed, spouse absent | 5 | 1 | 4 | 1 | 11 |
| 4. Mother unwed, single | 0 | 6 | 0 | 13 | 19 |
| 5. Mother unwed, not single | 0 | 2 | 0 | 3 | 5 |
| 6. Mother unwed, not single, father dead | 0 | 2 | 0 | 0 | 2 |
| Total with mother only | 11 | 12 | 6 | 17 | 46 |
| 7. Mother and mother's mother | 1 | 3 | 0 | 1 | 5 |
| 8. Mother and M's mother and father | 0 | 4 | 0 | 2 | 6 |
| 9. Mother and mother's father | 0 | 0 | 0 | 4 | 4 |
| 10. Mother and M's M's mother | 0 | 1 | 0 | 0 | 1 |
| 11. Mother and M's M's sister | 0 | 1 | 0 | 1 | 2 |
| 12. Mother and M's M's M's sister | 0 | 1 | 0 | 1 | 2 |
| 13. Mother and M's F's mother and father | 0 | 0 | 0 | 1 | 1 |
| 14. Mother and M's F's brother | 0 | 1 | 0 | 0 | 1 |
| 15. Mother and M's F's F's B's daughter | 0 | 0 | 0 | 1 | 1 |
| 16. Mother and M's absent father's spouse | 0 | 1 | 0 | 0 | 1 |
| 17. Mother and M's distant congatic kinsman | 0 | 1 | 0 | 1 | 2 |
| Total with mother and M's kin | 1 | 13 | 0 | 12 | 26 |
| TOTAL | 12 | 25 | 6 | 29 | 72 |

*L = Lawful, i.e., legitimate; U = Unlawful, i.e., illegitimate.

## TABLE 18

### FREQUENCY DISTRIBUTION OF DIFFERING TYPES OF DOMESTIC UNIT WITHIN THE SAMPLE

| | Households with Male Head | | | Households with Female Head | | | Total | | | |
|---|---|---|---|---|---|---|---|---|---|---|
| | No Others | Plus Others | Total | No Others | Plus Others | Total | No Others | Plus Others | Total | Per cent |
| 1. Single persons | 4 | 0 | 4 | 8 | 2 | 10 | 12 | 2 | 14 | 13.7 |
| 2. Siblings | 0 | 0 | 0 | 1 | 1 | 2 | 1 | 1 | 2 | 1.9 |
| 3. Household head and children | 3 | 0 | 3 | 9 | 2 | 11 | 12 | 2 | 14 | 13.7 |
| 4. Childless couples | 7 | 9 | 16 | 0 | 1 | 1 | 7 | 10 | 17 | 16.6 |
| 5. Couples and children | 20 | 8 | 28 | 0 | 1 | 1 | 20 | 9 | 29 | 28.5 |
| 6. Household head and grandchildren | 0 | 0 | 0 | 5 | 1 | 6 | 5 | 1 | 6 | 5.9 |
| 7. Couples and grandchildren | 0 | 0 | 0 | 0 | 0 | 0 | 0 | 0 | 0 | 0.0 |
| 8. Household head, children, and grandchildren | 2 | 0 | 2 | 7 | 2 | 9 | 9 | 2 | 11 | 10.9 |
| 9. Couples, children, and grandchildren | 4 | 2 | 6 | 0 | 0 | 0 | 4 | 2 | 6 | 5.9 |
| 10. Household head and issue to 4th generation | 0 | 0 | 0 | 1 | 1 | 2 | 1 | 1 | 2 | 1.9 |
| 11. Couples and issue to 4th generation | 1 | 0 | 1 | 0 | 0 | 0 | 1 | 0 | 1 | 1.0 |
| TOTAL | 41 | 19 | 60 | 31 | 11 | 42 | 72 | 30 | 102 | 100.0 |

## TABLE 19

### DOMESTIC UNITS OF STRUCTURALLY DIFFERING TYPES, CLASSIFIED BY SEX OF HEAD AND GENERATION RANGE

| | Households with Male Head | | | | | Households with Female Head | | | | | Total | | | | |
|---|---|---|---|---|---|---|---|---|---|---|---|---|---|---|---|
| | Generation Range | | | | | Generation Range | | | | | Generation Range | | | | |
| | 1 | 2 | 3 | 4 | Total | 1 | 2 | 3 | 4 | Total | 1 | 2 | 3 | 4 | Total |
| 1. Single persons | 4 | 0 | 0 | 0 | 4 | 8 | 1 | 1 | 0 | 10 | 12 | 1 | 1 | 0 | 14 |
| 2. Siblings | 0 | 0 | 0 | 0 | 0 | 1 | 1 | 0 | 0 | 2 | 1 | 1 | 0 | 0 | 2 |
| 3. Household head and children | 0 | 3 | 0 | 0 | 3 | 0 | 10 | 1 | 0 | 11 | 0 | 13 | 1 | 0 | 14 |
| 4. Childless couples | 7 | 5 | 4 | 0 | 16 | 0 | 1 | 0 | 0 | 1 | 7 | 6 | 4 | 0 | 17 |
| 5. Couples and children | 0 | 25 | 3 | 0 | 28 | 0 | 1 | 0 | 0 | 1 | 0 | 26 | 3 | 0 | 29 |
| 6. Household head and grandchildren | 0 | 0 | 0 | 0 | 0 | 0 | 0 | 6 | 0 | 6 | 0 | 0 | 6 | 0 | 6 |
| 7. Couples and grandchildren | 0 | 0 | 0 | 0 | 0 | 0 | 0 | 0 | 0 | 0 | 0 | 0 | 0 | 0 | 0 |
| 8. Household head, children, and grandchildren | 0 | 0 | 2 | 0 | 2 | 0 | 0 | 9 | 0 | 9 | 0 | 0 | 11 | 0 | 11 |
| 9. Couples, children, and grandchildren | 0 | 0 | 6 | 0 | 6 | 0 | 0 | 0 | 0 | 0 | 0 | 0 | 6 | 0 | 6 |
| 10. Household head and issue to 4th generation | 0 | 0 | 0 | 0 | 0 | 0 | 0 | 0 | 2 | 2 | 0 | 0 | 0 | 2 | 2 |
| 11. Couples and issue to 4th generation | 0 | 0 | 0 | 1 | 1 | 0 | 0 | 0 | 0 | 0 | 0 | 0 | 0 | 1 | 1 |
| TOTAL | 11 | 33 | 15 | 1 | 60 | 9 | 14 | 17 | 2 | 42 | 20 | 47 | 32 | 3 | 102 |
| PERCENTAGE | 18.0 | 55.0 | 25.0 | 2.0 | 100.0 | 21.0 | 33.0 | 41.0 | 5.0 | 100.0 | 20.0 | 46.0 | 31.0 | 3.0 | 100.0 |

# TABLE 20

CONJUGAL UNIONS IN THE SAMPLE HOUSEHOLDS, CLASSIFIED BY THEIR BASIS, THE TYPE OF DOMESTIC UNIT IN WHICH THEY OCCUR, AND THE SEX OF THE HOUSEHOLD HEAD*

| Morphological Types | Male Head | | | Female Head | | | Total | | |
|---|---|---|---|---|---|---|---|---|---|
| | Wed | Unwed | Total | Wed | Unwed | Total | Wed | Unwed | Total |
| 1a. Childless couples only | 1 | 6 | 7 | 0 | 0 | 0 | 1 | 6 | 7 |
| b. Childless couples plus others | 7 | 2 | 9 | 0 | 1 | 1 | 7 | 3 | 10 |
| Total childless couples | 8 | 8 | 16 | 0 | 1 | 1 | 8 | 9 | 17 |
| 2a. Couples and children only | 17 | 3 | 20 | 0 | 0 | 0 | 17 | 3 | 20 |
| b. Couples, children plus others | 7 | 1 | 8 | 1 | 0 | 1 | 7 | 2 | 9 |
| Total couples and children | 24 | 4 | 28 | 1 | 0 | 1 | 24 | 5 | 29 |
| 3a. Couples, children, and grandchildren only | 4 | 0 | 4 | 0 | 0 | 0 | 4 | 0 | 4 |
| b. Couples, children, grandchildren plus others | 2 | 0 | 2 | 0 | 0 | 0 | 2 | 0 | 2 |
| Total couples, children, and grandchildren | 6 | 0 | 6 | 0 | 0 | 0 | 6 | 0 | 6 |
| 4a. Couples and issue to 4th generation only | 1 | 0 | 1 | 0 | 0 | 0 | 1 | 0 | 1 |
| b. Couples, issue to 4th generation plus others | 0 | 0 | 0 | 0 | 0 | 0 | 0 | 0 | 0 |
| Total couples and issue to 4th generation | 1 | 0 | 1 | 0 | 0 | 0 | 1 | 0 | 1 |
| TOTAL | 39 | 12 | 51 | 2 | 2 | 2 | 39 | 14 | 53 |

*Couples tabulated are principals of the domestic units in which they live. Since our sample contains no couples with their grandchildren apart from their children, this category has been omitted.

# 4. Grenville

Grenville is a small town on the eastern coast of Grenada. In sailing ship days, it was an important port, and its French name, La Baye, is still used by the folk. Nowadays only schooners and sloops come into the harbor, and many of these sail from Carriacou for the weekly Saturday market. The town is hemmed in by large land holdings, some of which have changed hands recently. The land rises quickly to about 500 feet and then flattens out for a few miles before rising again in the inland mountain range. The coastal road passes through Grenville, and the main road across the island from St. George's joins the coast road at this place. Pearls Airport, the only one in Grenada, lies two miles to the north on an alluvial plain.

During the nineteenth century, Grenville rivaled St. George's in importance; since then motor transport has led to a concentration of elite activities in St. George's, the island capital. By 1953 Grenville was a town with a past, but little future. In 1946 its population was estimated at 1, 193. There has been a steady decline in population since 1891. Even if we assume a small rise after 1946, the sample which I studied at Grenville represents about 30 per cent of the townsfolk. During the two months of this household survey, several households moved into and out of the census area. Fortunately I collected complete data on each of them. However, since the great majority of these people had to move their wooden houses when they moved as units, the normal arrangement in this area being tenancy of a "house spot," the removal of household groups was less than it might otherwise have been. A further complication was caused by movement of individuals into and out of these homes during the course of the survey. Such mobility was governed by conditions of mating and employment; I was also able to collect the necessary data for all mobile individuals, and included those who had lived in the households for more than four days in the week preceding my initial visit. The census area contained nine households which employed domestic help; only one of these households belonged to a member of the Grenadian elite, a retired gentleman above the age of eighty. Much of the domestic labor was employed on a part-time or time-payment basis; and with the exception noted, the employers all belonged to the Grenadian lower-middle class. [1] Our urban sample is therefore representative of the Grenadian urban lower class, including its mobile upper fringe.

Population and the Distribution of Headship

The 113 households studied at Grenville included 380 individuals. Table 1 describes the distribution of this population by sex and age. Of the aggregate, 35 per cent are below fifteen years, 55 per cent are between fifteen and fifty-four years of age, and 10 per cent are above this. In the total sample the male-female ratio is 1 to 1.36; and within the reproductive age groups fifteen to fifty-four the ratio is 1 to 1.3. There is a marked female excess in the population of age group twenty-five to thirty-nine; presumably this excess arises in part through male emigration from Grenville, in part from female immigration. The presence of this surplus of mature women has obvious implications for domestic organization.

In Table 2 the heads of these sample households are classified by sex and age; and the following table sets out the relative distribution of headship within each age group and sex. More than half the sample households have female heads. Ten per cent of all household heads are below the age of twenty-four; over one quarter are persons of twenty-five to thirty-nine years; only 30 per cent are over fifty-five. Our household heads here are predominantly a young group. Urban conditions emphasize rental of rooms and dwelling quarters; such tenancies encourage individualism in domestic relations. In consequence, there are many small units under comparatively young heads.

The incidence of headship by sex and age as shown in Table 3 bears out these observations fully. Just under one fifth of the men and over one tenth of the women below twenty-four years of age are heads of their own households. Half the men between twenty-five and thirty-nine are household heads, together with 30 per cent of the women in this age group. Just over half the women between forty and fifty-four years old are heads of their own homes, as are 80 per cent of those between fifty-five and sixty-nine, and all twelve over seventy. Curiously, the highest incidence of headship in any male age group occurs between forty and fifty-four years, at which point nine tenths of the men are household heads. The incidence of headship among males declines gradually but steadily thereafter, and not all of the five men over seventy are heads of their homes. Presumably the continuing increase of headship with age among females and its continuing decrease among males over middle age may reflect the changed economic and social position of older men and women in urban conditions. Even so, 53 per cent of the adult males in this sample are household heads, as against 40 per cent of adult females.

Table 4 analyzes these households by the sex of their heads and the number of persons which they contain. There are seventeen single-person units among them, twelve of which contain females. Only one household contains ten or more people, and only seven in all contain seven or more persons each. Of these seven, only one has a female head. The modal household size is two persons. Of the thirty-one units with this size, fifteen have male heads. Of the twenty-two units which contain three persons, fourteen have female heads; and forty-two of the fifty-nine households with female heads contain three or less persons. In short, most households with female heads are quite small, even when compared with male-headed households of this urban sample. For the total sample, the average household size is 3.38 persons; those units with male heads having an average of 3.84, while those with female heads average 2.83. Even if we exclude the seventeen single-person units, the average size of the remaining ninety-six would only be 3.78 persons.

Table 5 analyzes in greater detail the population living in homes with heads of different sex. Units with male heads include five ninths of the sample; and in these homes the sexes are equally balanced, on the whole although not by age groups. Thus, there are only eleven women but twenty-two men in age group forty to fifty-four; however in age group twenty-five to thirty-nine there are twenty-seven women and eighteen men. We may infer that men cohabit with women some years their junior.

There are only fifteen men over twenty-four years of age living in homes with female heads; and both men above fifty-four years of age who are not heads of their own homes are dependents of female heads. Whereas 39 per cent of the residents in homes with male heads are below fifteen years of age, only 30 per cent of the population under female heads are children of this age. By and large, the female heads themselves represent nine in every ten persons over forty who live in these homes.

The seventeen solitary individuals are isolated in Table 6, which gives the details of their marital status, their sex, and their age. Of the five solitary men, two are less than thirty-nine years of age and neither has married; another pair are between forty and fifty-four, and both these are separated from their wives. The fifth, who is over fifty-four, had never married. Clearly, men who fail to marry or to maintain their marriage are likely to be domestic isolates. Of the twelve women living on their own, nine also had not married; they ranged in age from twenty-five to sixty-nine. The other three were widows. Our sample contains no woman below the age of twenty-four who lives on her own.

## The System of Mating Relations

Tables 7 to 9 inclusive describe the distribution of mating and parental experience and status among adults of differing age and sex who live in these households. Table 7 embraces the entire adult population, Table 8 isolates adults who are not household heads, and Table 9 deals with household heads only. Together these tables describe the linkages between household status and mating or parenthood. They contain no category for persons of unknown parental status, since our information on this point is precise.

Of the 102 adult males in these households, thirty-six are below twenty-four years of age. Probably fifteen of these youths had not yet entered on their mating careers; another fourteen were mating extraresidentially, and half of these were already parents. Five had married, but none was cohabiting consensually. Apparently young men are prone to marry after, or without, a short period of extraresidential mating.

Of the thirty men in this sample between twenty-five and thirty-nine years of age, ten were single, and six of these were mating extraresidentially. An equal number were childless single persons, and another six were cohabiting consensually at this time. Thirteen men of this age group had already married, and four of these were separated from their wives. Of these four, three had resumed consensual cohabitation. The other remained celibate. In addition, one man who had been cohabiting consensually had separated from his mate. Apparently domestic unions are highly unstable in this community.

Of the twenty-four men between the ages of forty and fifty-four, in this sample, only four had remained single. Two were fathers and two were childless; none of these men were mating extraresidentially at the time of survey. Five of their age mates were cohabiting consensually; of the remaining fifteen who had married, only eight were living with their wives; five had separated from their wives and two had absent spouses who did not revisit them during my three months' stay in this district. The rate of marital breakdown is thus extremely high.

Of the six men aged between fifty-five and sixty-nine who had married, one was a widower, one had separated from his wife, and four had resident spouses. The only single men of this age group in the sample continued to mate extraresidentially. Only one of the five men over sixty-nine had not married, and he was cohabiting consensually. None of the four who had married were living with their wives, but two of these were widowers.

Of the forty-three married men in this sample, three were widowers, twenty-six lived with their wives, and fourteen did not. Of the forty-six single men, twenty-one were mating extraresidentially, and fourteen were known to be parents. Of the twelve men whose marriages had clearly broken down, six were cohabiting consensually, while some of the remainder were mating extraresidentially.

It is instructive to compare the marital and parental condition among females with that already observed among males. There were thirty-eight young women below the age of twenty-four in these households, ten of whom had probably not yet begun their mating careers, and twenty-eight of whom were single. Of these single girls, fifteen were mating extraresidentially at the time of survey and nine were already mothers. Another who had been cohabiting consensually was no longer doing so. Three women of this age group were partners in consensual domestic unions. Another six had already married, and in one case the spouse remained absent throughout my visit. Apparently girls of this age practice any of the three forms of mating relation, but the extraresidential form is the mode.

Of the forty-nine women living in these households who were between twenty-five and thirty-nine years of age, seventeen were single; of these, eleven were mothers, and ten were mating extraresidentially at the time of survey. Another eleven had entered consensual cohabitation and one of these unions had broken down. Of the twenty-one who had married, five had absent spouses and three of these declared that they were separated.

There were thirty women between the ages of forty and fifty-four in these homes. Ten had remained single, and eight of these were mothers, four of whom were mating extraresidentially at the time of survey. Another nine had cohabited consensually, one being widowed from the union while four had left their mates. Eleven had been married and two of these were widows. Of the remaining nine, only five had resident husbands and two affirmed their separation.

Of the nine women aged between fifty-five and sixty-nine who had married, five were widows, and three lived with their husbands. The other was separated, as were all three women of this age group whose consensual unions had not led to marriage. Only three women of this age group had remained single throughout their lives.

Of the twelve women over seventy, only one had remained single; two had been widowed after consensual cohabitation, and one had separated from her mate. All seven women of this age group who had married were now widows.

Of the fifty-four women in this sample who had married, fourteen were widows, twenty-nine lived with their husbands, and eleven did not. None of the eleven women whose husbands were not with them had resumed consensual cohabitation, but some of the younger ones were mating extraresidentially. No widow had resumed consensual cohabitation, but two of the three widowers in this sample had done so. Of the thirty-one women whose consensual domestic unions had not developed into marriage, sixteen were over forty years of age, seventeen were still cohabiting; and eleven, all mothers, were separated from their mates. Of the fifty-nine single women in this sample, thirty were mothers. Of the twenty-nine childless single women, ten had not yet begun their mating careers, and nineteen were below twenty-four years of age. One half of these single women were mating extraresidentially at the time of survey.

The distribution of marital conditions among the sexes corresponds closely, as we would expect. This correspondence reveals a pervasive instability in mating relations at Grenville. The rate of breakdown in consensual domestic unions and in marriage is equally high. Obviously the rate of breakdown in extraresidential relations is likely to be even higher. Among both sexes, we find a random distribution of these mating forms within the reproductive age groups; and it is to this randomness that the marked instability of all forms of mating relation may most likely be due. Clearly if an individual has a free choice with regard to mating forms within the legal limit against bigamy, the distribution of these mating forms among persons of different age and sex may well be random; but this can only be the case if neither form of mating relation is permanent or defined by its place within a developmental series embracing them all.

Cohabiting males are free to dissolve their unions or abscond, and to contract new ones, extraresidentially or otherwise. There is no observable difference on this point between marriage and consensual domestic unions. Notably, widows and separated wives refrain from re-entering consensual domestic unions; but equally notable is the fact that widowers and separated husbands easily find single women willing to cohabit with them consensually. Clearly some females, the married ones, conceive the mating alternatives as a nonreversible status series; clearly unmarried women and most men do not, and in this situation principals may separate from consensual or legal domestic unions to re-enter others, or to mate extraresidentially, at any point in time. Likewise young persons may enter marriage without previous cohabitation or child-bearing. So long as individual relations are smooth, the union is likely to endure. At any serious difficulty it is likely to break down, since its principals have other alternatives open, except that, for status reasons, women once married tend to avoid consensual co-habitation.

We have here a systematic disorganization worth special at-tention. The disorganization is not haphazard, but arises in con-sequence of the fact that its three constituent mating alternatives have an equal validity for almost all adults at all points of their career. In consequence, these alternatives are in ceaseless com-petition. Structurally speaking, they dislocate one another. None has its set place in the individual life cycle; all are equally open, and mating relations are truly random. Apparently a mating system may function smoothly when its alternatives are ranked in serial order, and when each has its proper place in the total system and the individual's career alike. Such arrangements are inherently progressive and developmental. Alternatively, a mating system which excludes consensual cohabitation may integrate marriage and the extraresidential relation, given a certain female surplus. But when the extraresidential union, the consensual domestic union, and marriage have equal currency at all phases of the individual's development, something very akin to marital chaos emerges.

Tables 8 and 9 describe the relation between mating and house-hold status among these urban adults. Given the lack of orderly re-lations within the mating system, we can expect some disorder in its association with the distribution of household status. Of the seven single fathers under twenty-four, three were household heads. Of the five men of this age group who were married, four were household heads. Of the ten single males between the ages of twenty-five and thirty-nine, two were household heads; of the six males in this age group who were cohabiting consensually, only one was a household head. All twelve married men of this age group who were currently cohabiting were household heads, including three whose partners were not their wives. The man who had separated from his wife and remained single was not a household head. Two of the four single males aged between forty and fifty-four were household heads. All five who were cohabiting consensually and all fifteen who had married were heads of their own homes. The only males above this age who were not household heads were one single man and one living in a consensual union. Of the forty-three men who had married, forty were household heads; of the thirteen who had engaged in cohabitation without marrying, six were household heads. Eight of the forty-six single men in these homes were household heads. Marriage is strongly associated with male headship; neither the consensual domestic union nor single status is. In consequence, domestic mating relations are liable to break down since alternative forms are available to the principals, and since there is no clear agreement on the locus of authority within them.

Since men head households based on their marriages, we find no wives with resident husbands among the population of female heads. Nor are any of the wives whose absent husbands have not formally left them heads of their own homes; but five of the six separated wives and thirteen of the fourteen widows are household heads. Of the thirty single mothers, seventeen head their own homes and two of these are below twenty-four years of age. Another childless young woman is head of her home, together with one whose consensual union had already broken down. Of seventeen single women between twenty-five and thirty-nine years of age, eight were heads of their own homes; of ten in the age group forty to fifty-four, eight were household heads, together with all four above this age. Of the thirty-one women whose consensual cohabitation had not developed into marriage, eighteen were heads of their own homes. Five of these had resident mates, ten had separated and had children of the unions with them, and three had been widowed. In short, women become household heads after their twenty-fifth year, whether they remain single, are or have been cohabiting, have separated from their husbands, or have been widowed. The majority of these women have displayed their sexual maturity in one way or another, and apparently, unless they are living with their husbands, this maturity provides the basis and rationale for female headship and domestic independence in Grenville.

The Composition of Domestic Groups

The households with male heads contain a total of 152 dependents, thirty-nine of whom are mates of the heads, fourteen of these being unwed. Seventy-nine or 51 per cent of these dependents are off-spring of the heads, but only four of these are grandchildren. Of the remaining thirty-four persons, twelve are issue of the head's resident mate by former unions and another three are collateral kin of these mates. Ten are close collaterals of the heads themselves, five are employees and their children, and three are adoptees of the head. The extreme simplicity of these domestic units with male heads is apparent. The relevant chart represents this visually.

Of the 114 dependents living in homes with female heads, five are consensual mates of these women. Fifty-one per cent are children of the head, and another twenty-five are grandchildren or great-grandchildren. Altogether, homes with female heads contain more resident issue of the head than do those under males; 73 per cent of the dependents living in homes with female heads are lineal issue as against 51 per cent under males. The remaining twenty-five dependents in these homes include three issue of resident mates by former unions, ten collaterals of the heads themselves, seven adoptees and their kin, two unrelated persons, one boarder, one mother's mother, and one patrilateral kinsman.

Units with female heads have as simple a structure as those under males. In one case the domestic unit typically consists of the head, his mate, and their children, jointly or separately; in the other, it typically consists of the head and her children or grandchildren. We find no boarders, unrelated persons, remote patrikin or ancestors of the head in units with male heads; we find no employees or collateral kin of resident mates in units under females. Units of either type contain an equal number of close collateral kin of the head. Three of the seven resident siblings of male heads are maternal half siblings; none are paternal half siblings. Only one of the five resident siblings of female household heads is not a full sibling, and this is a maternal half brother. Paternal half siblings have no place in the homes of these heads. Adopted, unrelated, and employed persons represent nearly 7 per cent of the total dependent population in these homes; differences in their distribution in homes with male and female heads illustrate sex differences in economic and social condition.

Setting aside the lineal components of these units for the moment, we may examine their collateral components briefly. Table 11 isolates the resident collaterals of female principals and examines them in the familiar way. Only two of these fifteen collaterals are legitimate, and only one is patrilateral kin. None of the ten collaterals living with male household heads is known to be legitimate. Of the seven siblings resident in homes with male heads, four are sisters. All resident issue of these heads' siblings are issue of their sisters. Although men may accommodate their brothers in their homes, they exclude their brothers' offspring as well as their own illegitimate offspring. Of the five resident siblings of female household heads, four are brothers; but of the five resident issue of these heads' siblings, only one is a brother's child and only one is lawful. Of the nine residents descended from siblings of these household heads, eight are issue of the head's sisters or sisters' daughters, and seven of these are illegitimate. There are three cases of brothers living together, only one of sisters living together; but there are four cases in which brothers have sisters living with them in their own homes, and four more in which sisters have their brothers living with them in theirs. Remoter collateral kin are scarcely present.

We can summarize this analysis briefly. The typical domestic association of collaterals includes brothers and sisters in either's home. However, resident collateral kin of junior generation are almost always sisters' illegitimate offspring, and they are to be found in homes with male or female heads alike. Kinship obligations have a narrow range, and the brother-sister tie is one of three recognized alternatives. That between mates and that between a mother and her children, especially her daughters, are the others. Table 12 re-examines the lineal issue resident with these household heads and illustrates the point just made.

Only four of the seventy-nine resident issue of male heads are grandchildren. Of these, three are daughters' issue and all are legitimate. Men do not accommodate their daughters' illegitimate issue in their homes; apparently they exclude their own illegitimate issue also. Of the seventy-two children below the age of twenty-four who live in their fathers' homes, only three are illegitimate. Only three children above twenty-four years of age remain in their fathers' homes.

Of eighty-four resident issue of female household heads, fifteen are over twenty-four years of age, half of these being sons. Of the forty-eight children of these female heads who are less than twenty-four years, forty-one are illegitimate. All seven sons' issue resident with these heads are unlawful; and only one of the fourteen resident daughters' issue below the age of twenty-four is legitimate. Sixty-one of the sixty-nine resident junior offspring of these female heads are illegitimate. Almost all lineal issue living with female heads are illegitimate, just as almost all lineal issue living with male heads are legitimate. Given that marriage is only one of the

three alternative mating forms, it is clear that parental role definitions in the other two alternatives allocate children to women;
and also that the mothers of these children have to care for them
either alone, in their mothers' homes, or with their siblings. Consensual cohabitation and extraresidential mating operate similarly
in this respect, since the women are left with the children after
these domestic unions have come to grief. Apparently women may
take their children by former unions into their consensual unions,
less easily into their marriage; as the diagrams show, there were
only four resident offspring of the twenty consensual unions in
these homes. In other words, the majority of these consensual
cohabitations were childless, and many may have been short-lived.

The Distribution of Children
    Table 13 analyzes the distribution of children and parents in
these homes. It concentrates on their coresidence or separation
in relation to differences of birth status among the children. As
there are only three children living with widowed mothers in this
sample, I have included them among those living with their mothers
apart from their fathers. This residential category is larger than
any others in the classification. Of the 221 children enumerated in
Table 13, 80 or 36. 2 per cent lived with their mothers apart from
their fathers, excluding these three children of widows. A further
fifty-nine or 26. 7 per cent lived apart from both parents. Living
with both parents were 31. 6 per cent, and 4. 1 per cent with their
fathers apart from their mothers. Of those who lived with their
mothers apart from their fathers, five sixths were illegitimate
and a similar proportion lived in homes with female heads. Of
those who lived apart from both parents, at most one in eight are
legitimate, and 60 per cent live in homes with female heads. Only
one child lived with both parents in the home of which its mother
was head. Forty-three per cent of all these children are legitimate; only one in three lives with its father, with or without its
mother. Two thirds of the total live with their mothers, with or
without their fathers; and a quarter live apart from both parents.
Men only accommodate their legitimate children. They are more
likely to accommodate the illegitimate children of their resident
mates than their own or their children's unlawful issue. Yet marriage is only one of the three mating forms, and the offspring of the
others are illegitimate. Also, more than half the children are illegitimate. It follows that women have sole charge of most of their
children born out of wedlock, unless they are able to take some of
these into a domestic union.

Tables 14, 15, and 16 show how children below the age of twenty-four who live apart from either or both parents are distributed. Of forty-four children living apart from both parents, twenty-one live with their matrilateral kin and three with their mothers' siblings. Seven live with their patrilateral kin and thirteen live with unrelated persons. As already noted, men are more likely to accommodate unrelated persons in their homes than their own illegitimate issue. Of these forty-four children, eleven are of unspecified birth status; of the remainder, three are legitimate. Of the six children below the age of twenty-four who live with their fathers apart from their mothers, four live with their fathers only, two with their fathers and fathers' kin. Of the seventy-one children under twenty-four who live with their mothers apart from their fathers, fifty-five live with their mothers only and six of these are legitimate. Thirty-six of these fifty-five children live alone with their unwed mothers. Of the sixteen who live with their mothers in homes which contain other adult kin, only nine live with their mother and mother's mother. None live with the mother and mother's sister together.

The Variety of Domestic Forms

Tables 17 to 19 complete our analysis. These tables examine the morphology of domestic groups and the frequency of alternative domestic forms. Table 17 is especially interesting.

Of the 113 households in this sample, eighty-three or 73 per cent are pure forms of these structural categories. Twenty of these households or 17.7 per cent of the total are single-person units; another eight or 7.2 per cent are based on coresident siblings; six of these include no one else. Another twenty-two, or 19.5 per cent, contain a single parent and his or her children, and only three of these have male heads. There are also twenty-five units whose principals are childless couples, and twenty-one of these have male heads. These twenty-five units are 22.1 per cent of the total sample; and the aggregate of the four categories just listed is 66.5 per cent of all the households studied. Even if we exclude the category based on siblings, nearly three fifths of these Grenville households do not contain elementary families, and most of them cannot be derived from households which did.

We have seen that ten of the thirty-one women whose consensual cohabitation did not develop into marriage were mothers separated from their former mates. We have also seen that the great majority of current consensual unions are childless. Putting these facts together, it is obvious that consensual unions at Grenville either develop into marriage or break up shortly after children are born to them. The rate of breakdown is undoubtedly high, and perhaps one half of the mothers living alone with their children in these homes may have participated in consensual unions. Even without these, nearly one half the sample homes have never included elementary families in which their heads were principals.

The most intriguing feature of Table 17 is the relatively high incidence of units based on siblingship in this sample. Such units may be residues of former elementary families, but they may equally derive from groups consisting of a woman and her children. For present purposes, the important point is their frequency and constitution. These units, as already shown, contain a brother and sister in most cases. This brother-sister combination is economically just as viable as a conjugal union. Given the high rate of breakdown in cohabitation, the brother-sister unit offers marked security. Either or both siblings may mate extraresidentially, with the knowledge that their domestic unit will not be disturbed by the birth of children. In fact, most of the siblings who lived together were doing just this. They had employed siblingship as an alternative to cohabitation, since the latter was less stable than the former. This use of siblingship illustrates most vividly the instability of mating relations in Grenville, and the effect of this instability on domestic organization. There could be no clearer proof of the way in which mating patterns regulate the constitution and growth of domestic groups.

Of these 113 households, twenty contain couples and children. Four contain the head and the head's grandchildren; eleven include the head, his or her children, and grandchildren; the remaining three include the head and the head's issue to the fourth generation. No households having a depth of three or more generations have cohabiting couples as their principals. Only two of these seventeen three- and four-generation units have male heads. The units which contain three successive generations are nearly three times as frequent as those which include alternate generations. In all, households having a depth of three or more lineal generations inclusive of their head represent 15. 8 per cent of the total sample.

As Table 18 shows, only 21 per cent of these homes had a depth of three or more generations inclusive of collateral or affinal kin. Twenty of the fifty-four homes with male heads included members of one generation only; twenty-seven of these units had a depth of two generations. Only 29 per cent of the homes with female heads had a depth of three or more generations.

Table 19 shows that of the twenty-five childless couples in these homes, fifteen are unwed and fourteen live by themselves. Of the twenty couples who live with their children as principals in these homes, sixteen are married, and sixteen of these households do not contain accretions. All four unwed couples with children live by themselves. It is clear that childlessness is the usual condition of consensually cohabiting couples. Those couples who remain together after having children will normally be married. Presumably, therefore, consensual unions which do not develop into marriage shortly after children are born to them dissolve, leaving the mother and children on their own. Of these forty-five cohabiting couples, twenty-nine lived in households without accretions.

Conclusion

In Grenville we have a case of disorderly mating. Persons may mate by either of three forms, in two of which the women are responsible for accommodating the children. These mating alternatives are not related to one another in any coherent fashion, nor are they mutually exclusive. In consequence, mating relations are brittle and domestic unions of either sort have a high rate of breakdown. Under these conditions, domestic units are small, generationally shallow, and highly unstable. Some people seek to avoid these instabilities by living with a sibling of the opposite sex, others by living alone. Many consensual unions dissolve after children are born to them; others may develop into marriage. The residues of this disorganized mating complex are units which consist of single mothers and their children, or of women and their grandchildren, often including their daughters also. But for this disintegrated mating system, the frequency of such domestic units would be inexplicable. Small, unstable households having this composition are unavoidable concomitants of the Grenville patterns of mating and parenthood.

## TABLE 1

### POPULATION OF THE SAMPLE HOUSEHOLDS, CLASSIFIED BY SEX AND AGE

| Age | Number Male | Female | Total | Percentage Male | Female | Total | Females per Male |
|-----|------|--------|-------|------|--------|-------|------|
| 0- 4 | 27 | 29 | 56 | 7.1 | 7.6 | 14.7 | 1.07 |
| 5-14 | 33 | 45 | 78 | 8.7 | 11.8 | 20.5 | 1.35 |
| 15-24 | 36 | 38 | 74 | 9.5 | 10.0 | 19.5 | 1.05 |
| 25-39 | 30 | 49 | 79 | 7.9 | 12.9 | 20.8 | 1.63 |
| 40-54 | 24 | 30 | 54 | 6.3 | 7.9 | 14.2 | 1.25 |
| 55-69 | 7 | 15 | 22 | 1.9 | 3.9 | 5.8 | 2.05 |
| 70 and Over | 5 | 12 | 17 | 1.3 | 3.2 | 4.5 | 2.40 |
| TOTAL | 162 | 218 | 380 | 42.7 | 57.3 | 100.0 | 1.36 |

## TABLE 2

### HEADS OF THE SAMPLE HOUSEHOLDS, CLASSIFIED BY SEX AND AGE

| Age | Number Male | Female | Total | Percentage Male | Female | Total |
|-----|------|--------|-------|------|--------|-------|
| 15-24 | 7 | 4 | 11 | 6.5 | 3.5 | 10.0 |
| 25-39 | 15 | 15 | 30 | 13.3 | 13.3 | 26.6 |
| 40-54 | 22 | 16 | 38 | 19.2 | 14.2 | 33.4 |
| 55-69 | 6 | 12 | 18 | 5.1 | 10.7 | 15.8 |
| 70 and Over | 4 | 12 | 16 | 3.5 | 10.7 | 14.2 |
| TOTAL | 54 | 59 | 113 | 47.6 | 52.4 | 100.0 |

## TABLE 3

### DISTRIBUTION OF HOUSEHOLD HEADSHIP AMONG ADULT MEMBERS OF THE SAMPLE POPULATION, CLASSIFIED BY SEX AND AGE

| Age | Male Total | HHs* | %HHs | Female Total | HHs | %HHs | % HHs in Both Sexes |
|-----|------|------|------|------|-----|------|------|
| 15-24 | 36 | 7 | 19.3 | 38 | 4 | 10.5 | 14.9 |
| 25-39 | 30 | 15 | 50.0 | 49 | 15 | 30.3 | 37.8 |
| 40-54 | 24 | 22 | 91.5 | 30 | 16 | 53.2 | 70.3 |
| 55-69 | 7 | 6 | 85.5 | 15 | 12 | 80.0 | 81.8 |
| 70 and Over | 5 | 4 | 80.0 | 12 | 12 | 100.0 | 94.2 |
| TOTAL | 102 | 54 | 53.0 | 144 | 59 | 40.6 | 45.7 |

*HHs = Household heads.

## TABLE 4

HOUSEHOLDS OF THE SAMPLE, CLASSIFIED BY SEX OF HEAD AND NUMBER OF PERSONS

| Number of Persons | Sex of Head Male | Female | Total | Male HHs* | Total Female HHs | Total |
|---|---|---|---|---|---|---|
| 1 | 5 | 12 | 17 | 5 | 12 | 17 |
| 2 | 15 | 16 | 31 | 30 | 32 | 62 |
| 3 | 8 | 14 | 22 | 24 | 42 | 66 |
| 4 | 7 | 7 | 14 | 28 | 28 | 56 |
| 5 | 8 | 3 | 11 | 40 | 15 | 55 |
| 6 | 5 | 6 | 11 | 30 | 36 | 66 |
| 7 | 3 | 0 | 3 | 21 | 0 | 21 |
| 8 | 1 | 1 | 2 | 8 | 8 | 16 |
| 9 | 1 | 0 | 1 | 9 | 0 | 9 |
| 10 | 0 | 0 | 0 | 0 | 0 | 0 |
| 11 | 0 | 0 | 0 | 0 | 0 | 0 |
| 12 | 1 | 0 | 1 | 12 | 0 | 12 |
| TOTAL | 54 | 59 | 113 | 207 | 173 | 380 |

| Averages: including solitary persons | 3.84% | 2.83% | 3.38% |
|---|---|---|---|
| excluding solitary persons | 4.16% | 3.42% | 3.95% |

*HHs = Household heads.

## TABLE 5

AGE AND SEX DISTRIBUTION OF HOUSEHOLD POPULATION, CLASSIFIED ACCORDING TO THE SEX OF THE HEAD

| Age | Male Head Male | Fe-male | Total | Per cent | Female Head Male | Fe-male | Total | Per cent | Total Male %HHs* | Female %HHs |
|---|---|---|---|---|---|---|---|---|---|---|
| 0- 4 | 18 | 18 | 36 | 17.4 | 9 | 11 | 20 | 11.6 | 9.5 | 5.2 |
| 5-14 | 18 | 27 | 45 | 21.7 | 15 | 18 | 33 | 19.1 | 12.8 | 8.7 |
| 15-24 | 16 | 19 | 35 | 16.9 | 20 | 19 | 39 | 22.5 | 9.2 | 10.3 |
| 25-39 | 18 | 27 | 45 | 21.7 | 12 | 22 | 34 | 19.6 | 11.8 | 8.9 |
| 40-54 | 22 | 11 | 33 | 15.9 | 2 | 19 | 21 | 12.2 | 8.7 | 5.5 |
| 55-69 | 6 | 3 | 9 | 4.4 | 1 | 12 | 13 | 7.5 | 1.6 | 3.4 |
| 70 + | 4 | 0 | 4 | 2.0 | 1 | 12 | 13 | 7.5 | 1.0 | 3.4 |
| TOTAL | 102 | 105 | 207 | 100.0 | 60 | 113 | 173 | 100.0 | 54.6 | 45.4 |

*HHs = Household heads.

## TABLE 6

HOUSEHOLDERS LIVING ALONE, CLASSIFIED BY AGE, SEX, AND MARITAL STATUS

| | Male -24 | -39 | -54 | -69 | 70+ | Total | Female -24 | -39 | -54 | -69 | 70+ | Total |
|---|---|---|---|---|---|---|---|---|---|---|---|---|
| Never married | 1 | 1 | 0 | 1 | 0 | 3 | 0 | 3 | 3 | 3 | 0 | 9 |
| Marital status n/k* | 0 | 0 | 0 | 0 | 0 | 0 | 0 | 0 | 0 | 0 | 0 | 0 |
| Married, spouse absent | 0 | 0 | 0 | 0 | 0 | 0 | 0 | 0 | 0 | 0 | 0 | 0 |
| Married, separated | 0 | 0 | 2 | 0 | 0 | 2 | 0 | 0 | 0 | 0 | 0 | 0 |
| Married, widowed | 0 | 0 | 0 | 0 | 0 | 0 | 0 | 0 | 1 | 0 | 2 | 3 |
| TOTAL | 1 | 1 | 2 | 1 | 0 | 5 | 0 | 3 | 4 | 3 | 2 | 12 |

*n/k = Not known.

## TABLE 7

ALL ADULT MEMBERS OF THE SAMPLE POPULATION, CLASSIFIED BY SEX, AGE, MARITAL CONDITION, AND PARENTAL STATUS

| Mating and Parental Status | Male | | | | | | Female | | | | | |
|---|---|---|---|---|---|---|---|---|---|---|---|---|
| | -24 | -39 | -54 | -69 | 70+ | Total | -24 | -39 | -54 | -69 | 70+ | Total |
| **1. Childless single persons** | | | | | | | | | | | | |
| a. Mating now n/k* | 9 | 3 | 1 | 0 | 0 | 13 | 4 | 1 | 1 | 0 | 0 | 6 |
| b. Never mated | 6 | 1 | 1 | 0 | 0 | 8 | 6 | 2 | 0 | 2 | 0 | 10 |
| c. Not mating in 1953 | 2 | 0 | 0 | 0 | 0 | 2 | 3 | 2 | 1 | 0 | 0 | 6 |
| d. Mating in 1953 | 7 | 2 | 0 | 0 | 0 | 9 | 6 | 1 | 0 | 0 | 0 | 7 |
| Total childless single persons | 24 | 6 | 2 | 0 | 0 | 32 | 19 | 6 | 2 | 2 | 0 | 29 |
| **2. Single parents** | | | | | | | | | | | | |
| a. Mating now n/k | 0 | 0 | 1 | 0 | 0 | 1 | 0 | 1 | 0 | 0 | 0 | 1 |
| b. Not mating now | 0 | 0 | 1 | 0 | 0 | 1 | 0 | 1 | 4 | 1 | 1 | 7 |
| c. Mating in 1953 | 7 | 4 | 0 | 1 | 0 | 12 | 9 | 9 | 4 | 0 | 0 | 22 |
| Total single parents | 7 | 4 | 2 | 1 | 0 | 14 | 9 | 11 | 8 | 1 | 1 | 30 |
| **3. Consensually wed** | | | | | | | | | | | | |
| a. In 1953 | 0 | 6 | 5 | 0 | 1 | 12 | 3 | 10 | 4 | 0 | 0 | 17 |
| b. Separated, with children | 0 | 1 | 0 | 0 | 0 | 1 | 1 | 1 | 4 | 3 | 2 | 11 |
| c. Widowed, single | 0 | 0 | 0 | 0 | 0 | 0 | 0 | 0 | 1 | 0 | 2 | 3 |
| Total consensually wed | 0 | 7 | 5 | 0 | 1 | 13 | 4 | 11 | 9 | 3 | 4 | 31 |
| **4. Married persons** | | | | | | | | | | | | |
| a. Spouse present | 5 | 9 | 8 | 4 | 0 | 26 | 5 | 16 | 5 | 3 | 0 | 29 |
| b. Spouse absent | 0 | 0 | 2 | 0 | 0 | 2 | 1 | 2 | 2 | 0 | 0 | 5 |
| c. Separated, single | 0 | 1 | 2 | 1 | 2 | 6 | 0 | 3 | 2 | 1 | 0 | 6 |
| d. Separated, not single | 0 | 3 | 3 | 0 | 0 | 6 | 0 | 0 | 0 | 0 | 0 | 0 |
| Total married persons | 5 | 13 | 15 | 5 | 2 | 40 | 6 | 21 | 9 | 4 | 0 | 40 |
| **5. Widowed persons** | | | | | | | | | | | | |
| a. Widowed, single | 0 | 0 | 0 | 0 | 1 | 1 | 0 | 0 | 2 | 5 | 7 | 14 |
| b. Widowed, not single | 0 | 0 | 0 | 1 | 1 | 2 | 0 | 0 | 0 | 0 | 0 | 0 |
| Total widowed persons | 0 | 0 | 0 | 1 | 2 | 3 | 0 | 0 | 2 | 5 | 7 | 14 |
| GRAND TOTAL | 36 | 30 | 24 | 7 | 5 | 102 | 38 | 49 | 30 | 15 | 12 | 144 |

*n/k = Not known.

## TABLE 8

ADULT MEMBERS OF THE SAMPLE POPULATION OTHER THAN HOUSEHOLD HEADS, CLASSIFIED BY SEX, AGE, MARITAL CONDITION, AND PARENTAL STATUS

| Mating and Parental Status | Male | | | | | | Female | | | | | |
|---|---|---|---|---|---|---|---|---|---|---|---|---|
| | -24 | -39 | -54 | -69 | 70+ | Total | -24 | -39 | -54 | -69 | 70+ | Total |
| **1. Childless single persons** | | | | | | | | | | | | |
| a. Mating now n/k* | 9 | 3 | 1 | 0 | 0 | 13 | 4 | 0 | 0 | 0 | 0 | 4 |
| b. Never mated | 6 | 0 | 1 | 0 | 0 | 7 | 6 | 2 | 1 | 0 | 0 | 8 |
| c. Not mating in 1953 | 2 | 0 | 0 | 0 | 0 | 2 | 3 | 2 | 1 | 0 | 0 | 6 |
| d. Mating in 1953 | 7 | 1 | 0 | 0 | 0 | 8 | 5 | 0 | 1 | 0 | 0 | 5 |
| Total childless single persons | 24 | 4 | 2 | 0 | 0 | 30 | 18 | 4 | 1 | 0 | 0 | 23 |
| **2. Single parents** | | | | | | | | | | | | |
| a. Mating now n/k | 0 | 0 | 0 | 0 | 0 | 0 | 0 | 0 | 0 | 0 | 0 | 0 |
| b. Not mating now | 0 | 0 | 0 | 0 | 0 | 0 | 0 | 0 | 0 | 0 | 0 | 0 |
| c. Mating in 1953 | 4 | 4 | 0 | 0 | 0 | 8 | 7 | 5 | 1 | 0 | 0 | 13 |
| Total single parents | 4 | 4 | 0 | 0 | 0 | 8 | 7 | 5 | 1 | 0 | 0 | 13 |
| **3. Consensually wed** | | | | | | | | | | | | |
| a. In 1953 | 0 | 5 | 0 | 0 | 1 | 6 | 3 | 5 | 4 | 0 | 0 | 12 |
| b. Separated, with children | 0 | 1 | 0 | 0 | 0 | 1 | 0 | 0 | 0 | 0 | 1 | 1 |
| c. Widowed, single | 0 | 0 | 0 | 0 | 0 | 0 | 0 | 0 | 0 | 0 | 0 | 0 |
| Total consensually wed | 0 | 6 | 0 | 0 | 1 | 7 | 3 | 5 | 4 | 0 | 1 | 13 |
| **4. Married persons** | | | | | | | | | | | | |
| a. Spouse present | 1 | 0 | 0 | 0 | 0 | 1 | 5 | 16 | 5 | 3 | 0 | 29 |
| b. Spouse absent | 0 | 0 | 0 | 0 | 0 | 0 | 1 | 2 | 2 | 0 | 0 | 5 |
| c. Separated, single | 0 | 1 | 0 | 1 | 0 | 2 | 0 | 1 | 0 | 0 | 0 | 1 |
| d. Separated, not single | 0 | 0 | 0 | 0 | 0 | 0 | 0 | 0 | 0 | 0 | 0 | 0 |
| Total married persons | 1 | 1 | 0 | 1 | 0 | 3 | 6 | 19 | 7 | 3 | 0 | 35 |
| **5. Widowed persons** | | | | | | | | | | | | |
| a. Widowed, single | 0 | 0 | 0 | 0 | 0 | 0 | 0 | 0 | 1 | 0 | 0 | 1 |
| b. Widowed, not single | 0 | 0 | 0 | 0 | 0 | 0 | 0 | 0 | 0 | 0 | 0 | 0 |
| Total widowed persons | 0 | 0 | 0 | 0 | 0 | 0 | 0 | 0 | 1 | 0 | 0 | 1 |
| **GRAND TOTAL** | 29 | 15 | 2 | 1 | 1 | 48 | 34 | 33 | 14 | 3 | 1 | 85 |

*n/k = Not known.

## TABLE 9

### HOUSEHOLD HEADS, CLASSIFIED BY SEX, AGE, MARITAL CONDITION, AND PARENTAL STATUS

| Mating and Parental Status | Male | | | | | | Female | | | | | |
|---|---|---|---|---|---|---|---|---|---|---|---|---|
| | -24 | -39 | -54 | -69 | 70+ | Total | -24 | -39 | -54 | -69 | 70+ | Total |
| **1. Childless single persons** | | | | | | | | | | | | |
| a. Mating now n/k* | 0 | 0 | 0 | 0 | 0 | 0 | 0 | 1 | 1 | 0 | 0 | 2 |
| b. Never mated | 0 | 1 | 0 | 0 | 0 | 1 | 0 | 0 | 0 | 2 | 0 | 2 |
| c. Not mating in 1953 | 0 | 0 | 0 | 0 | 0 | 0 | 0 | 0 | 0 | 0 | 0 | 0 |
| d. Mating in 1953 | 0 | 1 | 0 | 0 | 0 | 1 | 1 | 1 | 0 | 0 | 0 | 2 |
| Total childless single persons | 0 | 2 | 0 | 0 | 0 | 2 | 1 | 2 | 1 | 2 | 0 | 6 |
| **2. Single parents** | | | | | | | | | | | | |
| a. Mating now n/k | 0 | 0 | 1 | 0 | 0 | 1 | 0 | 1 | 0 | 0 | 0 | 1 |
| b. Not mating in 1953 | 0 | 0 | 1 | 0 | 0 | 1 | 0 | 1 | 4 | 1 | 1 | 7 |
| c. Mating in 1953 | 3 | 0 | 0 | 1 | 0 | 4 | 2 | 4 | 3 | 0 | 0 | 9 |
| Total single parents | 3 | 0 | 2 | 1 | 0 | 6 | 2 | 6 | 7 | 1 | 1 | 17 |
| **3. Consensually wed** | | | | | | | | | | | | |
| a. In 1953 | 0 | 1 | 5 | 0 | 0 | 6 | 0 | 5 | 0 | 0 | 1 | 6 |
| b. Separated, with children | 0 | 0 | 0 | 0 | 0 | 0 | 1 | 1 | 4 | 3 | 0 | 9 |
| c. Widowed, single | 0 | 0 | 0 | 0 | 0 | 0 | 0 | 0 | 1 | 0 | 2 | 3 |
| Total consensually wed | 0 | 1 | 5 | 0 | 0 | 6 | 1 | 6 | 5 | 3 | 3 | 18 |
| **4. Married persons** | | | | | | | | | | | | |
| a. Spouse present | 4 | 9 | 8 | 4 | 0 | 25 | 0 | 0 | 0 | 0 | 0 | 0 |
| b. Spouse absent | 0 | 0 | 2 | 0 | 0 | 2 | 0 | 0 | 0 | 0 | 0 | 0 |
| c. Separated, single | 0 | 0 | 2 | 0 | 2 | 4 | 0 | 2 | 2 | 1 | 0 | 5 |
| d. Separated, not single | 0 | 3 | 3 | 0 | 0 | 6 | 0 | 0 | 0 | 0 | 0 | 0 |
| Total married persons | 4 | 12 | 15 | 4 | 2 | 37 | 0 | 2 | 2 | 1 | 0 | 5 |
| **5. Widowed persons** | | | | | | | | | | | | |
| a. Widowed, single | 0 | 0 | 0 | 0 | 1 | 1 | 0 | 0 | 1 | 5 | 7 | 13 |
| b. Widowed, not single | 0 | 0 | 0 | 1 | 1 | 2 | 0 | 0 | 0 | 0 | 0 | 0 |
| Total widowed persons | 0 | 0 | 0 | 1 | 2 | 3 | 0 | 0 | 1 | 5 | 7 | 13 |
| GRAND TOTAL | 7 | 15 | 22 | 6 | 4 | 54 | 4 | 16 | 16 | 12 | 11 | 59 |

*n/k = Not known.

TABLE 10

POPULATION OF THE SAMPLE HOUSEHOLDS, CLASSIFIED BY RELATIONSHIP TO
THE HOUSEHOLD HEAD AND SEX OF HEAD

| Categories of Kin | Male Head Number | Per cent | Female Head Number | Per cent | Total Number | Per cent |
|---|---|---|---|---|---|---|
| 1. Spouses and mates | 40 | 26.0 | 5 | 4.8 | 45 | 16.8 |
| 2. HH's* sons | 33 | 21.6 | 32 | 28.0 | 65 | 24.3 |
| 3. HH's daughters | 42 | 27.3 | 27 | 23.2 | 69 | 25.8 |
|    HH's children | 75 | 48.9 | 59 | 51.2 | 134 | 50.1 |
| 4. HH's sons' sons | 1 | 0.7 | 3 | 2.6 | 4 | 1.5 |
| 5. HH's sons' daughters | 0 | 0.0 | 4 | 3.5 | 4 | 1.5 |
| 6. HH's daughters' sons | 1 | 0.7 | 7 | 6.1 | 8 | 3.0 |
| 7. HH's daughters' daughters | 2 | 1.2 | 10 | 8.8 | 12 | 4.5 |
|    HH's grandchildren | 4 | 2.6 | 24 | 21.0 | 28 | 10.5 |
| 8. HH's daughters' grandchildren | 0 | 0.0 | 1 | 0.9 | 1 | 0.4 |
|    Total lineal issue of HH | 79 | 51.5 | 84 | 73.1 | 163 | 61.0 |
| 9. HH's mates' sons by others | 3 | 2.0 | 1 | 0.9 | 4 | 1.5 |
| 10. HH's mates' daughters by others | 4 | 2.6 | 0 | 0.0 | 4 | 1.5 |
| 11. HH's mates' daughters' sons | 2 | 1.3 | 1 | 0.9 | 3 | 1.1 |
| 12. HH's mates' daughters' daughters | 3 | 2.0 | 1 | 0.9 | 4 | 1.5 |
|     Issue of HH's mates by others | 12 | 7.9 | 3 | 2.7 | 15 | 5.7 |
| 13. HH's brothers | 3 | 2.0 | 4 | 3.5 | 7 | 2.5 |
| 14. HH's sisters | 4 | 2.6 | 1 | 0.9 | 5 | 1.9 |
| 15. HH's brothers' issue | 0 | 0.0 | 1 | 0.9 | 1 | 0.4 |
| 16. HH's sisters' issue | 3 | 2.0 | 4 | 3.5 | 7 | 2.5 |
|     HH's siblings and their issue | 10 | 6.6 | 10 | 8.8 | 20 | 7.3 |
| 17. HH's mother's mother | 0 | 0.0 | 1 | 0.9 | 1 | 0.4 |
| 18. HH's patrilateral kin | 0 | 0.0 | 1 | 0.9 | 1 | 0.4 |
| 19. HH's mate's daughter's mate | 1 | 0.7 | 0 | 0.0 | 1 | 0.4 |
| 20. Other kin of HH's mate or spouse | 3 | 2.0 | 0 | 0.0 | 3 | 1.1 |
| 21. HH's adopted children and their kin | 3 | 2.0 | 7 | 6.1 | 10 | 3.8 |
| 22. Unrelated persons | 0 | 0.0 | 2 | 1.8 | 2 | 0.8 |
| 23. Employees and their children | 5 | 3.3 | 0 | 0.0 | 5 | 1.9 |
| 24. Boarders | 0 | 0.0 | 1 | 0.9 | 1 | 0.4 |
|     Categories 17 to 24 | 12 | 8.0 | 12 | 10.6 | 24 | 9.2 |
| TOTAL | 153 | 100.0 | 114 | 100.0 | 267 | 100.0 |

*HH = Household head.

# TABLE 11

RESIDENT COLLATERALS OF FEMALE PRINCIPALS, CLASSIFIED BY KINSHIP CATEGORY, BIRTH STATUS, AND SEX OF HOUSEHOLD HEAD

| Kinship Category | Male Head L* | Male Head U* | Male Head N/K* | Male Head All | Female Head L | Female Head U | Female Head N/K | Female Head All | Total |
|---|---|---|---|---|---|---|---|---|---|
| Full siblings | 0 | 0 | 0 | 0 | 1 | 1 | 2 | 4 | 4 |
| Issue of full siblings | 0 | 2 | 0 | 2 | 0 | 2 | 0 | 2 | 4 |
| Matrilateral kin | 0 | 0 | 0 | 0 | 1 | 4 | 0 | 5 | 5 |
| Patrilateral kin | 0 | 1 | 0 | 1 | 0 | 0 | 1 | 1 | 2 |
| TOTAL | 0 | 3 | 0 | 3 | 2 | 7 | 3 | 12 | 15 |

*L = Lawful, i.e., legitimate; U = Unlawful, i.e., illegitimate; N/K = Birth status not known.

# TABLE 12

RESIDENT LINEAL ISSUE OF THE HOUSEHOLD HEAD, CLASSIFIED BY SEX, BIRTH STATUS, GENERATION, SEX OF PARENT THROUGH WHOM DESCENT IS TRACED, AND SEX OF THE HOUSEHOLD HEAD

| Sex and Birth Status | Households with Male Head Own Issue | Households with Male Head Sons' Issue | Households with Male Head Daughters' Issue | Households with Male Head Total | Households with Female Head Own Issue | Households with Female Head Sons' Issue | Households with Female Head Daughters' Issue | Households with Female Head Total | Total Own Issue | Total Sons' Issue | Total Daughters' Issue | Total |
|---|---|---|---|---|---|---|---|---|---|---|---|---|
| Males L* | 31 | 0 | 1 | 32 | 4 | 0 | 0 | 4 | 35 | 0 | 1 | 36 |
| Males U* | 1 | 1 | 0 | 2 | 23 | 3 | 5 | 31 | 24 | 4 | 5 | 33 |
| Males N/K* | 1 | 0 | 0 | 1 | 5 | 0 | 2 | 7 | 6 | 0 | 2 | 8 |
| All males | 33 | 1 | 1 | 35 | 32 | 3 | 7 | 42 | 65 | 4 | 8 | 77 |
| Females L | 38 | 0 | 2 | 40 | 3 | 0 | 1 | 4 | 41 | 0 | 3 | 44 |
| Females U | 2 | 0 | 0 | 2 | 18 | 4 | 8 | 30 | 20 | 4 | 8 | 32 |
| Females N/K | 2 | 0 | 0 | 2 | 6 | 0 | 2 | 8 | 8 | 0 | 2 | 10 |
| All females | 42 | 0 | 2 | 44 | 27 | 4 | 11 | 42 | 69 | 4 | 13 | 86 |
| Total L | 69 | 0 | 3 | 72 | 7 | 0 | 1 | 8 | 76 | 0 | 4 | 80 |
| Total U | 3 | 1 | 0 | 4 | 41 | 7 | 13 | 61 | 44 | 8 | 13 | 65 |
| Total N/K | 3 | 0 | 0 | 3 | 11 | 0 | 4 | 15 | 14 | 0 | 4 | 18 |
| GRAND TOTAL | 75 | 1 | 3 | 79 | 59 | 7 | 18 | 84 | 134 | 8 | 21 | 163 |

*L = Lawful, i.e., legitimate; U = Unlawful, i.e., illegitimate; N/K = Birth status not known.

## TABLE 13

DISTRIBUTION OF CHILDREN WITHIN THE SAMPLE HOUSEHOLDS, CLASSIFIED BY SEX OF HEAD, WITH SPECIAL REFERENCE TO THE PRESENCE OF EITHER PARENT IN THE HOUSEHOLD, AND TO THE AGE AND BIRTH STATUS OF THE CHILDREN OF EITHER SEX

| Age | Households with Male Head | | | | | | | Households with Female Head | | | | | | | Total | | | | | | |
|---|---|---|---|---|---|---|---|---|---|---|---|---|---|---|---|---|---|---|---|---|---|
| | LS* | LD* | US* | UD* | N/KS* | N/KD* | Total | LS | LD | US | UD | N/KS | N/KD | Total | LS | LD | US | UD | N/KS | N/KD | Total |
| **a. Both parents present** | | | | | | | | | | | | | | | | | | | | | |
| 0– 4 | 15 | 15 | 0 | 1 | 0 | 0 | 31 | 1 | 0 | 0 | 0 | 0 | 0 | 1 | 16 | 15 | 0 | 1 | 0 | 0 | 32 |
| 5–14 | 14 | 19 | 0 | 0 | 0 | 0 | 33 | 0 | 0 | 0 | 0 | 0 | 0 | 0 | 14 | 19 | 0 | 0 | 0 | 0 | 33 |
| 15–24 | 2 | 3 | 0 | 0 | 0 | 0 | 5 | 0 | 0 | 0 | 0 | 0 | 0 | 0 | 2 | 3 | 0 | 0 | 0 | 0 | 5 |
| 25–39 | 0 | 0 | 0 | 0 | 0 | 0 | 0 | 0 | 0 | 0 | 0 | 0 | 0 | 0 | 0 | 0 | 0 | 0 | 0 | 0 | 0 |
| 40 + | 0 | 0 | 0 | 0 | 0 | 0 | 0 | 0 | 0 | 0 | 0 | 0 | 0 | 0 | 0 | 0 | 0 | 0 | 0 | 0 | 0 |
| Total | 31 | 37 | 0 | 1 | 0 | 0 | 69 | 1 | 0 | 0 | 0 | 0 | 0 | 1 | 32 | 37 | 0 | 1 | 0 | 0 | 70 |
| **b. Both parents absent** | | | | | | | | | | | | | | | | | | | | | |
| 0– 4 | 0 | 0 | 0 | 0 | 0 | 0 | 0 | 0 | 0 | 1 | 1 | 0 | 0 | 2 | 0 | 0 | 1 | 1 | 0 | 0 | 2 |
| 5–14 | 0 | 0 | 3 | 1 | 0 | 0 | 4 | 0 | 1 | 4 | 2 | 1 | 0 | 8 | 0 | 1 | 7 | 3 | 1 | 0 | 12 |
| 15–24 | 0 | 1 | 2 | 3 | 3 | 3 | 12 | 0 | 1 | 8 | 5 | 3 | 1 | 18 | 0 | 2 | 10 | 8 | 6 | 4 | 30 |
| 25–39 | 0 | 2 | 1 | 1 | 2 | 1 | 7 | 1 | 1 | 5 | 0 | 1 | 0 | 7 | 0 | 3 | 6 | 1 | 3 | 1 | 14 |
| 40 + | 0 | 0 | 0 | 0 | 0 | 0 | 0 | 1 | 0 | 0 | 0 | 0 | 0 | 1 | 1 | 0 | 0 | 0 | 0 | 0 | 1 |
| Total | 0 | 3 | 6 | 5 | 5 | 4 | 23 | 1 | 3 | 18 | 8 | 5 | 1 | 36 | 1 | 6 | 24 | 13 | 10 | 5 | 59 |
| **c. Mothers only present** | | | | | | | | | | | | | | | | | | | | | |
| 0– 4 | 1 | 2 | 2 | 0 | 0 | 0 | 5 | 0 | 0 | 6 | 9 | 0 | 0 | 15 | 1 | 2 | 8 | 9 | 0 | 0 | 20 |
| 5–14 | 0 | 0 | 1 | 5 | 0 | 0 | 6 | 1 | 3 | 10 | 11 | 0 | 0 | 25 | 1 | 3 | 11 | 16 | 0 | 0 | 31 |
| 15–24 | 0 | 0 | 1 | 2 | 0 | 0 | 3 | 2 | 1 | 9 | 5 | 0 | 0 | 17 | 2 | 1 | 10 | 7 | 0 | 0 | 20 |
| 25–39 | 0 | 0 | 0 | 0 | 0 | 0 | 0 | 1 | 2 | 2 | 2 | 0 | 0 | 7 | 1 | 2 | 2 | 2 | 0 | 0 | 7 |
| 40 + | 0 | 0 | 0 | 0 | 0 | 0 | 0 | 1 | 1 | 1 | 2 | 0 | 0 | 5 | 1 | 1 | 1 | 2 | 0 | 0 | 5 |
| Total | 1 | 2 | 4 | 7 | 0 | 0 | 14 | 6 | 9 | 28 | 29 | 0 | 0 | 69 | 6 | 9 | 32 | 36 | 0 | 0 | 83 |

## TABLE 13 (continued)

DISTRIBUTION OF CHILDREN WITHIN THE SAMPLE HOUSEHOLDS, CLASSIFIED BY SEX OF HEAD, WITH SPECIAL REFERENCE TO THE PRESENCE OF EITHER PARENT IN THE HOUSEHOLD, AND TO THE AGE AND BIRTH STATUS OF THE CHILDREN OF EITHER SEX

| Age | Households with Male Head | | | | | | | Households with Female Head | | | | | | | Total | | | | | | |
|---|---|---|---|---|---|---|---|---|---|---|---|---|---|---|---|---|---|---|---|---|---|
| | LS* | LD* | US* | UD* | N/KS* | N/KD* | Total | LS | LD | US | UD | N/KS | N/KD | Total | LS | LD | US | UD | N/KS | N/KD | Total |
| **d. Fathers only present** | | | | | | | | | | | | | | | | | | | | | |
| 0- 4 | 0 | 0 | 0 | 0 | 0 | 0 | 0 | 0 | 0 | 1 | 1 | 0 | 0 | 2 | 0 | 0 | 1 | 1 | 0 | 0 | 2 |
| 5-14 | 0 | 0 | 0 | 2 | 0 | 0 | 2 | 0 | 0 | 0 | 0 | 0 | 0 | 0 | 0 | 0 | 0 | 2 | 0 | 0 | 2 |
| 15-24 | 0 | 1 | 1 | 0 | 0 | 0 | 2 | 0 | 0 | 0 | 0 | 0 | 0 | 0 | 0 | 1 | 1 | 0 | 0 | 0 | 2 |
| 25-39 | 1 | 1 | 0 | 0 | 0 | 0 | 2 | 0 | 0 | 0 | 0 | 0 | 0 | 0 | 1 | 1 | 0 | 0 | 0 | 0 | 2 |
| 40 + | 0 | 1 | 0 | 0 | 0 | 0 | 1 | 0 | 0 | 0 | 0 | 0 | 0 | 0 | 0 | 1 | 0 | 0 | 0 | 0 | 1 |
| Total | 1 | 3 | 1 | 2 | 0 | 0 | 7 | 0 | 0 | 1 | 1 | 0 | 0 | 2 | 1 | 3 | 2 | 3 | 0 | 0 | 9 |
| **e. With mothers, fathers dead** | | | | | | | 0 | | | | | | | 0 | | | | | | | 0 |
| **f. With fathers, mothers dead** | | | | | | | 0 | | | | | | | 0 | | | | | | | 0 |
| **Totals by sex of household head** | | | | | | | | | | | | | | | | | | | | | |
| 0- 4 | 16 | 17 | 2 | 1 | 0 | 0 | 36 | 1 | 0 | 8 | 11 | 0 | 0 | 20 | 17 | 17 | 10 | 12 | 0 | 0 | 56 |
| 5-14 | 14 | 19 | 4 | 8 | 0 | 0 | 45 | 1 | 4 | 13 | 13 | 1 | 1 | 33 | 15 | 23 | 18 | 21 | 1 | 1 | 78 |
| 15-24 | 2 | 5 | 4 | 5 | 3 | 3 | 22 | 1 | 2 | 17 | 10 | 1 | 3 | 35 | 4 | 7 | 21 | 15 | 6 | 6 | 57 |
| 25-39 | 1 | 3 | 1 | 1 | 1 | 2 | 9 | 1 | 3 | 7 | 2 | 0 | 1 | 14 | 2 | 6 | 8 | 3 | 3 | 3 | 23 |
| 40 + | 0 | 1 | 0 | 0 | 0 | 0 | 1 | 2 | 1 | 1 | 2 | 0 | 0 | 6 | 2 | 2 | 1 | 2 | 0 | 0 | 7 |
| TOTAL | 33 | 45 | 11 | 15 | 4 | 5 | 113 | 7 | 10 | 47 | 38 | 1 | 5 | 108 | 40 | 55 | 58 | 53 | 10 | 10 | 221 |

*LS = Lawful son; LD = Lawful daughter; US = Unlawful son; UD = Unlawful daughter; N/KS = Son, birth status not known; N/KD = Daughter, birth status not known.

## TABLE 14

CHILDREN SEPARATED FROM BOTH PARENTS, CLASSIFIED BY SEX, BIRTH STATUS AND
KINSHIP TO PRINCIPALS IN WHOSE HOMES THEY LIVE

| Guardians | Wards Male L* | U* | Female L | U | N/K* Male | Female | Total |
|---|---|---|---|---|---|---|---|
| 1. Mother's mother | 0 | 4 | 0 | 1 | 0 | 0 | 5 |
| 2. Mother's full brother | 0 | 0 | 0 | 1 | 0 | 0 | 1 |
| 3. M's maternal half brother | 0 | 1 | 0 | 0 | 0 | 0 | 1 |
| 4. M's full sister and her spouse | 0 | 1 | 1 | 1 | 0 | 0 | 3 |
| 5. M's maternal half sister | 0 | 1 | 1 | 0 | 0 | 0 | 2 |
| 6. M's mother and her husband | 0 | 2 | 0 | 1 | 0 | 0 | 3 |
| 7. M's mother's mate's wife | 0 | 1 | 0 | 1 | 0 | 0 | 2 |
| 8. M's M's maternal half sister | 0 | 1 | 0 | 1 | 0 | 0 | 2 |
| 9. M's maternal half sister's daughter | 0 | 1 | 0 | 0 | 0 | 0 | 1 |
| 10. M's paternal half brother's daughter | 0 | 0 | 0 | 1 | 0 | 0 | 1 |
| Matrilateral kin | 0 | 12 | 2 | 7 | 0 | 0 | 21 |
| 11. Mother's full sister | 0 | 0 | 1 | 0 | 0 | 0 | 1 |
| 12. Mother's full brother | 0 | 1 | 0 | 0 | 1 | 0 | 2 |
| Mother's siblings | 0 | 1 | 1 | 0 | 1 | 0 | 3 |
| 13. Father's father | 0 | 1 | 0 | 0 | 0 | 0 | 1 |
| 14. Father's mother | 0 | 3 | 0 | 3 | 0 | 0 | 6 |
| Patrilateral kin | 0 | 4 | 0 | 3 | 0 | 0 | 7 |
| 15. Unrelated persons | 0 | 1 | 0 | 2 | 3 | 7 | 13 |
| TOTAL | 0 | 18 | 3 | 12 | 4 | 7 | 44 |

*L = Lawful, i.e., legitimate; U = Unlawful, i.e., illegitimate; N/K = Birth
status not known.

TABLE 15

CHILDREN LESS THAN 24 YEARS OF AGE, LIVING WITH THEIR FATHERS APART
FROM THEIR MOTHERS, CLASSIFIED BY SEX, BIRTH STATUS, AND
STATUS OF FATHER OR KIN WITH WHOM THEY LIVE

|  | Male | | Female | | |
|---|---|---|---|---|---|
|  | L* | U* | L | U | Total |
| 1. Father unwed, mother dead | 0 | 0 | 0 | 2 | 2 |
| 2. Father unwed, mother alive | 0 | 1 | 0 | 0 | 1 |
| 3. Father widowed | 0 | 0 | 1 | 0 | 1 |
| Total with father only | 0 | 1 | 1 | 2 | 4 |
| 4. Father and father's mother | 0 | 0 | 0 | 1 | 1 |
| 5. Father and father's maternal half sister | 0 | 1 | 0 | 0 | 1 |
| TOTAL | 0 | 2 | 1 | 3 | 6 |

*L = Lawful, i.e., legitimate; U = Unlawful, i.e., illegitimate.


TABLE 16

CHILDREN LESS THAN 24 YEARS OF AGE, LIVING WITH THEIR MOTHERS APART
FROM THEIR FATHERS, CLASSIFIED BY SEX, BIRTH STATUS, AND
STATUS OF MOTHER OR KIN WITH WHOM THEY LIVE

|  | Male | | Female | | |
|---|---|---|---|---|---|
|  | L* | U* | L | U | Total |
| 1. Mother widowed | 2 | 0 | 1 | 0 | 3 |
| 2. Mother wed | 0 | 0 | 0 | 1 | 1 |
| 3. Mother wed, father dead | 0 | 1 | 0 | 0 | 1 |
| 4. Mother unwed, father dead | 0 | 0 | 0 | 1 | 1 |
| 5. Mother unwed, not single† | 0 | 6 | 0 | 4 | 10 |
| 6. Mother unwed, single | 1 | 19 | 0 | 17 | 36 |
| 7. Mother wed, spouse absent | 1 | 0 | 2 | 0 | 3 |
| Total with mother only | 3 | 26 | 3 | 23 | 55 |
| 8. Mother and mother's adopted mother | 0 | 0 | 0 | 1 | 1 |
| 9. Mother and mother's mother | 0 | 2 | 1 | 6 | 9 |
| 10. Mother and mother's father | 1 | 0 | 2 | 0 | 3 |
| 11. Mother and mother's mother's mate | 0 | 0 | 0 | 1 | 1 |
| 12. Mother and mother's brother | 0 | 1 | 0 | 1 | 2 |
| Total with mother and mother's kin | 1 | 3 | 3 | 9 | 16 |
| TOTAL | 4 | 29 | 6 | 32 | 71 |

*L = Lawful, i.e., legitimate; U = Unlawful, i.e., illegitimate.
†Mother unwed, not single: that is, cohabiting consensually with another mate.

TABLE 17

FREQUENCY DISTRIBUTION OF DIFFERING TYPES OF DOMESTIC UNIT WITHIN THE SAMPLE

| | Households with Male Head | | | Households with Female Head | | | Total | | | Per cent |
|---|---|---|---|---|---|---|---|---|---|---|
| | No Others | Plus Others | Total | No Others | Plus Others | Total | No Others | Plus Others | Total | |
| 1. Single persons | 5 | 0 | 5 | 12 | 3 | 15 | 17 | 3 | 20 | 17.7 |
| 2. Siblings | 3 | 1 | 4 | 3 | 1 | 4 | 6 | 2 | 8 | 7.2 |
| 3. Household head and children | 1 | 2 | 3 | 16 | 3 | 19 | 17 | 5 | 22 | 19.5 |
| 4. Childless couples | 12 | 9 | 21 | 2 | 2 | 4 | 14 | 11 | 25 | 22.1 |
| 5. Couples and children | 14 | 5 | 19 | 1 | 0 | 1 | 15 | 5 | 20 | 17.7 |
| 6. Household head and grandchildren | 1 | 0 | 1 | 2 | 1 | 3 | 3 | 1 | 4 | 3.5 |
| 7. Couples and grandchildren | 0 | 0 | 0 | 0 | 0 | 0 | 0 | 0 | 0 | 0.0 |
| 8. Household head, children, and grandchildren | 0 | 1 | 1 | 8 | 2 | 10 | 8 | 3 | 11 | 9.7 |
| 9. Couples, children, and grandchildren | 0 | 0 | 0 | 0 | 0 | 0 | 0 | 0 | 0 | 0.0 |
| 10. Household head and issue to 4th generation | 0 | 0 | 0 | 3 | 0 | 3 | 3 | 0 | 3 | 2.6 |
| 11. Couples and issue to 4th generation | 0 | 0 | 0 | 0 | 0 | 0 | 0 | 0 | 0 | 0.0 |
| TOTAL | 36 | 18 | 54 | 47 | 12 | 59 | 83 | 30 | 113 | 100.0 |

TABLE 18

DOMESTIC UNITS OF STRUCTURALLY DIFFERING TYPES, CLASSIFIED BY SEX OF HEAD AND GENERATION RANGE

| | Households with Male Head | | | | | Households with Female Head | | | | | Total | | | | |
|---|---|---|---|---|---|---|---|---|---|---|---|---|---|---|---|
| | Generation Range | | | | Total | Generation Range | | | | Total | Generation Range | | | | Total |
| | 1 | 2 | 3 | 4 | | 1 | 2 | 3 | 4 | | 1 | 2 | 3 | 4 | |
| 1. Single persons | 5 | 0 | 0 | 0 | 5 | 12 | 2 | 1 | 0 | 15 | 17 | 2 | 1 | 0 | 20 |
| 2. Siblings | 3 | 1 | 0 | 0 | 4 | 2 | 2 | 0 | 0 | 4 | 5 | 3 | 0 | 0 | 8 |
| 3. Household head and children | 0 | 3 | 0 | 0 | 3 | 0 | 19 | 0 | 0 | 19 | 0 | 22 | 0 | 0 | 22 |
| 4. Childless couples | 12 | 6 | 3 | 0 | 21 | 2 | 2 | 0 | 0 | 4 | 14 | 8 | 3 | 0 | 25 |
| 5. Couples and children | 0 | 17 | 2 | 0 | 19 | 0 | 1 | 0 | 0 | 1 | 0 | 18 | 2 | 0 | 20 |
| 6. Household head and grandchildren | 0 | 0 | 1 | 0 | 1 | 0 | 0 | 3 | 0 | 3 | 0 | 0 | 4 | 0 | 4 |
| 7. Couples and grandchildren | 0 | 0 | 0 | 0 | 0 | 0 | 0 | 0 | 0 | 0 | 0 | 0 | 0 | 0 | 0 |
| 8. Household head, children, and grandchildren | 0 | 0 | 1 | 0 | 1 | 0 | 0 | 10 | 0 | 10 | 0 | 0 | 11 | 0 | 11 |
| 9. Couples, children, and grandchildren | 0 | 0 | 0 | 0 | 0 | 0 | 0 | 0 | 0 | 0 | 0 | 0 | 0 | 0 | 0 |
| 10. Household head and issue to 4th generation | 0 | 0 | 0 | 0 | 0 | 0 | 0 | 0 | 3 | 3 | 0 | 0 | 0 | 3 | 3 |
| 11. Couples and issue to 4th generation | 0 | 0 | 0 | 0 | 0 | 0 | 0 | 0 | 0 | 0 | 0 | 0 | 0 | 0 | 0 |
| TOTAL | 20 | 27 | 7 | 0 | 54 | 16 | 26 | 14 | 3 | 59 | 36 | 53 | 21 | 3 | 113 |
| PERCENTAGE | 37.0 | 50.0 | 13.0 | 0.0 | 100.0 | 27.0 | 44.0 | 24.0 | 5.0 | 100.0 | 32.0 | 47.0 | 18.0 | 3.0 | 100.0 |

## TABLE 19

CONJUGAL UNIONS IN THE SAMPLE HOUSEHOLDS, CLASSIFIED BY THEIR BASIS, THE TYPE OF DOMESTIC UNIT IN WHICH THEY OCCUR, AND THE SEX OF THE HOUSEHOLD HEAD*

| Morphological Types | Male Head | | | Female Head | | | Total | | |
|---|---|---|---|---|---|---|---|---|---|
| | Wed | Unwed | Total | Wed | Unwed | Total | Wed | Unwed | Total |
| 1a. Childless couples only | 5 | 7 | 12 | 0 | 3 | 3 | 5 | 10 | 15 |
| b. Childless couples plus others | 5 | 4 | 9 | 0 | 2 | 2 | 5 | 6 | 11 |
| Total childless couples | 10 | 11 | 21 | 0 | 5 | 5 | 10 | 16 | 26 |
| 2a. Couples and children only | 11 | 3 | 14 | 0 | 1 | 1 | 11 | 4 | 15 |
| b. Couples, children plus others | 5 | 0 | 5 | 0 | 0 | 0 | 5 | 0 | 5 |
| Total couples and children | 16 | 3 | 19 | 0 | 1 | 1 | 16 | 4 | 20 |
| TOTAL | 26 | 14 | 40 | 0 | 6 | 6 | 26 | 20 | 46 |

*Our sample at Grenville contains no households which include grandchildren or great grandchildren of the resident couple; hence the omission of these categories from the present table.

# 5. Rural Jamaica

Jamaica is the largest and perhaps the best known of the British Caribbean islands. It lies in the Greater Antilles, opposite Cuba and Haiti, and has an area of 4,400 square miles. It was captured by the British in 1655 and has remained British since then. In 1955, when I conducted the surveys described in this and the following chapter, the population was estimated at 1,550,000. Of these, approximately 400,000 lived in towns, and about 300,000 were settled on the sugar-producing plains near plantations. Nearly a million Jamaicans live in the hilly interior, and perhaps four fifths of those who do so may be classified as peasants or members of peasant communities. In this chapter I shall only discuss the family organization of these peasant communities.

As already mentioned, in 1955 I was assigned the task of surveying labor problems in rural Jamaica. Eight districts were selected for detailed study, each from a different parish, scattered throughout the length and breadth of the island. The boundaries of each area were defined by maps. I made a census in each, and in the course of this collected materials on household composition as well as on problems of labor supply and demand. The survey periods in these areas averaged about twelve days each, and in consequence my information on certain aspects of the family system is by no means as complete as I would wish. Nonetheless, the data collected and presented below are quite definitive of the family structure. I shall mention the gaps in our information as we come to them.

In my Survey Report I have described the economic conditions of four of these areas in some detail. This summary of economic conditions was based on fairly detailed estimates of the income in cash and kind of all households in these four areas over the twelve months preceding survey. The salient features of these data are worth mention here. Of the 551 households in these four areas, 40 per cent had annual incomes of less than fifty pounds sterling, in cash and kind; 29 per cent had incomes of fifty-one pounds to one hundred pounds for the year; 15 per cent had incomes of more than one hundred but less than one hundred and fifty pounds per year, and the remaining 16 per cent had incomes of more than one hundred and fifty pounds per year. This last group includes 4 per cent with incomes of more than three hundred pounds a year. Only 10 per cent of these 550 households had no land; 28 per cent had less than one acre, 16 per cent had between one and two acres, and 22 per cent had from two to five acres. Two thirds of the remainder had less than ten acres, 6 per cent had between ten and twenty acres, and less than 3 per cent had more than twenty acres. [1]

Population and the Distribution of Headship

The population of these 1,015 households is analyzed by sex and age in Table 1. Children under fourteen years of age form 42.4 per cent of the total. Adults of more than fifty-five years are 9.7 per cent. Adults between the ages of fifteen and fifty-four are 47.9 per cent. Of this population, 50.1 per cent are males. Of the 4,326 individuals in these homes, 2,167 are males, 2,159 are females. There is an almost perfect balance of the sexes in this sample, and even within the reproductive age groups between fifteen and fifty-four years there are 1.04 females per male.

Of these 1,015 households, eight defied further classification; in some of them I could not determine the locus of headship; in others I could not determine the unit boundary. These eight households together contain twenty-eight persons. Although they are included in Table 1 for completeness, I have omitted them from the subsequent analysis. The heads of the remaining 1,007 households are classified by sex and age in Table 2, and the distribution of headship among the remaining 4,298 persons classified by sex and age is given in Table 3.

Seven in every ten households have male heads. Two thirds of these male household heads are over forty years of age; and 40 per cent of all male household heads are between forty and fifty-four. Only 4 per cent of these male heads are under twenty-four, and less than 5.5 per cent are over sixty-nine years of age. Of the 305 female heads, 73 per cent are over forty, and 35 per cent are between forty and fifty-four years old. Thirteen per cent are over sixty-nine and about 2 per cent under twenty-four.

Only one in twelve men below the age of twenty-four is a household head; and only one in fifty women of this age group. But among the men of twenty-five to thirty-nine years of age, nearly two thirds are heads of their own homes. This striking rise in the incidence of headship among men over twenty-four denotes a general constraint on males of this age group to establish their own homes. Obviously, many will not be able to do so, and one third in fact do not; clearly many of those who conform to this rule will find it a strain. Ninety-one per cent of the males between forty and fifty-four years and between fifty-five and sixty-nine years are heads of their own homes; only 76 per cent of those above sixty-nine have this status. Apparently men who do not attain headship by their fortieth year are unlikely to do so thereafter. Of the 1,220 adult males in these homes, 57.6 per cent are household heads. Of the 1,273 adult females in these homes, only 23.9 per cent are household heads.

The incidence of headship increases by equal intervals among women between their twenty-fourth and sixty-ninth year. Just under one in every five women of twenty-five to thirty-nine heads her own home; just over one in three of those between forty and fifty-four do so, and just over one half of those between fifty-five and sixty-nine. There is no further change in the relative incidence of headship among women. Of the heads in both sexes, 284 are over fifty-five, and of these 169 are males. We may therefore expect a relatively high incidence of units containing three lineal generations inclusive of male as well as female heads. However, nearly 38 per cent of these 305 female household heads are over fifty-five, but only 24 per cent of the males; in consequence, the incidence of these three-generation households will probably be higher within the category of units under female heads than in those under males. This difference in relative incidence should not obscure absolute frequencies of these three-generation units in the two household categories. Percentages do not tell the whole story.

Table 4 classifies these 1,007 households by size as well as sex of their head. There are 116 single-person units among them. Of these, 120 contain males, and units of this size are more frequent than any other. Households containing only two persons come next, with a total of 162; those with three and four persons number 138 and 152, respectively. There is a steady decrease in the frequency of households of increasing size beyond this point, but our sample, being a large one, includes some freaks such as units with sixteen and twenty-five people.

The average size of all these 1,007 households is 4.3 persons. Units with male heads average 4.42 persons, those with female heads, 3.92. There are many more units containing four or more persons under male heads than there are under females; but the

relative incidence of larger households in the total with female
heads is sufficiently high to show that females may just as easily be
heads of large households as of small ones.

Of these 4, 298 persons, 3, 104 or 72 per cent live in homes with
male heads. In these units, men outnumber women by 1. 15 to 1.
In units with female heads, women outnumber men by 2. 3 to 1.
However, the ratios of children under fifteen in either group of
households are strikingly similar, being 42. 2 per cent in units
with male heads, and 43. 2 per cent in those under females. The
absolute numbers of children involved differ sharply, there being
1, 310 children below fifteen years of age in homes with male heads,
and 515 in those with female heads.

I was not able to collect accurate information about the marital
status of all 166 individuals who lived on their own. In Table 6
these persons are therefore classified by sex and age only. Of the
120 males, forty are between twenty-five and thirty-nine years of
age and an equal number are between forty and fifty-four. The high
incidence of solitary males in these age groups illustrates the
strength of the pressure on men to establish their own homes, and
the number who cannot do so adequately. Of the forty-six solitary
females, only one was less than twenty-four, and only eight were
between twenty-five and thirty-nine years old. One third were
women between forty and fifty-four and twenty-one were above
this age. Solitary women are usually past their prime. Solitary
men are more usually in theirs. These features are not random,
nor are the differing distributions of isolation between the sexes.
All alike are governed by principles of family structure.

## The System of Mating Relations

Gaps in the data are most noticeable in regard to the mating
and parental condition of the adult population. As we have seen,
it proved impossible to collect adequate data on all persons who
lived by themselves. Eleven males and nine females who were on
visits to these homes have also been excluded from the following
analysis; even so, there is a large number of people, especially
males, whose parental status and mating relations remain unknown.
Females are better documented, since their children or pregnancies
are observable. The large groups of childless single persons,
entered in Tables 7 to 9 as probably never having mated, are ado-
lescents whose experimental activities do not merit description
as mating in this analysis. To facilitate interpretation I have reduced the principal categories of Table 7 to percentage ratios in
a brief supplementary table, 7a.

Table 7 summarized my data on the mating and parental condition
of all but a few adults of different sex and age in these households.
Of the 1,209 males in this sample, 315 or 26.2 per cent were childless single persons, and of these 242 or 19.8 per cent of the sample
total may not yet have begun their mating careers. I cannot specify
the parental status of a further 156 or 12.9 per cent of the total.
Another 131 of these 1,209 men, that is 10.8 per cent, were single
parents; 251 had engaged in consensual cohabitation; 338 were
married; and eighteen were widowed. Of the 356 young men of less
than twenty-four, only eighteen were known to have entered domestic unions. Sixteen of these were cohabiting consensually and
two had married. The parental status of forty-one remained unknown; 288 were childless single persons. Of the 338 single males
in this age group, fifty-one were known to be mating extraresidentially, including eight of the nine known parents among them.

Of the 357 males aged between twenty-five and thirty-nine, we
lack details on the parental status of fifty-five, and we have no information on the mating condition of forty-seven of these men.
Of the remaining 302, ninety-three were single persons, seventy-
one of these being parents also. Another 123 had entered consensual
cohabitation, and the remaining eighty-six had married. Consensual
cohabitation is more frequent among men of this age group for
whom we have adequate knowledge than marriage or single status.
Of the ninety-three single men, seventy-one were mating extraresidentially. We lack details on both mating and parental status
of twenty-two of the 302 men between forty and fifty-four; and we
lack details of the parental status of another three. Of the remaining
277, 152 had married, and four of these were widowers. A further
eighty-four had cohabited consensually, and only seven of these
were not then doing so. Of the forty-one men known to have remained single, thirty-six were parents and fifteen were mating
extraresidentially. Clearly, marriage is the modal form of mating
for men in middle age and single status is anomalous among them.

For the 144 men between fifty-five and sixty-nine, we have adequate information on 122 only. For the remainder, we lack details
of mating and parental status alike. Twelve of the 122 documented
males were single, and all of them were parents. Of the remainder,
twenty-five had cohabited consensually without marrying, and
twenty-one of these were still doing so. Of the eighty-five men who
had married, six were widowers. Excluding the thirteen men over
seventy, for whom we lack details of parental status, and for most
of whom we lack details of mating condition also, there remain
thirty-seven, only three of whom, all fathers, had remained single,

and only three of whom had cohabited consensually without marrying. Eight of the remainder were widowers.

It is clear that young men under twenty-four do not normally
enter domestic unions, but mate extraresidentially as a rule. Between the ages of twenty-five and thirty-nine men are expected
to establish domestic unions, and most of them do so consensually,
those who marry at this age being little fewer than those whom we
know to have remained always single. Between the ages of forty
and fifty-four, most men will marry, and two thirds of the remainder will by then have participated in consensual domestic
unions, the great majority of these still doing so. After they are
past fifty-five, few men continue single, and most have already
married.

We have here a developmental series of mating alternatives
very like that of Latante. Mating forms for males are serially
successive, and each has its mode at a particular point in the individual life cycle. There is a normal pattern of male development
which includes movement from the extraresidential mating form
into and through consensual cohabitation to marriage. This development assumes high degrees of stability in domestic unions of
either type. Our data confirm this expectation.

Of 251 men with experience of consensual cohabitation, 239 were
living in these unions at the time of study; five had been widowed
from these unions and had remained single. Only seven were known
to have separated from their consensual mates. The consensual
union is much more likely to develop into marriage than to dissolve,
in rural Jamaica. Alternatively, persons whose consensual unions
have broken down re-enter others shortly after.

Marriages in this population are also stable. Of the 356 married
men in this sample, eighteen were widowers and 322 were living
with their wives. Eleven had absent spouses, and in most of these
cases there was little doubt that the marriage persisted. Only
five were known to have separated from their wives, and only one
of these had resumed consensual cohabitation. Apparently in this
population consensual domestic unions and marriages are irreversible status conditions. Men who have participated in either of these
types of union seldom reverse their mating development, unless
they live by themselves. Interesting evidence in support of this
view is provided by the decrease in the number of senior men whose
parental status remains unknown. The analysis of male mating
patterns accordingly demonstrates a serial arrangement of extraresidential mating, consensual cohabitation, and marriage, which

has high actual observance. This mating order is thus clearly normative.

As indicated above, we have fuller data for the population of female adults than for the males. None the less, we lack knowledge about the mating and parental status of 70 women, or 5. 6 per cent of the 1, 264 adult females under review. Another 211 or 16. 7 per cent were childless single women, and of these, 149 or 11.4 per cent of the total sample had probably not yet begun their mating careers. Three hundred and three or 24. 1 per cent of the total were single mothers; 258 or 20. 3 per cent had cohabited consensually, and of these, 237 were still doing so. Another 348 or 27. 6 per cent were married, and seventy-two or 5. 7 per cent were widows.

Of the 366 young women under twenty-four in these homes, 149 may not yet have begun mating. Another thirty-seven were childless single persons, and two were of unknown parental or mating status. Eighty-six were single mothers, and seventy-seven of these were then mating extraresidentially. Another seventy were engaged in consensual cohabitation, and twenty-two had married, one of these being already a widow. Clearly, it is more usual for young women in this age group to remain single than for them to cohabit; moreover, most of those who cohabit will do so consensually. In all there were 274 single females under twenty-four, of whom 110 were mating extraresidentially.

Of the 375 women between twenty-five and thirty-nine years of age, we lack adequate data on the parental and mating condition of fourteen. Of the remaining 361, 107 had not cohabited, and 91 or these were mothers. Of these 107 single women, 71 were mating extraresidentially. Women of this age group living in consensual domestic unions numbered 107, and another one had separated from her former mate. Of the 146 married women, six were widows, ten had absent spouses, and 129 were living with their husbands. Only one of these 146 women had separated from her husband. Clearly, cohabitation is usual among women of this age group; and although marriage has a greater frequency than consensual unions, the latter are quite important. Set beside the number of young women under twenty-four who have entered domestic unions, the frequency of consensual and legal cohabitation among women of age group twenty-five to thirty-nine suggests that many of the married women of this age began cohabiting consensually before their twenty-fourth year; and many women of this age who are cohabiting consensually only began doing so after their twenty-fourth year.

Our data are inadequate for nineteen of the 296 women aged between forty and fifty-four. Of the remaining 277, seventy may never
have cohabited, sixty-five are single mothers, and only eleven still
continue to mate extraresidentially. The remaining 207 with experience of cohabitation include sixty who had not married and twenty-
three widows. Marriage is the modal mating form for women of this
age group; and presumably many of those still living in consensual
domestic unions either adopted this form of mating late or resumed
it after an early union had broken down.

Excluding the eighteen women between fifty-five and sixty-nine
for whom our data are inadequate, forty-eight of the remaining
128 have always been single; and forty-four of these forty-eight
women are mothers. None mate extraresidentially. Of the remaining eighty, twelve had not married and seven of these were
cohabiting consensually at the time of survey. Sixteen of the sixty-
eight women of this age group who had married, were widows.
Marriage is clearly the predominant mating status of these senior
women. Consensual cohabitation is anomalous among them. Our
data include no information to suggest that there are any women
of this age group whose consensual unions have broken down, except
for those eighteen persons of unknown mating and parental status.
We must conclude that women living in consensual domestic unions
strive to convert these into marriages at the latest by their fifty-
fourth year.

Of the eighty-one women over seventy in this sample, nineteen
were single mothers and another seventeen were of unknown mating
and parental status. Eight had cohabited consensually without marrying thereafter; of these only two remained with their mates, and
only one had left her mate, the remainder being widowed from this
form of union. Of the thirty-seven women in this age group who
were known to have married, twenty-six were widows.

The distribution of mating conditions among women confirms
the analysis of mating derived from the study of these conditions
among men. There is only one important difference between the
sexes, namely, that women move through different stages of the
mating cycle slightly ahead of men, and end this cycle with widowhood more frequently. The extraresidential mating mode predominates among young women below twenty-four years of age and
among single women of twenty-five to thirty-nine years; but many
of these women under twenty-four have already entered domestic
unions, mainly in the consensual form. Among their immediate
seniors we find more women living in marriage than singly or in
consensual unions. Beyond this point, the incidence of marriage

increases steadily with each age group, and beyond the fifty-fifth
year there is a sharp decline in the incidence of consensual cohabitation. Marriage is the appropriate mating mode for middle-
aged or senior women. Its only acceptable alternative among senior
women is reassumed single status; but in point of fact, most women
who have been cohabiting consensually seem to succeed in marrying
by their fifty-fifth year. Extraresidential mating is the appropriate
mode for young women; and domestic unions, consensual or other,
are equally acceptable for mature women between twenty-five and
thirty-nine.

The irreversibility of this mating order is neatly illustrated by
the data at hand. Of the 258 women whose consensual cohabitation
had not developed into marriage, only seven had separated from
their mates, and fourteen had been widowed; the remainder were
still cohabiting. Of the 348 women whose husbands were alive, only
six had separated. Twenty had absent spouses but there was little
indication that these unions were insecure. The remaining 322 lived
with their husbands. No separated wife had resumed consensual
cohabitation. Only four of the seventy-two widows in this sample
had resumed consensual cohabitation, and these were all women
in youth or early middle age. Of the 194 women in these households
who were mating extraresidentially, only eleven were over forty,
seventy-three were between twenty-five and thirty-nine, and 110
were under twenty-four. With this analysis of the mating system
behind us, we may now turn to Tables 8 and 9, which together
describe the relations between mating and household status.

Table 8 isolates all adults other than household heads, and classifies them by sex, age, and mating condition. Table 9 does likewise for the residue of household heads. Of the 338 married men
and 18 widowers in this sample, 324 married men and 15 widowers were heads of their own homes. Clearly marriage and male
headship go together, and widowhood of men does not seriously
interfere with this. Of the 239 couples cohabiting consensually
at the time of survey, 197 or 82 per cent had male heads, eighteen
or 7.5 per cent had female heads and the remaining twenty-four or
10 per cent lived in other peoples' homes. Men are more likely to
head households based on their marriage than on their consensual
union, but most consensual unions have male heads. Of the 702
male household heads, ninety-eight are known to be single and fifty-
seven are of unspecified parental or mating status. Only fifteen of
these household heads are single men below twenty-four years of
age. Of the 148 men of single or unknown status between the ages
of twenty-five and thirty-nine, another fifty-one are heads of their

own homes. Of the sixty-six men not cohabiting who are between forty and fifty-four years of age, fifty-three are household heads; of thirty-four men between fifty-five and sixty-nine in a similar position, twenty-six are household heads. Of the remaining sixteen men in this condition, who are over sixty-nine, only ten are household heads. In short, age and male headship go together; so does cohabitation, especially marriage, and male headship. Young men who marry are likely to be household heads, while old men who have remained single may not be heads. Normally, cohabitation and male maturity are linked with one another and with household headship. In short, these frequency distributions describe a normative order, a set of regulatory principles.

Of the 305 female household heads in this sample, fifty-three were widows, but only five had husbands living with them. Eighteen had absent husbands, and three of these were separated. Fifteen of the twenty-one women whose consensual unions had already ended were heads of their own homes; only eighteen of the 237 unwed women who were cohabiting consensually were household heads. Women are rarely heads of units based on their cohabitation.

Of 586 single women in these homes, 196 were household heads. Of 305 single mothers, 146 were household heads. There were thirty-four female heads of indeterminate mating and parental status. Only sixteen of these single female heads were childless persons. Of 274 single women below the age of twenty-four, only six were household heads. Of 121 between twenty-five and thirty-nine, fifty-one were heads of their own homes. Of eighty-nine between forty and fifty-four years of age, sixty-six were heads of their own homes; of sixty-six between fifty-five and sixty-nine years of age, forty-five were household heads; and of the thirty-six single women of seventy years or more, twenty-five were household heads. Seniority by age is the basis for the distribution of headship among females who remain outside of cohabitation, but within this group, motherhood and its responsibilities are also important. The incidence of headship among single mothers in each age group is notably higher than among women of childless or indeterminate parental status. For those women who have entered cohabitation, widowhood or separation provides the general basis for headship. Very few cohabiting women have charge of their own homes.

The Composition of Domestic Groups

The 702 households with male heads contain 2,402 dependents

and mates. The 305 units with female heads include 865 resident dependents. In Table 10, these dependent populations are classified by relationship to the heads with whom they live. Despite the forty-five categories in this table, it does not distinguish all varieties of relations involved. The two kinship charts attached represent these relationships and their frequencies exactly.

One fifth of the dependents living with male household heads are mates of the heads, roughly 40 per cent of these being consensual. Just over half of the dependent populations of these units are children of the head, and the 196 resident grandchildren or great-grandchildren of these heads are less than one twelfth of their total dependents. There are 152 persons in these homes who are descended from resident mates of the head by former unions; together they represent 6.4 per cent of the total. Of this group, 108 are the mates' children, forty-one are grandchildren, and three are great-grandchildren. The presence of these grandchildren and great-grandchildren demonstrates the assumption of social fatherhood by these women's mates. In addition, there are another seventy-seven kin of resident mates living in homes with male heads. Together they represent 3.5 per cent of the total dependents; and one in eleven of all dependents in these homes traces kinship exclusively to the mate of the head. Of these seventy-seven kinsfolk of the heads' mates, nine are the mates' mothers, and the remaining sixty-eight are collateral kin.

These homes with male heads include nineteen mothers and four fathers of their heads; in addition, there are two mothers' mothers and one father's mother present. Besides these, there are eighty-four resident collateral kin of the household heads. Of these, nineteen are full siblings, eight are maternal half siblings and only one is a paternal half sibling. Thirty-two are the issue of full siblings, nine are the issue of maternal half siblings, and only one is descended from a paternal half sibling. There are also eight matrilateral and six patrilateral kin of the heads living in these homes.

Junior affines, including resident mates of the head's children or grandchildren, and their kin, represent less than 1 per cent of the dependent total. Resident employees and their issue number thirty-two, and these homes also include thirty-six adopted and thirty-two unrelated persons among the 103 miscellaneous members itemized in categories 41-45 of Table 10. Only two boarders and one person whose relation to the head was not clearly determined live in these homes. In short, apart from the heads' mates and issue, these units include a variety of collateral, affinal, and ancestral kin of their heads, together with a fair number of nonkin. Excluding the heads' mates and issue, the largest category of dependents is the issue of resident mates by their former unions. Next come the collateral kin of the head and his mate.

The twenty-four resident mates of female household heads represent less than 3 per cent of the dependent population in these homes. Resident children of the household head are 47 per cent of the dependent total, and resident grandchildren are 27 per cent. Thus the ratio of grandchildren in homes with female heads is 3.5 times that in units under males. In absolute terms, these differences are far less; homes with male heads contain 186 grandchildren of the heads as against 240 in units with female heads. Ratios can mislead unless the totals to which they refer are kept in mind. The thirty-nine resident great-grandchildren of female household heads bring the ratio of lineal issue in these homes to 77 per cent of all dependents. Collateral kin of the heads account for almost half of the remainder, with a total of ninety persons. These homes contain nine mothers and four fathers of their heads, but no ancestors of remoter generation. The issue and kin of resident mates represent less than 1 per cent of their total membership; but junior affines and their kin are one fortieth of the total. Most of these are resident mates of the heads' children. Of the thirty-seven miscellaneous persons living in these homes, twenty-four are adopted and four are employees. No boarders or kin of indeterminate relation are found within them. We can summarize the constitution of these households with female heads as primarily lineal. Their collateral components are the only other important element, apart from a few resident spouses of the heads or their children.

Tables 11 and 12 examine the resident collaterals of male household heads and female principals in homes of either type. Siblings and collaterals of senior generation are included in Table 11, which focuses attention on the differing frequencies of kinship and birth status within this group. These senior collaterals and siblings are both excluded from Table 12, which seeks to determine the relative frequency with which collaterals are connected with these principals through their fathers or mothers.

Of the eighty-four resident collaterals of male household heads, nineteen were full siblings and thirty-three were the issue of full siblings; eight were maternal half siblings and nine were their issue. There were only two residents connected with the head by ties of paternal half siblingship, five others by patrikinship and eight by matrikinship. It is already evident that maternal kinship predominates among collaterals. We lack details on the birth status of forty-eight of these eighty-four collateral residents in homes with male heads. None of the remaining thirty-six was legitimate; nor were any of the eighty-three resident collaterals of female principals for whom we have adequate data legitimate. Of the seventy-six resident collateral kin of the mates of male household heads, nine were full siblings and fifty were their issue; eleven were maternal half siblings or their issue; two were remote patrikin, and there were four matrikin. Of the eighty-seven resident collaterals of female household heads, twenty-two were full siblings, forty-eight were their issue. There were nine maternal half siblings and their issue in these homes as against three issue of paternal half siblings. The remaining six persons were equally distributed between patrikin and matrikin. Issue of full siblings predominate among resident collaterals of male or female principals in all these homes; next come the full siblings themselves, followed by maternal half siblings and their issue.

Table 12 analyzes these collaterals, with the exceptions already mentioned, by their generation remove from the principals with whom they live, by birth status, sex, and by the sex of the parent through whom kinship is traced. Of the sixty-four resident collaterals of male heads, included in this table, forty-one are male and forty trace kinship to these household heads through their mothers. Half of these resident collaterals of male heads belong to the immediately junior generation, but there are a few of the second generation removed. Of the sixty-six resident collaterals of the mates of these male heads, thirty-one are females and thirty-six trace kinship through their mothers. Forty-nine of these collaterals belong to the generation immediately junior to that of the principals with whom they live. We lack birth-status details for thirty resident collaterals of male heads, and for twenty-three resident collaterals of their mates. The thirty-four kin of these men and the forty-three kin of their mates for whom our data are adequate are all illegitimate. Of the sixty-five resident collaterals of female household heads included in Table 12, thirty-four are males and forty-six trace kinship through their mothers. Thirty-seven belong to the generation immediately junior to that of the head. All thirty-eight whose birth status is known are illegitimate. Of the aggregate of 195 resident collaterals just discussed, 122 or 63 per cent trace kinship to these principals through their mothers, and 118 belong to the immediately junior generation. None of these people are known to be legitimate. Two thirds live with their kinswomen. The preponderance of materterine kinship in the domestic placement of collaterals is fully evident, as also is the preponder-

ance of illegitimates among them. In comparing these samples, I
shall discuss these features more fully.

The Distribution of Children

In view of the preponderance of the illegitimate issue of kinswomen among these resident collaterals, careful analysis of the
composition of lineal descendants of the heads of these homes is
necessary. Table 13 presents our data on this population. Of 1,424
resident descendants of male household heads, 86.3 per cent or
1,230 are children of the head, 3.7 per cent or 51 are issue of the
head's sons, and 10 per cent are daughters' issue. Eighteen resident issue below the age of twenty-four are of unknown birth status.
The remaining sixty-nine entered as of unknown birth status in
Table 13 are over twenty-four years of age, and of these fifty-one
are children of the head.

Of the resident lineal issue of female household heads, 60 per
cent or 417 are children of the head, 8.7 per cent or sixty-one
are sons' issue, and 31.3 per cent or 218 are daughters' issue.
In these homes there are only six persons below the age of twenty-
four among the 111 entered as of unknown birth status in Table 13.
Of the remaining 105 who are above twenty-four years of age,
seventy-three are children of the heads themselves.

Of the 1,424 resident issue of male household heads, 57.3 per
cent are legitimate, 36.6 per cent are not, and 6.1 per cent are
of unspecified birth status. Of the 1,230 resident children of these
men, 794 or 63.5 per cent are legitimate. Of the fifty-one resident
children of these men's sons, seventeen or 33 per cent are legitimate; but of the 143 resident daughters' issue, only seven or less
than 5 per cent are legitimate. Three important points emerge
from this. Men have many illegitimate children of their consensual
or extraresidential unions living with them in their homes. They
are not as willing to accommodate their sons' children as their
daughters'; they freely accommodate their daughters' illegitimate
offspring, only rarely their daughters' lawful children.

Of the total 696 resident issue of female household heads, 111
or 15.9 per cent are of unspecified birth status, 121 or 17.4 per
cent are legitimate, and 464 or 66.7 per cent are not. Of the 417
resident children of these women, seventy-nine or 19 per cent are
of unspecified birth status, ninety-eight or 23.4 per cent are legitimate, and 240 or 57.2 per cent are not. None of the resident
sixty-one sons' issue is known to be lawful. Of the 218 resident
daughters' issue, twenty-three or 10.5 per cent are lawful, sixteen
or 7.3 per cent are of unspecified birth status, and the remaining

179 or 82.2 per cent are illegitimate. Even so, the illegitimacy ratio among daughers' issue living in homes with male heads is higher than in homes with female heads; and there are more illegitimate descendants of male household heads living with them than live under females. As already mentioned, only about 60 per cent of the resident mates of male household heads are married. The high incidence of consensual domestic unions among this population insures a high ratio of illegitimate offspring living with both parents in their fathers' homes. Similarly, the organization of mating among these populations assumes extraresidential mating among young persons. In consequence of parental role definitions within this mating form, there are many illegitimate daughters' issue living in the homes of their mothers' fathers as well as those of their mothers' mothers. Conversely, in view of the parental role definition associated with domestic unions, and especially with marriage, there are few legitimate issue of either sons or daughters in these homes. Such as there are occur in domestic units which include young married couples or young widowed persons.

Table 14 isolates all dependents in these homes who have one or more parents alive. These dependents are analyzed by their sex, age, and birth status, and by their residence with or separation from either or both of their parents in homes with heads of different sex. Of the 2,691 individuals classified here, 1,010 or 37.6 per cent are legitimate, and 320 or nearly 12 per cent are of unspecified birth status. The majority of these dependents are therefore illegitimate.

Of these 2,691 persons, 1,152 or 42.8 per cent live with both parents and 40.6 per cent of them live in their fathers' homes. Of these 1,152 individuals living with both parents, 824 or 71 per cent are lawful. All the remainder are illegitimate. The 634 children living apart from both parents are 23.5 per cent of the total. Only four persons known to be legitimate are included in this group; but for 297 children in this position we lack adequate data on birth status. Many of these 297 children live with their senior collateral kin.

There are 670 children living with their mothers apart from their fathers in this population. They represent 24.9 per cent of the total. Only eighty-eight or 13 per cent of this group are legitimate. Of the 158 children living with their fathers apart from their mothers, only twenty-six or 16.5 per cent are legitimate. Children living with their fathers apart from their mothers represent 5.9 per cent of the total population.

The sixty-three children living with widowed mothers are 2 per cent of the total, and fifty-five of these are legitimate. Another fourteen children, thirteen of whom are legitimate, live with their widowed fathers.

Of 1,853 children living in homes with male heads, 1,090 or approximately 59 per cent live with both parents. Three hundred and seventy-three or about 20 per cent live apart from both parents; 220 or about 12 per cent live with their mothers apart from their fathers; and 147 or about 8 per cent live with their fathers apart from their mothers.

Of the 838 children living in homes with female heads, sixty-two or 7.4 per cent live with both parents, 261 or 31 per cent live apart from both parents, 450 or 53.7 per cent live with their mothers apart from their fathers, and eleven or 1.3 per cent live with their fathers apart from their mothers. The children of widowed parents are not included in these calculations.

The great majority of children living apart from both parents, or with their mothers apart from their fathers, are illegitimate; the great majority of those who live with both parents are otherwise, and live in their fathers' homes. Most of the children separated from both their parents also live in homes with male heads, together with one third of those who live with their mothers apart from their fathers. In addition, there are many children living with their fathers in the latter's homes apart from their mothers, and most of these are illegitimate also. Of the total number of legitimates in this population, 804 or 73 per cent live with both parents. Of the 1,361 illegitimates in this population, 328 or 24 per cent live with both parents, 333 live apart from both parents, 577 or 42 per cent live with their mothers apart from their fathers, 119 or 8.7 per cent live with their fathers apart from their mothers. Most of the legitimates live with both parents, and most of those who live in homes with both their parents are legitimate. Most of the illegitimate members of this population also live in homes with male heads and many illegitimate offspring also live with both parents. The disparity by birth status is most marked for the group who are separated from both parents, and among the group living with their mothers apart from their fathers. But significant portions of both these groups reside in homes with male heads. The prevalence of consensual domestic unions insures that a large number of the illegitimate offspring will share conditions similar to those of the legitimate. Illegitimate offspring include persons begotten in consensual domestic unions as well as the offspring of extraresidential matings, and the parental roles which characterize these two sorts of union are strikingly different. Given

their equal prevalence, it follows that there will be no simple consistent pattern governing the residential placement of illegitimate
children and their parents.

Tables 15 and 16 enumerate the children who live apart from
either or both of their parents with different categories of kin.
Table 15 presents the kinship distribution of those children under
twenty-four who live apart from both parents. Sex and birth status
are included in this classification. Of the 493 individuals enumerated in this table, only four are known to be legitimate and 176 are
of unspecified birth status. Of these 493 individuals, 250 live with
their mothers' kin, 136 of these with their mothers' mothers or
mothers' parents. One hundred and thirty-four live with their fathers' kin, forty-seven of these with their fathers' mothers or
fathers' parents. Twenty live with the mother's sister, twenty-five
with the father's sister. Another 109 live with unrelated persons.

Of the 602 children under twenty-four included in Table 16, as
living with their mothers apart from their fathers, ninety are lawful, the remainder are not. Of the ninety lawful children, eighty-
five live with their mothers in homes which contain no other adult
kin. Two hundred and seventy-two illegitimate offspring also live
with their mothers alone. Of the 245 who live with their mothers
in homes containing adult consanguine kin, 240 are illegitimate;
fifty-nine of these live with the mother and both her parents, eighty-
six with the mother and mother's mother only; sixteen with the
mother and her brother; twelve with the mother and her father.

Table 17 isolates the 157 children below the age of twenty-four
who live with their fathers apart from their mothers. Thirty-five
of these are legitimate, and all these legitimate issue, together
with another eighty-eight illegitimate issue, live with their fathers
only, or with their fathers and fathers' wives, often second wives.
Of the remaining thirty-three, who live with their fathers and fathers' kin, sixteen live with their fathers and fathers' mothers.
Clearly, women who live apart from the fathers of their children
get more assistance from their kin than do men who keep their children after parting from the mothers. Twice as many children separated from both parents live in the homes of their mothers' kin
as live with their fathers' kin. Forty per cent of the children who
live with their mothers apart from their fathers do so in homes
of which their mothers' kin are heads. Surely the kinship facilities
so readily available to single mothers and so scarce for fathers in
a similar position encourage women to retain their illegitimate
offspring of extraresidential or broken consensual unions and dis-
courage men from doing so. Such men must manage on their own,

or rely on a subsequent mate to care for these children. For the women, collateral kinship provides ample opportunities of placing their children with close kinswomen. Our previous analysis has shown that most resident collaterals trace kinship to the principals with whom they live through their mothers. Materterine kinship serves to place junior illegitimate kin in these homes. Men find it less easy to place their children even in their parents' homes than women do to place theirs with their collateral kin.

## The Variety of Domestic Forms

Tables 18, 19, and 20 analyze the sample households by structural type. The categories of this taxonomy will by now be familiar. Of these 1,007 households, 65.5 per cent are pure cases of the eleven structural types. Of households with female heads, 74 per cent are pure types; of those with male heads, 62 per cent. Difference in the incidence of pure types between these two groups indicates a higher degree of accretions in homes with male heads.

Two hundred and fifteen or 21.4 per cent of these units are single-person households. Only twenty-two or 2.2 per cent are based on the siblingship of principals. Only 107 or 10.6 per cent have single parents and their children as structural cores; of these, eighty-one have female heads and twenty-six have male heads. One hundred and eighty-seven of these households contain childless couples as their principals. In all, these four structurally distinct types of domestic unit represent 52.7 per cent of the total sample. Of these only the sibling units are directly derivable from households formerly containing elementary families; and, as previously pointed out, sibling units may quite well be continuations of others based on single parents and their children. The high incidence of single-person units accounts for this large total of "deviant" household types.

Units containing the elementary families of their principals are 28 per cent of the total sample, and this is the modal household form. Of the 282 units of this class, 168 are exclusive elementary families. Units under single heads containing three successive lineally connected generations inclusive of the head are twice as frequent as those which lack the intermediate generation. Altogether there are 123 units of both types in the sample, only seventeen of which have male heads. However, there are fifty-five units of similar type whose male heads are cohabiting. Units of four-generation depth are rare, those under single female heads being twice as frequent as those under cohabiting males. In all, there are 178 units containing three successive generations inclusive of the heads and fourteen with a depth of four lineally connected generations.

Table 19 classifies all these households by morphological type and the number of generations, lineal or collateral, present within them. Two hundred and ten or 29. 8 per cent of the homes with male heads contain one generation only; 339 or 48. 2 per cent have a depth of two generations, and 144 or 20. 5 per cent contain three generations, exactly half of these being based on collateral rather than lineal descent from the head. Nine have a depth of four generations. Of the 305 homes under female heads, sixty-five or 21. 3 per cent contain one generation only, 105 or 34. 4 per cent have a depth of two generations, 122 or 40 per cent have a depth of three generations, and thirteen or 4. 3 per cent contain members of four generations. Of the total sample, 71 per cent contain one or two generations only, and of the 266 units having a depth of three generations, eighty-seven owe this depth to the presence of collateral kin.

Table 20 concludes our analysis. It enumerates by marital basis those conjugal unions whose members are household principals and whose domestic groups differ structurally. Of the 187 childless couples analyzed in this table, only seventy-three live by themselves and sixty-eight of these do so in homes with male heads. Eighty-seven of these childless couples are wed and of these only one couple lives in a unit with a female head. Of the 282 couples with children, 168 live in units which contain no accretions, and 171 are married. Only two of these married couples live in units with female heads and only six of all 282 couples do so.

Another two couples live in units with female heads, and both of these were married and had the couples' children and grandchildren living with them. Certainly cohabiting couples marry before their grandchildren are born if the union persists. The majority of the couples with children are married; but 39 per cent are not. Conversely, 47 per cent of the childless couples in these households are also married. Marriage takes place whether or not a domestic union is fertile, at the appropriate period of the partners' life cycles.

Conclusion

There is an obvious resemblance in the family structures of rural Jamaica and Latante. Both populations have a similar mating organization, within which each of the three alternative mating forms has its proper place in the individual life cycle, and couples may ideally move from extraresidential mating into consensual cohabitation and so to marriage. In consequence of this mating system, the two populations share similar patterns of domestic organization, and with the sole exception of single-person units, the frequencies of these differing forms are rather similar. In both populations illegitimacy has differing connotations according to the types of union between parents. In consequence, there is no simple residential dichotomy observable between legitimate and illegitimate in either population. Collateral kinship traced through women is an important basis for the domestic placement of the illegitimate offspring of extraresidential or broken consensual unions alike. In both populations marriage is an irreversible status and highly stable. In both fathers keep a certain proportion of their illegitimate offspring in their homes.

In each system, the mating and domestic alternatives are synchronized within the individual life cycle, and adults normally move from extraresidential mating into domestic unions shortly before or after the death of their parents or senior collateral kin, with whom they have been living. In both these populations, the coresidence of collaterals assumes the domestic separation of elementary family units and the practice of extraresidential mating among young folk.

## TABLE 1

### POPULATION OF THE SAMPLE HOUSEHOLDS, CLASSIFIED BY SEX AND AGE

| Age | Number Male | Number Female | Total | Percentage Male | Percentage Female | Percentage Total | Females per Male |
|---|---|---|---|---|---|---|---|
| 0- 4 | 360 | 324 | 684 | 8.3 | 7.5 | 15.8 | 0.85 |
| 5-14 | 587 | 562 | 1,149 | 13.6 | 13.0 | 26.6 | 0.96 |
| 15-24 | 360 | 369 | 729 | 8.3 | 8.5 | 16.8 | 1.02 |
| 25-39 | 364 | 378 | 742 | 8.4 | 8.8 | 17.2 | 1.04 |
| 40-54 | 302 | 299 | 601 | 7.0 | 6.9 | 13.9 | 0.99 |
| 55-69 | 144 | 146 | 290 | 3.3 | 3.4 | 6.7 | 1.01 |
| 70 and Over | 50 | 81 | 131 | 1.2 | 1.8 | 3.0 | 1.60 |
| TOTAL | 2,167 | 2,159 | 4,326 | 50.1 | 49.9 | 100.0 | 0.995 |

## TABLE 2

### HEADS OF THE SAMPLE HOUSEHOLDS, CLASSIFIED BY SEX AND AGE*

| Age | Number Male | Number Female | Total | Percentage Male | Percentage Female | Percentage Total |
|---|---|---|---|---|---|---|
| 15-24 | 29 | 8 | 37 | 2.9 | 0.7 | 3.6 |
| 25-39 | 229 | 75 | 304 | 22.7 | 7.4 | 30.1 |
| 40-54 | 275 | 107 | 382 | 27.4 | 10.6 | 38.0 |
| 55-69 | 131 | 74 | 205 | 13.1 | 7.3 | 20.4 |
| 70 and Over | 38 | 41 | 79 | 3.8 | 4.1 | 7.9 |
| TOTAL | 702 | 305 | 1,007 | 69.9 | 30.1 | 100.0 |

*Households with indeterminate headship are excluded from this table.

## TABLE 3

### DISTRIBUTION OF HOUSEHOLD HEADSHIP AMONG ADULT MEMBERS OF THE SAMPLE POPULATION, CLASSIFIED BY SEX AND AGE

| Age | Total | Male HHs* | %HHs | Total | Female HHs | %HHs | % HHs in Both Sexes |
|---|---|---|---|---|---|---|---|
| 15-24 | 360 | 29 | 8.0 | 369 | 8 | 2.1 | 5.0 |
| 25-39 | 364 | 229 | 63.0 | 378 | 75 | 19.8 | 41.0 |
| 40-54 | 302 | 275 | 91.0 | 299 | 107 | 35.8 | 63.5 |
| 55-69 | 144 | 131 | 91.0 | 146 | 74 | 50.6 | 70.5 |
| 70 and Over | 50 | 38 | 76.0 | 81 | 41 | 50.6 | 60.2 |
| TOTAL | 1,220 | 702 | 57.6 | 1,273 | 305 | 23.9 | 40.4 |

*HHs = Household heads.

TABLE 4

HOUSEHOLDS OF THE SAMPLE, CLASSIFIED BY SEX OF HEAD AND NUMBER OF PERSONS†

| Number of Persons | Sex of Head | | | Total | | |
|---|---|---|---|---|---|---|
| | Male | Female | Total | Male HHs* | Female HHs | Total |
| 1 | 120 | 46 | 166 | 120 | 46 | 166 |
| 2 | 97 | 65 | 162 | 194 | 130 | 324 |
| 3 | 90 | 48 | 138 | 270 | 144 | 414 |
| 4 | 104 | 48 | 152 | 416 | 192 | 608 |
| 5 | 82 | 38 | 120 | 410 | 190 | 600 |
| 6 | 58 | 19 | 77 | 348 | 114 | 462 |
| 7 | 37 | 10 | 47 | 259 | 70 | 329 |
| 8 | 38 | 12 | 50 | 304 | 96 | 400 |
| 9 | 29 | 7 | 36 | 261 | 63 | 324 |
| 10 | 22 | 3 | 25 | 220 | 30 | 250 |
| 11 | 11 | 5 | 16 | 121 | 55 | 176 |
| 12 | 6 | 1 | 7 | 72 | 12 | 84 |
| 13 | 5 | 1 | 6 | 65 | 13 | 78 |
| 14 | 2 | 1 | 3 | 28 | 14 | 42 |
| 15 | 0 | 0 | 0 | 0 | 0 | 0 |
| 16 | 1 | 0 | 1 | 16 | 0 | 16 |
| 25 | 0 | 1 | 1 | 0 | 25 | 25 |
| TOTAL | 702 | 305 | 1,007 | 3,104 | 1,194 | 4,298 |

| Averages: | including solitary persons | 4.42% | 3.92% | 4.30% |
|---|---|---|---|---|
| | excluding solitary persons | 5.13% | 4.44% | 4.92% |

†Households of indeterminate headship are not included in this table.
*HHs = Household heads.

TABLE 5

AGE AND SEX DISTRIBUTION OF HOUSEHOLD POPULATION, CLASSIFIED ACCORDING TO THE SEX OF THE HEAD

| Age | Male Head | | | | Female Head | | | | Total | |
|---|---|---|---|---|---|---|---|---|---|---|
| | Male | Fe-male | Total | Per cent | Male | Fe-male | Total | Per cent | Male %HHs* | Female %HHs |
| 0- 4 | 248 | 225 | 473 | 15.3 | 110 | 99 | 209 | 17.5 | 10.9 | 4.9 |
| 5-14 | 426 | 411 | 837 | 26.9 | 155 | 151 | 306 | 25.7 | 19.4 | 7.2 |
| 15-24 | 242 | 264 | 506 | 16.4 | 114 | 102 | 216 | 18.1 | 11.8 | 5.1 |
| 25-39 | 301 | 254 | 555 | 17.8 | 56 | 121 | 177 | 14.8 | 12.9 | 4.2 |
| 40-54 | 281 | 172 | 453 | 14.6 | 21 | 124 | 145 | 12.1 | 10.5 | 3.3 |
| 55-69 | 136 | 64 | 200 | 6.4 | 8 | 82 | 90 | 7.5 | 4.6 | 2.1 |
| 70 + | 43 | 37 | 80 | 2.6 | 7 | 44 | 51 | 4.3 | 1.9 | 1.2 |
| TOTAL | 1,677 | 1,427 | 3,104 | 100.0 | 471 | 723 | 1,194 | 100.0 | 72.0 | 28.0 |

*HHs = Household heads.

TABLE 6

HOUSEHOLDERS LIVING ALONE, CLASSIFIED BY AGE AND SEX

| Age | Male | Female | Total |
|---|---|---|---|
| 15-24 | 11 | 1 | 12 |
| 25-39 | 40 | 8 | 48 |
| 40-54 | 40 | 16 | 56 |
| 55-69 | 22 | 8 | 30 |
| 70 + | 7 | 13 | 20 |
| TOTAL | 120 | 46 | 166 |

# TABLE 7

## ALL ADULT MEMBERS OF THE SAMPLE POPULATION, CLASSIFIED BY SEX, AGE, MARITAL CONDITION, AND PARENTAL STATUS

| Mating and Parental Status | Male | | | | | | Female | | | | | |
|---|---|---|---|---|---|---|---|---|---|---|---|---|
| | -24 | -39 | -54 | -69 | 70+ | Total | -24 | -39 | -54 | -69 | 70+ | Total |
| **1. Childless single persons** | | | | | | | | | | | | |
| a. Mating now n/k* | 3 | 2 | 2 | 0 | 0 | 7 | 0 | 0 | 0 | 0 | 0 | 0 |
| b. Not mating now | 8 | 5 | 2 | 0 | 0 | 15 | 4 | 7 | 4 | 4 | 0 | 19 |
| c. Probably never mated | 242 | 0 | 0 | 0 | 0 | 242 | 149 | 0 | 0 | 0 | 0 | 149 |
| d. Mating now | 35 | 15 | 1 | 0 | 0 | 51 | 33 | 9 | 1 | 0 | 0 | 43 |
| Total childless single persons | 288 | 22 | 5 | 0 | 0 | 315 | 186 | 16 | 5 | 4 | 0 | 211 |
| **2. Single persons, parental status n/k** | | | | | | | | | | | | |
| a. Mating now n/k | 33 | 47 | 22 | 22 | 12 | 136 | 2 | 13 | 19 | 18 | 17 | 69 |
| b. Not mating now | 0 | 0 | 1 | 0 | 0 | 1 | 0 | 1 | 0 | 0 | 0 | 1 |
| c. Mating now | 8 | 8 | 2 | 0 | 1 | 19 | 0 | 0 | 0 | 0 | 0 | 0 |
| Total single persons, parental status n/k | 41 | 55 | 25 | 22 | 13 | 156 | 2 | 14 | 19 | 18 | 17 | 70 |
| **3. Single parents** | | | | | | | | | | | | |
| a. Mating now n/k | 1 | 12 | 19 | 5 | 0 | 37 | 8 | 21 | 22 | 3 | 0 | 54 |
| b. Not mating now | 0 | 3 | 3 | 5 | 3 | 14 | 1 | 6 | 33 | 41 | 19 | 100 |
| c. Mating now | 8 | 56 | 14 | 2 | 0 | 80 | 77 | 64 | 10 | 0 | 0 | 151 |
| Total single parents | 9 | 71 | 36 | 12 | 3 | 131 | 86 | 91 | 65 | 44 | 19 | 305 |
| **4. Consensually wed** | | | | | | | | | | | | |
| a. In 1955 | 16 | 122 | 77 | 21 | 3 | 239 | 70 | 107 | 51 | 7 | 2 | 237 |
| b. Separated, childless | 0 | 1 | 1 | 1 | 0 | 3 | 0 | 0 | 1 | 1 | 0 | 2 |
| c. Separated, with children | 0 | 0 | 4 | 1 | 0 | 5 | 0 | 1 | 4 | 0 | 0 | 5 |
| d. Widowed, single | 0 | 0 | 2 | 2 | 0 | 4 | 0 | 0 | 4 | 5 | 5 | 14 |
| Total consensually wed | 16 | 123 | 84 | 25 | 3 | 251 | 70 | 108 | 60 | 12 | 8 | 258 |
| **5. Married persons** | | | | | | | | | | | | |
| a. Spouse present | 2 | 82 | 139 | 76 | 23 | 322 | 19 | 129 | 115 | 48 | 11 | 322 |
| b. Spouse absent | 0 | 3 | 7 | 1 | 0 | 11 | 1 | 10 | 6 | 3 | 0 | 20 |
| c. Separated, single | 0 | 1 | 1 | 2 | 0 | 4 | 1 | 1 | 3 | 1 | 0 | 6 |
| d. Separated, not single | 0 | 0 | 1 | 0 | 0 | 1 | 0 | 0 | 0 | 0 | 0 | 0 |
| Total married persons | 2 | 86 | 148 | 79 | 23 | 338 | 21 | 140 | 124 | 52 | 11 | 348 |
| **6. Widowed persons** | | | | | | | | | | | | |
| a. Widowed, single | 0 | 0 | 4 | 6 | 8 | 18 | 1 | 5 | 20 | 16 | 26 | 68 |
| b. Widowed, not single | 0 | 0 | 0 | 0 | 0 | 0 | 0 | 1 | 3 | 0 | 0 | 4 |
| Total widowed persons | 0 | 0 | 4 | 6 | 8 | 18 | 1 | 6 | 23 | 16 | 26 | 72 |
| GRAND TOTAL | 356 | 357 | 302 | 144 | 50 | 1,209 | 366 | 375 | 296 | 146 | 81 | 1,264 |

*n/k = Not known.

TABLE 7a

RELATIVE INCIDENCE OF DIFFERING MARITAL AND PARENTAL CONDITIONS
AMONG THE TOTAL ADULT POPULATION OF THE SAMPLE

| Mating and Parental Condition | Percentage of Population | |
|---|---|---|
| | Male | Female |
| 1. Childless single persons | 26.2 | 16.7 |
| 2. Single persons, parental status n/k* | 12.9 | 5.6 |
| 3. Single parents | 10.8 | 24.1 |
| 4. Consensually wed, etc. | 20.8 | 20.3 |
| 5. Married persons | 27.9 | 27.6 |
| 6. Widowed persons | 1.4 | 5.7 |
| TOTAL | 100.0 | 100.0 |
| 1c. Probably never mated | 19.8 | 11.4 |
| 1. Childless persons less than 24 years | 24.0 | 14.7 |
| Total single persons, parents, etc. | 49.9 | 46.4 |
| Single persons mating in 1955 | 150-12.3 | 194-15.3 |

*n/k = Not known.

## TABLE 8

### ADULT MEMBERS OF THE SAMPLE POPULATION OTHER THAN HOUSEHOLD HEADS, CLASSIFIED BY SEX, AGE, MARITAL CONDITION, AND PARENTAL STATUS

| Mating and Parental Status | Male | | | | | | Female | | | | | |
|---|---|---|---|---|---|---|---|---|---|---|---|---|
| | -24 | -39 | -54 | -69 | 70+ | Total | -24 | -39 | -54 | -69 | 70+ | Total |
| **1. Childless single persons** | | | | | | | | | | | | |
| a. Mating now n/k* | 0 | 0 | 0 | 0 | 0 | 0 | 0 | 0 | 0 | 0 | 0 | 0 |
| b. Probably never mated | 242 | 0 | 0 | 0 | 0 | 242 | 149 | 0 | 0 | 0 | 0 | 149 |
| c. Not mating now | 7 | 4 | 1 | 0 | 0 | 12 | 3 | 4 | 2 | 0 | 0 | 9 |
| d. Mating now | 32 | 12 | 0 | 0 | 0 | 44 | 32 | 5 | 0 | 0 | 0 | 37 |
| Total childless single persons | 281 | 16 | 1 | 0 | 0 | 298 | 184 | 9 | 2 | 0 | 0 | 195 |
| **2. Single persons, parental status n/k** | | | | | | | | | | | | |
| a. Mating now n/k | 27 | 38 | 7 | 8 | 5 | 85 | 2 | 9 | 7 | 11 | 6 | 35 |
| b. Not mating now | 0 | 0 | 0 | 0 | 0 | 0 | 0 | 1 | 0 | 0 | 0 | 1 |
| c. Mating now | 8 | 6 | 0 | 0 | 0 | 14 | 0 | 0 | 0 | 0 | 0 | 0 |
| Total single persons, parental status n/k | 35 | 44 | 7 | 8 | 5 | 99 | 2 | 10 | 7 | 11 | 6 | 36 |
| **3. Single parents** | | | | | | | | | | | | |
| a. Mating now n/k | 1 | 4 | 0 | 0 | 0 | 5 | 8 | 11 | 4 | 1 | 0 | 24 |
| b. Not mating now | 0 | 3 | 2 | 0 | 1 | 6 | 1 | 2 | 8 | 6 | 5 | 22 |
| c. Mating now | 6 | 30 | 3 | 0 | 0 | 39 | 73 | 38 | 2 | 0 | 0 | 113 |
| Total single parents | 7 | 37 | 5 | 0 | 1 | 50 | 82 | 51 | 14 | 7 | 5 | 159 |
| **4. Consensually wed** | | | | | | | | | | | | |
| a. In 1955 | 3 | 25 | 11 | 3 | 0 | 42 | 70 | 97 | 45 | 5 | 2 | 219 |
| b. Separated, childless | 0 | 1 | 0 | 0 | 0 | 1 | 0 | 0 | 0 | 0 | 0 | 0 |
| c. Separated, with children | 0 | 0 | 0 | 0 | 0 | 0 | 0 | 0 | 1 | 0 | 0 | 1 |
| d. Widowed, single | 0 | 0 | 0 | 0 | 0 | 0 | 0 | 0 | 1 | 1 | 3 | 5 |
| Total consensually wed | 3 | 26 | 11 | 3 | 0 | 43 | 70 | 97 | 47 | 6 | 5 | 225 |
| **5. Married persons** | | | | | | | | | | | | |
| a. Spouse present | 1 | 5 | 2 | 2 | 3 | 13 | 19 | 129 | 112 | 46 | 11 | 317 |
| b. Spouse absent | 0 | 0 | 1 | 0 | 0 | 1 | 0 | 3 | 2 | 0 | 0 | 5 |
| c. Separated, single | 0 | 0 | 0 | 0 | 0 | 0 | 1 | 0 | 2 | 0 | 0 | 3 |
| d. Separated, not single | 0 | 0 | 0 | 0 | 0 | 0 | 0 | 0 | 0 | 0 | 0 | 0 |
| Total married persons | 1 | 5 | 3 | 2 | 3 | 14 | 20 | 132 | 116 | 46 | 11 | 325 |
| **6. Widowed persons** | | | | | | | | | | | | |
| a. Widowed, single | 0 | 0 | 0 | 0 | 3 | 3 | 0 | 1 | 2 | 2 | 13 | 18 |
| b. Widowed, not single | 0 | 0 | 0 | 0 | 0 | 0 | 0 | 0 | 1 | 0 | 0 | 1 |
| Total widowed persons | 0 | 0 | 0 | 0 | 3 | 3 | 0 | 1 | 3 | 2 | 13 | 19 |
| GRAND TOTAL | 327 | 128 | 27 | 13 | 12 | 507 | 358 | 300 | 189 | 72 | 40 | 959 |

*n/k = Not known.

## TABLE 9

HOUSEHOLD HEADS, CLASSIFIED BY SEX, AGE, MARITAL CONDITION, AND PARENTAL STATUS

| Mating and Parental Status | Male | | | | | | Female | | | | | |
|---|---|---|---|---|---|---|---|---|---|---|---|---|
| | -24 | -39 | -54 | -69 | 70+ | Total | -24 | -39 | -54 | -69 | 70+ | Total |
| **1. Childless single persons** | | | | | | | | | | | | |
| a. Mating now n/k* | 3 | 2 | 2 | 0 | 0 | 7 | 0 | 0 | 0 | 0 | 0 | 0 |
| b. Not mating now | 1 | 1 | 1 | 0 | 0 | 3 | 1 | 3 | 2 | 4 | 0 | 10 |
| c. Mating now | 3 | 3 | 1 | 0 | 0 | 7 | 1 | 4 | 1 | 0 | 0 | 6 |
| Total childless single persons | 7 | 6 | 4 | 0 | 0 | 17 | 2 | 7 | 3 | 4 | 0 | 16 |
| **2. Single persons, parental status n/k** | | | | | | | | | | | | |
| a. Mating now n/k | 6 | 9 | 15 | 14 | 7 | 51 | 0 | 4 | 12 | 7 | 11 | 34 |
| b. Not mating now | 0 | 0 | 1 | 0 | 0 | 1 | 0 | 0 | 0 | 0 | 0 | 0 |
| c. Mating now | 0 | 2 | 2 | 0 | 1 | 5 | 0 | 0 | 0 | 0 | 0 | 0 |
| Total single persons, parental status n/k | 6 | 11 | 18 | 14 | 8 | 57 | 0 | 4 | 12 | 7 | 11 | 34 |
| **3. Single parents** | | | | | | | | | | | | |
| a. Mating now n/k | 0 | 8 | 19 | 5 | 0 | 32 | 0 | 10 | 18 | 2 | 0 | 30 |
| b. Not mating now | 0 | 0 | 1 | 5 | 2 | 8 | 0 | 4 | 25 | 35 | 14 | 78 |
| c. Mating now | 2 | 26 | 11 | 2 | 0 | 41 | 4 | 26 | 8 | 0 | 0 | 38 |
| Total single parents | 2 | 34 | 31 | 12 | 2 | 81 | 4 | 40 | 51 | 37 | 14 | 146 |
| **4. Consensually wed** | | | | | | | | | | | | |
| a. In 1955 | 13 | 97 | 66 | 18 | 3 | 197 | 0 | 10 | 6 | 2 | 0 | 18 |
| b. Separated, childless | 0 | 0 | 1 | 0 | 0 | 1 | 0 | 0 | 1 | 0 | 1 | 2 |
| c. Separated, with children | 0 | 0 | 4 | 1 | 0 | 5 | 0 | 1 | 3 | 0 | 0 | 4 |
| d. Widowed, single | 0 | 0 | 2 | 3 | 0 | 5 | 0 | 0 | 3 | 4 | 2 | 9 |
| Total consensually wed | 13 | 97 | 73 | 22 | 3 | 208 | 0 | 11 | 13 | 6 | 3 | 33 |
| **5. Married persons** | | | | | | | | | | | | |
| a. Spouse present | 1 | 77 | 137 | 74 | 20 | 309 | 0 | 0 | 3 | 2 | 0 | 5 |
| b. Spouse absent | 0 | 3 | 6 | 1 | 0 | 10 | 1 | 7 | 4 | 3 | 0 | 15 |
| c. Separated, single | 0 | 1 | 1 | 2 | 0 | 4 | 0 | 1 | 1 | 1 | 0 | 3 |
| d. Separated, not single | 0 | 0 | 1 | 0 | 0 | 1 | 0 | 0 | 0 | 0 | 0 | 0 |
| Total married persons | 1 | 81 | 145 | 77 | 20 | 324 | 1 | 8 | 8 | 6 | 0 | 23 |
| **6. Widowed persons** | | | | | | | | | | | | |
| a. Widowed, single | 0 | 0 | 4 | 6 | 5 | 15 | 1 | 4 | 18 | 14 | 13 | 50 |
| b. Widowed, not single | 0 | 0 | 0 | 0 | 0 | 0 | 0 | 1 | 2 | 0 | 0 | 3 |
| Total widowed persons | 0 | 0 | 4 | 6 | 5 | 15 | 1 | 5 | 20 | 14 | 13 | 53 |
| GRAND TOTAL | 29 | 229 | 275 | 131 | 38 | 702 | 8 | 75 | 107 | 74 | 41 | 305 |

*n/k = Not known.

## TABLE 10

### POPULATION OF THE SAMPLE HOUSEHOLDS, CLASSIFIED BY RELATIONSHIP TO THE HOUSEHOLD HEAD AND SEX OF HEAD

| Categories of Kin | Male Head Number | Male Head Per cent | Female Head Number | Female Head Per cent | Total Number | Total Per cent |
|---|---|---|---|---|---|---|
| 1. Spouses and mates | 507 | 21.3 | 24 | 2.78 | 531 | 16.05 |
| 2. HH's* sons | 643 | 26.7 | 212 | 23.9 | 855 | 25.7 |
| 3. HH's daughters | 587 | 24.5 | 205 | 23.5 | 792 | 24.3 |
| HH's children | 1,230 | 51.2 | 417 | 47.4 | 1,647 | 50.0 |
| 4. HH's sons' sons | 26 | 1.08 | 31 | 3.43 | 57 | 1.73 |
| 5. HH's sons' daughters | 20 | 0.82 | 22 | 2.47 | 42 | 1.28 |
| 6. HH's daughters' sons | 64 | 2.55 | 91 | 10.6 | 155 | 4.7 |
| 7. HH's daughters' daughters | 76 | 3.1 | 96 | 10.9 | 172 | 5.22 |
| HH's grandchildren | 186 | 7.75 | 240 | 27.4 | 426 | 12.93 |
| 8. HH's sons' grandchildren | 6 | 0.24 | 8 | 0.9 | 14 | 0.44 |
| 9. HH's daughters' grandchildren | 4 | 0.16 | 31 | 2.48 | 35 | 1.05 |
| HH's great-grandchildren | 10 | 0.40 | 39 | 3.38 | 49 | 1.49 |
| 10. HH's mates' sons by others | 56 | 2.34 | 2 | 0.22 | 58 | 1.71 |
| 11. HH's mates' daughters by others | 52 | 2.16 | 2 | 0.22 | 54 | 1.64 |
| 12. HH's mates' sons' children | 13 | 0.64 | 0 | 0.0 | 13 | 0.49 |
| 13. HH's mates' daughters' children | 28 | 1.16 | 1 | 0.11 | 29 | 0.88 |
| 14. HH's mates' sons' grandchildren | 2 | 0.08 | 0 | 0.0 | 2 | 0.04 |
| 15. HH's mates' daughters' grandchildren | 1 | 0.04 | 0 | 0.0 | 1 | 0.02 |
| Issue of HH's mates by others | 152 | 6.42 | 5 | 0.55 | 157 | 4.78 |
| 16. HH's full brothers | 12 | 0.48 | 11 | 1.23 | 23 | 0.69 |
| 17. HH's full sisters | 7 | 0.28 | 11 | 1.23 | 18 | 0.67 |
| 18. HH's maternal half siblings | 8 | 0.32 | 3 | 0.33 | 11 | 0.34 |
| 19. HH's paternal half siblings | 1 | 0.04 | 0 | 0.0 | 1 | 0.02 |
| 20. HH's full siblings' children and grandchildren | 32 | 1.33 | 48 | 5.4 | 80 | 2.43 |
| 21. HH's maternal half siblings' children and grandchildren | 9 | 0.36 | 6 | 0.67 | 15 | 0.45 |
| 22. HH's paternal half siblings' children and grandchildren | 1 | 0.04 | 3 | 0.33 | 4 | 0.12 |
| HH's siblings and their issue | 70 | 2.76 | 82 | 9.19 | 152 | 4.72 |

*HH = Household head.

## TABLE 10 (continued)

### POPULATION OF THE SAMPLE HOUSEHOLDS, CLASSIFIED BY RELATIONSHIP TO THE HOUSEHOLD HEAD AND SEX OF HEAD

| Categories of Kin | Male Head Number | Male Head Per cent | Female Head Number | Female Head Per cent | Total Number | Total Per cent |
|---|---|---|---|---|---|---|
| 23. HH's mother | 19 | 0.77 | 9 | 1.01 | 28 | 0.86 |
| 24. HH's mother's mother | 2 | 0.08 | 0 | 0.0 | 2 | 0.04 |
| 25. HH's other matrilateral kin | 8 | 0.36 | 4 | 0.44 | 12 | 0.38 |
| HH's mother and maternal kin | 29 | 1.21 | 13 | 1.45 | 42 | 1.28 |
| 26. HH's father | 4 | 0.16 | 4 | 0.45 | 8 | 0.24 |
| 27. HH's father's mother | 1 | 0.04 | 0 | 0.0 | 1 | 0.03 |
| 28. HH's other patrilateral kin | 6 | 0.24 | 4 | 0.45 | 10 | 0.3 |
| HH's father and patrilateral kin | 11 | 0.44 | 8 | 0.9 | 19 | 0.57 |
| 29. HH's mates' full siblings | 9 | 0.36 | 0 | 0.0 | 9 | 0.27 |
| 30. HH's mates' full siblings' children and grandchildren | 50 | 2.07 | 2 | 0.22 | 52 | 1.61 |
| 31. HH's mates' maternal half siblings | 4 | 0.16 | 0 | 0.0 | 4 | 0.12 |
| 32. HH's mates' maternal half siblings' children | 7 | 0.28 | 0 | 0.0 | 7 | 0.21 |
| 33. HH's mates' mothers | 9 | 0.36 | 0 | 0.0 | 9 | 0.27 |
| 34. HH's mates' matrilateral kin | 6 | 0.24 | 0 | 0.0 | 6 | 0.18 |
| 35. HH's mates' patrilateral kin | 2 | 0.08 | 0 | 0.0 | 2 | 0.04 |
| Consanguineal kin of HH's mates | 87 | 3.55 | 2 | 0.22 | 89 | 2.7 |
| 36. HH's children's mates or spouses | 10 | 0.4 | 15 | 1.7 | 25 | 0.76 |
| 37. HH's grandchildren's mates or spouses | 1 | 0.04 | 2 | 0.22 | 3 | 0.09 |
| 38. Mates of issue or kin of HH's mate | 2 | 0.08 | 0 | 0.0 | 2 | 0.06 |
| 39. Mates or spouses of HH's kin | 2 | 0.08 | 1 | 0.11 | 3 | 0.09 |
| 40. Kin of 36 to 39 | 2 | 0.08 | 4 | 0.44 | 6 | 0.18 |
| Junior affines | 17 | 0.68 | 22 | 2.47 | 39 | 1.18 |
| 41. HH's kin, relationship not known | 1 | 0.04 | 0 | 0.0 | 1 | 0.02 |
| 42. Employees and their children | 32 | 1.33 | 4 | 0.45 | 36 | 1.07 |
| 43. Unrelated persons and their children | 32 | 1.33 | 9 | 1.01 | 41 | 1.25 |
| 44. Adopted persons and their children | 36 | 1.51 | 24 | 2.81 | 60 | 1.9 |
| 45. Boarders | 2 | 0.08 | 0 | 0.0 | 2 | 0.06 |
| Miscellaneous residents | 103 | 4.29 | 37 | 4.26 | 140 | 4.3 |
| TOTAL | 2,402 | 100.0 | 889 | 100.0 | 3,291 | 100.0 |

# TABLE 11

RESIDENT COLLATERALS OF HOUSEHOLD PRINCIPALS, CLASSIFIED BY SEX OF PRINCIPAL AND HOUSEHOLD HEAD, BY BIRTH STATUS, AND BY KINSHIP TO THE LINKED PRINCIPAL

| Kinship Category | Households with Male Head | | | | | | | | Households with Female Head | | | | Total Kin of: | |
| --- | --- | --- | --- | --- | --- | --- | --- | --- | --- | --- | --- | --- | --- | --- |
| | Principal Male HH* | | | | Principal HH's Mate | | | | Principal HH | | | | All Principals | Female Principals |
| | L* | U* | N/K* | All | L | U | N/K | All | L | U | N/K | All | | |
| Full siblings | 0 | 3 | 16 | 19 | 0 | 0 | 9 | 9 | 0 | 1 | 21 | 22 | 50 | 31 |
| Issue of full siblings | 0 | 19 | 14 | 33 | 0 | 32 | 18 | 50 | 0 | 27 | 21 | 48 | 131 | 58 |
| Maternal half siblings | 0 | 5 | 3 | 8 | 0 | 1 | 3 | 4 | 0 | 3 | 0 | 3 | 15 | 7 |
| Issue of maternal half siblings | 0 | 6 | 3 | 9 | 0 | 6 | 1 | 7 | 0 | 4 | 2 | 6 | 22 | 13 |
| Paternal half siblings | 0 | 0 | 1 | 1 | 0 | 0 | 0 | 0 | 0 | 0 | 0 | 0 | 1 | 0 |
| Issue of paternal half siblings | 0 | 0 | 1 | 1 | 0 | 0 | 0 | 0 | 0 | 3 | 0 | 3 | 4 | 3 |
| Other patrilateral kin | 0 | 1 | 4 | 5 | 0 | 0 | 2 | 2 | 0 | 0 | 3 | 3 | 10 | 5 |
| Other matrilateral kin | 0 | 2 | 6 | 8 | 0 | 4 | 0 | 4 | 0 | 2 | 0 | 2 | 14 | 6 |
| TOTAL | 0 | 36 | 48 | 84 | 0 | 43 | 33 | 76 | 0 | 40 | 47 | 87 | 247 | 164 |

*HH = Household head; L = Lawful, i.e., legitimate; U = Unlawful, i.e., illegitimate; N/K = Birth status not known.

# TABLE 12

RESIDENT COLLATERALS OF HOUSEHOLD PRINCIPAL, CLASSIFIED BY SEX, BIRTH STATUS, GENERATION, SEX OF PARENT THROUGH WHOM KINSHIP IS TRACED, AND SEX OF HOUSEHOLD HEAD AND LINKED PRINCIPAL

| Generation | Sex of Linking Parent | Households with Male Head | | | | | | | | Households with Mate of Male Head | | | | | | | | Households with Female Head | | | | | | | | Total | | | | | | | | | Total |
|---|---|---|---|---|---|---|---|---|---|---|---|---|---|---|---|---|---|---|---|---|---|---|---|---|---|---|---|---|---|---|---|---|---|---|
| | | L* | | U* | | N/K* | | All | | L | | U | | N/K | | All | | L | | U | | N/K | | All | | L | | U | | N/K | | All | | |
| | | M | F | M | F | M | F | M | F | M | F | M | F | M | F | M | F | M | F | M | F | M | F | M | F | M | F | M | F | M | F | M | F | |
| +1 | Male | 0 | 0 | 0 | 0 | 0 | 0 | 0 | 0 | 0 | 0 | 0 | 0 | 0 | 0 | 0 | 0 | 0 | 0 | 0 | 0 | 0 | 0 | 0 | 0 | 0 | 0 | 0 | 0 | 0 | 0 | 0 | 0 | 0 |
| | Female | 0 | 0 | 0 | 0 | 0 | 0 | 0 | 0 | 0 | 0 | 0 | 0 | 0 | 0 | 0 | 0 | 0 | 0 | 0 | 0 | 0 | 0 | 0 | 0 | 0 | 0 | 0 | 0 | 0 | 0 | 0 | 0 | 0 |
| | Total | 0 | 0 | 0 | 0 | 0 | 0 | 0 | 0 | 0 | 0 | 0 | 0 | 0 | 0 | 0 | 0 | 0 | 0 | 0 | 0 | 0 | 0 | 0 | 0 | 0 | 0 | 0 | 0 | 0 | 0 | 0 | 0 | 0 |
| 0 | Male | 0 | 0 | 0 | 1 | 1 | 1 | 1 | 2 | 0 | 0 | 0 | 0 | 1 | 0 | 1 | 0 | 0 | 0 | 0 | 0 | 0 | 1 | 0 | 1 | 0 | 0 | 0 | 1 | 2 | 2 | 2 | 3 | 5 |
| | Female | 0 | 0 | 5 | 1 | 6 | 2 | 11 | 3 | 0 | 0 | 0 | 2 | 0 | 3 | 0 | 5 | 0 | 0 | 3 | 1 | 1 | 1 | 4 | 2 | 0 | 0 | 8 | 4 | 7 | 6 | 15 | 10 | 25 |
| | Total | 0 | 0 | 5 | 2 | 7 | 3 | 12 | 5 | 0 | 0 | 0 | 2 | 1 | 3 | 1 | 5 | 0 | 0 | 3 | 1 | 1 | 2 | 4 | 3 | 0 | 0 | 8 | 5 | 9 | 8 | 17 | 13 | 30 |
| −1 | Male | 0 | 0 | 4 | 5 | 5 | 2 | 9 | 7 | 0 | 0 | 5 | 10 | 4 | 5 | 9 | 15 | 0 | 0 | 7 | 3 | 3 | 5 | 10 | 8 | 0 | 0 | 16 | 18 | 12 | 12 | 28 | 30 | 58 |
| | Female | 0 | 0 | 4 | 8 | 3 | 1 | 7 | 9 | 0 | 0 | 10 | 7 | 4 | 4 | 14 | 11 | 0 | 0 | 0 | 10 | 7 | 2 | 7 | 12 | 0 | 0 | 14 | 25 | 14 | 7 | 28 | 32 | 60 |
| | Total | 0 | 0 | 8 | 13 | 8 | 3 | 16 | 16 | 0 | 0 | 15 | 17 | 8 | 9 | 23 | 26 | 0 | 0 | 7 | 13 | 10 | 7 | 17 | 20 | 0 | 0 | 30 | 43 | 26 | 19 | 56 | 62 | 118 |
| −2 | Male | 0 | 0 | 0 | 0 | 3 | 0 | 3 | 0 | 0 | 0 | 3 | 0 | 0 | 0 | 3 | 0 | 0 | 0 | 0 | 1 | 0 | 1 | 0 | 2 | 0 | 0 | 3 | 1 | 3 | 1 | 6 | 2 | 8 |
| | Female | 0 | 0 | 3 | 1 | 5 | 1 | 8 | 2 | 0 | 0 | 7 | 4 | 3 | 3 | 10 | 7 | 0 | 0 | 3 | 2 | 1 | 1 | 4 | 3 | 0 | 0 | 13 | 7 | 9 | 5 | 22 | 12 | 34 |
| | Total | 0 | 0 | 3 | 1 | 8 | 1 | 11 | 2 | 0 | 0 | 10 | 4 | 3 | 3 | 13 | 7 | 0 | 0 | 3 | 3 | 1 | 2 | 4 | 5 | 0 | 0 | 16 | 8 | 12 | 6 | 28 | 14 | 42 |
| −3 | Male | 0 | 0 | 2 | 0 | 0 | 0 | 2 | 0 | 0 | 0 | 0 | 0 | 0 | 0 | 0 | 0 | 0 | 0 | 0 | 0 | 0 | 0 | 0 | 0 | 0 | 0 | 2 | 0 | 0 | 0 | 2 | 0 | 2 |
| | Female | 0 | 0 | 0 | 0 | 0 | 0 | 0 | 0 | 0 | 0 | 3 | 0 | 0 | 0 | 3 | 0 | 0 | 0 | 0 | 0 | 0 | 0 | 0 | 0 | 0 | 0 | 3 | 0 | 0 | 0 | 3 | 0 | 3 |
| | Total | 0 | 0 | 2 | 0 | 0 | 0 | 2 | 0 | 0 | 0 | 3 | 0 | 0 | 0 | 3 | 0 | 0 | 0 | 0 | 0 | 0 | 0 | 0 | 0 | 0 | 0 | 5 | 0 | 0 | 0 | 5 | 0 | 5 |
| GRAND TOTAL | | 0 | 0 | 18 | 16 | 23 | 7 | 41 | 23 | 0 | 0 | 21 | 22 | 10 | 13 | 31 | 35 | 0 | 0 | 20 | 18 | 14 | 13 | 34 | 31 | 0 | 0 | 59 | 56 | 47 | 33 | 106 | 89 | 195 |

*L = Lawful, i.e., legitimate; U = Unlawful, i.e., illegitimate; N/K = Birth status not known; M = Male; F = Female.

## TABLE 13

RESIDENT LINEAL ISSUE OF THE HOUSEHOLD HEAD, CLASSIFIED BY SEX, BIRTH STATUS, GENERATION, SEX OF PARENT THROUGH WHOM DESCENT IS TRACED, AND SEX OF THE HOUSEHOLD HEAD

| Sex and Birth Status | Households with Male Head | | | | Households with Female Head | | | | Total | | | |
|---|---|---|---|---|---|---|---|---|---|---|---|---|
| | Own Issue | Sons' Issue** | Daughters' Issue† | Total | Own Issue‡ | Sons' Issue | Daughters' Issue†† | Total | Own Issue | Sons' Issue | Daughters' Issue | Total |
| Males L* | 402 | 8 | 3 | 413 | 62 | 0 | 12 | 74 | 464 | 8 | 15 | 487 |
| Males U* | 197 | 15 | 57 | 269 | 114 | 29 | 93 | 236 | 311 | 44 | 150 | 505 |
| Males N/K* | 44 | 4 | 5 | 53 | 36 | 7 | 9 | 52 | 80 | 11 | 14 | 105 |
| All males | 643 | 27 | 65 | 735 | 212 | 36 | 114 | 362 | 855 | 63 | 179 | 1,097 |
| Females L | 392 | 9 | 4 | 405 | 36 | 0 | 11 | 47 | 428 | 9 | 15 | 452 |
| Females U | 168 | 13 | 69 | 250 | 126 | 16 | 86 | 228 | 294 | 29 | 155 | 478 |
| Females N/K | 27 | 2 | 5 | 34 | 43 | 9 | 7 | 59 | 70 | 11 | 12 | 93 |
| All females | 587 | 24 | 78 | 689 | 205 | 25 | 104 | 334 | 792 | 49 | 182 | 1,023 |
| Total L | 794 | 17 | 7 | 818 | 98 | 0 | 23 | 121 | 892 | 17 | 30 | 939 |
| Total U | 365 | 28 | 126 | 519 | 240 | 45 | 179 | 464 | 605 | 73 | 305 | 983 |
| Total N/K | 71 | 6 | 10 | 87 | 79 | 16 | 16 | 111 | 150 | 22 | 26 | 198 |
| GRAND TOTAL | 1,230 | 51 | 143 | 1,424 | 417 | 61 | 218 | 696 | 1,647 | 112 | 361 | 2,120 |

*L = Lawful, i.e., legitimate; U = Unlawful, i.e., illegitimate; N/K = Birth status not known.

**Includes 2 unlawful sons, and 3 unlawful daughters of household head's lawful son's N/K daughter.

†Includes 1 unlawful son of household head's lawful daughter's unlawful daughter; also 2 unlawful sons and 1 unlawful daughter of household head's lawful daughter's lawful daughter.

‡Includes 31 great-grandchildren descended from household head's daughter (3 LMs, 2 LFs, 19 UMs, 6 UFs, and 1 N/K male).

††Includes 8 great-grandchildren, offspring of household head's sons (4 UMs, 3 UFs, 1 N/K M).

## TABLE 14

DISTRIBUTION OF CHILDREN WITHIN THE SAMPLE HOUSEHOLDS, CLASSIFIED BY SEX OF HEAD, WITH SPECIAL REFERENCE TO THE PRESENCE OF EITHER PARENT IN THE HOUSEHOLD, AND TO THE AGE AND BIRTH STATUS OF THE CHILDREN OF EITHER SEX

| Age | Households with Male Head | | | | | | | Households with Female Head | | | | | | | Total | | | | | | |
|---|---|---|---|---|---|---|---|---|---|---|---|---|---|---|---|---|---|---|---|---|---|
| | LS* | LD* | US* | UD* | N/KS* | N/KD* | Total | LS | LD | US | UD | N/KS | N/KD | Total | LS | LD | US | UD | N/KS | N/KD | Total |
| **a. Both parents present** | | | | | | | | | | | | | | | | | | | | | |
| 0-- 4 | 94 | 83 | 74 | 70 | 0 | 0 | 321 | 6 | 2 | 10 | 12 | 0 | 0 | 30 | 100 | 85 | 84 | 82 | 0 | 0 | 351 |
| 5--14 | 201 | 200 | 60 | 50 | 0 | 0 | 511 | 4 | 4 | 8 | 7 | 0 | 0 | 23 | 205 | 204 | 68 | 57 | 0 | 0 | 534 |
| 15--24 | 93 | 96 | 15 | 14 | 0 | 0 | 218 | 1 | 3 | 0 | 3 | 0 | 0 | 7 | 94 | 99 | 15 | 17 | 0 | 0 | 225 |
| 25--39 | 24 | 10 | 0 | 3 | 0 | 0 | 37 | 0 | 0 | 2 | 0 | 0 | 0 | 2 | 24 | 10 | 2 | 3 | 0 | 0 | 39 |
| 40 + | 0 | 3 | 0 | 0 | 0 | 0 | 3 | 0 | 0 | 0 | 0 | 0 | 0 | 0 | 0 | 3 | 0 | 0 | 0 | 0 | 3 |
| Total | 412 | 392 | 149 | 137 | 0 | 0 | 1,090 | 11 | 9 | 20 | 22 | 0 | 0 | 62 | 423 | 401 | 169 | 159 | 0 | 0 | 1,152 |
| **b. Both parents absent** | | | | | | | | | | | | | | | | | | | | | |
| 0-- 4 | 1 | 1 | 14 | 18 | 9 | 5 | 48 | 0 | 0 | 18 | 9 | 2 | 2 | 31 | 1 | 1 | 32 | 27 | 11 | 7 | 79 |
| 5--14 | 1 | 0 | 49 | 44 | 30 | 27 | 151 | 0 | 0 | 42 | 32 | 14 | 28 | 116 | 1 | 0 | 91 | 76 | 44 | 55 | 267 |
| 15--24 | 0 | 0 | 19 | 20 | 39 | 30 | 108 | 0 | 0 | 18 | 15 | 20 | 18 | 71 | 0 | 0 | 37 | 35 | 59 | 48 | 179 |
| 25--39 | 0 | 0 | 11 | 6 | 25 | 13 | 55 | 0 | 0 | 8 | 6 | 9 | 7 | 30 | 0 | 0 | 19 | 12 | 34 | 20 | 85 |
| 40 + | 0 | 0 | 0 | 0 | 5 | 6 | 11 | 0 | 0 | 3 | 1 | 4 | 4 | 13 | 0 | 0 | 3 | 1 | 9 | 10 | 24 |
| Total | 2 | 1 | 93 | 88 | 108 | 81 | 373 | 2 | 1 | 89 | 63 | 49 | 59 | 261 | 3 | 1 | 182 | 151 | 157 | 140 | 634 |
| **c. Mothers only present** | | | | | | | | | | | | | | | | | | | | | |
| 0-- 4 | 1 | 2 | 42 | 37 | 0 | 0 | 82 | 7 | 8 | 62 | 62 | 0 | 0 | 139 | 8 | 10 | 104 | 99 | 0 | 0 | 221 |
| 5--14 | 0 | 1 | 41 | 45 | 0 | 1 | 88 | 18 | 8 | 51 | 59 | 1 | 0 | 137 | 18 | 9 | 92 | 104 | 1 | 1 | 225 |
| 15--24 | 1 | 1 | 15 | 19 | 0 | 0 | 36 | 17 | 7 | 41 | 41 | 2 | 0 | 108 | 18 | 8 | 56 | 60 | 2 | 0 | 144 |
| 25--39 | 2 | 0 | 4 | 7 | 0 | 0 | 13 | 5 | 8 | 15 | 24 | 1 | 0 | 53 | 7 | 8 | 19 | 31 | 1 | 0 | 66 |
| 40 + | 0 | 0 | 0 | 1 | 0 | 0 | 1 | 1 | 1 | 4 | 7 | 0 | 0 | 13 | 1 | 1 | 4 | 8 | 0 | 0 | 14 |
| Total | 4 | 4 | 102 | 109 | 0 | 1 | 220 | 48 | 32 | 173 | 193 | 4 | 0 | 450 | 52 | 36 | 275 | 302 | 4 | 1 | 670 |
| **d. Fathers only present** | | | | | | | | | | | | | | | | | | | | | |
| 0-- 4 | 0 | 1 | 11 | 3 | 1 | 2 | 18 | 0 | 0 | 0 | 0 | 0 | 0 | 0 | 0 | 1 | 11 | 3 | 1 | 2 | 18 |
| 5--14 | 6 | 4 | 29 | 27 | 5 | 4 | 75 | 0 | 0 | 5 | 6 | 0 | 0 | 11 | 6 | 4 | 34 | 33 | 5 | 4 | 86 |
| 15--24 | 8 | 5 | 17 | 10 | 1 | 0 | 41 | 0 | 0 | 0 | 0 | 0 | 0 | 0 | 8 | 5 | 17 | 10 | 1 | 0 | 41 |
| 25--39 | 2 | 0 | 6 | 3 | 0 | 0 | 11 | 0 | 0 | 0 | 0 | 0 | 0 | 0 | 2 | 0 | 6 | 3 | 0 | 0 | 11 |
| 40 + | 0 | 0 | 1 | 1 | 0 | 0 | 2 | 0 | 0 | 0 | 0 | 0 | 0 | 0 | 0 | 0 | 1 | 1 | 0 | 0 | 2 |
| Total | 16 | 10 | 64 | 44 | 7 | 6 | 147 | 0 | 0 | 5 | 6 | 0 | 0 | 11 | 16 | 10 | 69 | 50 | 7 | 6 | 158 |

TABLE 14 (continued)

DISTRIBUTION OF CHILDREN WITHIN THE SAMPLE HOUSEHOLDS, CLASSIFIED BY SEX OF HEAD, WITH SPECIAL REFERENCE TO THE PRESENCE OF EITHER PARENT IN THE HOUSEHOLD, AND TO THE AGE AND BIRTH STATUS OF THE CHILDREN OF EITHER SEX

| Age | Households with Male Head | | | | | | | Households with Female Head | | | | | | | Total | | | | | | |
|---|---|---|---|---|---|---|---|---|---|---|---|---|---|---|---|---|---|---|---|---|---|
| | LS* | LD* | US* | UD* | N/KS* | N/KD* | Total | LS | LD | US | UD | N/KS | N/KD | Total | LS | LD | US | UD | N/KS | N/KD | Total |
| **e. With mothers, fathers dead** | | | | | | | | | | | | | | | | | | | | | |
| 0- 4 | 0 | 2 | 0 | 0 | 0 | 0 | 2 | 5 | 4 | 0 | 0 | 0 | 0 | 9 | 5 | 6 | 0 | 0 | 0 | 0 | 11 |
| 5-14 | 2 | 2 | 0 | 0 | 0 | 0 | 4 | 10 | 7 | 1 | 0 | 1 | 0 | 19 | 12 | 9 | 1 | 0 | 1 | 0 | 23 |
| 15-24 | 2 | 0 | 0 | 0 | 0 | 0 | 2 | 6 | 4 | 0 | 0 | 3 | 1 | 14 | 8 | 4 | 0 | 0 | 3 | 1 | 16 |
| 25-39 | 1 | 0 | 0 | 0 | 0 | 0 | 1 | 8 | 1 | 0 | 2 | 0 | 0 | 11 | 9 | 1 | 0 | 2 | 0 | 0 | 12 |
| 40 + | 0 | 0 | 0 | 0 | 0 | 0 | 0 | 0 | 1 | 0 | 0 | 0 | 0 | 1 | 0 | 1 | 0 | 0 | 0 | 0 | 1 |
| Total | 5 | 4 | 0 | 0 | 0 | 0 | 9 | 29 | 17 | 1 | 2 | 4 | 1 | 54 | 34 | 21 | 1 | 2 | 4 | 1 | 63 |
| **f. With fathers, mothers dead** | | | | | | | | | | | | | | | | | | | | | |
| 0- 4 | 1 | 1 | 0 | 0 | 0 | 0 | 2 | | | | | | | | 1 | 1 | 0 | 0 | 0 | 0 | 2 |
| 5-14 | 1 | 6 | 1 | 0 | 0 | 0 | 8 | | | | | | | | 1 | 6 | 1 | 0 | 0 | 0 | 8 |
| 15-24 | 3 | 0 | 0 | 0 | 0 | 0 | 3 | | | | | | | | 3 | 0 | 0 | 0 | 0 | 0 | 3 |
| 25-39 | 1 | 0 | 0 | 0 | 0 | 0 | 1 | | | | | | | | 1 | 0 | 0 | 0 | 0 | 0 | 1 |
| 40 + | 0 | 0 | 0 | 0 | 0 | 0 | 0 | | | | | | | | 0 | 0 | 0 | 0 | 0 | 0 | 0 |
| Total | 6 | 7 | 1 | 0 | 0 | 0 | 14 | | | | | | | | 6 | 7 | 1 | 0 | 0 | 0 | 14 |
| **Totals by sex of household head** | | | | | | | | | | | | | | | | | | | | | |
| 0- 4 | 97 | 90 | 141 | 128 | 10 | 7 | 473 | 18 | 14 | 90 | 83 | 2 | 2 | 209 | 115 | 104 | 231 | 211 | 12 | 9 | 682 |
| 5-14 | 211 | 213 | 180 | 166 | 35 | 32 | 837 | 32 | 19 | 107 | 104 | 16 | 28 | 306 | 243 | 232 | 287 | 270 | 51 | 60 | 1,143 |
| 15-24 | 107 | 102 | 66 | 63 | 40 | 30 | 408 | 24 | 14 | 59 | 59 | 25 | 19 | 200 | 131 | 116 | 125 | 122 | 65 | 49 | 608 |
| 25-39 | 30 | 10 | 21 | 19 | 25 | 13 | 118 | 13 | 9 | 25 | 32 | 10 | 7 | 96 | 43 | 19 | 46 | 51 | 35 | 20 | 214 |
| 40 + | 0 | 3 | 1 | 2 | 5 | 6 | 17 | 2 | 2 | 7 | 8 | 4 | 4 | 27 | 2 | 5 | 8 | 10 | 9 | 10 | 44 |
| TOTAL | 445 | 418 | 409 | 378 | 115 | 88 | 1,853 | 89 | 58 | 288 | 286 | 57 | 60 | 838 | 534 | 476 | 697 | 664 | 172 | 148 | 2,691 |

*LS = Lawful son; LD = Lawful daughter; US = Unlawful son; UD = Unlawful daughter; N/KS = Son, birth status not known; N/KD = Daughter, birth status not known.

## TABLE 15

DEPENDENTS BELOW THE AGE OF 24 WHO LIVE APART FROM BOTH PARENTS IN THE SAMPLE HOUSEHOLDS, CLASSIFIED BY SEX, BIRTH STATUS, AND RELATION TO THE HOUSEHOLD PRINCIPALS WHO ARE THEIR KIN

### Matrilateral Kin

| Matrilateral Kin | Male L* | Male U* | Male N/K* | Female L | Female U | Female N/K | All |
|---|---|---|---|---|---|---|---|
| 1. Mother's mother | 0 | 43 | 1 | 0 | 31 | 10 | 85 |
| 2. M's F and M | 1 | 17 | 5 | 0 | 21 | 7 | 51 |
| 3. M's father | 0 | 7 | 1 | 0 | 8 | 0 | 16 |
| 4. M's sister | 0 | 6 | 3 | 0 | 8 | 3 | 20 |
| 5. M's brother | 0 | 5 | 0 | 0 | 4 | 1 | 10 |
| 6. M's M's sister | 0 | 0 | 3 | 0 | 0 | 3 | 6 |
| 7. M's F's sister | 0 | 0 | 0 | 0 | 4 | 0 | 4 |
| 8. M's F's brother | 0 | 2 | 1 | 0 | 0 | 1 | 4 |
| 9. M's F's M | 0 | 0 | 2 | 0 | 1 | 0 | 3 |
| 10. M's F's F | 0 | 0 | 0 | 0 | 3 | 0 | 3 |
| 11. M's M's M | 0 | 0 | 0 | 0 | 1 | 0 | 1 |
| 12. M's M's brother | 0 | 1 | 0 | 0 | 3 | 0 | 4 |
| 13. M's M and M's M's F and M | 0 | 2 | 0 | 0 | 3 | 0 | 5 |
| 14. M's mat. half brother | 0 | 4 | 0 | 0 | 1 | 0 | 5 |
| 15. M's mat. half sister | 0 | 0 | 1 | 0 | 1 | 1 | 3 |
| 16. M and M's brother | 0 | 0 | 0 | 0 | 3 | 0 | 3 |
| 17. M's M and M's M's M | 0 | 1 | 0 | 0 | 1 | 0 | 2 |
| 18. M's M's brother and M's M's sister | 0 | 0 | 0 | 0 | 1 | 0 | 1 |
| 19. M and M's B and M's S | 0 | 1 | 0 | 0 | 1 | 0 | 2 |
| 20. M's M's M and others | 0 | 4 | 3 | 0 | 0 | 0 | 7 |
| 21. M's F and M's F's sister | 0 | 1 | 0 | 0 | 1 | 0 | 2 |
| 22. M's F's brother's daughter's D | 0 | 0 | 0 | 0 | 1 | 0 | 1 |
| 23. M's sister's D | 0 | 0 | 0 | 0 | 0 | 1 | 1 |
| 24. M's M and M's sister | 0 | 3 | 0 | 0 | 6 | 0 | 9 |
| 25. M's brother's son | 0 | 0 | 0 | 0 | 0 | 1 | 1 |
| 26. M's sister's D | 0 | 0 | 0 | 0 | 2 | 0 | 2 |
| 27. M's brother's daughter's D | 0 | 0 | 0 | 0 | 1 | 0 | 1 |
| 28. M's M's sister's daughter's son | 0 | 2 | 0 | 0 | 0 | 0 | 2 |
| 29. M's M and mat. half brother | 0 | 1 | 0 | 0 | 0 | 0 | 1 |
| 30. M's M's brother's spouse | 0 | 0 | 1 | 0 | 0 | 0 | 1 |

### Patrilateral Kin

| Patrilateral Kin | Male L | Male U | Male N/K | Female L | Female U | Female N/K | All |
|---|---|---|---|---|---|---|---|
| 1. Father's M and F | 1 | 6 | 0 | 1 | 4 | 0 | 12 |
| 2. F's M | 0 | 20 | 0 | 0 | 15 | 0 | 35 |
| 3. F's F | 1 | 4 | 1 | 0 | 5 | 0 | 11 |
| 4. F's sister | 0 | 10 | 0 | 0 | 13 | 2 | 25 |
| 5. F's brother | 0 | 4 | 0 | 0 | 3 | 0 | 7 |
| 6. F's brother and sister | 0 | 0 | 0 | 0 | 1 | 0 | 1 |
| 7. F's pat. half brother | 0 | 0 | 0 | 0 | 1 | 0 | 1 |
| 8. F's pat. half sister | 0 | 1 | 0 | 0 | 2 | 0 | 3 |
| 9. F's mat. half brother | 0 | 0 | 0 | 0 | 2 | 1 | 3 |
| 10. F's mat. half sister | 0 | 2 | 0 | 0 | 1 | 0 | 3 |
| 11. F's M's M | 0 | 0 | 0 | 0 | 2 | 1 | 3 |
| 12. F's M's brother | 0 | 1 | 0 | 0 | 0 | 0 | 1 |
| 13. F's M's mat. half brother | 0 | 1 | 0 | 0 | 0 | 0 | 1 |
| 14. F's sister and F's sister's son | 0 | 0 | 0 | 0 | 1 | 0 | 1 |
| 15. F's M and F's sister | 0 | 4 | 0 | 0 | 1 | 0 | 5 |
| 16. F's M's sister | 0 | 0 | 0 | 0 | 3 | 0 | 3 |
| 17. F's M and F's brother | 0 | 4 | 1 | 0 | 2 | 0 | 7 |
| 18. F's F's brother's daughter | 0 | 0 | 0 | 0 | 1 | 0 | 1 |
| 19. F's F's sister's D | 0 | 1 | 0 | 0 | 0 | 0 | 1 |
| 20. F's M and M's M's sister | 0 | 1 | 0 | 0 | 0 | 0 | 1 |
| 21. F's F's F's brother's son | 0 | 0 | 0 | 0 | 1 | 0 | 1 |
| 22. F's brother's mate | 0 | 0 | 0 | 0 | 1 | 0 | 1 |
| 23. F's spouse | 0 | 2 | 0 | 0 | 2 | 0 | 4 |
| 24. F's paternal kinsman | 0 | 0 | 0 | 0 | 1 | 0 | 1 |
| 25. F's kinswoman, kinship n/k | 0 | 0 | 0 | 0 | 1 | 0 | 1 |
| 26. F's sister's husband | 0 | 0 | 0 | 0 | 1 | 0 | 1 |
| | | | | | | | |
| Total father's kin | 2 | 63 | 5 | 1 | 54 | 9 | 134 |
| Total mother's kin | 1 | 99 | 25 | 0 | 89 | 36 | 250 |
| Total unrelated persons | 0 | 6 | 54 | 0 | 0 | 49 | 109 |
| GRAND TOTAL | 3 | 168 | 84 | 1 | 143 | 94 | 493 |

*L = Lawful, i.e., legitimate; U = Unlawful, i.e., illegitimate; N/K = Birth status not known.

## TABLE 16

CHILDREN LESS THAN 24 YEARS OF AGE, LIVING WITH THEIR FATHERS APART FROM THEIR MOTHERS, CLASSIFIED BY SEX, BIRTH STATUS, AND STATUS OF FATHER OR KIN WITH WHOM THEY LIVE

| | Male | | | Female | | | Total | | |
|---|---|---|---|---|---|---|---|---|---|
| | L* | U* | N/K* | L | U | N/K | Total | L | U |
| 1. Father widowed | 1 | 0 | 0 | 0 | 0 | 0 | 1 | 1 | 0 |
| 2. Father wed | 20 | 11 | 0 | 12 | 8 | 0 | 51 | 32 | 19 |
| 3. Father wed, spouse absent | 0 | 0 | 0 | 2 | 0 | 0 | 2 | 2 | 0 |
| 4. Father unwed | 0 | 39 | 0 | 0 | 30 | 0 | 69 | 0 | 69 |
| 5. Father, status not known | 0 | 0 | 1 | 0 | 0 | 0 | 1 | 0 | 0 |
| Total with father only | 21 | 50 | 1 | 14 | 38 | 0 | 124 | 35 | 88 |
| 6. Father and father's mother and father | 0 | 2 | 0 | 0 | 2 | 0 | 4 | 0 | 4 |
| 7. Father and father's father | 0 | 2 | 0 | 0 | 1 | 0 | 3 | 0 | 3 |
| 8. Father and father's mother | 0 | 7 | 0 | 0 | 9 | 0 | 16 | 0 | 16 |
| 9. Father and mother's mother | 0 | 1 | 0 | 0 | 1 | 0 | 2 | 0 | 2 |
| 10. Father and F's M and M's mother | 0 | 0 | 0 | 0 | 1 | 0 | 1 | 0 | 1 |
| 11. Father and F's mother and sister | 0 | 1 | 0 | 0 | 0 | 0 | 1 | 0 | 1 |
| 12. Father and F's M's sister | 0 | 1 | 0 | 0 | 1 | 0 | 2 | 0 | 2 |
| 13. Father and F's M's F's brother | 0 | 1 | 0 | 0 | 0 | 0 | 1 | 0 | 1 |
| 14. Father and F's B's mother and sister | 0 | 1 | 0 | 0 | 1 | 0 | 2 | 0 | 2 |
| 15. Father and F's mat. half sister | 0 | 1 | 0 | 0 | 0 | 0 | 1 | 0 | 1 |
| Total with father and F's kin | 0 | 17 | 0 | 0 | 16 | 0 | 33 | 0 | 33 |
| TOTAL | 21 | 67 | 1 | 14 | 54 | 0 | 157 | 35 | 121 |

*L = Lawful, i.e., legitimate; U = Unlawful, i.e., illegitimate; N/K = Birth status not known.

## TABLE 17

CHILDREN LESS THAN 24 YEARS OF AGE, LIVING WITH THEIR MOTHERS APART FROM THEIR FATHERS, CLASSIFIED BY SEX, BIRTH STATUS, AND STATUS OF MOTHER OR KIN WITH WHOM THEY LIVE

| | Male | | | Female | | | Total | L | U |
|---|---|---|---|---|---|---|---|---|---|
| | L* | U* | N/K* | L | U | N/K | | | |
| 1. Mother widowed | 30 | 0 | 0 | 21 | 1 | 0 | 52 | 51 | 1 |
| 2. Mother wed | 13 | 14 | 0 | 13 | 20 | 0 | 60 | 26 | 34 |
| 3. Mother wed, separated | 8 | 0 | 0 | 0 | 1 | 0 | 9 | 8 | 1 |
| 4. Mother unwed | 0 | 119 | 0 | 0 | 117 | 0 | 236 | 0 | 236 |
| Total with mother only | 51 | 133 | 0 | 34 | 139 | 0 | 357 | 85 | 272 |
| 5. Mother and M's mother and father | 0 | 25 | 0 | 0 | 34 | 0 | 59 | 0 | 59 |
| 6. Mother and mother's mother | 1 | 48 | 0 | 0 | 38 | 0 | 87 | 1 | 86 |
| 7. Mother and mother's brother | 2 | 8 | 0 | 0 | 8 | 0 | 18 | 2 | 16 |
| 8. Mother and mother's sister | 0 | 6 | 0 | 0 | 4 | 0 | 10 | 0 | 10 |
| 9. Mother and mother's father | 0 | 3 | 0 | 0 | 9 | 0 | 12 | 0 | 12 |
| 10. Mother and maternal half brother | 0 | 1 | 0 | 0 | 0 | 0 | 1 | 0 | 1 |
| 11. Mother and M's mat. half sister | 0 | 1 | 0 | 0 | 1 | 0 | 2 | 0 | 2 |
| 12. Mother and M's F's mother | 0 | 1 | 0 | 0 | 2 | 0 | 3 | 0 | 3 |
| 13. Mother and M's F's sister | 0 | 6 | 0 | 0 | 0 | 0 | 6 | 0 | 6 |
| 14. Mother and M's F's brother and sister | 0 | 1 | 0 | 0 | 0 | 0 | 1 | 0 | 1 |
| 15. Mother and M's F's sister's son | 0 | 0 | 0 | 0 | 1 | 0 | 1 | 0 | 1 |
| 16. Mother and M's father and brother | 0 | 1 | 0 | 0 | 0 | 0 | 1 | 0 | 1 |
| 17. Mother and M's F's parents | 0 | 1 | 0 | 0 | 4 | 0 | 5 | 0 | 5 |
| 18. Mother and M's M and M's M's father | 0 | 0 | 0 | 0 | 1 | 0 | 1 | 0 | 1 |
| 19. Mother and M's M's F's sister | 0 | 1 | 0 | 0 | 0 | 0 | 1 | 0 | 1 |
| 20. Mother and M's brother and sister | 0 | 1 | 0 | 0 | 4 | 0 | 5 | 0 | 5 |
| 21. Mother and M's mother and brother | 1 | 3 | 0 | 1 | 5 | 0 | 10 | 2 | 8 |
| 22. Mother and M's B and M's M's mother | 0 | 3 | 0 | 0 | 0 | 0 | 3 | 0 | 3 |
| 23. Mother and M's M's sister | 0 | 2 | 0 | 0 | 1 | 0 | 3 | 0 | 3 |
| 24. Mother and M's M's parents | 0 | 1 | 0 | 0 | 0 | 0 | 1 | 0 | 1 |
| 25. Mother and M's M and M's M's mother | 0 | 1 | 0 | 0 | 0 | 0 | 1 | 0 | 1 |
| 26. Mother and M's B and M's M's sister | 0 | 0 | 0 | 0 | 1 | 0 | 1 | 0 | 1 |
| 27. Mother and M's M's mother | 0 | 4 | 0 | 0 | 1 | 0 | 5 | 0 | 5 |
| 28. Mother and M's sister's son | 0 | 1 | 0 | 0 | 2 | 0 | 3 | 0 | 3 |
| 29. Mother and M's M's sister's son | 0 | 0 | 0 | 0 | 1 | 0 | 1 | 0 | 1 |
| 30. Mother and M's S's husband | 0 | 0 | 0 | 0 | 1 | 0 | 1 | 0 | 1 |
| 31. Mother and M's M and B and M's F's B | 0 | 1 | 0 | 0 | 1 | 0 | 2 | 0 | 2 |
| 32. Mother and M's F's spouse | 0 | 1 | 0 | 0 | 0 | 0 | 1 | 0 | 1 |
| Total with mother and M's kin | 4 | 121 | 0 | 1 | 119 | 0 | 245 | 5 | 240 |
| TOTAL | 55 | 254 | 0 | 35 | 258 | 0 | 602 | 90 | 512 |

*L = Lawful, i.e., legitimate; U = Unlawful, i.e., illegitimate; N/K = Birth status not known.

## TABLE 18

### FREQUENCY DISTRIBUTION OF DIFFERING TYPES OF DOMESTIC UNIT WITHIN THE SAMPLE

| | Households with Male Head | | | Households with Female Head | | | Total | | | |
|---|---|---|---|---|---|---|---|---|---|---|
| | No Others | Plus Others | Total | No Others | Plus Others | Total | No Others | Plus Others | Total | Per cent |
| 1. Single persons | 120 | 28 | 148 | 46 | 21 | 67 | 166 | 49 | 215 | 21.4 |
| 2. Siblings | 4 | 3 | 7 | 5 | 10 | 15 | 9 | 13 | 22 | 2.2 |
| 3. Household head and children | 19 | 7 | 26 | 67 | 14 | 81 | 86 | 21 | 107 | 10.6 |
| 4. Childless couples | 68 | 101 | 169 | 5 | 13 | 18 | 73 | 114 | 187 | 18.5 |
| 5. Couples and children | 164 | 112 | 276 | 4 | 2 | 6 | 168 | 114 | 282 | 28.0 |
| 6. Household head and grandchildren | 3 | 4 | 7 | 26 | 8 | 34 | 29 | 12 | 41 | 4.1 |
| 7. Couples and grandchildren | 2 | 6 | 8 | 0 | 0 | 0 | 2 | 6 | 8 | 0.8 |
| 8. Household head, children, and grandchildren | 9 | 1 | 10 | 61 | 11 | 72 | 70 | 12 | 82 | 8.1 |
| 9. Couples, children, and grandchildren | 41 | 6 | 47 | 1 | 1 | 2 | 42 | 7 | 49 | 4.9 |
| 10. Household head and issue to 4th generation | 0 | 0 | 0 | 10 | 0 | 10 | 10 | 0 | 10 | 1.0 |
| 11. Couples and issue to 4th generation | 3 | 1 | 4 | 0 | 0 | 0 | 3 | 1 | 4 | 0.4 |
| TOTAL | 433 | 269 | 702 | 225 | 80 | 305 | 660 | 349 | 1,007 | 100.0 |
| PERCENTAGE | 62.0 | 38.0 | 100.0 | 74.0 | 26.0 | 100.0 | 65.5 | 34.5 | 100.0 | |

## TABLE 19

### DOMESTIC UNITS OF STRUCTURALLY DIFFERING TYPES, CLASSIFIED BY SEX OF HEAD AND GENERATION RANGE

| | Households with Male Head | | | | | Households with Female Head | | | | | Total | | | | |
|---|---|---|---|---|---|---|---|---|---|---|---|---|---|---|---|
| | Generation Range | | | | | Generation Range | | | | | Generation Range | | | | |
| | 1 | 2 | 3 | 4 | Total | 1 | 2 | 3 | 4 | Total | 1 | 2 | 3 | 4 | Total |
| 1. Single persons | 134 | 12 | 2 | 0 | 148 | 52 | 10 | 4 | 1 | 67 | 186 | 22 | 6 | 1 | 215 |
| 2. Siblings | 4 | 3 | 0 | 0 | 7 | 5 | 6 | 4 | 0 | 15 | 9 | 9 | 4 | 0 | 22 |
| 3. Household head and children | 0 | 22 | 4 | 0 | 26 | 8 | 78 | 2 | 1 | 81 | 0 | 100 | 6 | 1 | 107 |
| 4. Childless couples | 72 | 59 | 36 | 2 | 169 | 8 | 5 | 5 | 0 | 18 | 80 | 64 | 41 | 2 | 187 |
| 5. Couples and children | 0 | 243 | 30 | 3 | 276 | 0 | 6 | 0 | 0 | 6 | 0 | 249 | 30 | 3 | 282 |
| 6. Household head and grandchildren | 0 | 0 | 7 | 0 | 7 | 0 | 0 | 34 | 0 | 34 | 0 | 0 | 41 | 0 | 41 |
| 7. Couples and grandchildren | 0 | 0 | 8 | 0 | 8 | 0 | 0 | 0 | 0 | 0 | 0 | 0 | 8 | 0 | 8 |
| 8. Household head, children, and grandchildren | 0 | 0 | 10 | 0 | 10 | 0 | 0 | 71 | 1 | 72 | 0 | 0 | 81 | 1 | 82 |
| 9. Couples, children, and grandchildren | 0 | 0 | 47 | 0 | 47 | 0 | 0 | 2 | 0 | 2 | 0 | 0 | 49 | 0 | 49 |
| 10. Household head and issue to 4th generation | 0 | 0 | 0 | 0 | 0 | 0 | 0 | 0 | 10 | 10 | 0 | 0 | 0 | 10 | 10 |
| 11. Couples and issue to 4th generation | 0 | 0 | 0 | 4 | 4 | 0 | 0 | 0 | 0 | 0 | 0 | 0 | 0 | 4 | 4 |
| TOTAL | 210 | 339 | 144 | 9 | 702 | 65 | 105 | 122 | 13 | 305 | 275 | 444 | 266 | 22 | 1,007 |
| PERCENTAGE | 29.8 | 48.2 | 20.5 | 1.5 | 100.0 | 21.3 | 34.4 | 40.0 | 4.2 | 100.0 | 27.3 | 44.1 | 26.5 | 2.2 | 100.0 |

TABLE 20

CONJUGAL UNIONS IN THE SAMPLE HOUSEHOLDS, CLASSIFIED BY THEIR BASIS, THE TYPE OF DOMESTIC UNIT IN WHICH THEY OCCUR, AND THE SEX OF THE HOUSEHOLD HEAD

| Morphological Types | Male Head | | | Female Head | | | Total | | |
|---|---|---|---|---|---|---|---|---|---|
| | Wed | Unwed | Total | Wed | Unwed | Total | Wed | Unwed | Total |
| 1a. Childless couples only | 27 | 41 | 68 | 1 | 4 | 5 | 28 | 45 | 73 |
| b. Childless couples plus others | 59 | 44 | 103 | 0 | 11 | 11 | 59 | 55 | 114 |
| Total childless couples | 86 | 85 | 171 | 1 | 15 | 16 | 87 | 100 | 187 |
| 2a. Couples and children only | 110 | 54 | 164 | 2 | 2 | 4 | 112 | 56 | 168 |
| b. Couples, children plus others | 59 | 53 | 112 | 0 | 2 | 2 | 59 | 55 | 114 |
| Total couples and children | 169 | 107 | 276 | 2 | 4 | 6 | 171 | 111 | 282 |
| 3a. Couples and grandchildren only | 2 | 0 | 2 | 0 | 0 | 0 | 2 | 0 | 2 |
| b. Couples, grandchildren plus others | 5 | 1 | 6 | 0 | 0 | 0 | 5 | 1 | 6 |
| Total couples and grandchildren | 7 | 1 | 8 | 0 | 0 | 0 | 7 | 1 | 8 |
| 4a. Couples, children, and grandchildren only | 36 | 5 | 41 | 1 | 0 | 1 | 37 | 5 | 42 |
| b. Couples, children, grandchildren plus others | 6 | 0 | 6 | 1 | 0 | 1 | 7 | 0 | 7 |
| Total couples, children, and grandchildren | 42 | 5 | 47 | 2 | 0 | 2 | 44 | 5 | 49 |
| 5a. Couples and issue to 4th generation only | 3 | 0 | 3 | 0 | 0 | 0 | 3 | 0 | 3 |
| b. Couples, issue to 4th generation plus others | 1 | 0 | 1 | 0 | 0 | 0 | 1 | 0 | 1 |
| Total couples and issue to 4th generation | 4 | 0 | 4 | 0 | 0 | 0 | 4 | 0 | 4 |
| TOTAL | 308 | 198 | 506 | 5 | 19 | 24 | 313 | 217 | 530 |

# 6. Kingston

⊠⊠⊠⊠⊠⊠⊠⊠⊠⊠⊠⊠⊠⊠

Kingston, the capital of Jamaica, now includes several square miles of the neighboring parish, St. Andrew, to form one contiguous urban area. The city limits now contain about 350,000 people. The upper and middle classes are mostly to be found in the newer residential suburbs. The old city and its fast-growing West End are the most densely populated areas, and it is in these areas that we find the greatest concentration of working-class households.

I was able to study a sample of 425 lower-income households of Kingston in December, 1955. I wished to study these lower-class Kingston households for comparison with other groups in rural Jamaica and outside of it. To secure a systematic sample which would be representative of the Kingston lower class, I approached the Department of Statistics, Jamaica, whose officials kindly offered me a subsample of their own construction which had been used for a survey of housing conditions among the lower-income urban population in March that year. As mentioned in the introduction, the units of this sample frame were dwelling quarters marked on diagrams of buildings, scattered proportionately over the city according to the density of working-class households within it. The occupants of these sample units were listed, and this list was made available to me for use in my survey. By comparing the occupants of these quarters in March and December, 1955, it is therefore possible to estimate the minimum annual residential mobility of this urban lower class. Table 1 sets out the frequency with which the three enumerators working in different sections of the city had to make substitutions of differing types. Of the 425 units analyzed below, 142 were substitutes for an equal number in the sample frame furnished to me. Of these 142, only six were substitutes for refusals; another six were substitutes for listed

occupants who remained unavailable throughout the survey period.
Five substitutes replaced the occupants of dwelling units which had
either been demolished or were then under repair. A further 124
replaced listed occupants who had moved elsewhere. In all, the
substitution rate of dwelling units was only 4. 2 per cent while the
substitution rate for occupants was 33. 4 per cent. Thus, 29. 2 per
cent of the listed occupants of these 425 units had moved elsewhere
during the months between March and December, 1955. The minimum annual rate of residential mobility among this urban lower
class is therefore equal to 40 per cent of the total number of households. This rate varies between city districts; in western Kingston
substitutes occupying the sample rooms were 37 per cent of the
total, giving an annual minimum mobility of 50 per cent. In central
Kingston, the Area B of Table 1, the substitutes living on sample
premises were 27. 4 per cent of the total, giving a minimum annual
mobility of 36 per cent; in eastern Kingston or Area C, new occupants of the sample premises represented 21. 3 per cent of the
total, and the minimum annual mobility rate for this area is accordingly 28. 4 per cent. These regional differences agree with
the general character of the three areas; since the sample is
weighted for varying densities of working-class settlement in all
areas, the average sample mobility of 40 per cent represents the
urban lower-class population as a whole. This remarkable rate
of residential movement cannot fail to reflect and influence the
character of domestic organization within this urban working class.

Population and the Distribution of Headship
      These 425 households contain 1, 340 souls, distributed by sex
and age as shown in Table 2. The male-female ratio for all age
groups is 1 to 1. 36, females forming 57. 7 per cent of the total.
However, within the reproductive age groups between fifteen and
fifty-four years of age, there are 495 females and 317 males, or
1. 55 women per male. Children under fourteen represent only
32. 7 per cent of the sample population, and within this group there
are ninety-nine girls to every 100 boys. It seems therefore that the
excess of active adult females may be due to immigration of women
from the rural areas as well as to some emigration of urban males.
Probably the movement of countrywomen into town is of greater
significance, despite considerable male emigration from Kingston
to Britain since 1953. [1] The low incidence of children under fourteen
in these homes may be due to many women sending some of their
children to kinsfolk in the country, or leaving them there when
they come to town themselves. These practices are known to be

fairly common among the working-class women in Jamaican towns. [2] Only 6.7 per cent of the population of these sample households are over fifty-five years of age; this low ratio of aged persons may reflect the withdrawal of many rural folk who came into town to work, as their earning power declines. Within this framework of intraisland migration, the high rates of residential mobility among this urban lower class become more intelligible.

Tables 3 and 4 classify the heads of these sample households by sex and age, and describe the relative incidence of headship among persons of differing sex and age. Of the 425 households, 216 or 50.8 per cent have male heads. Of the household heads, only fourteen or 3.3 per cent are over seventy years of age, and another forty-eight or 11.4 per cent are above fifty-five. Less than 15 per cent of these households have heads of the two senior age groups.

Thirty-three of the 425 household heads are under twenty-four years of age, and they form 7.8 per cent of the total, the women outnumbering males slightly. One hundred and ninety-three or 45.3 per cent of all household heads are between twenty-five and thirty-nine years of age, and three in every five of these are males. The remaining 137 household heads, just under a third of the total, are between forty and fifty-four years of age, and among these women slightly outnumber men.

Of the ninety-eight young men under twenty-four in this sample, 15.3 per cent were heads of their own homes; of the 163 young women under twenty-four, 9 per cent were household heads. Among the 145 men aged 25 to 39 in this sample, 115 or 79 per cent were household heads. Of the 214 women of this age group, 36.4 per cent were heads of their own homes. Between the ages of forty and fifty-four, 85 per cent of the males and 62 per cent of the females were household heads. There is little further change in the incidence of headship beyond this point. The two notable features of this changing incidence of headship are the sudden increase among young men after their twenty-fourth year and the two sharp consecutive increases among women after their twenty-fifth and fortieth years. The majority of our household heads are young people, and the majority of their homes will thus contain one or two generations at most. Although approximately half of these homes have female heads, only 37.5 per cent of the adult females are household heads as compared with 62.7 per cent of the males.

Table 5 classifies these households by the head's sex and the numbers of persons within them. Of the 425 households, 75 or 17.5 per cent contain solitary individuals; a further 114 or 27.8 per cent contain two persons only, while 95 or 22.2 per cent contain three persons each. Thus 67.5 per cent of the households in this sample contain three persons or less. Units containing two persons are the sample mode, and these units are equally divided under heads of different sex. So are households which contain three or four people; but nearly two thirds of the individuals who live alone are women. There are two households containing ten or more people, both under male heads, and twenty-seven which contain between seven and nine persons, ten of these households having female heads. However, of fifty-four households which include five or six persons, thirty-seven have male heads. These data reveal a tendency for large households to have male rather than female heads; but the preponderance of male heads is greatest among units which have five or six members. The distribution before us suggests that after units pass this size, they are more likely to split than to persist. The splitting of these larger units may account for the relatively large numbers of homes including three or four persons under female heads.

The average size of household in this sample is small, being 3.16 persons. Homes with female heads average 2.86 persons each, those under males average 3.43. As regards size, there is little to choose between units with heads of different sex.

Table 6 classifies by age and sex the members of households having heads of different sex. Of the population living in homes with male heads, 34 per cent are under fourteen, and of the remaining 489 adults, 230 are women. Only 5.1 per cent of this household population is above fifty-five years of age. The larger number of males in each adult age group but the lowest indicates that men mate with women somewhat their junior in years. Of the 599 members of homes with female heads, 30.4 per cent are under fourteen. Only 8.8 per cent are above fifty-five; of the 413 adults in these homes, only eighty-five or 20.6 per cent are males. Either the large number of women of reproductive age in these homes includes many childless persons, or it includes many who do not have all their children living with them. Of the 1,340 individuals in the total sample, 741 or 55.5 per cent live in homes with male heads.

Lacking adequate data on the marital condition and parental status of the seventy-five solitary individuals in this sample, I have confined my analysis to their distribution by age and sex. Only seven of these isolates are under twenty-four years of age, and of these five are females. Only three are over seventy, two being women. Thirty-four of these solitary persons are between twenty-five and thirty-nine years of age; and the twenty-two women of this condition and age group are rather more than one tenth of all women of this

age in the sample. Another twenty-one persons aged between forty
and sixty-four live on their own, eleven of these being males; these
males are a little less than a sixth of the men in their age group.
More than two thirds of all those who live on their own are between
twenty-five and fifty-four years of age, and together these isolates
represent one tenth of all members of these age groups in our
sample. It is difficult to imagine that economic conditions alone
produce this ratio and concentration of isolated individuals among
persons between twenty-five and fifty-four; yet if economic explanations are not adequate, the distribution of this isolation would
seem to be linked with the family structure.

The System of Mating Relations

Tables 8, 9, and 10 present my data on the distribution of marital
and parental experience among the sample adults. These data are
seriously incomplete owing to the scatter of the sample through
the town as well as to the anonymity of its adult elements, especially where previous mating experience was concerned. Those
persons for whom we lack adequate data on mating and parental
status are entered separately in Tables 8 to 10. Many of these
persons may have separated from their consensual or legal mates,
and accordingly our categories for consensually wed and separated
persons, and also for separated married persons, are left blank.
In the circumstances of this survey, it was well-nigh impossible
to gather accurate information on many persons who had no mates
living with them. We lacked the necessary contacts with knowl-
edgeable neighbors which were so useful in the rural areas.

Of the ninety-eight young men under twenty-four in these homes,
twelve were cohabiting consensually and three were married at the
time of survey. Only one of the remainder was known to be a father,
and he was the only person of his age known to be mating extraresidentially. For the other eighty-two young men, parental and
mating status remains obscure. Of 145 men between twenty-five
and thirty-nine years of age in this sample, forty-two were single
persons, and our data were incomplete for thirty-nine of these.
Fifty-eight were cohabiting consensually and forty-five were married at the time of survey. Of seventy-four men between forty and
fifty-four years of age, sixteen were single and our data are incomplete for fifteen of these. Of the remainder, thirty-four had
married and twenty-four were cohabiting consensually. We lack
adequate data on all six men aged between fifty-five and sixty-nine
who continued single. Four of the remainder were cohabiting but
had never married. Of the twelve who had married, one was a

widower. Three of the five men over seventy years of age had married and were living with their wives.

Of these 344 men, 149 were ostensibly single and of these approximately one tenth were known to be childless persons, while five were known to be parents. For the remainder we lack adequate knowledge; none the less, more than half of these single persons were below the age of twenty-four, at which age few men may yet have entered domestic unions. The remaining 197 men were divided equally between marriage and consensual cohabitation. There is a tendency for the incidence of marriage among men to increase with their age, and for the proportions living without mates, or with consensual mates, to decline. Most of the young men live without mates; most men between twenty-five and thirty-nine years of age or older live in domestic unions, consensual or legal; but our data do not reveal the number of ostensibly single men whose domestic unions, legal or other, had broken down; nor does it tell us how many of them were mating extraresidentially or were already parents. Many of these "single" men may well have been widowers. Our data on male mating in this town are largely limited to direct observation. Since females are better subjects for these observations and inquiries, we shall probably find data on their mating and parental condition more illuminating.

Our sample households contain 163 young women below twenty-four years of age. Of these, we lack definite information on the mating and parental status of 106, many of whom had not yet begun their mating careers. Nineteen were already mothers, and of these, thirteen were mating extraresidentially at the time of survey. Twenty-four were cohabiting consensually and fourteen had married, in one case the husband being absent. Of the 214 women aged between twenty-five and thirty-nine in this sample, eighty-nine were single at the time of study, and for sixty-four of these we lack details of mating and parental status. The other twenty-five were single mothers, and eight had extraresidential mates at the time of study. One hundred and twenty-five women were in this age group, sixty cohabiting consensually, fifty living with their husbands; eleven had absent husbands and four were widows. There were in these homes one hundred and eighteen women forty to fifty-four years of age. Fifty-six of these were single at the time of survey, and of these fifty-six, thirty-four were known to be mothers. Fifteen were cohabiting consensually and forty-seven had wed, only twenty-one of these latter living with their husbands at the time of survey. Half of the forty-eight women between fifty-five and sixty-nine were ostensibly single. We do not know how many of these twenty-five "single" women had previously taken part in domestic unions. The parental status as well as the mating history of thirteen of these women remains obscure. The other twelve were single mothers. No women of this age group were cohabiting consensually; and of the twenty-three who were married, only ten lived with their husbands, five of the remainder being widows. Of the fifteen women over seventy in these homes, seven were single at the time of survey and five of these were single mothers. Of eight who had married, none lived with their husbands, but only two were widowed. Three hundred and two of these 558 women were single at time of survey. One hundred and seventy-seven were over twenty-four years of age and ninety-five known to be mothers. Only thirty were known to be mating extraresidentially, a clear underestimate. We do not know how many of the mature "single" women had been principals in broken domestic unions of either sort; however, if we are to judge from the proportion of wives who report their husbands' absence, the number of women whose consensual domestic unions had broken down should be fairly substantial. Of the 142 married women in this sample, forty-eight had absent husbands and a good many of these were in effect separated; some were mating extraresidentially.

Even with these defective data, it is clear that the system of mating relations within this urban working class is complex and unstable. Young people mate extraresidentially rather than by domestic forms; women tend to enter domestic unions, consensual or other, at an earlier age than men; they also withdraw from consensual cohabitation earlier than men. Often these withdrawals mark the end of the woman's mating career rather than the beginning of her marriage. Former consensual mates resume their single status anonymously. It is thus likely that much of the residential mobility in this working class is linked with the formation and dissolution of consensual unions; but change of residence may secure anonymity for married persons also.

Since men rarely keep their children with them, their paternal status and responsibilities remain obscure in the early stages of their subsequent unions, owing to this urban anonymity. Since women have children by extraresidential as well as by domestic unions, the history of their cohabitation is equally obscure, despite the presence of children; but those women who dispatch their offspring to rural kin thereby obscure their parental as well as their mating record.

These obscurities which perplex the field worker are essential conditions of this mating organization, with its concurrent alternative forms. Marriage is certainly brittle, as the number of women with absent husbands indicates; anonymity is prized, as shown by the fact that only two men admit having absent wives. Consensual cohabitation is probably more liable to break down in these conditions than to develop into marriage. These breakdowns of marriage and consensual unions are in large part due to the facility with which extraresidential mating can be established by persons of all reproductive ages, and by the facility with which domestic unions of either sort can be terminated or established.

In this urban society, there are three mating forms: the extra-residential relation, consensual cohabitation, and marriage. None has exclusive place within a series, nor in the development of the individual life cycle. Despite a tendency for adults to begin their mating career extraresidentially and to complete it with marriage, there is ample evidence that many begin by marrying and later resume extraresidential or consensual mating as "single persons." Consensual cohabitation will be singularly unstable in these conditions, since marriage establishes no permanent union, and since other alternative mating forms are always open to both partners. Under these conditions, the definition and fulfilment of parental roles by persons of either sex becomes uncertain, and accordingly many women dispatch the offspring of their unions, past and present, to rural kinsfolk.

Tables 9 and 10 examine the association between mating and parental condition on the one hand, and household status on the other, among adults of differing sex and age in this urban population. Of the ninety-eight young men below twenty-four, only fifteen are household heads. Of the eighty-three single males of this age group, five are heads of their homes, and of twelve males cohabiting consensually at time of survey, seven are household heads. All three young men under twenty-four who had married were heads of their own homes, as were forty-four of the forty-five men aged between twenty-five and thirty-nine whose wives lived with them. Of the fifty-eight men between twenty-five and thirty-nine who were cohabiting consensually, fifty were household heads; but of the forty-two "single" men in this age group, only one half were heads of their own homes. Of seventy-four men between forty and fifty-four, sixty-three were household heads. Of sixteen "single persons" in this age group, fourteen were household heads; but of twenty-four men who were cohabiting consensually, only seventeen were household heads. The incidence of headship among "single" men of this age group exceeds that among those who live in consensual unions. Of the thirty-four married men between forty and

fifty-four, thirty-two are household heads. Marriage and male
headship go together here, as elsewhere. Of the three dependent
males between fifty-five and sixty-nine, one lives with his wife,
one with a consensual partner, and one as a single man. The only
dependent male above sixty-nine years of age lives with his wife.
There is a clear tendency for senior men to head their own homes,
but some of these men may be living alone. There is another tendency for senior men to be married, but this is by no means universal. The rule is that married men are household heads, while of the
ninety-eight men living in consensual unions, only seventy-seven
were heads of their homes. The ambiguous character of consensual
unions in this urban society is illustrated by this irregular distribution of headship within them.

Of the 207 single females of indeterminate mating and parental
status, 106 were less than twenty-four years of age, and only fourteen of these were household heads. Of the remaining 101, sixty-
four were heads of their own homes. Women in indeterminate mating and parental status are more likely than not to be heads of their
own homes. Of the twenty-four young women under twenty-four
who were cohabiting consensually, two were household heads, and
another married woman of this age group whose husband was absent
was also a household head. Of the fifteen widows in this sample,
twelve were household heads; of the forty-eight women with absent
spouses, thirty-six were household heads; and of ninety-four women
living with their husbands, three were household heads; of ninety-
nine women cohabiting consensually, nineteen were household heads;
and more than one sixth of the women aged between twenty-five and
thirty-nine who participated in unions of this sort were heads of
their own homes. Of the ninety-five single mothers in this sample,
sixty-one were household heads. If we exclude the nineteen single
mothers under twenty-four, sixty of the remaining seventy-six
single mothers were household heads. Among single women over
twenty-five years of age, headship is the norm; among married
women living with their husbands, it is exceptional; but one fifth
of the women engaged in consensual cohabitation are heads of their
own homes.

In view of the gaps in our data on the mating and parental condition of this urban population, I have abstracted certain information
on the conjugal status of women from a sample study of Kingston
carried out by the Department of Statistics in 1933.[3] These depart-
mental studies are in some respects comparable with my data on
mating and parental status. They enable us to check on the gaps in
my data, and to make certain adjustments thereto, especially be-

cause the parental and mating condition of women has been a major preoccupation of Jamaican censuses and population surveys for some years.

Table 11 accordingly summarizes the distribution of women of differing age groups in the categories used by the Department of Statistics in its population survey, and converts the absolute numbers into percentage frequencies among women of each age group. Table 12 estimates the distribution of the women in my Kingston sample within the system of categories used by the Department of Statistics on the basis of the percentages set out in Table 11. Table 13 refines the Department's classification to fit the categories I have been using; it also adjusts the raw estimates given in Table 12 to incorporate information presented in Table 8 of my sample. Items of this revised estimate in Table 13 which may need further upward adjustment are asterisked; those which are dubious in the light of Table 8 are marked by queries. Despite uncertainties, the distribution presented in Table 13 provides a useful check on Table 8, and is worth some attention.

By this estimate, our sample contained 164 childless single women and twenty-seven childless women who were living in consensual unions, and another twelve who had married. There were probably 121 single mothers in the sample, and seventy-two mothers living in consensual cohabitation. One hundred and twenty-seven of the married women were mothers also, and another thirty-five were probably widows. These estimates help to reduce the number of women whose parental status remained unspecified in Table 8; they are suggestive about the breakdown of consensual unions, but they shed little light on its rate, or on the rate of breakdown in marriage. Nonetheless, the 121 single mothers of this revised estimate must have mated by the extraresidential and consensual forms. This total indicates a high incidence of extraresidential mating among these women, and also a high incidence of breakdown in consensual unions. In short, the data collected by the Department of Statistics strengthen our preceding analysis of mating organization among this urban population.

The Composition of Domestic Groups

In Table 14 the dependent populations of the sample households are analyzed by their relationship to the heads with whom they live, and by the sex of the household head. They are also included in the two charts which present these relationships in greater detail and in genealogical form. There are 525 resident dependents of male, and 389 dependents of female household heads. Of those living in homes with male heads, 31. 3 per cent are mates of the head and almost one half of these are consensual mates. Children of male heads comprise 43. 4 per cent, and 4. 6 per cent are their grandchildren; thus four fifths of the people living in homes with male heads are the mates or issue of these men, and less than 5 per cent are their grandchildren. Of the remainder, the kin and issue of resident mates by other unions are nearly half; and the consanguineal kin of the male head are a third. Of the total dependents in these homes, 4. 4 per cent are adopted or unrelated persons, eight of these being employees and six boarders.

Of the 389 resident dependents of female household heads, twenty-two or about 5 per cent are the mates of these women, and nineteen of these are consensual partners. Exactly one half of the total dependent population are children of the female heads, and if remoter issue are included, exactly two thirds of all resident dependents are descended from the heads of these homes. Only one great-grandchild is included in these remoter issue. Altogether, resident mates and issue represent about 70 per cent of the dependent population in homes with female heads. Half the remainder are the heads' siblings or their issue, another 4 per cent are other consanguineal kin of the heads. The kin or issue of resident mates include only three persons, and five others are mates of the heads' children or the children of such mates. Miscellaneous members of these units are 7. 5 per cent of the dependent total. Only one is an employee, seven are boarders, eight are adopted persons or their issue, and thirteen are unrelated.

Neither category of household includes any father of the household head. In four homes with male heads we find the head's mother; six women live in homes of which their daughters are heads, and an equal number live in homes of which their daughters' husbands are heads. Two female household heads have their mothers' mothers living with them. As the charts show, the average generation depth and spread of homes with female heads is greater than that of homes under males. Homes with female heads contain nearly three times as many grandchildren and siblings and their issue of the head as do units under males. Homes with male heads contain five times as many affines as do homes with female heads, excluding offspring of the heads' mates by other unions, for whom the ratios are even more unequal. The resident consanguineal kin of male household heads are not quite equal to the number of issue brought into their homes by these men's mates. One fifth of the dependent members in all these households are unrelated persons. Men are obliged to accommodate the kin and other issue of their resident

mates, as well as these mates and their joint offspring. In consequence, they have fewer kinsmen of their own living with them
than do female heads, in whose homes male mates and their kin or
other issue are correspondingly rare. Of the male household heads,
fifty have no mates living with them, but only twenty-nine live
entirely by themselves. Thus, one in every ten male heads only
has his consanguineal kin or issue with him, or has some unrelated
person in the home. Of the 187 female household heads who lack
resident mates, forty-six live by themselves; thus thirteen in every
nineteen female heads will be found living with their issue and/or
kin, or with some unrelated person. In homes with female heads,
sisters' issue outnumber brothers' issue by five to one, and resident sisters outnumber brothers by four to one. In homes with male
heads, siblings' issue are rare, but resident brothers outnumber
sisters slightly. Men accommodate their brothers more frequently
than their sisters. Among women, materterine and uterine kinship
governs the domestic placement of collaterals.

Table 15 isolates the resident collaterals of household principals
and classifies them by relationship to the principals with whom they
live, and by birth status. Of the twenty-one resident collateral kin
of male heads, three are full siblings, eleven are maternal half-
siblings, and two are paternal half-siblings. These homes include
only three issue of the head's siblings of either sort. The remaining
two collaterals are matrilateral relatives. Clearly, male household
heads are unlikely to have their full siblings, paternal half-siblings,
patrilateral or matrilateral kin living with them, as well as the
issue of their siblings. However, maternal half-siblings of these
male heads are rather frequent, in consequence of women's domestic responsibilities for the issue of their unions. Of these twenty-
one resident collaterals of male heads, four were legitimate, fifteen
were not, and the birth status of two remained obscure. Ten of the
eleven maternal half-siblings in these homes were illegitimate.

Of the twenty-six resident collaterals of mates of male heads,
four were full siblings and another twelve were their issue. Four
were maternal half-siblings, and one was the child of a maternal
half-sibling. The other five were matrilateral kin. Women are
not responsible for the domestic accommodation of their patrilateral kin, including paternal half-siblings, when living in the
homes of their mates. Of the twenty-six collaterals of the mates
of male household heads, seven were legitimate, seventeen were
not, and the birth status of two remained obscure. Ten of the twelve
issue of these women's siblings were illegitimate.

There were sixty-six resident collaterals of female household heads. Twenty-one of these were full siblings and seventeen were their issue. Five were maternal half-siblings and twelve were their issue. One was a paternal half-sibling and three others were the issue of paternal half-siblings. There were seven other matrilateral kin in these homes, but no patrilateral kin. Of these sixty-six collaterals, eleven were legitimate, thirty-three were not, and the birth status of twenty-two was obscure. The prevalence of illegitimacy and matrilateral kinship among these resident collaterals indicates the need for further analysis to determine the exact nature of the collateral tie, and its relation with birth status. Table 16 presents this analysis, full siblings being excluded as their kinship is traced through both parents, together with collaterals of senior generation for whom we lack adequate data on birth status.

Of the remaining twenty-two resident collaterals of females living with male household heads, only three trace kinship to these women through their fathers. Fifteen of the nineteen resident issue of these principals' kinswomen are illegitimate, and almost all their mothers are maternal relatives of the linked principal. Of the forty-five collaterals of female household heads classified in Table 16, only seven trace relationship through their fathers; and of the twenty-seven kinswomen's issue whose birth status is known, only two are legitimate. In all, fifty-seven of the sixty-seven resident collaterals of female principals are kinswomen's issue, and of those forty-five whose birth status is known, only five are legitimate. Materterine kinship provides women with opportunities the placement of their illegitimate offspring.

Table 17 analyzes resident issue of these household heads by sex, descent, and birth status. Of the 254 resident descendants of male household heads, 231 are children, sixteen are sons' children, and only seven are daughters' children. All seven daughters' children are illegitimate, but only two of the sixteen sons' children are unlawful. Given a high incidence of consensual cohabitation, many of the children living in their fathers' homes will be illegitimate. Of the sixty-one illegitimate children of male household heads, only ten are offspring of former unions.

Female household heads have 194 children living with them. Of these, twenty-eight are of unspecified birth status, being mainly above twenty-four years of age. Only seven are offspring of these women and their resident mates jointly; seventy-three are legitimate and ninety-three are not. Of the eight resident issue of these women's sons, only one was legitimate. Of the fifty-five resident issue of their daughters, thirty-eight were illegitimate. Of fifty-four resident illegitimate grandchildren of all our household heads, forty-five lived in homes with female heads and five sixths of these were daughters' issue. Virtually, men exclude their sons' illegiti-mate issue from their homes and only rarely will they accommodate their daughters' illegitimate issue. Contrariwise, women are more likely to accommodate their sons' illegitimate issue in their own homes; but the majority of the grandchildren in these women's homes are daughters' illegitimate children. Uterine kinship pro-vides a basis for the placement of illegitimate offspring, but it is slightly less important than materterine kinship.

The Distribution of Children

Our sample contains 708 dependents who have one or both parents living. In Table 18 these dependents are analyzed by reference to their residence with or separation from either or both parents, as well as by age, sex, birth status, and sex of the household head with whom they live. Of these 708 dependents, 225 or 31.9 per cent live with both parents, and 214 of these are in homes with male heads. One hundred and ninety-five or 27.5 per cent live apart from both parents, and of these eighty are found in homes with male heads. Two hundred and thirty-six or 33.4 per cent live with their mothers apart from their fathers, and only thirty-seven of these are found in homes with male heads. Twenty live with their fathers only, and the mothers of four of these are dead; seventeen of these twenty live in homes with male heads. Another thirty-two live with their widowed mothers, thirty-one of these in homes with female heads.

Of this dependent total, 24.6 per cent are legitimate persons who live with both parents, and almost all of these do so in homes with male heads; but another 17 per cent who are also legitimate live either apart from both parents or with their mothers apart from their fathers. Marriage being brittle, legitimacy does not insure coresidence of elementary families. In addition, domestic unions are often consensual, and one quarter of those who live with both parents are illegitimate offspring of these unions. Homes with male heads contain twice as many legitimates under twenty-four years of age as do homes with female heads; but there are not many more illegitimate dependents living under female heads than live with males. The most striking feature of Table 18 is the evi-dence that less than one third of all these dependents live with both their parents, and more than two thirds live apart from their fathers.

Tables 19, 20, and 21 analyze the distribution of children under twenty-four who live in these homes apart from either or both parents but with differing categories of kin. Sex and birth status of the children are included in this classification.

Table 19 shows that eighty-seven of the 153 dependents below the age of twenty-four who live in these homes apart from both parents remain with their matrilateral kin, nineteen of these with their mother's mother, and sixty-two of the eighty-seven are illegitimate. Thirty-three others live with their patrilateral kin, and of these twenty-two are illegitimate. Another thirty-three live with unrelated persons, and of these, twenty-nine are of unspecified birth status. A close examination of those 120 persons who live apart from their parents with their paternal or maternal kin shows that the great majority of them live with their materterine kin. Only nineteen live with their mother's mother, and twenty with their father's parents.

Of the twenty children who lived with their fathers apart from their mothers, six are legitimate, and only four live in homes which contain other adult kin of their father. Of 237 who live with their mothers apart from their fathers, eighty-two are legitimate, and 185 live in homes which contain no other adult kin of their mother, seventy-one of these latter being legitimate also. Of the fifty-two who live with their mother and other adult maternal kin, thirty-two live with the mother and mother's mother alone, and seven live with the mother and mother's parents. The total number of children living with their mother's mother, with or without their mother, is sixty. This is only two more than the number who live apart from both their parents with their mother's materterine kinswomen only; and another twelve live apart from both parents with their materterine kinsmen. In short, materterine kinship is more frequently used as a basis for placing children than are ties with the maternal grandmother.

The Variety of Domestic Forms

Table 22 classifies the households of this sample into eleven structurally distinct types, and reports their frequencies. The bases and character of this taxonomy will by now be familiar. Units which are pure types of these structural categories represent approximately 70 per cent of the total sample, and are slightly more frequent among households with female heads than in the other group.

Seventy-five of these households are single-person units, and another thirty-two contain the heads and individuals not linked with them by ties of siblingship, mating, or descent. All are in-

cluded in category 1 of Table 22. These 107 households are 25.1
per cent of the sample. Another twenty-one households representing 4.9 per cent of the sample have siblings as their principals.
Seventy have single parents and their children as the structural
core, and these represent 16.4 per cent of the sample. In addition
there are eighty-seven units having childless couples as their principals, and they are 20.5 per cent of the total. Thus 66.9 per cent
of these homes do not contain elementary families, and at least one
half of these units cannot be derived directly from units which formerly contained elementary families. We have already seen how
frequently maternal half-siblings live together in Kingston. Many
units which have maternal half-siblings as their principals are
unlikely to have contained the fathers of these persons. Many of
the childless couples in this sample were young persons cohabiting
consensually and who were most unlikely to have had children in
common. In Western Kingston all couples living together outside
of wedlock were childless; and their principals were rarely over
thirty-nine. The uniform lack of children among these units indicates that the arrival of offspring may promote their dissolution.
It is clear that the elementary family is neither the normal domestic unit nor the normal basis for domestic units in this urban
population.

There are ninety-one households whose cores are couples and
their children. Thirty-six of these contain accretions, and all
ninety-one represent 21.4 per cent of the total sample. In nine
cases single heads and their grandchildren formed the structural
core; in three cases this core contained couples and grandchildren.
Together these two categories represent less than 3 per cent of the
total. Thirty-one units had single heads, their children and grandchildren as the structural core; another four had couples, their
children and grandchildren as the core. These two categories together represent 8.3 per cent of all our households. Only two homes
had a depth of four lineal generations. Of all forty-nine homes
with a depth of three or more lineal generations inclusive of their
heads, thirty-nine had female heads and ten had male. Units with
single heads which include three successive generations are three
times as frequent as those which lack the intermediate generation.

As already shown, these households do not depend entirely on
the head's lineal issue for extended generational depth. They contain
many junior collaterals and other persons one or two generations
removed from the head. Table 23 enumerates households of varying
generation depth and structural type having heads of different sex.
Of the 216 units with male heads, 40.3 per cent contain one gener-

ation only, and fifty of these principals are childless couples. One hundred and seven or 50 per cent of all homes with male heads have a depth of two generations, and in eighty of these the core consists of a couple and their children. Another twenty homes with male heads have a three-generation span and there is one which includes members of four generations. Together these units with extended depth are 9.7 per cent of all homes with male heads.

Of the 209 homes with female heads, seventy-two or 34.4 per cent contain one generation only, and of these fifty-three are single-person units, nine are sibling units and ten are childless couples with females as heads. Another ninety-six or 45.9 per cent contain two generations, and in sixty-four of these mothers and children are the core. Thirty-eight households have a three-generation depth, and another three include members of four generations. To-gether these homes with extended depth represent 19.7 per cent of all units with female heads. For the whole sample, just over one third of the homes include members of one generation only; just under one half include two generations; and only sixty-two homes or 14.6 per cent of the total have a depth of three or more generations.

Table 24 classifies couples who are principals of these sample households by the type of domestic group in which they live, and by the basis of their conjugal union. Of the seventy-one childless couples living in homes with male heads, forty-six are unwed and forty-five live by themselves alone. Of the sixteen childless couples living in homes with female heads, fourteen are unwed and nine live by themselves. In all, sixty of the eighty-seven childless couples in these homes are unwed and fifty-four live by themselves. Childless couples are not usually married. Of eighty-six couples who have children and live in homes with male heads, twenty-eight are unwed and fifty-three live by themselves. All five couples who have children and live in homes with female heads are unwed, and of these only two live by themselves. Of the ninety-one couples having children, thirty-three are unwed and fifty-five live by themselves. The incidence of accretions in homes which contain couples and their children is just as great as in homes whose principals are childless; however, among couples who live together with their children marriage is twice as common as consensual cohabitation. Among childless couples, consensual cohabitation is twice as fre-quent as marriage. Of the four couples whose children and grand-children live with them, two are married, two are not.

Conclusion

The family conditions we have just analyzed reveal a certain order within the context of unstable mating. Such order as there is consists in a series of substitutes for unfulfilled parental roles. The coexistence of unstable extraresidential unions, consensual cohabitation, and marriage confuses definitions of parenthood appropriate to either form and produces substantial evasion or failure to accept the obligations of parenthood. In consequence, uterine and materterine kinship ties are invoked by women as substitutes, and they are especially important in providing alternative domestic placement for the issue of broken unions. Men accommodate the kin and outside issue of their resident mates, together with some of their own kin, but very few of their children by former unions. Many adults of both sexes withdraw from this family complex into domestic isolation; a few seek stability by living with their siblings rather than with mates. The mating system has no inherent order by which the alternative mating forms are arranged in an irreversible series. In consequence, these alternatives have equal validity for all individuals at most points of their career; they compete with and dislocate one another. In consequence, the totality of mating relations is in systematic disorder. For this reason the character of this totality is highly stable and little subject to change, since it consists in an equilibrium of competing elements. The domestic alternatives just mentioned are necessary adjustments to this mating context with its unstable parenthood; and since this system of mating is a selfregulating disorder liable to little further change, it follows that the varieties of substitute parenthood and the frequencies of alternative domestic forms tend to be fixed.

## TABLE 1

### REPLACEMENTS, REFUSALS, AND SUBSTITUTIONS IN THE SAMPLE RESURVEY BY REASONS, AND AREAS ASSIGNED TO INDIVIDUAL WORKERS

| Reason for Substitution | Area A | B | C | Total | Source of Substitue |
|---|---|---|---|---|---|
| Refusal | 0 | 3 | 3 | 6 | Unit of same type |
| Addressee no longer lives in unit | 49 | 29 | 29 | 107 | Present occupants |
| Addressee no longer lives in unit | 10 | 7 | 0 | 17 | Occupant next door |
| Dwelling unit demolished | 0 | 0 | 1 | 1 | Occupant next door |
| Dwelling unit empty, under repair | 1 | 0 | 3 | 4 | Occupant next door |
| Listed occupant present, but not available | 1 | 3 | 2 | 6 | Occupant next door |
| Reason for substitution not known | 1 | 0 | 0 | 1 | Unknown |
| TOTAL | 62 | 42 | 38 | 142 | |
| Total units surveyed | 158 | 131 | 136 | 425 | |
| Substitution rate in persons | 39.0% | 32.0% | 28.0% | 33.4% | |
| Substitution rate in dwelling units | 2.0% | 4.6% | 6.7% | 4.2% | |

## TABLE 2

### POPULATION OF THE SAMPLE HOUSEHOLDS, CLASSIFIED BY SEX AND AGE

| Age | Number Male | Female | Total | Percentage Male | Female | Total | Females per Male |
|---|---|---|---|---|---|---|---|
| 0- 4 | 87 | 78 | 165 | 6.5 | 5.9 | 12.4 | 0.90 |
| 5-14 | 135 | 138 | 273 | 10.1 | 10.2 | 20.3 | 1.01 |
| 15-24 | 98 | 163 | 261 | 7.3 | 12.2 | 19.5 | 1.66 |
| 25-39 | 145 | 214 | 359 | 10.8 | 16.0 | 26.8 | 1.48 |
| 40-54 | 74 | 118 | 192 | 5.5 | 8.8 | 14.3 | 1.59 |
| 55-69 | 22 | 48 | 70 | 1.6 | 3.6 | 5.2 | 2.18 |
| 70 and Over | 5 | 15 | 20 | 0.5 | 1.0 | 1.5 | 3.00 |
| TOTAL | 566 | 774 | 1,340 | 42.3 | 57.7 | 100.0 | 1.36 |

## TABLE 3

### HEADS OF THE SAMPLE HOUSEHOLDS, CLASSIFIED BY SEX AND AGE

| Age | Number Male | Female | Total | Percentage Male | Female | Total |
|---|---|---|---|---|---|---|
| 15-24 | 15 | 18 | 33 | 3.5 | 4.3 | 7.8 |
| 25-39 | 115 | 78 | 193 | 27.0 | 18.3 | 45.3 |
| 40-54 | 63 | 74 | 137 | 14.8 | 17.4 | 32.2 |
| 55-69 | 19 | 29 | 48 | 4.5 | 6.9 | 11.4 |
| 70 and Over | 4 | 10 | 14 | 1.0 | 2.3 | 3.3 |
| TOTAL | 216 | 209 | 425 | 50.8 | 49.2 | 100.0 |

## TABLE 4

### DISTRIBUTION OF HOUSEHOLD HEADSHIP AMONG ADULT MEMBERS OF THE SAMPLE POPULATION, CLASSIFIED BY SEX AND AGE

| Age | Total | Male HHs* | %HHs | Total | Female HHs | %HHs | % HHs in Both Sexes |
|---|---|---|---|---|---|---|---|
| 15-24 | 98 | 15 | 15.3 | 163 | 18 | 9.0 | 12.6 |
| 25-39 | 145 | 115 | 79.2 | 214 | 78 | 36.4 | 53.6 |
| 40-54 | 74 | 63 | 85.0 | 118 | 74 | 62.6 | 71.1 |
| 55-69 | 22 | 19 | 86.5 | 48 | 29 | 60.5 | 69.7 |
| 70 and Over | 5 | 4 | 80.0 | 15 | 10 | 66.7 | 70.0 |
| TOTAL | 344 | 216 | 62.7 | 558 | 209 | 37.5 | 47.2 |

*HHs = Household heads.

## TABLE 5

### HOUSEHOLDS OF THE SAMPLE, CLASSIFIED BY SEX OF HEAD AND NUMBER OF PERSONS

| Number of Persons | Sex of Head | | | | Total | |
|---|---|---|---|---|---|---|
| | Male | Female | Total | Male HHs* | Female HHs | Total |
| 1 | 29 | 46 | 75 | 29 | 46 | 75 |
| 2 | 58 | 56 | 114 | 116 | 112 | 228 |
| 3 | 46 | 49 | 95 | 138 | 147 | 285 |
| 4 | 27 | 30 | 57 | 108 | 120 | 228 |
| 5 | 26 | 15 | 41 | 130 | 75 | 205 |
| 6 | 11 | 2 | 13 | 66 | 12 | 78 |
| 7 | 8 | 7 | 15 | 56 | 49 | 105 |
| 8 | 5 | 2 | 7 | 40 | 16 | 56 |
| 9 | 4 | 1 | 5 | 36 | 9 | 45 |
| 10 | 1 | 0 | 1 | 10 | 0 | 10 |
| 11 | 0 | 0 | 0 | 0 | 0 | 0 |
| 12 | 1 | 1 | 2 | 12 | 12 | 24 |
| TOTAL | 216 | 209 | 425 | 741 | 599 | 1,340 |

| Averages: | including solitary persons | 3.43% | 2.86% | 3.16% |
|---|---|---|---|---|
| | excluding solitary persons | 3.80% | 3.39% | 3.60% |

*HHs = Household heads.

## TABLE 6

### AGE AND SEX DISTRIBUTION OF HOUSEHOLD POPULATION, CLASSIFIED ACCORDING TO THE SEX OF THE HEAD

| Age | Male Head | | | | Female Head | | | | Total | |
|---|---|---|---|---|---|---|---|---|---|---|
| | Male | Female | Total | Per cent | Male | Female | Total | Per cent | Male %HHs* | Female %HHs |
| 0- 4 | 62 | 48 | 110 | 14.8 | 25 | 30 | 55 | 8.4 | 8.3 | 4.1 |
| 5-14 | 67 | 75 | 142 | 19.2 | 68 | 63 | 131 | 22.0 | 10.6 | 9.7 |
| 15-24 | 51 | 77 | 128 | 17.3 | 47 | 86 | 133 | 22.4 | 9.6 | 9.9 |
| 25-39 | 120 | 105 | 225 | 30.4 | 25 | 109 | 134 | 22.6 | 16.8 | 10.0 |
| 40-54 | 64 | 34 | 98 | 13.2 | 10 | 84 | 94 | 15.8 | 7.3 | 7.0 |
| 55-69 | 20 | 13 | 33 | 4.4 | 2 | 35 | 37 | 6.3 | 2.5 | 2.7 |
| 70 + | 4 | 1 | 5 | 0.7 | 1 | 14 | 15 | 2.5 | 0.4 | 1.1 |
| TOTAL | 388 | 353 | 741 | 100.0 | 178 | 421 | 599 | 100.0 | 55.5 | 44.5 |

*HHs = Household heads.

## TABLE 7

### HOUSEHOLDERS LIVING ALONE, CLASSIFIED BY AGE AND SEX

| Age | Male | Female | Total |
|---|---|---|---|
| 15-24 | 2 | 5 | 7 |
| 25-39 | 12 | 22 | 34 |
| 40-54 | 11 | 10 | 21 |
| 55-69 | 3 | 7 | 10 |
| 70 + | 1 | 2 | 3 |
| TOTAL | 29 | 46 | 75 |

## TABLE 8

ALL ADULT MEMBERS OF THE SAMPLE POPULATION, CLASSIFIED BY SEX, AGE, MARITAL CONDITION, AND PARENTAL STATUS

| Mating and Parental Status | Male -24 | -39 | -54 | -69 | 70+ | Total | Female -24 | -39 | -54 | -69 | 70+ | Total | Total |
|---|---|---|---|---|---|---|---|---|---|---|---|---|---|
| **1. Single persons, parental status n/k*** | | | | | | | | | | | | | |
| a. Mating now n/k | 79 | 37 | 12 | 2 | 0 | 130 | 106 | 62 | 15 | 0 | 0 | 183 | 313 |
| b. Mating now | 3 | 2 | 3 | 0 | 0 | 8 | 0 | 2 | 0 | 0 | 0 | 2 | 10 |
| c. Not mating now | 0 | 0 | 0 | 4 | 2 | 6 | 0 | 0 | 7 | 13 | 2 | 22 | 28 |
| Total single persons, parental status n/k | 82 | 39 | 15 | 6 | 2 | 144 | 106 | 64 | 22 | 13 | 2 | 207 | 351 |
| **2. Single parents** | | | | | | | | | | | | | |
| a. Mating now n/k | 0 | 2 | 1 | 0 | 0 | 3 | 6 | 17 | 21 | 0 | 0 | 44 | 47 |
| b. Not mating now | 0 | 0 | 0 | 0 | 0 | 0 | 0 | 0 | 11 | 12 | 5 | 28 | 28 |
| c. Mating now | 1 | 1 | 0 | 0 | 0 | 2 | 13 | 8 | 2 | 0 | 0 | 23 | 25 |
| Total single parents | 1 | 3 | 1 | 0 | 0 | 5 | 19 | 25 | 34 | 12 | 5 | 95 | 100 |
| **3. Consensually wed, etc.** | | | | | | | | | | | | | |
| a. In 1955 | 12 | 58 | 24 | 4 | 0 | 98 | 24 | 60 | 15 | 0 | 0 | 99 | 197 |
| b. Separated, with children | 0 | 0 | 0 | 0 | 0 | 0 | 0 | 0 | 0 | 0 | 0 | 0 | 0 |
| c. Separated, childless | 0 | 0 | 0 | 0 | 0 | 0 | 0 | 0 | 0 | 0 | 0 | 0 | 0 |
| d. Separated, not single | 0 | 0 | 0 | 0 | 0 | 0 | 0 | 0 | 0 | 0 | 0 | 0 | 0 |
| Total consensually wed, etc. | 12 | 58 | 24 | 4 | 0 | 98 | 24 | 60 | 15 | 0 | 0 | 99 | 197 |
| **4. Married persons** | | | | | | | | | | | | | |
| a. Spouse present | 3 | 45 | 33 | 10 | 3 | 94 | 13 | 50 | 21 | 10 | 0 | 94 | 188 |
| b. Spouse absent | 0 | 0 | 1 | 1 | 0 | 2 | 1 | 11 | 22 | 8 | 6 | 48 | 50 |
| c. Separated, single | 0 | 0 | 0 | 0 | 0 | 0 | 0 | 0 | 0 | 0 | 0 | 0 | 0 |
| d. Separated, not single | 0 | 0 | 0 | 0 | 0 | 0 | 0 | 0 | 0 | 0 | 0 | 0 | 0 |
| Total married persons | 3 | 45 | 34 | 11 | 3 | 96 | 14 | 61 | 43 | 18 | 6 | 142 | 238 |
| **5. Widowed persons** | | | | | | | | | | | | | |
| a. Widowed, single | 0 | 0 | 0 | 1 | 0 | 1 | 0 | 4 | 4 | 5 | 2 | 15 | 16 |
| b. Widowed, not single | 0 | 0 | 0 | 0 | 0 | 0 | 0 | 0 | 0 | 0 | 0 | 0 | 0 |
| Total widowed persons | 0 | 0 | 0 | 1 | 0 | 1 | 0 | 4 | 4 | 5 | 2 | 15 | 16 |
| **GRAND TOTAL** | 98 | 145 | 74 | 22 | 5 | 344 | 163 | 214 | 118 | 48 | 15 | 558 | 902 |

*n/k = Not known.

## TABLE 9

ADULT MEMBERS OF THE SAMPLE POPULATION OTHER THAN HOUSEHOLD HEADS, CLASSIFIED
BY SEX, AGE, MARITAL CONDITION, AND PARENTAL STATUS

| Mating and Parental Status | Male | | | | | | Female | | | | | | Total |
|---|---|---|---|---|---|---|---|---|---|---|---|---|---|
| | -24 | -39 | -54 | -69 | 70+ | Total | -24 | -39 | -54 | -69 | 70+ | Total | |
| 1. Single persons, parental status n/k* | | | | | | | | | | | | | |
| a. Mating now n/k | 75 | 19 | 2 | 0 | 0 | 96 | 92 | 28 | 5 | 0 | 0 | 125 | 221 |
| b. Mating in 1955 | 2 | 0 | 0 | 0 | 0 | 2 | 0 | 0 | 0 | 0 | 0 | 0 | 2 |
| c. Not mating in 1955 | 0 | 0 | 0 | 1 | 0 | 1 | 0 | 0 | 1 | 3 | 0 | 4 | 5 |
| Total single persons, parental status n/k | 77 | 19 | 2 | 1 | 0 | 99 | 92 | 28 | 6 | 3 | 0 | 129 | 228 |
| 2. Single parents | | | | | | | | | | | | | |
| a. Mating now n/k | 0 | 2 | 0 | 0 | 0 | 2 | 5 | 3 | 4 | 0 | 0 | 12 | 14 |
| b. Not mating now | 0 | 0 | 0 | 0 | 0 | 0 | 0 | 0 | 1 | 4 | 1 | 6 | 6 |
| c. Mating now | 1 | 0 | 0 | 0 | 0 | 1 | 13 | 3 | 0 | 0 | 0 | 16 | 17 |
| Total single parents | 1 | 2 | 0 | 0 | 0 | 3 | 18 | 6 | 5 | 4 | 1 | 34 | 37 |
| 3. Consensually wed, etc.† | | | | | | | | | | | | | |
| a. In 1955 | 5 | 8 | 7 | 1 | 0 | 21 | 22 | 49 | 9 | 0 | 0 | 80 | 101 |
| Total consensually wed, etc. | 5 | 8 | 7 | 1 | 0 | 21 | 22 | 49 | 9 | 0 | 0 | 80 | 101 |
| 4. Married persons‡ | | | | | | | | | | | | | |
| a. Spouse present | 0 | 1 | 2 | 1 | 1 | 5 | 13 | 50 | 21 | 7 | 0 | 91 | 96 |
| b. Spouse absent | 0 | 0 | 0 | 0 | 0 | 0 | 0 | 2 | 3 | 3 | 4 | 12 | 12 |
| Total married persons | 0 | 1 | 2 | 1 | 1 | 5 | 13 | 52 | 24 | 10 | 4 | 103 | 108 |
| 5. Widowed persons | | | | | | | | | | | | | |
| a. Widowed, single | 0 | 0 | 0 | 0 | 0 | 0 | 0 | 1 | 0 | 2 | 0 | 3 | 3 |
| b. Widowed, not single | 0 | 0 | 0 | 0 | 0 | 0 | 0 | 0 | 0 | 0 | 0 | 0 | 0 |
| Total widowed persons | 0 | 0 | 0 | 0 | 0 | 0 | 0 | 1 | 0 | 2 | 0 | 3 | 3 |
| GRAND TOTAL | 83 | 30 | 11 | 3 | 1 | 128 | 145 | 136 | 44 | 19 | 5 | 349 | 477 |

*n/k = Not known.

†For reasons given above, we lack data on consensually wed and separated parents or childless persons.

‡We lack reliable data on married persons who have separated or divorced.

## TABLE 10

### HOUSEHOLD HEADS, CLASSIFIED BY SEX, AGE, MARITAL CONDITION, AND PARENTAL STATUS

| Mating and Parental Status | Male | | | | | | Female | | | | | | Total |
|---|---|---|---|---|---|---|---|---|---|---|---|---|---|
| | -24 | -39 | -54 | -69 | 70+ | Total | -24 | -39 | -54 | -69 | 70+ | Total | |
| 1. Single persons, parental status n/k* | | | | | | | | | | | | | |
| a. Mating now n/k | 4 | 18 | 10 | 2 | 0 | 34 | 14 | 34 | 10 | 0 | 0 | 58 | 92 |
| b. Mating in 1955 | 1 | 2 | 3 | 0 | 0 | 6 | 0 | 2 | 0 | 0 | 0 | 2 | 8 |
| c. Not mating in 1955 | 0 | 0 | 0 | 3 | 2 | 5 | 0 | 0 | 6 | 10 | 2 | 18 | 23 |
| d. Never mated | 0 | 0 | 0 | 0 | 0 | 0 | 0 | 0 | 0 | 0 | 0 | 0 | 0 |
| Total single persons, parental status n/k | 5 | 20 | 13 | 5 | 2 | 45 | 14 | 36 | 16 | 10 | 2 | 78 | 123 |
| 2. Single parents | | | | | | | | | | | | | |
| a. Mating now n/k | 0 | 0 | 1 | 0 | 0 | 1 | 1 | 14 | 17 | 0 | 0 | 32 | 33 |
| b. Not mating now | 0 | 0 | 0 | 0 | 0 | 0 | 0 | 0 | 10 | 8 | 4 | 22 | 22 |
| c. Mating now | 0 | 1 | 0 | 0 | 0 | 1 | 0 | 5 | 2 | 0 | 0 | 7 | 8 |
| Total single parents | 0 | 1 | 1 | 0 | 0 | 2 | 1 | 19 | 29 | 8 | 4 | 61 | 63 |
| 3. Consensually wed, etc. | | | | | | | | | | | | | |
| a. In 1955 | 7 | 50 | 17 | 3 | 0 | 77 | 2 | 11 | 6 | 0 | 0 | 19 | 96 |
| b. Separated, with children | 0 | 0 | 0 | 0 | 0 | 0 | 0 | 0 | 0 | 0 | 0 | 0 | 0 |
| c. Widowed, single | 0 | 0 | 0 | 0 | 0 | 0 | 0 | 0 | 0 | 0 | 0 | 0 | 0 |
| Total consensually wed, etc. | 7 | 50 | 17 | 3 | 0 | 77 | 2 | 11 | 6 | 0 | 0 | 19 | 96 |
| 4. Married persons | | | | | | | | | | | | | |
| a. Spouse present | 3 | 44 | 31 | 9 | 2 | 89 | 0 | 0 | 0 | 3 | 0 | 3 | 92 |
| b. Spouse absent | 0 | 0 | 1 | 1 | 0 | 2 | 1 | 9 | 19 | 5 | 2 | 36 | 38 |
| c. Separated, single | 0 | 0 | 0 | 0 | 0 | 0 | 0 | 0 | 0 | 0 | 0 | 0 | 0 |
| d. Separated, not single | 0 | 0 | 0 | 0 | 0 | 0 | 0 | 0 | 0 | 0 | 0 | 0 | 0 |
| Total married persons | 3 | 44 | 32 | 10 | 2 | 91 | 1 | 9 | 19 | 8 | 2 | 39 | 130 |
| 5. Widowed persons | | | | | | | | | | | | | |
| a. Widowed, single | 0 | 0 | 0 | 1 | 0 | 1 | 0 | 3 | 4 | 3 | 2 | 12 | 13 |
| b. Widowed, not single | 0 | 0 | 0 | 0 | 0 | 0 | 0 | 0 | 0 | 0 | 0 | 0 | 0 |
| Total widowed persons | 0 | 0 | 0 | 1 | 0 | 1 | 0 | 3 | 4 | 3 | 2 | 12 | 13 |
| GRAND TOTAL | 15 | 115 | 63 | 19 | 4 | 216 | 18 | 78 | 74 | 29 | 10 | 209 | 425 |

*n/k = Not known.

## TABLE 11

### THE ADULT FEMALE POPULATION OF KINGSTON IN 1953, CLASSIFIED BY AGE AND PARENTAL AND MARITAL STATUS*

| Parental Status | Number | | | | | Percentage | | | | |
|---|---|---|---|---|---|---|---|---|---|---|
| | -24 | -39 | -54 | -69 | 70+ | -24 | -39 | -54 | -69 | 70+ |
| All women | 35,687 | 46,747 | 24,009 | 9,061 | 4,389 | 100.0 | 100.0 | 100.0 | 100.0 | 100.0 |
| All mothers | 11,623 | 33,794 | 18,618 | 7,695 | 4,386 | 32.5 | 72.3 | 77.2 | 84.6 | 100.0 |
| Conjugal Status of Mothers | | | | | | | | | | |
| Single mothers | 6,402 | 10,557 | 5,176 | 1,954 | 731 | 17.9 | 22.6 | 21.5 | 21.5 | 16.7 |
| Consensually wed | 3,211 | 8,901 | 3,010 | 635 | 345 | 8.9 | 19.0 | 12.5 | 7.0 | 7.7 |
| Married, divorced, etc. | 1,806 | 13,214 | 8,128 | 2,828 | 1,026 | 5.5 | 28.3 | 33.8 | 31.1 | 23.4 |
| Widowed | 0 | 455 | 1,908 | 2,823 | 2,120 | 0.0 | 1.0 | 7.9 | 24.5 | 48.4 |
| Not stated | 204 | 567 | 296 | 45 | 164 | 0.2 | 1.4 | 1.5 | 0.5 | 3.8 |

*Information abstracted from Report on A Sample Survey of the Population of Jamaica Oct.-Nov., 1953, Department of Statistics, Kingston, Jamaica, Table 14, pp. 31-32, and Table 18, p. 40.

## TABLE 12

### ESTIMATED DISTRIBUTION OF ADULT FEMALES OF THE HOUSEHOLD SAMPLE BY AGE AND PARENTAL AND MARITAL STATUS

| Parental Status | -24 | -39 | -54 | -69 | 70+ | Total |
|---|---|---|---|---|---|---|
| Population by age groups | 163 | 214 | 118 | 48 | 15 | 558 |
| Number of mothers | 53 | 155 | 91 | 41 | 15 | 355 |
| Childless women | 110 | 59 | 27 | 7 | 0 | 203 |
| Conjugal Status of Mothers | | | | | | |
| Single persons | 30 | 49 | 25 | 11 | 3 | 118 |
| Consensually wed | 15 | 42 | 15 | 3 | 1 | 76 |
| Married, divorced, or separated | 8 | 62 | 40 | 15 | 3 | 128 |
| Widowed | 0 | 2 | 11 | 12 | 8 | 33 |

## TABLE 13

### ADULT FEMALES OF THE SAMPLE POPULATION, CLASSIFIED BY AGE AND PARENTAL AND MARITAL STATUS

| Parental and Marital Status | -24 | -39 | -54 | -69 | 70+ | Total |
|---|---|---|---|---|---|---|
| 1. Childless single persons | 95 | 40 | 22 | 7 | 0 | 164† |
| 2. Single parents | 30 | 49 | 27 | 11 | 4 | 121 |
| 3. a. Consensually wed, childless persons | 9 | 18 | ? | ? | ? | 27* |
| b. Consensually wed, parents | 15 | 42 | 15 | 0 | 0 | 72 |
| 4. a. Married, separated, divorced, childless | 6 | ? | 3 | 3 | 0 | 12* |
| b. Married, separated, divorced, parents | 8 | 61 | 40 | 15 | 3 | 127 |
| 5. Widowed persons | 0 | 4 | 11 | 12 | 8 | 35 |
| TOTAL | 163 | 214 | 118 | 48 | 15 | 558 |

(Items marked by an asterisk may require further upward adjustment at the expense of the first category on this table, marked thus †.)

# TABLE 14

## POPULATION OF THE SAMPLE HOUSEHOLDS, CLASSIFIED BY RELATIONSHIP TO THE HOUSEHOLD HEAD AND SEX OF HEAD

| Categories of Kin | Male Head Number | Male Head Per cent | Female Head Number | Female Head Per cent | Total Number | Total Per cent |
|---|---|---|---|---|---|---|
| 1. Spouses and mates | 166 | 31.3 | 22 | 5.6 | 188 | 20.3 |
| 2. HH's* sons | 118 | 22.1 | 93 | 24.0 | 211 | 23.2 |
| 3. HH's daughters | 113 | 21.3 | 101 | 25.9 | 214 | 23.6 |
| 4. HH's children | 231 | 43.4 | 194 | 49.9 | 425 | 46.8 |
| 5. HH's sons' sons | 4 | 0.8 | 4 | 1.0 | 8 | 0.9 |
| 6. HH's sons' daughters | 12 | 2.4 | 4 | 1.0 | 16 | 1.7 |
| 7. HH's daughters' sons | 3 | 0.6 | 28 | 7.2 | 31 | 3.4 |
| 8. HH's daughters' daughters | 4 | 0.8 | 26 | 6.6 | 30 | 3.3 |
| HH's grandchildren | 23 | 4.6 | 62 | 15.8 | 85 | 9.3 |
| HH's daughters' grandchildren | 0 | 0.0 | 1 | 0.3 | 1 | 0.1 |
| Total lineal issue of HH | 254 | 48.0 | 257 | 66.0 | 511 | 56.2 |
| 9. HH's mates' sons by others | 18 | 3.6 | 2 | 0.6 | 20 | 2.2 |
| 10. HH's mates' daughters by others | 6 | 1.2 | 0 | 0.0 | 6 | 0.7 |
| 11. HH's mates' daughters' daughters | 2 | 0.4 | 0 | 0.0 | 2 | 0.2 |
| Issue of HH's mates by others | 26 | 5.2 | 2 | 0.6 | 28 | 3.1 |
| 12. HH's brothers | 9 | 1.8 | 5 | 1.3 | 14 | 1.5 |
| 13. HH's sisters | 7 | 1.4 | 21 | 5.4 | 28 | 3.1 |
| 14. HH's brothers' children | 1 | 0.2 | 5 | 1.3 | 6 | 0.7 |
| 15. HH's sisters' children | 2 | 0.4 | 25 | 6.3 | 27 | 2.9 |
| 16. HH's brothers' grandchildren | 0 | 0.0 | 2 | 0.6 | 2 | 0.2 |
| HH's siblings and their issue | 19 | 3.8 | 58 | 14.9 | 77 | 8.4 |
| 17. HH's mother | 4 | 0.8 | 6 | 1.5 | 10 | 1.1 |
| 18. HH's mother's mother | 0 | 0.0 | 2 | 0.6 | 2 | 0.2 |
| 19. HH's other matrilateral kin | 2 | 0.4 | 7 | 1.8 | 9 | 1.0 |
| HH's other consanguineal kin | 6 | 1.2 | 15 | 3.9 | 21 | 2.3 |
| 20. HH's sons' mates or spouses | 0 | 0.0 | 2 | 0.5 | 2 | 0.2 |
| 21. HH's daughters' mates or spouses | 0 | 0.0 | 2 | 0.5 | 2 | 0.2 |
| 22. HH's son's mate's child by another | 0 | 0.0 | 1 | 0.2 | 1 | 0.1 |
| 23. Other kin of HH's mate or spouse | 32 | 6.1 | 1 | 0.2 | 33 | 3.6 |
| Other affinal kin | 32 | 6.1 | 6 | 1.5 | 38 | 4.1 |
| 24. Adopted persons and their issue | 4 | 0.8 | 8 | 2.2 | 12 | 1.3 |
| 25. Unrelated persons and their issue | 4 | 0.8 | 13 | 3.3 | 17 | 1.9 |
| 26. Boarders | 6 | 1.2 | 7 | 1.8 | 13 | 1.4 |
| 27. Employees | 8 | 1.6 | 1 | 0.2 | 9 | 1.0 |
| Total miscellaneous persons | 22 | 4.4 | 29 | 7.5 | 51 | 5.6 |
| TOTAL | 525 | 100.0 | 389 | 100.0 | 914 | 100.0 |

*HH = Household head.

## TABLE 15

RESIDENT COLLATERALS OF HOUSEHOLD PRINCIPALS, CLASSIFIED BY SEX OF PRINCIPAL AND HOUSEHOLD HEAD, BY BIRTH STATUS, AND BY KINSHIP TO THE LINKED PRINCIPAL

| Kinship Category | Households with Male Head | | | | | | | | Households with Female Head | | | | Total Kin of: | |
| | Principal Male HH* | | | | Principal HH's Mate | | | | Principal HH | | | | | |
| | L* | U* | N/K* | All | L | U | N/K | All | L | U | N/K | All | All Principals | Female Principals |
|---|---|---|---|---|---|---|---|---|---|---|---|---|---|---|
| Full siblings | 2 | 0 | 1 | 3 | 3 | 1 | 0 | 4 | 8 | 3 | 10 | 21 | 28 | 25 |
| Issue of full siblings | 1 | 0 | 0 | 1 | 1 | 10 | 1 | 12 | 0 | 14 | 3 | 17 | 30 | 29 |
| Maternal half siblings | 0 | 10 | 1 | 11 | 2 | 2 | 0 | 4 | 0 | 0 | 5 | 5 | 20 | 9 |
| Issue of maternal half siblings | 1 | 0 | 0 | 1 | 0 | 1 | 0 | 1 | 0 | 10 | 2 | 12 | 14 | 13 |
| Paternal half siblings | 0 | 2 | 0 | 2 | 0 | 0 | 0 | 0 | 0 | 0 | 1 | 1 | 3 | 1 |
| Issue of paternal half siblings | 0 | 1 | 0 | 1 | 0 | 0 | 0 | 0 | 1 | 2 | 0 | 3 | 4 | 3 |
| Other patrilateral kin | 0 | 0 | 0 | 0 | 0 | 0 | 0 | 0 | 0 | 0 | 0 | 0 | 0 | 0 |
| Other matrilateral kin† | 0 | 2 | 0 | 2 | 1 | 3 | 1 | 5 | 2 | 4 | 1 | 7 | 14 | 12 |
| TOTAL | 4 | 15 | 2 | 21 | 7 | 17 | 2 | 26 | 11 | 33 | 22 | 66 | 113 | 92 |

*HH = Household head; L = Lawful, i.e., legitimate; U = Unlawful, i.e., illegitimate; N/K = Birth status not known.
†This does not include the 4 resident mothers of male HH's, or the 6 resident mothers of the mates of these men, or the 6 resident mothers and 2 resident grandmothers of female spouses.

# TABLE 16

RESIDENT COLLATERALS OF FEMALE PRINCIPALS, CLASSIFIED BY SEX, BIRTH STATUS, GENERATION, SEX OF PARENT THROUGH WHOM KINSHIP IS TRACED, AND SEX OF HOUSEHOLD HEAD

| Generation | Sex of Linking Parent | MH L* M* | MH L* F* | MH U* M | MH U* F | MH N/K* M | MH N/K* F | MH All M | MH All F | FH L M | FH L F | FH U M | FH U F | FH N/K M | FH N/K F | FH All M | FH All F | Tot L M | Tot L F | Tot U M | Tot U F | Tot N/K M | Tot N/K F | Tot All M | Tot All F | Total |
|---|---|---|---|---|---|---|---|---|---|---|---|---|---|---|---|---|---|---|---|---|---|---|---|---|---|---|
| +1 | Male | 0 | 0 | 0 | 0 | 0 | 0 | 0 | 0 | 0 | 0 | 0 | 0 | 0 | 0 | 0 | 0 | 0 | 0 | 0 | 0 | 0 | 0 | 0 | 0 | 0 |
|  | Female | 0 | 0 | 0 | 0 | 0 | 1 | 0 | 1 | 0 | 0 | 0 | 0 | 0 | 0 | 0 | 0 | 0 | 0 | 0 | 0 | 0 | 1 | 0 | 1 | 1 |
|  | Total | 0 | 0 | 0 | 0 | 0 | 1 | 0 | 1 | 0 | 0 | 0 | 0 | 0 | 0 | 0 | 0 | 0 | 0 | 0 | 0 | 0 | 1 | 0 | 1 | 1 |
| 0 | Male | 0 | 1 | 0 | 0 | 0 | 0 | 0 | 1 | 0 | 1 | 0 | 1 | 0 | 1 | 0 | 3 | 0 | 2 | 0 | 1 | 0 | 1 | 0 | 4 | 4 |
|  | Female | 2 | 0 | 3 | 2 | 0 | 0 | 5 | 2 | 0 | 1 | 0 | 1 | 0 | 6 | 0 | 8 | 2 | 1 | 3 | 3 | 0 | 6 | 5 | 10 | 15 |
|  | Total | 2 | 1 | 3 | 2 | 0 | 0 | 5 | 3 | 0 | 2 | 0 | 2 | 0 | 7 | 0 | 11 | 2 | 3 | 3 | 4 | 0 | 7 | 5 | 14 | 19 |
| -1 | Male | 0 | 0 | 0 | 0 | 0 | 1 | 0 | 1 | 0 | 1 | 1 | 2 | 0 | 0 | 1 | 3 | 0 | 1 | 1 | 2 | 0 | 1 | 1 | 4 | 5 |
|  | Female | 0 | 1 | 1 | 4 | 0 | 0 | 1 | 5 | 0 | 1 | 9 | 13 | 1 | 4 | 10 | 18 | 0 | 2 | 10 | 17 | 1 | 4 | 11 | 23 | 34 |
|  | Total | 0 | 1 | 1 | 4 | 0 | 1 | 1 | 6 | 0 | 2 | 10 | 15 | 1 | 4 | 11 | 21 | 0 | 3 | 11 | 19 | 1 | 5 | 12 | 27 | 39 |
| -2 | Male | 0 | 0 | 0 | 0 | 0 | 1 | 0 | 1 | 0 | 0 | 0 | 0 | 0 | 0 | 0 | 0 | 0 | 0 | 0 | 0 | 0 | 1 | 0 | 1 | 1 |
|  | Female | 0 | 0 | 1 | 4 | 0 | 0 | 1 | 4 | 0 | 0 | 2 | 0 | 0 | 0 | 2 | 0 | 0 | 0 | 3 | 4 | 0 | 0 | 3 | 4 | 7 |
|  | Total | 0 | 0 | 1 | 4 | 0 | 1 | 1 | 5 | 0 | 0 | 2 | 0 | 0 | 0 | 2 | 0 | 0 | 0 | 3 | 4 | 0 | 1 | 3 | 5 | 8 |
| All generations | Male | 0 | 1 | 0 | 0 | 0 | 2 | 0 | 3 | 0 | 2 | 1 | 3 | 0 | 1 | 1 | 6 | 0 | 3 | 1 | 3 | 0 | 3 | 1 | 9 | 10 |
|  | Female | 2 | 1 | 5 | 10 | 0 | 1 | 7 | 12 | 0 | 2 | 11 | 14 | 1 | 10 | 12 | 26 | 2 | 3 | 16 | 24 | 1 | 11 | 19 | 38 | 57 |
|  | TOTAL | 2 | 2 | 5 | 10 | 0 | 3 | 7 | 15 | 0 | 4 | 12 | 17 | 1 | 11 | 13 | 32 | 2 | 6 | 17 | 27 | 1 | 14 | 20 | 47 | 67 |

*L = Lawful, i.e., legitimate; U = Unlawful, i.e., illegitimate; N/K = Birth status not known; M = Male; F = Female.

## TABLE 17

RESIDENT LINEAL ISSUE OF THE HOUSEHOLD HEAD, CLASSIFIED BY SEX, BIRTH STATUS, GENERATION, SEX OF PARENT THROUGH WHOM DESCENT IS TRACED, AND SEX OF THE HOUSEHOLD HEAD

| Sex and Birth Status | Households with Male Head | | | | Households with Female Head | | | | Total | | | |
|---|---|---|---|---|---|---|---|---|---|---|---|---|
| | Own Issue | Sons' Issue | Daughters' Issue | Total | Own Issue | Sons' Issue | Daughters' Issue | Total | Own Issue | Sons' Issue | Daughters' Issue | Total |
| Males L* | 88 | 4 | 0 | 92 | 42 | 1 | 8 | 51 | 130 | 5 | 8 | 143 |
| U* | 29 | 0 | 3 | 32 | 40 | 3 | 19 | 62 | 69 | 3 | 22 | 94 |
| N/K* | 1 | 0 | 0 | 1 | 11 | 0 | 2 | 13 | 12 | 0 | 2 | 14 |
| All males | 118 | 4 | 3 | 125 | 93 | 4 | 29 | 126 | 211 | 8 | 32 | 251 |
| Females L | 79 | 10 | 0 | 89 | 31 | 0 | 7 | 38 | 110 | 10 | 7 | 127 |
| U | 32 | 2 | 4 | 38 | 53 | 4 | 19 | 76 | 85 | 6 | 23 | 114 |
| N/K | 2 | 0 | 0 | 2 | 17 | 0 | 0 | 17 | 19 | 0 | 0 | 19 |
| All females | 113 | 12 | 4 | 129 | 101 | 4 | 26 | 131 | 214 | 16 | 30 | 260 |
| Total L | 167 | 14 | 0 | 181 | 73 | 1 | 15 | 89 | 240 | 15 | 15 | 270 |
| U | 61 | 2 | 7 | 70 | 93 | 7 | 38 | 138 | 154 | 9 | 45 | 208 |
| N/K | 3 | 0 | 0 | 3 | 28 | 0 | 2 | 30 | 31 | 0 | 2 | 33 |
| GRAND TOTAL | 231 | 16 | 7 | 254 | 194 | 8 | 55 | 257 | 425 | 24 | 62 | 511 |

*L = Lawful, i.e., legitimate; U = Unlawful, i.e., illegitimate; N/K = Birth status not known.

## TABLE 18

DISTRIBUTION OF CHILDREN WITHIN THE SAMPLE HOUSEHOLDS, CLASSIFIED BY SEX OF HEAD, WITH SPECIAL REFERENCE TO THE PRESENCE OF EITHER PARENT IN THE HOUSEHOLD, AND TO THE AGE AND BIRTH STATUS OF THE CHILDREN OF EITHER SEX

| Age | Households with Male Head | | | | | | | Households with Female Head | | | | | | | Total | | | | | | |
|---|---|---|---|---|---|---|---|---|---|---|---|---|---|---|---|---|---|---|---|---|---|
| | LS* | LD* | US* | UD* | N/KS* | N/KD* | Total | LS | LD | US | UD | N/KS | N/KD | Total | LS | LD | US | UD | N/KS | N/KD | Total |
| **a. Both parents present** | | | | | | | | | | | | | | | | | | | | | |
| 0– 4 | 36 | 21 | 16 | 14 | 0 | 0 | 87 | 0 | 0 | 2 | 4 | 0 | 0 | 6 | 36 | 21 | 18 | 18 | 0 | 0 | 93 |
| 5–14 | 34 | 41 | 9 | 6 | 0 | 0 | 90 | 1 | 1 | 0 | 0 | 0 | 0 | 2 | 35 | 42 | 9 | 6 | 0 | 0 | 92 |
| 15–24 | 15 | 14 | 1 | 4 | 0 | 0 | 34 | 0 | 0 | 1 | 0 | 0 | 0 | 1 | 15 | 14 | 2 | 4 | 0 | 0 | 35 |
| 25–39 | 1 | 2 | 0 | 0 | 0 | 0 | 3 | 1 | 1 | 0 | 0 | 0 | 0 | 2 | 2 | 3 | 0 | 0 | 0 | 0 | 5 |
| 40 + | 0 | 0 | 0 | 0 | 0 | 0 | 0 | 0 | 0 | 0 | 0 | 0 | 0 | 0 | 0 | 0 | 0 | 0 | 0 | 0 | 0 |
| Total | 86 | 78 | 26 | 24 | 0 | 0 | 214 | 2 | 2 | 3 | 4 | 0 | 0 | 11 | 88 | 80 | 29 | 28 | 0 | 0 | 225 |
| **b. Both parents absent** | | | | | | | | | | | | | | | | | | | | | |
| 0– 4 | 1 | 3 | 3 | 4 | 0 | 0 | 11 | 1 | 0 | 3 | 4 | 0 | 1 | 9 | 2 | 3 | 6 | 8 | 0 | 1 | 20 |
| 5–14 | 3 | 8 | 6 | 7 | 2 | 1 | 27 | 2 | 2 | 12 | 11 | 3 | 4 | 34 | 5 | 10 | 18 | 18 | 5 | 5 | 61 |
| 15–24 | 5 | 6 | 3 | 5 | 2 | 8 | 29 | 4 | 7 | 7 | 15 | 2 | 8 | 43 | 9 | 13 | 10 | 20 | 4 | 16 | 72 |
| 25–39 | 0 | 1 | 0 | 1 | 3 | 4 | 9 | 2 | 3 | 3 | 4 | 1 | 3 | 16 | 2 | 4 | 3 | 5 | 4 | 7 | 25 |
| 40 + | 1 | 0 | 0 | 0 | 1 | 2 | 4 | 0 | 1 | 0 | 1 | 2 | 9 | 13 | 1 | 1 | 0 | 1 | 3 | 11 | 17 |
| Total | 10 | 18 | 12 | 17 | 8 | 15 | 80 | 9 | 13 | 25 | 35 | 8 | 25 | 115 | 19 | 31 | 37 | 52 | 16 | 40 | 195 |
| **c. Mothers only present** | | | | | | | | | | | | | | | | | | | | | |
| 0– 4 | 0 | 0 | 5 | 5 | 0 | 0 | 10 | 5 | 2 | 13 | 18 | 0 | 0 | 38 | 5 | 2 | 18 | 23 | 0 | 0 | 48 |
| 5–14 | 0 | 0 | 11 | 6 | 0 | 0 | 17 | 20 | 16 | 20 | 23 | 0 | 0 | 79 | 20 | 16 | 31 | 29 | 0 | 0 | 96 |
| 15–24 | 0 | 0 | 7 | 2 | 0 | 0 | 9 | 11 | 10 | 17 | 21 | 0 | 0 | 59 | 11 | 10 | 24 | 23 | 0 | 0 | 68 |
| 25–39 | 0 | 0 | 1 | 0 | 0 | 0 | 1 | 2 | 4 | 6 | 11 | 0 | 0 | 23 | 2 | 4 | 7 | 11 | 0 | 0 | 24 |
| 40 + | 0 | 0 | 0 | 0 | 0 | 0 | 0 | 0 | 0 | 0 | 0 | 0 | 0 | 0 | 0 | 0 | 0 | 0 | 0 | 0 | 0 |
| Total | 0 | 0 | 24 | 13 | 0 | 0 | 37 | 38 | 32 | 56 | 73 | 0 | 0 | 199 | 38 | 32 | 80 | 86 | 0 | 0 | 236 |
| **d. Fathers only present** | | | | | | | | | | | | | | | | | | | | | |
| 0– 4 | 0 | 0 | 1 | 1 | 0 | 0 | 2 | 0 | 0 | 1 | 0 | 0 | 0 | 1 | 0 | 0 | 2 | 1 | 0 | 0 | 3 |
| 5–14 | 0 | 1 | 2 | 4 | 0 | 0 | 7 | 0 | 0 | 1 | 1 | 0 | 0 | 2 | 0 | 1 | 3 | 5 | 0 | 0 | 9 |
| 15–24 | 1 | 0 | 0 | 3 | 0 | 0 | 4 | 0 | 0 | 0 | 0 | 0 | 0 | 0 | 1 | 0 | 0 | 3 | 0 | 0 | 4 |
| 25–39 | 0 | 0 | 0 | 0 | 0 | 0 | 0 | 0 | 0 | 0 | 0 | 0 | 0 | 0 | 0 | 0 | 0 | 0 | 0 | 0 | 0 |
| 40 + | 0 | 0 | 0 | 0 | 0 | 0 | 0 | 0 | 0 | 0 | 0 | 0 | 0 | 0 | 0 | 0 | 0 | 0 | 0 | 0 | 0 |
| Total | 1 | 1 | 3 | 8 | 0 | 0 | 13 | 0 | 0 | 2 | 1 | 0 | 0 | 3 | 1 | 1 | 5 | 9 | 0 | 0 | 16 |

## TABLE 18 (continued)

DISTRIBUTION OF CHILDREN WITHIN THE SAMPLE HOUSEHOLDS, CLASSIFIED BY SEX OF HEAD, WITH SPECIAL REFERENCE TO THE PRESENCE OF EITHER PARENT IN THE HOUSEHOLD, AND TO THE AGE AND BIRTH STATUS OF THE CHILDREN OF EITHER SEX

| Age | Households with Male Head | | | | | | | Households with Female Head | | | | | | | Total | | | | | | |
|---|---|---|---|---|---|---|---|---|---|---|---|---|---|---|---|---|---|---|---|---|---|
| | LS* | LD* | US* | UD* | N/KS* | N/KD* | Total | LS | LD | US | UD | N/KS | N/KD | Total | LS | LD | US | UD | N/KS | N/KD | Total |
| **e. With mothers, fathers dead** | | | | | | | | | | | | | | | | | | | | | |
| 0- 4 | 0 | 0 | 0 | 0 | 0 | 0 | 0 | 0 | 0 | 0 | 1 | 0 | 0 | 1 | 0 | 0 | 0 | 1 | 0 | 0 | 1 |
| 5-14 | 0 | 0 | 0 | 0 | 0 | 0 | 0 | 8 | 2 | 1 | 3 | 0 | 0 | 14 | 8 | 2 | 1 | 3 | 0 | 0 | 14 |
| 15-24 | 0 | 0 | 0 | 1 | 0 | 0 | 1 | 2 | 6 | 0 | 1 | 0 | 0 | 9 | 2 | 6 | 0 | 2 | 0 | 0 | 10 |
| 25-39 | 0 | 0 | 0 | 0 | 0 | 0 | 0 | 2 | 5 | 0 | 0 | 0 | 0 | 7 | 2 | 5 | 0 | 0 | 0 | 0 | 7 |
| 40 + | 0 | 0 | 0 | 0 | 0 | 0 | 0 | 0 | 0 | 0 | 0 | 0 | 0 | 0 | 0 | 0 | 1 | 0 | 0 | 0 | 0 |
| Total | 0 | 0 | 0 | 1 | 0 | 0 | 1 | 12 | 13 | 1 | 5 | 0 | 0 | 31 | 12 | 13 | 1 | 6 | 0 | 0 | 32 |
| **f. With fathers, mothers dead** | | | | | | | | | | | | | | | | | | | | | |
| 0- 4 | 0 | 0 | 0 | 0 | 0 | 0 | 0 | 0 | 0 | 0 | 0 | 0 | 0 | 0 | 0 | 0 | 0 | 0 | 0 | 0 | 0 |
| 5-14 | 0 | 1 | 0 | 0 | 0 | 0 | 1 | 0 | 0 | 0 | 0 | 0 | 0 | 0 | 0 | 1 | 0 | 0 | 0 | 0 | 1 |
| 15-24 | 2 | 1 | 0 | 0 | 0 | 0 | 3 | 0 | 0 | 0 | 0 | 0 | 0 | 0 | 2 | 1 | 0 | 0 | 0 | 0 | 3 |
| 25-39 | 0 | 0 | 0 | 0 | 0 | 0 | 0 | 0 | 0 | 0 | 0 | 0 | 0 | 0 | 0 | 0 | 0 | 0 | 0 | 0 | 0 |
| 40 + | 0 | 2 | 0 | 0 | 0 | 0 | 0 | 0 | 0 | 0 | 0 | 0 | 0 | 0 | 0 | 2 | 0 | 0 | 0 | 0 | 0 |
| Total | 2 | 2 | 0 | 0 | 0 | 0 | 4 | 0 | 0 | 0 | 0 | 0 | 0 | 0 | 2 | 2 | 0 | 0 | 0 | 0 | 4 |
| **Totals by sex of household head** | | | | | | | | | | | | | | | | | | | | | |
| 0- 4 | 37 | 24 | 25 | 24 | 0 | 0 | 110 | 6 | 2 | 19 | 27 | 0 | 1 | 55 | 43 | 26 | 44 | 51 | 0 | 1 | 165 |
| 5-14 | 37 | 51 | 28 | 23 | 2 | 1 | 142 | 31 | 21 | 34 | 38 | 3 | 4 | 131 | 68 | 72 | 62 | 61 | 5 | 5 | 273 |
| 15-24 | 23 | 21 | 11 | 15 | 2 | 8 | 80 | 17 | 23 | 25 | 37 | 2 | 8 | 112 | 40 | 44 | 36 | 52 | 4 | 16 | 192 |
| 25-39 | 1 | 3 | 1 | 1 | 3 | 4 | 13 | 7 | 13 | 9 | 15 | 1 | 3 | 48 | 8 | 16 | 10 | 16 | 4 | 7 | 61 |
| 40 + | 1 | 0 | 0 | 0 | 1 | 2 | 4 | 0 | 1 | 0 | 1 | 2 | 9 | 13 | 1 | 1 | 0 | 1 | 3 | 11 | 17 |
| TOTAL | 99 | 99 | 65 | 63 | 8 | 15 | 349 | 61 | 60 | 87 | 118 | 8 | 25 | 359 | 160 | 159 | 152 | 181 | 16 | 40 | 708 |

*LS = Lawful son; LD = Lawful daughter; US = Unlawful son; UD = Unlawful daughter; N/KS = Son, birth status not known; N/KD = Daughter, birth status not known.

# TABLE 19

DEPENDENTS BELOW THE AGE OF 24 WHO LIVE APART FROM BOTH PARENTS IN THE SAMPLE HOUSEHOLDS, CLASSIFIED BY SEX, BIRTH STATUS, AND RELATION TO THE HOUSEHOLD PRINCIPALS WHO ARE THEIR KIN

| Matrilateral Kin | Male L* | Male U* | Male N/K* | Female L | Female U | Female N/K | All |
|---|---|---|---|---|---|---|---|
| 1. Mother's mother | 3 | 8 | 0 | 1 | 7 | 0 | 19 |
| 2. M's M's full sister | 0 | 4 | 0 | 0 | 5 | 0 | 9 |
| 3. M's M's mat. half brother | 1 | 0 | 0 | 0 | 0 | 0 | 1 |
| 4. M's mat. half sister | 0 | 2 | 0 | 0 | 5 | 0 | 7 |
| 5. M's pat. half sister | 0 | 1 | 0 | 1 | 0 | 0 | 2 |
| 6. M's full brother | 0 | 0 | 0 | 2 | 0 | 0 | 2 |
| 7. M's full sister | 3 | 0 | 0 | 5 | 3 | 0 | 11 |
| 8. M's mat. half brother | 0 | 5 | 0 | 0 | 2 | 0 | 7 |
| 9. M's sister's mate | 0 | 1 | 1 | 1 | 3 | 0 | 6 |
| 10. M's mat. half sister's mate | 0 | 0 | 0 | 0 | 1 | 0 | 1 |
| 11. M's mat. half sister's mate | 0 | 3 | 0 | 0 | 2 | 0 | 5 |
| 12. M's pat. half sister's mate | 2 | 0 | 0 | 0 | 0 | 0 | 2 |
| 13. M's mat. half brother's mate | 0 | 0 | 0 | 0 | 1 | 0 | 1 |
| 14. M's sister's daughter | 0 | 0 | 0 | 1 | 1 | 0 | 2 |
| 15. M's sister's mate | 1 | 1 | 0 | 2 | 0 | 0 | 4 |
| 16. M's M and M's M's mate | 0 | 1 | 0 | 0 | 2 | 0 | 2 |
| 17. M's father's sister | 0 | 1 | 0 | 0 | 1 | 0 | 2 |
| 18. M's F's sister's mate | 0 | 1 | 0 | 0 | 0 | 0 | 1 |
| 19. M's adopted mother | 0 | 1 | 0 | 0 | 0 | 0 | 1 |
| 20. M's adopted father | 1 | 0 | 0 | 0 | 0 | 0 | 1 |

| Patrilateral Kin | Male L | Male U | Male N/K | Female L | Female U | Female N/K | All |
|---|---|---|---|---|---|---|---|
| 1. Father's M and F | 4 | 1 | 0 | 10 | 2 | 0 | 17 |
| 2. Father's mother | 1 | 0 | 0 | 0 | 2 | 0 | 3 |
| 3. F's mat. half sister | 0 | 1 | 0 | 0 | 2 | 0 | 3 |
| 4. F's pat. half brother | 0 | 1 | 0 | 0 | 1 | 0 | 2 |
| 5. F's pat. half sister | 0 | 0 | 0 | 0 | 1 | 0 | 1 |
| 6. F's sister's daughter | 0 | 0 | 0 | 1 | 1 | 0 | 2 |
| 7. F's sister's mate | 0 | 0 | 0 | 0 | 1 | 0 | 1 |
| 8. F's F's sister's mate | 0 | 0 | 1 | 0 | 0 | 0 | 1 |
| 9. F's mate | 0 | 2 | 0 | 0 | 0 | 0 | 2 |
| 10. F's mat. half S's daughter's mate | 0 | 0 | 0 | 1 | 0 | 0 | 1 |

| | Male L | Male U | Male N/K | Female L | Female U | Female N/K | All |
|---|---|---|---|---|---|---|---|
| Total father's kin | 5 | 5 | 1 | 12 | 10 | 0 | 33 |
| Total mother's kin | 11 | 29 | 1 | 13 | 33 | 0 | 87 |
| Total unrelated persons | 0 | 0 | 8 | 1 | 3 | 21 | 33 |
| **GRAND TOTAL** | 16 | 34 | 10 | 26 | 46 | 21 | 153 |

*L = Lawful, i.e., legitimate; U = Unlawful, i.e., illegitimate; N/K = Birth status not known.

## TABLE 20

CHILDREN LESS THAN 24 YEARS OF AGE, LIVING WITH THEIR FATHERS APART
FROM THEIR MOTHERS, CLASSIFIED BY SEX, BIRTH STATUS, AND
STATUS OF FATHER OR KIN WITH WHOM THEY LIVE

|  | Male | | Female | | |
|---|---|---|---|---|---|
|  | L* | U* | L | U | Total |
| 1. Father widowed | 2 | 0 | 2 | 0 | 4 |
| 2. Father wed | 0 | 0 | 0 | 1 | 1 |
| 3. Father wed, spouse absent | 1 | 0 | 1 | 0 | 2 |
| 4. Father unwed, single | 0 | 0 | 0 | 0 | 0 |
| 5. Father unwed, not single | 0 | 3 | 0 | 6 | 9 |
| Total with father only | 3 | 3 | 3 | 7 | 16 |
| 6. Father and father's father and mother | 0 | 2 | 0 | 2 | 4 |
| TOTAL | 3 | 5 | 3 | 9 | 20 |

*L = Lawful, i.e., legitimate; U = Unlawful, i.e., illegitimate.

## TABLE 21

CHILDREN LESS THAN 24 YEARS OF AGE, LIVING WITH THEIR MOTHERS APART
FROM THEIR FATHERS, CLASSIFIED BY SEX, BIRTH STATUS, AND
STATUS OF MOTHER OR KIN WITH WHOM THEY LIVE

|  | Male | | Female | | |
|---|---|---|---|---|---|
|  | L* | U* | L | U | Total |
| 1. Mother wed | 0 | 6 | 0 | 2 | 8 |
| 2. Mother wed, spouse absent | 25 | 0 | 17 | 0 | 42 |
| 3. Mother wed, father dead | 0 | 0 | 0 | 1 | 1 |
| 4. Mother widowed | 16 | 0 | 13 | 0 | 29 |
| 5. Mother unwed, single | 0 | 37 | 0 | 44 | 81 |
| 6. Mother unwed, father dead | 0 | 1 | 0 | 6 | 7 |
| 7. Mother unwed, not single | 0 | 13 | 0 | 4 | 17 |
| Total with mother only | 41 | 57 | 30 | 57 | 185 |
| 8. Mother and mother's father and mother | 0 | 3 | 0 | 4 | 7 |
| 9. Mother and mother's mother | 4 | 10 | 5 | 13 | 32 |
| 10. Mother and mother's M's mother | 1 | 1 | 1 | 0 | 3 |
| 11. Mother and mother's sister | 0 | 0 | 0 | 3 | 3 |
| 12. Mother and M's sister's mate | 0 | 1 | 0 | 0 | 1 |
| 13. M's and M's M's mat. half S's daughter | 0 | 1 | 0 | 0 | 1 |
| 14. Mother and M's mate's mother | 0 | 0 | 0 | 1 | 1 |
| 15. Mother and M's F's sister's mate | 0 | 0 | 0 | 2 | 2 |
| 16. Mother and M's sister's mate | 0 | 0 | 0 | 1 | 1 |
| 17. Mother and M's F's sister's daughter | 0 | 1 | 0 | 0 | 1 |
| Total with mother and M's kin | 5 | 17 | 6 | 24 | 52 |
| TOTAL | 46 | 74 | 36 | 81 | 237 |

*L = Lawful, i.e., legitimate; U = Unlawful, i.e., illegitimate.

## TABLE 22

### FREQUENCY DISTRIBUTION OF DIFFERING TYPES OF DOMESTIC UNIT WITHIN THE SAMPLE

| | Households with Male Head | | | Households with Female Head | | | Total | | | |
|---|---|---|---|---|---|---|---|---|---|---|
| | No Plus Others | Others | Total | No Plus Others | Others | Total | No Plus Others | Others | Total | Per cent |
| 1. Single persons | 29 | 11 | 40 | 46 | 21 | 67 | 75 | 32 | 107 | 25.1 |
| 2. Siblings | 5 | 0 | 5 | 8 | 8 | 16 | 13 | 8 | 21 | 4.9 |
| 3. Household head and children | 3 | 1 | 4 | 58 | 8 | 66 | 61 | 9 | 70 | 16.4 |
| 4. Childless couples | 45 | 26 | 71 | 9 | 7 | 16 | 54 | 33 | 87 | 20.5 |
| 5. Couples and children | 53 | 33 | 86 | 2 | 3 | 5 | 55 | 36 | 91 | 21.4 |
| 6. Household head and grandchildren | 0 | 1 | 1 | 5 | 3 | 8 | 5 | 4 | 9 | 2.1 |
| 7. Couples and grandchildren | 3 | 0 | 3 | 0 | 0 | 0 | 3 | 0 | 3 | 0.8 |
| 8. Household head, children, and grandchildren | 2 | 1 | 3 | 22 | 6 | 28 | 24 | 7 | 31 | 7.3 |
| 9. Couples, children, and grandchildren | 2 | 1 | 3 | 0 | 1 | 1 | 2 | 2 | 4 | 1.0 |
| 10. Household head and issue to 4th generation | 0 | 0 | 0 | 2 | 0 | 2 | 2 | 0 | 2 | 0.5 |
| 11. Couples and issue to 4th generation | 0 | 0 | 0 | 0 | 0 | 0 | 0 | 0 | 0 | 0.0 |
| TOTAL | 142 | 74 | 216 | 152 | 57 | 209 | 294 | 131 | 425 | 100.0 |
| PERCENTAGE | 66.5 | 33.5 | 100.0 | 72.5 | 27.5 | 100.0 | 69.5 | 30.5 | 100.0 | |

## TABLE 23

### DOMESTIC UNITS OF STRUCTURALLY DIFFERING TYPES, CLASSIFIED BY SEX OF HEAD AND GENERATION RANGE

| | Households with Male Head | | | | | Households with Female Head | | | | | Total | | | | |
|---|---|---|---|---|---|---|---|---|---|---|---|---|---|---|---|
| | Generation Range | | | | Total | Generation Range | | | | Total | Generation Range | | | | Total |
| | 1 | 2 | 3 | 4 | | 1 | 2 | 3 | 4 | | 1 | 2 | 3 | 4 | |
| 1. Single persons | 33 | 7 | 0 | 0 | 40 | 53 | 14 | 0 | 0 | 67 | 86 | 21 | 0 | 0 | 107 |
| 2. Siblings | 5 | 0 | 0 | 0 | 5 | 9 | 7 | 0 | 0 | 16 | 14 | 7 | 0 | 0 | 21 |
| 3. Household head and children | 0 | 3 | 1 | 0 | 4 | 0 | 64 | 2 | 0 | 66 | 0 | 67 | 3 | 0 | 70 |
| 4. Childless couples | 50 | 17 | 4 | 0 | 71 | 10 | 6 | 0 | 0 | 16 | 60 | 23 | 4 | 0 | 87 |
| 5. Couples and children | 0 | 80 | 6 | 0 | 86 | 0 | 5 | 0 | 0 | 5 | 0 | 85 | 6 | 0 | 91 |
| 6. Household head and grandchildren | 0 | 0 | 1 | 0 | 1 | 0 | 0 | 8 | 0 | 8 | 0 | 0 | 9 | 0 | 9 |
| 7. Couples and grandchildren | 0 | 0 | 3 | 0 | 3 | 0 | 0 | 0 | 0 | 0 | 0 | 0 | 3 | 0 | 3 |
| 8. Household head, children, and grandchildren | 0 | 0 | 2 | 1 | 3 | 0 | 0 | 28 | 0 | 28 | 0 | 0 | 30 | 1 | 31 |
| 9. Couples, children, and grandchildren | 0 | 0 | 3 | 0 | 3 | 0 | 0 | 0 | 1 | 1 | 0 | 0 | 3 | 1 | 4 |
| 10. Household head and issue to 4th generation | 0 | 0 | 0 | 0 | 0 | 0 | 0 | 0 | 2 | 2 | 0 | 0 | 0 | 2 | 2 |
| 11. Couples and issue to 4th generation | 0 | 0 | 0 | 0 | 0 | 0 | 0 | 0 | 0 | 0 | 0 | 0 | 0 | 0 | 0 |
| TOTAL | 88 | 107 | 20 | 1 | 216 | 72 | 96 | 38 | 3 | 209 | 160 | 203 | 58 | 4 | 425 |
| PERCENTAGE | 40.3 | 50.0 | 9.2 | 0.5 | 100.0 | 34.4 | 45.9 | 18.2 | 1.5 | 100.0 | 37.7 | 47.7 | 13.6 | 1.0 | 100.0 |

# TABLE 24

## CONJUGAL UNIONS IN THE SAMPLE HOUSEHOLDS, CLASSIFIED BY THEIR BASIS, THE TYPE OF DOMESTIC UNIT IN WHICH THEY OCCUR, AND THE SEX OF THE HOUSEHOLD HEAD

| Morphological Types | Male Head | | | Female Head | | | Total | | |
|---|---|---|---|---|---|---|---|---|---|
| | Wed | Unwed | Total | Wed | Unwed | Total | Wed | Unwed | Total |
| 1a. Childless couples only | 16 | 29 | 45 | 1 | 8 | 9 | 17 | 37 | 54 |
| b. Childless couples plus others | 9 | 17 | 26 | 1 | 6 | 7 | 10 | 23 | 33 |
| Total childless couples | 25 | 46 | 71 | 2 | 14 | 16 | 27 | 60 | 87 |
| 2a. Couples and children only | 38 | 15 | 53 | 0 | 2 | 2 | 38 | 17 | 55 |
| b. Couples, children plus others | 20 | 13 | 33 | 0 | 3 | 3 | 20 | 16 | 36 |
| Total couples and children | 58 | 28 | 86 | 0 | 5 | 5 | 58 | 33 | 91 |
| 3a. Couples, children, and grandchildren only | 2 | 0 | 2 | 0 | 0 | 0 | 2 | 0 | 2 |
| b. Couples, children, grandchildren plus others | 0 | 1 | 1 | 0 | 1 | 1 | 0 | 2 | 2 |
| Total couples, children, and grandchildren | 2 | 1 | 3 | 0 | 1 | 1 | 2 | 2 | 4 |
| 4 Couples and issue to 4th generation | 0 | 0 | 0 | 0 | 0 | 0 | 0 | 0 | 0 |
| TOTAL | 85 | 75 | 160 | 2 | 20 | 22 | 87 | 95 | 182 |

# 7. Comparison

In the preceding chapters, I have analyzed each of the five household samples independently, In this chapter I shall compare them, to determine their variability or similarity. To be adequate, this comparison must proceed on several levels. I shall have to consider variations in the frequencies of particular conditions within the sample series. I shall have to seek evidence of covariations within them. However, frequencies require explanation; and I shall have to seek these explanations of similarity or difference at the structural level, in the principles which regulate family relations within these samples.

Our samples are drawn from three differing ecological situations. Grenville and Kingston are urban environments; the populations studied in rural Jamaica and Latante are peasants, cultivating their own holdings for subsistence and exchange alike; the Carriacou folk depend heavily on emigration and seafaring as well as on peasant agriculture. It is possible that these differing ecological situations may be reflected in parallel differences of family structure between the samples. If such differences exist, the problem of their determination has to be faced. In her study of family organization in three ecologically distinct Jamaican communities, Miss Edith Clarke has found remarkable differences which she attributes to economic conditions.[1] In this chapter, we must see whether the similarity or difference of familial organization in these five populations is reducible to economic context.

Our samples vary quite widely in their demographic structure. All five populations are formally monogamous. Given these monogamous commitments, it may be argued that their differences or similarities in family organization are attributable to demographic conditions. We shall test this hypothesis also.

Various writers have offered hypotheses which seek to account for West Indian family forms. Until recently it was taken for granted that in the West Indies the "grandmother family, " consisting of a woman and her grandchildren, with or without the intermediate generation, was typical and self-perpetuating. Various psychological and historical explanations have been offered for the prevalence and form of this family type.[2] Discussing similar forms among American Negroes, Professor Franklin Frazier emphasizes economic determinants much as Miss Edith Clarke does for Jamaica.[3] In his studies of British Guiana Negroes, Dr. R. T. Smith treats this "grandmother family" as one phase in a general developmental cycle which governs the forms of household group and their frequencies. As mentioned above, the developing unit from which Dr. Smith derives the variety and frequency of alternative domestic groups is a household which contains an elementary family. Dr. Smith supplements this genetic hypothesis with another which incorporates economic factors. This second hypothesis holds that the status deprivation of the Guianese Negroes reduces male effectiveness and familial responsibility, thereby producing deformities in the normal developmental cycle of elementary family units. The frequency of households with female heads and varying generational depth is thus attributable to "male marginality" and "matrifocality" alike. In this chapter and the next, I shall consider these hypotheses in the light of our data.[4]

To facilitate the fluent comparison of our five samples, I have converted their absolute distributions into averages, or standard percentage ratios. This allows us to discern regularities or variations by simple inspection. Where one set of ratios seemed somewhat misleading, I have not hesitated to give others with different bases. For example, Tables 10, 11, and 12 of the Appendix to this chapter rework the frequencies of differing categories of kin in these households from different angles. On the assumption that the comparative tables in the Appendix to this chapter are reasonably clear, and that the reader is already familiar with most of the sample details, I shall not attempt to review these figures or to discuss each table in detail, but shall concentrate on those salient features which express similarity or variation, or which bear on either of the hypotheses outlined above.

The Demographic Factor

Table 1 describes the sample populations. In the samples from Carriacou, Latante, and rural Jamaica, 40 per cent are below fourteen years of age. In the two urban samples this ratio is signif-

icantly lower. However, this does not mean that the urban samples
have a higher average age than others, since they contain fewer
old people. Within this urban group, differences in age and sex
ratios seem to be correlated with township size. Kingston, which
is far larger than Grenville, has a lower proportion of children
under fourteen, a lower proportion of old people above fifty-five,
and a more extreme sex disparity. Kingston households are also
smaller on average than those in Grenville. On the ecological hypothesis, these differences could be attributed to degrees of urbanization.

Our samples vary in absolute size, and also in the proportions
of the universes which they represent. The Carriacou sample includes approximately one seventh of the island folk, Latante represents one in 110 of the Grenadian peasants, the Grenville sample
is one thirtieth of the urban population of Grenada, the Kingston
sample is about one in 200 of the Kingston lower class, and the
sample in rural Jamaica would be about one in 170 of the Jamaican peasantry. Whatever their varying representativeness, these
samples have an equal validity, being, with the exception of Kingston, local censuses studied by uniform methods.

Apart from the absolute differences in the size of the various
samples, the most striking variations presented in Table 1 are
those which describe the sex ratios among adults. In this series,
rural Jamaica, with an almost exact equivalence among adults of
both sexes represents one extreme, while Carriacou, where there
are twice as many women as men, represents the other. Apart
from Carriacou, Kingston contains the largest female surplus in
the reproductive age groups. There is some difference between
Latante and Grenville in this respect, but the difference between
Kingston and rural Jamaica is remarkable evidence of the flow of
women from country to town. Apparently Grenville attracts far
fewer country folk. In Carriacou the female surplus is due to male
emigration. In rural Jamaica the sex parity is due to female emigration.

In terms of the demographic hypothesis, these differences in the
adult sex ratio will be linked with variations in family structure,
and will be expressed by variations in the frequencies of alternative types of domestic unit. Samples with similar sex ratios
should therefore have similar family organization; those with differing sex ratios should differ in proportion. In these terms, the
family structure and domestic forms of Latante and Grenville on
the one hand, and Kingston and Carriacou on the other, should

resemble one another, while those in rural Jamaica should differ widely. We already know broadly that this is not so; the details and the reasons for this will be mentioned in due course.

In view of the equal balance of the sexes in rural Jamaica and the large surplus of adult females in Kingston, the lower proportion of children in Kingston might suggest that the surplus urban females include few single mothers. We already know that many single women in Kingston are mothers, and that many of these urban women have their children living with their rural kin. This is not so at Grenville. In consequence, the apparently lower ratio of young people in these two urban populations cannot be attributed to urbanization. Indeed, Carriacou, with the highest ratio of surplus females, and rural Jamaica with the most perfect equivalence, both have the same proportion of children under fourteen. Adult sex ratios may vary but have no necessary connection with the ratios of children in these populations. The number of children varies as a function of fertile matings; mating organizations vary independently of demographic ratios. If these populations were polygynous and women were obliged to marry, differences in sample sex ratios might conceivably be linked with differences in the proportions of children among them; conversely, if these populations were rigorously monogamous and all men were obliged to marry, the differences in their sex ratios might also govern differences in the relative size of their junior population. Since neither of these conditions obtain, it is clear that the mating system of these populations is neither pure polygyny nor rigid monogamy. Moreover, since the ratios of children within these samples vary independently of their sex ratios, it is clear that there are differences between the mating systems of these samples. We cannot determine the nature of these mating differences from demographic data alone; but we can distinguish between the two urban samples with their high sex disparity and low child ratios, Carriacou, with an even greater sex disparity but a high child ratio, and rural Jamaica and Latante with lower sex disparities and high child ratios. Presumably Kingston and Grenville may have similar sorts of mating organization. Carriacou is unique in this series, and rural Jamaica and Latante resemble one another closely as regards mating. Demographic conditions offer inadequate grounds of explanation.

Presumably demographic conditions may govern the distribution of household headship and the size of household units. Table 2 presents the relevant data. Carriacou, with the highest ratio of surplus females, also has the highest ratio of female household heads. Rural Jamaica, with the minimum sex disparity, has the lowest ratio of female heads. Latante comes next with another low sex disparity. However, Kingston, with a greater female surplus, has a lower incidence of female headship than Grenville. Carriacou households are larger, on average, than those in rural Jamaica, Kingston, or Grenville, despite the Carriacou female surplus. Sex ratios govern neither the average household size nor the distribution of headship.

Household headship is a culturally defined status. In polygynous societies, such as the Hausa, women cannot be household heads, simply on grounds of sex. Among these Caribbean populations we always find heads of both sexes. This is an important constant. The polygynous Hausa identify marriage and adult status; all unmarried adults of either sex are classified as "prostitutes" *(karuwai);* [5] their relative number is no greater than that of the Carriacou couples who cohabit consensually in "wooden" (men's) houses and who are also classified by Carriacou society as "prostitutes." Thus among the Hausa, mating relations are all contained within the framework of domestic organization. In this framework, polygyny invests males with precedence; consequently household heads are all male. The concurrence of male and female headship in West Indian societies indicates that mating relations are not confined within the domestic framework of these populations. Carriacou illustrates this well. There, consensual cohabitation is taboo, but men are simultaneously expected to marry and mate extraresidentially. Demographic abnormalities certainly facilitate this mating organization, even if they do not necessitate it. Demographically Carriacou is well suited to domestic polygyny; but in fact the sole acceptable alternative to marriage in this society is the extraresidential union; and it is just there that we find the greatest incidence of female headship, as well as the highest incidence of marriage. In rural Jamaica and Latante, consensual cohabitation commonly precedes marriage. Accordingly, the position and frequency of extraresidential relations within the mating system differs from that in Carriacou; so does the incidence of female headship. In Kingston and Grenville the larger ratios of female household heads may therefore be due to differences in mating pattern rather than to sex disparity.

Nonetheless, Grenville and Kingston differ from the other samples in having a higher incidence of headship among people under twenty-four and a lower incidence among those over fifty-five. In Carriacou, Latante, and rural Jamaica alike, we find few household heads below twenty-four years of age and many above fifty-five. One common feature of all five samples is that approxi-

mately one third of the household heads in each are between forty
and fifty-four years of age. Within this uniformity, there are important differences in the distribution of headship by sex. Carriacou
is peculiar in the low incidence of headship among persons aged
twenty-five to thirty-nine. The similarity in distribution of headship by age and sex in Latante and rural Jamaica is marked, and
this implies corresponding similarity in their mating and family
organization. Kingston and Grenville differ greatly in the distribution of headship among their different age groups. Less than
15 per cent of the Kingston heads are over fifty-five years of age,
as against 30 per cent of those at Grenville. Forty-five per cent
of the Kingston heads are between twenty-five and thirty-nine years
of age, as against 27 per cent at Grenville. Presumably differences
in average household size may be attributable to differing degrees
of urbanization, since the households in Grenville and Kingston,
respectively, are far smaller than elsewhere. These differences
of household size are not directly associated with the varying incidence of female headship since Grenville, with its higher ratio
of female heads, has households of larger average size than Kingston, and Carriacou homes are also larger than those in rural Jamaica.

The higher incidence of household headship among urban women
is associated with an increase in the relative number of those who
live alone. Of the Latante household heads, 11. 8 per cent live on
their own, and 7. 9 per cent are women. One in every 5. 3 female
heads at Latante lives by herself. At Grenville, single-person
households are 15. 1 per cent of the total, 10. 7 per cent having
female heads. The ratio of solitary females among female heads is
thus one in 4. 9. In rural Jamaica 15 per cent of all female household heads live alone, as against 22 per cent in Kingston. Such
increases in the number of solitary women are matched by others
in the number of mature women who live without mates; and the increase of both these groups connotes an increase in the incidence
of extraresidential unions.

The remarkable incidence of solitary males in rural Jamaica
cannot be derived from the demographic structure, since the population contains an even larger number of single adult females.
The distribution of these solitary males by age defines them as
persons who can no longer remain household dependents but who
have no stable groups dependent on them. Presumably many of
these solitary males also mate extraresidentially, and their distribution and condition are functions of the family structure.

Demographic factors influence but do not govern the generation structure of household units. Nor does the distribution of headship by age do so directly. It is quite possible for old people to have no grandchildren living with them; it is equally possible for them to have some of their children and grandchildren in their homes. In Tables 3 and 4 I have classified the household samples by genera- tion depth. In Table 3, the head's generation has a value of one; in Table 4, which gives the proportion of the population in each gener- ation, the head's generation is the reference point and has the value of zero. Our urban samples contain more households of one generation only and fewer of three or four generations than do the others. In all samples about 45 per cent of the homes have a depth of two generations. The incidence of units with varying generation depth is similar for Latante and rural Jamaica on the one hand, and for Grenville and Kingston on the other. Carriacou deviates, with a very low ratio of generationally shallow units and a very high ratio of extended ones. Given the similarities in age structure between Carriacou and Latante, these differences are not reducible to age. Given the similar sex disparities of Carriacou and Kingston, differences in the frequencies of units of varying generational span are not reducible to sex ratios. In short, they do not reflect the influence of demographic factors directly.

Table 4 shows that Carriacou households contain larger propor- tions of the second and third descending generation than the other samples, together with smaller proportions belonging to the gen- eration of the household head. The generation structure of house- holds in rural Jamaica and Latante are again similar, and so are those at Grenville and Kingston, which have the lowest proportion of persons belonging to the second and third descending generation. It remains to be seen whether the variations and continuities which distinguish Carriacou from Latante and rural Jamaica, and the two latter from Grenville and Kingston, can be reduced to ecolog- ical conditions. Certainly the demographic explanation can be dis- missed as inadequate.

The ecological extremes in this sample series are Kingston and Carriacou. Kingston is a large town which receives migrants from the country. Carriacou is an island of seafarers and depends heavily on emigration. Male migration from Carriacou and female movement into Kingston produce comparable female surpluses in both populations. Within the adult age groups, the age distri- butions are also broadly similar. However, Kingston and Carriacou have quite dissimilar family organizations. The direct demographic effect of their differing ecological situation corresponds more closely than do the family systems. It seems unlikely therefore that the ecological situation operates as a uniform determining factor.

The Regulation of Mating

Given these inadequacies in the demographic and ecological hypotheses, we must seek the bases of similarity and variation among
these samples within their family structures. It is thus appropriate
to examine the mating organization. However, my data are uneven
in this respect. For Grenville, Latante, and one third of the Carriacou sample I have full records of the mating careers of all adults.
For the remainder of the Carriacou sample, my information is less
complete, and for Kingston and rural Jamaica it is defective, especially with regard to single persons without resident issue. Owing
to this unevenness, the Grenada samples include no persons of
indeterminate parental and mating status, while those from Jamaica
give minimum figures for single parents and for persons currently
engaged in mating. The superior data from Latante and Grenville
permit estimates of the breakdowns of domestic unions. Such estimates are also possible for Carriacou; but in Kingston and rural
Jamaica many persons classified as single individuals may have
had broken domestic unions. Nonetheless, the data presented in
Tables 5 to 9 allow us to define and compare the mating systems
of these populations.

Table 5 summarizes the distribution of mating and parental conditions among all adults in each sample. Table 6 isolates those
adults under twenty-four in each sample and classifies them similarly. The majority of these junior adults may not yet have entered
on their mating careers, and their inclusion in Table 5 somewhat
misrepresents the distribution of mating and parental condition
among the mature adults of these populations. Table 6 allows us to
correct this by subtracting its ratios from those in the previous
table. Table 7 isolates the populations of household heads and classifies them identically. In the two following tables I have enumerated the currently married and the evermarried adults of these
samples by sex and age. In this tabulation the currently married
are defined as all whose marriages are not known definitely to
have broken down. Accordingly, most of the Kingston wives with
absent husbands are included as currently married. The evermarried in each age group include those who have separated from
their spouses or been widowed, together with the currently married.

Carriacou contains the highest ratios of single adults, married
and widowed persons, the lowest ratio of consensually wed persons.
The two Jamaican samples have the highest incidence of consensual

cohabitation and the lowest incidence of marriage or widowhood. Latante and Grenville have very similar proportions of married persons and of widows. However, the ratio of separated married persons in Grenville is twice as high as that at Latante. The ratio of married persons with absent spouses in Kingston is more than three times as high as that in rural Jamaica. Marriage is less stable in Grenville and Kingston than in Latante or rural Jamaica. In Carriacou marriage has the greatest stability, and most of the women whose spouses are absent have no reason to doubt that they will return as soon as they have realized the objectives of their emigration. In Latante and rural Jamaica we find few broken consensual unions, in Grenville many, and in Kingston almost certainly more, despite the lack of data on this point.

Thirty per cent of the Carriacou adults are childless single persons. So are 37 per cent of those at Latante, but only 25 per cent of those in Grenville. Our Jamaican estimates of this category and of its opposite, the single parents, are lower owing to lack of information on the parental status of many adults. These deficiencies of data are acute in Kingston especially, 34 per cent of these adults being of unknown parental status. Even so, Carriacou has the greatest proportion of single adults, owing to its exclusion of consensual unions. In Carriacou, the ratios of single males and females are very similar. In Kingston, with the next highest incidence of single adults, there is a substantial difference between the proportion of women and men who are single. Once again there is a close correspondence between Latante and rural Jamaica in the proportions of single adults. These two samples differ most sharply in their ratios of married and consensually cohabiting adults. Of the Latante population, 11. 5 per cent have cohabited consensually without marrying as against 20. 6 per cent in rural Jamaica. Of the Latante folk, 39. 5 per cent have married, as against 31. 3 per cent of those in rural Jamaica. These differences disappear when the married and consensually cohabiting ratios are added together, within the single category of domestic unions. Of the Jamaican adults, 51. 3 per cent have participated in domestic unions; so have 51 per cent of those at Latante, 46. 8 per cent of those in Carriacou, 57. 2 per cent of those in Grenville, and, on the data available, at least 50. 6 per cent of those in Kingston. Clearly the incidence of extraresidential mating is high in all these populations; clearly, too, variations between rural Jamaica and Latante in the relative incidence of marriage and consensual cohabitation occur within a common framework of stable domestic unions having a similar frequency.

Of the Carriacou females, 16.6 per cent are single mothers; so are 15.8 per cent and 21 per cent of those at Latante and Grenville, respectively. In rural Jamaica this category includes 24.2 per cent of the adult females, in Kingston its minimum incidence is 16.9 per cent but it may well be twice as high. The important point for our purposes is the presence of a large number of single mothers. Since consensual cohabitation is ruled out in Carriacou, these single mothers will contain few who have experience of domestic unions. Since more than half the Carriacou females have never entered domestic unions, and less than one third of them are single mothers, extraresidential mating in Carriacou must be subject to effective social control. Indeed, as it is the only acceptable alternative to marriage in this society, it would be surprising if it remained uncontrolled. The very low proportion of single mothers at Latante indicates that women enter consensual or legal cohabitation shortly after the birth of their first child. In Grenville, one fifth of the adult females have cohabited consensually, but an equal proportion are single mothers who have not. Moreover many women who were cohabiting consensually no longer do so; many wives also live apart from their husbands. It seems clear that in Grenville extraresidential mating and consensual cohabitation are less durable and controlled than at Latante. Marriage is also more unstable. The position in rural Jamaica is similar to that at Latante. Consensual cohabitation and marriage are stable, but about one quarter of the adult females are single mothers. In short, extraresidential mating is prevalent in this population, and most women probably have their first child before entering domestic unions. In Kingston marriage is unstable, and it is certain that consensual cohabitation is even more so, despite the lack of quantities in Table 5. One quarter of the Kingston women for whom we have adequate data are single mothers; probably this proportion also applies to those of indeterminate status. Thus many of the remaining women in this indeterminate category will be separated from their consensual mates or husbands; in short, we can infer an even higher instability in the domestic unions of Kingston than is evident at Grenville.

We have three mating systems with differing modalities in this sample series; that of Carriacou includes marriage and the extraresidential union, but excludes consensual cohabitation. That which is common to Latante and rural Jamaica includes consensual domestic unions as well as marriage and extraresidential mating; in this system, domestic unions of either sort are stable, and consensual cohabitation normally precedes marriage. In Grenville and

Kingston all three forms of mating coexist, and each is highly
unstable. They do not form a developmental series in these urban
societies.

Table 6 isolates adults under twenty-four in these samples. The
percentage ratios are proportions of the total adult populations of
either and both sexes in each sample. Adults of this age group are
30 per cent of the Carriacou sample. Women of this age group
are 27 per cent of the Carriacou sample. Of these, one tenth were
single parents and one thirteenth were cohabiting; the remainder
were childless. At Latante, two in nine of these young women were
single mothers; one in fourteen was cohabiting, and more than one
in three were mating extraresidentially. In Grenville, one quarter
of the single women were mothers and rather more than a quarter
were cohabiting. Two in five were mating extraresidentially. For
Kingston our data on parental status are especially weak for single
women; however, one quarter of those under twenty-four were cohabiting. In rural Jamaica rather more than a fifth of these young
women were single mothers, one quarter were cohabiting, and a
third were mating extraresidentially. Less than one tenth of those
in Carriacou were mating extraresidentially. Carriacou differs
from the other samples as much by its firm regulation of extraresidential mating as by its rejection of consensual cohabitation. In all
four remaining samples, cohabitation and extraresidential mating
have equal validity for the young; but as we have already seen,
Latante and rural Jamaica share a common system, the critical
feature of which is a serial arrangement of these mating alternatives in a theoretically irreversible order. In this system, extraresidential relations are appropriate for young people at the beginning of their mating careers; from this, many move into consensual
cohabitation, and thence to marriage, which is appropriate for mature persons, and is conceived as permanent. Other young folk
sometimes marry early and regret it, leaving their spouses soon
after. In this system, few senior people continue in consensual cohabitation; fewer mate extraresidentially, and a relation which
begins extraresidentially may develop into marriage through the
consensual domestic form.

In Grenville and Kingston we found no such developmental order.
Persons of different sex and age mate by any of the three forms.
There is a tendency for the extraresidential union to be prevalent
among younger folk, and for marriage to be prevalent among the
older ones, but there is no consistent pattern in either case. With
regard to consensual cohabitation, the age distribution is even more
random. In these two populations, we found a high incidence of

broken consensual unions and broken marriages. Widowed and separated married persons often reverted to consensual cohabitation and/or extraresidential mating. Excluding widows, nearly 60 per cent of the adult women in these two samples were living without resident mates as against 50.2 per cent and 53.2 per cent in rural Jamaica and Latante, respectively.

The differences in mating organization between these rural and urban samples may conceivably be attributed to urbanization. This seems unnecessary, and on general grounds improbable. Other urban populations similar in size to Grenville and Kingston may have widely dissimilar mating patterns. Likewise, rural populations in circumstances similar to those of Latante and rural Jamaica may have quite different mating systems. There is evidence that the mating conditions characteristic of Grenville and Kingston are also characteristic of the Jamaican sugar proletariat.[6] In consequence, differences in the mating organizations of Grenville and Latante or Kingston and rural Jamaica are no more attributable to urbanization than to ecological factors, unless sugar plantations be equated with townships. What is clear is that mating relations are important elements of family structure and that differences in mating organization are very likely to be linked with differences in family structure.

The marital and parental conditions of household heads in these various samples are compared in Table 7. Many uniformities are immediately apparent. Few married males are not heads of their own homes, and most male household heads are cohabiting, legally or otherwise. Widows and women of single status are the overwhelming majority of female household heads. In areas of conjugal instability, such as Grenville and Kingston, these "single" female heads include many whose domestic unions have broken down. Women with absent spouses tend to assert headship of their own homes; the greater proportion of single female household heads are single parents also, in so far as our data permit judgment. Continence has little value among either sex; and only in Carriacou is there any notable emphasis on chastity among females.

Among consensually cohabiting couples, females are sometimes household heads. In Latante and rural Jamaica, the incidence of this female headship in units based on consensual cohabitation is lower than in Grenville and Kingston. In these two rural communities the ratio of female household heads engaged in extraresidential mating at the time of survey is lower than at Grenville, and presumably Kingston also.

Comparison of the evermarried and currently married ratios in Tables 8 and 9 underlines the differences in marital stability which distinguish Grenville and Kingston from other sample units. Jamaican marriage ratios are lower than those of Grenada and Carriacou; and I have classified among the currently married all married members of the Kingston sample whose marriages were not definitely broken. In consequence, these tables give a more favorable impression of marital stability in Kingston than is actually warranted.

The Composition of Domestic Groups

We have seen that the similarities and variations between these samples cannot be explained by demographic or ecological conditions, nor can they be regarded as correlates of urbanization. This leaves us with the hypotheses which explain West Indian family forms developmentally, by reference to the "grandmother family," or the elementary family, or both. We need not worry with the supplementary historical, cultural, or structural hypotheses which are employed to account for the initial or current peculiarities of this family organization until we have tested the applicability of their underlying assumptions. In reviewing the domestic composition of these sample populations, we shall see how far these elementary and grandmother family forms predominate or enter into the composition of these domestic units.

Tables 10, 11, and 12 compare the composition of these household samples from slightly different points of view. Table 10 summarizes the distribution of dependents in households having heads of different sex, by reference to the relation between the dependents and heads. In Table 11 the heads are included, and the kinship distribution of all household members is expressed as percentage ratios of the total populations under heads of differing sex. Table 12 restates the ratios in Table 11, using the total sample population as the basis for these ratios. Table 12, therefore, gives an accurate picture of the absolute distribution of differing categories of kin in the separate samples. In these three tables spouses and consensual mates are grouped together.

Table 10 shows that in Latante, Carriacou, and rural Jamaica, resident mates and spouses of male household heads are 18.2 per cent, 18.8 per cent, and 21.3 per cent of their dependents, respectively. In Grenville and Kingston the ratios are 26 per cent and 31.3 per cent, respectively. Thus, in the two urban samples resident mates are a larger proportion of the dependent members of units with male heads than elsewhere. In these two urban samples, resident mates of female household heads also form a larger proportion of the dependents in those homes than elsewhere.

The ratios for resident mates of female household heads in the two urban samples are more than twice as great as those in peasant samples from the same territory. In aggregate, 10.4 per cent of all dependent members of the Carriacou households are mates of their heads. For rural Jamaica and Latante this ratio is 16 per cent and 14 per cent, respectively; for Grenville and Kingston it is 16.8 per cent and 20.3 per cent. Carriacou has the lowest ratio of resident mates and the two urban samples have the highest.

The total resident issue of male heads are 66 per cent of the Carriacou units of this type. In Latante they are 69 per cent, in rural Jamaica 59 per cent. In Grenville they are 51 per cent, in Kingston 48 per cent. Thus the relative incidence of lineal issue of male household heads varies inversely with the relative incidence of their resident mates. To test this, we have only to add together the ratios for resident mates and lineal issue of male household heads. The inversion of these ratios is not quite exact, but impressive. It shows that whatever may be the relation between urbanization and cohabitation ratios, an inverse relation between the proportions of coresident mates and lineal issue of male heads is a condition of the family structure common to all our samples. Quite possibly, increased cohabitation in these populations involves more junior persons whose short reproductive careers diminish their opportunities for parenthood. However, we know that many single young people have children before cohabiting, and that many who cohabit are childless. Even so, such cohabitation may lead to a removal of some grandchildren as well as children from the parental homes, with a resulting drop in the ratio of lineal issue in these homes and a simultaneous increase in the cohabitation ratio. Thus the relation of these two ratios illustrates the logical closure of this family system; it does so by showing necessary interdependencies among its components such that changes occur in one variable when another is changed. It is easy to see the interdependence of mating and parental forms, and the relation of these two factors to domestic organization. In consequence, we may reasonably expect that societies with differing mating systems will tend to differ in their domestic organization and parental patterns alike.

Average household size is a simple function of the number of units in a given population aggregate. Increases in the number of households reduce average household size correspondingly; and

---

these increases tend to be due to increasing cohabitation rates which remove children as well as grandchildren from older units. To test this formula, we need only look at the ratios of resident children and remoter issue of male household heads. Table 10 shows that the incidence of resident children of male heads declines steadily as the ratios of resident mates increase; the general tendency is also for the resident grandchildren and great-grandchildren of these male household heads to decline.

Only one half of the dependents living under males in Grenville and Kingston are the issue of these men. In rural Jamaica, Latante, and Carriacou these lineal issue are three fifths and two thirds of the dependent populations. In homes with female heads, resident lineal issue represent three quarters of the dependent population, except for Kingston, where they are two thirds. In all samples except Carriacou resident children of female household heads are nearly one half of their total dependents. In Latante and rural Jamaica, resident grandchildren of these women are 24 per cent and 27 per cent of their dependents, respectively. In Grenville and Kingston these grandchildren are only 21 per cent and 16 per cent of the dependents of female household heads. In Carriacou there are almost as many resident grandchildren of female household heads as resident children, the two groups being 36.1 per cent and 38.5 per cent of the dependent totals, respectively. Thus, Carriacou differs sharply from the other samples in the constitution of its lineal components; likewise, Latante and rural Jamaica differ sharply from Grenville and Kingston. In Latante and rural Jamaica resident children of female heads outnumber grandchildren by two to one, in Grenville by two and one half to one, in Kingston by three to one. In Latante and rural Jamaica resident grandchildren of female heads outnumber resident great-grandchildren by seven to one and six to one, respectively; in Grenville and Kingston, by twenty-three to one and fifty to one. Clearly, the principles which govern the distribution of lineal issue of female household heads in these rural and urban samples differ in form or in effect owing to other elements in the family structure.·

The peculiar lineal constitution of Carriacou households requires little explanation. Carriacou men are often overseas for long periods; some take their wives, and many of these couples leave their children behind. Those who remain in the island are generally married, and have children by other women also. These "outside" children remain in their mothers' care and often live in homes of which their mothers' mothers are the heads, many of these senior women being widows themselves. Hence the re-

markable concentration of grandchildren in homes with female
heads in Carriacou.

In all five samples, resident kin and issue of the head's mate
are an important element. In Carriacou and rural Jamaica these
categories are 7. 6 per cent and 7. 5 per cent of the total dependent
populations of all households. In Grenville and Kingston they are
6. 8 per cent and 6. 7 per cent; at Latante they are only 6 per cent.
However, the distribution of these affines in the male-headed homes
of Grenville and Kingston resembles the distribution in Carriacou
more closely than in the two remaining samples. In Carriacou
13 per cent of the dependents of male household heads are kin or
issue of mates. In Grenville and Kingston, this ratio is 10. 6 per
cent and 11. 3 per cent. This similarity reflects the effects of similar frequencies of extraresidential mating in these samples rather
than similar levels of urbanization. In Carriacou, Kingston, and
rural Jamaica the kin or "outside" issue of resident mates of female heads are an insignificant proportion of their dependents;
in Grenville and Latante these affines are 2. 7 per cent and 4. 3 per
cent of the dependent totals, respectively. There is no consistent
difference between rural and urban samples in the relative incidence of affines other than issue of mates living in homes with
male heads.

In Carriacou 0. 9 per cent of the dependents of male household
heads are consanguineal kin of the head, as against 18. 3 per cent
of those in homes with female heads. In Kingston 5 per cent of the
dependents in male-headed homes are consanguineal kin of the
head, and 18. 8 per cent of those in homes with female heads. This
resemblance between Kingston and Carriacou can only be explained
in terms of family structure. Of all dependents in these Kingston
households, 10. 7 per cent are consanguine kin of the head, as
against 6. 6 per cent of those in rural Jamaican homes. In Latante
6. 75 per cent are consanguine kin of the head, in Grenville 8. 1
per cent. By adding ratios for resident kin of the heads and their
mates, and by subtracting their parents, we can estimate the relative incidence of collaterals living with these household principals.
For Carriacou, the ratio is 13. 3 per cent, for Latante 10 per cent,
for Grenville 9. 2 per cent, for rural Jamaica 8. 1 per cent, and for
Kingston 13. 2 per cent. The two urban samples diverge from their
rural cousins in differing directions; otherwise the collateral ratios
just set out reveal no simple pattern. However, we shall return to
this problem later.

The "miscellaneous" members of these sample households include junior affines (children or junior kin of resident mates of the

heads), adopted, employed, or unrelated persons. These miscellaneous components are extremely marginal in Carriacou and Latante, least so in Grenville and Kingston. Notably, Grenville and
Kingston households have very few resident junior affines, by comparison with the others.

We can now summarize the regularities and variations in the
composition of these households. Between 75 per cent and 80 per
cent of all dependents in each sample consist of the mates and issue
of the heads themselves. In homes with male heads, the majority of
the remaining members are likely to be issue and kin of the heads'
resident mates, and these affines generally outnumber resident
consanguineal kin of the heads themselves by two to one, except
in Carriacou, where the ratio is fourteen to one. In homes with
female heads, the majority of the dependents other than the head's
lineal issue are their consanguine kin, the sample ratios varying
between 10. 6 per cent and 18. 8 per cent. Only in rural Jamaica
are patrilateral kin of male household heads living with them.

Of the resident consanguineal kin of these household heads, full
siblings and their issue are clearly dominant; however, Carriacou
homes with male heads include very few of these; and they are proportionately more frequent in units with female heads in all five
samples.

Besides testing hypotheses which may account for the variations
or similarities of family organization in these samples, we have
also to determine whether or not these five populations have a
common family system, and to analyze their system or systems.
Irregularities or differences in mating and domestic organization
are the evidence necessary for classification and analysis alike.
Some recapitulation is therefore unavoidable, and indeed essential
for comparison. However, we need not dwell on Tables 11 and 12
unduly, since these restate the data just reviewed, in simpler
form and as ratios of the total samples.

Table 11 shows that the relative incidence of the resident children
of male heads by women other than their resident mates is of the
same order as the ratio descended from female heads and their
resident mates in all five samples. In absolute terms, the numbers
involved in either category are quite small. In Latante and Carriacou resident joint issue of male household heads and their mates
are approximately equal in ratio to the resident lineal issue of
female household heads; in the other three samples, the lineal issue
of female household heads is a substantially larger ratio of the
dependent population than are the joint issue of male heads and
their mates in other units. These differences imply other dif-

ferences between these samples in the stability or incidence of domestic units based on cohabitation. We shall examine this feature later.

The resident consanguineal kin of male heads and their mates are a relatively constant fraction of the total population of these homes in all five samples. In Carriacou homes with male heads they are 7. 3 per cent, at Latante and Grenville they are 6. 3 per cent and 6. 7 per cent respectively, in Kingston 7. 7 per cent, and in rural Jamaica 6. 5 per cent. We seem to have isolated a structural constant of relatively invariant character.

In units with female heads, these consanguine ratios are more variable; and their variations are also linked with changes in the ratios of consanguineal kin of female principals living in homes with male heads. In Carriacou, which has the highest ratio of resident collaterals of female household heads, the ratio of resident collaterals of the mates of male heads is also highest, and the ratio of resident collaterals of these heads is lowest. In Grenville, which has the lowest ratio of resident collaterals of female heads, the incidence of collateral kin of mates of male household heads is also lowest; but the resident kin of the male heads themselves have a higher ratio than in other samples. The ratios of these three types of collateral dependents seem to vary interdependently within fixed limits. The stronger the claims of consanguineal kinship on female household heads, as illustrated by the ratio of these kin resident with them, the greater the incidence of wives' and mates' kin in homes with male heads, and the lower the incidence of resident collateral kin of these heads themselves. The converse is true; greater emphasis on collateral kinship with male household heads, as illustrated by the resident ratios, is linked to reduced emphasis on collateral kinship with female principals. Moreover, the relative size of the total collateral component in all these samples is a relatively constant fraction of their population. We have already seen that materterine kinship is dominant among resident collaterals; and that the great majority of these dependents are illegitimate offspring of kinswomen of the principals with whom they live. It is therefore worth while to examine the distribution of children who live with their mothers only, or with their mothers and mothers' mates, or with their mothers' mothers, with or without their mothers, or with their paternal or maternal collateral kin. The actual numbers of persons in these categories are set out on page 216.

The category totals given below have been extracted from the

relevant tables for each sample. Children living with their mothers'
mothers and the latter's mates have been differentiated in categories 3 and 4 according to the presence or absence of their own
mother. These two categories include all children living with their
mother's mother whether or not their mother's father or collateral
kin were present also. They exclude no child who lives with its
mother's mother apart from its father. No children living with their
fathers are included in this table, nor are those who live with their
father's parents.

KINSHIP DISTRIBUTION OF CHILDREN UNDER 24 NOT LIVING WITH FATHERS

|  |  |  |  | Rural |  |
| --- | --- | --- | --- | --- | --- |
|  | Carriacou | Latante | Grenville | Jamaica | Kingston |
| 1. With mother alone | 78 | 46 | 55 | 272 | 185 |
| 2. With mother and mother's mate | 14 | 6 | 7 | 108 | 24 |
| 3. With mother and her mother, alone or with others | 51 | 11 | 10 | 159 | 39 |
| 4. With mother's mother and any-one except mother | 74 | 21 | 8 | 157 | 21 |
| 5. With mother's collateral kin only | 57 | 20 | 16 | 61 | 54 |
| 6. With mother and mother's col-lateral kin | 17 | 8 | 2 | 52 | 5 |
| 7. With father's collateral kin | 17 | 6 | 0 | 54 | 14 |
| TOTAL | 308 | 118 | 98 | 863 | 342 |
| Total with collaterals | 91 | 34 | 18 | 167 | 73 |
| All in categories 3 and 4 in | 100 | 25 | 18 | 226 | 55 |
| homes with female heads | of 125 | of 32 | of 18 | of 316 | of 60 |

The preceding table enables us to examine the significance of
differing types of kinship in the placement of children who do not
live with their fathers. It concentrates attention on maternal grandmothers, since this domestic association has been regarded as the
typical West Indian family form, and since theories about West
Indian family organization have been developed on this assumption.
   Children who live with their maternal grandmothers are 40 per
cent of the 308 listed above for Carriacou; they are 27 per cent and
37 per cent of the Latante and rural Jamaica totals, respectively;
for Grenville and Kingston these children are 18.5 per cent and
17 per cent of the total living apart from their fathers. Not all the
children who live with their mother's mother live in homes of which
females are heads. In Carriacou 31 per cent, and in rural Jamaica
and Latante 27 per cent and 21 per cent, do so. In Grenville and
Kingston the ratios are 18.5 per cent and 16 per cent. In all samples
excepting Carriacou the number of children who live apart from

their fathers with their mothers alone or with the mother's mate outnumber those who live with their grandmothers. The number living with their collateral kin and with their mother and mother's mate is always larger than the number who live with their grandmothers in homes having female heads. At Latante, Grenville, and Kingston, those children living with their collaterals are equal to, or more than, those who live with their mother's mother in homes with heads of either sex; in Carriacou the children living with their collaterals are three quarters of the number of all who live with their mother's mother, and are nearly equal to the number living with their mother's mother in homes with female heads. In Latante, Grenville, and Kingston those children living with their mother alone outnumber the totals living with their mother's mother. In these three communities, the children who live with their mother's collateral kin outnumber those who live with their mother's mothers in homes having female heads. It is clear that the importance of maternal grandmothers in the West Indian family organization has been greatly overemphasized. On our data, collateral kin are equally important in the placement of children who do not live with their fathers.

The rural Jamaican sample contains 316 children who live with their mothers' mothers, but only 167 who live with their collateral kin. It may seem that these facts invalidate the points just made; however, we know that many Kingston women have their children with kin in the country. This pattern has no parallel in the Latante, Grenville, or Carriacou samples. It also serves to inflate the significance of the grandmother in rural Jamaica while reducing her significance in Kingston. To present an accurate picture of the role of the maternal grandmother in Jamaica, we must therefore combine the data from Kingston and rural Jamaica. Fortunately our samples permit this by simple addition. Our Kingston sample represents one in 200 of the urban lower class; our rural Jamaican sample is one in 170 of the peasantry. These sample fractions allow us to add the Kingston and rural Jamaican data directly. This addition brings the total number of children living with their maternal grandmothers in our Jamaican samples to 376, of whom 281 live in homes with female heads. Another 240 children live with their collaterals, and 132 live with the mother and mother's mate. Thus, 372 live with their collaterals or with their mother and mother's mate, as against 376 with their maternal grandmothers. The maternal grandmother in Jamaica and in Grenada occupies a similar position. In both societies the combination of male responsibility for the issue of resident mates with collateral kinship is just as

important as uterine ties two generations deep. In these two soci-
ieties, more children live with their mother alone than live with
their mother's mother and their collateral kin together; in Carriacou this is not the case, and the reasons for it are clear. Carriacou
men must marry, and do so, after building their homes. Their
extraresidential mates are drawn from the island's surplus of
single women, and although some of these women live by themselves, more live with their parents or collateral kin. In consequence, the offspring of these extraresidential unions are heavily
concentrated in the homes of their maternal grandparents and collateral kin. This concentration is further increased by exclusion
of men's collaterals from their homes in favor of their wives'
collateral kin.

The maternal grandmother is far from being the central domi-
nating figure of the West Indian family. Even without considering
single women who care for their children alone, the collateral kin
and later mates of mothers are quite as important as the maternal
grandmother in caring for the children of broken unions. Many
women who have their daughters' children with them are not themselves household heads. In all our samples we find that the number
of children who live apart from their mothers and with their collateral kin exceed those who live apart from their mothers and with
their mother's mother. In the two Jamaican samples 178 children
live apart from their mother with their mother's mother, while
183 live apart from their mother with collateral kin. Apart from
parents themselves, the maternal grandmother may be a child's
most likely guardian; but the child is even more likely to live with
its collateral kin than with its mother's mother alone.

Theories which have assumed the central position of the maternal
grandmother, or the modal distribution of "grandmother families"
in the British Caribbean thus need little attention. Neither does the
maternal grandmother occupy a central position nor is the "grandmother family" the modal family form. Consequently those historical, cultural, structural, and psychological theories developed
with such care to "explain" this peculiar family system are primarily of value as items in the history of social thought.

The significance of collateral ties in the placement of children
will now be clear. The constancy of the collateral components of
these household samples has already been noted. This constancy
is attributable to the fact that collateral kinship has a fixed place
and function in these family systems. As a basis for domestic
placement, collateral kinship emphasizes materterine ties and
responsibilities for the illegitimate offspring of kinswomen. Most

of these offspring are the products of broken consensual and extraresidential unions. Thus the fixity of the collateral component in
domestic groups is directly associated with the regulation of mating. In Carriacou, where consensual cohabitation is excluded,
collateral kinship is less significant as a basis for domestic placement than are uterine ties three generations deep. It is also less
significant in Carriacou than in those populations which practice
consensual cohabitation and extraresidential mating as well as
marriage. Thus, the significance of the maternal grandmother,
like that of materterine kin, varies directly with the mating organization.

We have already shown how the proportions of resident lineal
issue of household heads vary inversely with the incidence of cohabitation. It is clear that the mating organization governs the
form of the domestic system and provides the central principle
of the family structure. Differences in the mating organization
entail differences in the distribution and significance of kinship
roles and domestic forms. Similarities of mating organization, such
as we have found between Latante and rural Jamaica on the one
hand, and Grenville and Kingston on the other, entail similarities
of domestic grouping and kinship roles. The mating system operates
as a formative principle in family structure because it establishes
relations between as well as within household groups, changing
their composition and mediating the establishment of new units.
Moreover, relations between mates include allocation of rights and
responsibilities towards offspring; these definitions of parental
roles govern the domestic placement of children in all sorts of
unions; they also vary with unions of differing types; and the resulting varieties of parenthood, as well as of mating relations, are
the dynamic conditions which shape and change domestic units.

Given a mating system which contains three equally valid alternative forms, there will be six divergent forms of parenthood,
one for each sex in each type of union. Given these six varieties
of parenthood, a variety of kinship ties will be invoked as supplements to, or substitutes for, marginal parenthood. Obviously, all
varieties of parenthood will not be equally effective, and their
differences in this respect are aspects of the alternative mating
relations themselves. Obviously, if these mating alternatives are
equally widespread, no one kinship relation will be able to supplement or discharge all these varieties of parenthood adequately.
In consequence, a variety of kinship relations is brought into play
to discharge or supplement parenthood in differing situations.

We can list the more important parental substitutes simply. They include a woman's mother, her subsequent mates, her collateral, especially her materterine kin, and the parents and kin of the child's father. In addition, many women have to look after their children single-handedly, and many others live with the fathers of all their children. Carriacou, with its simple dichotomy of mating forms, invests the mother's mother with the major responsibility for substitute parenthood. The other four samples, with their more complex mating organizations, distribute these responsibilities more widely and lay greater stress on collateral kin. Differences in the stability of domestic unions within these populations express themselves as differing proportions of children who do not live with both their parents; these latter differences also express themselves in the ratios of children who live alone with their mothers, since the level of conjugal stability itself regulates the capacity of grandmothers and collaterals to act as substitute parents. The preceding table illustrates this nicely.

Of the 308 Carriacou children under 24 who do not live with their fathers, 78 or 25 per cent live with the mother alone. Of the 863 children living apart from their fathers in rural Jamaica, 272 or 31.5 per cent live with their mothers alone. Of 118 children in Latante, 46 or 39 per cent live with their mothers alone. Of 98 in Grenville, 55 or 56 per cent live with their mothers only. Of 342 in Kingston, 185 or 54 per cent live with their mothers only.

The marital stability of these populations has three modes. Domestic unions are most stable in Carriacou, least so in Grenville and Kingston. In Latante and rural Jamaica the level of stability is similar. We already know that the Carriacou mating system enjoins lifelong marriage for all males, and excludes consensual cohabitation. Hence the stability of mating relations in Carriacou. We also know that in Latante and rural Jamaica the alternative forms of mating are arranged in irreversible series, each having its proper place in the development of the individual life cycle. This regulation of mating also has its peculiar level of stability. So does the less controlled system practiced in Grenville and Kingston. In these urban populations, the three alternative forms of mating do not form a developmental series, but have an equal validity throughout most of the individual life cycle, and compete incessantly with one another. In consequence, the level of conjugal instability is remarkably high. Where a family structure is based on alternative mating forms and these forms are neither integrated with one another as in Carriacou nor serially exclusive as in Latante or rural Jamaica, the levels of conjugal instability will be high; and if the kinship system is a bilateral one formally based on monogamy, there will be then a correspondingly large proportion of mothers living alone with their children. Where the family structure is based on alternative mating forms, the domestic organization will differ correspondingly.

The Development of Domestic Varieties

Tables 13 to 19 are a systematic presentation of the data on the domestic placement of children, which we have just discussed. I shall therefore not linger upon them, beyond pointing out that the legal category of illegitimates includes three quite distinct sets of issue, the offspring of at least three distinct types of situation. The offspring of consensual domestic unions and of extraresidential unions are legally, but not socially, illegitimate in this family system. The offspring of promiscuous sex relations are socially as well as legally illegitimate within it. This last group of children can have no effective fathers; they are thus distinguished structurally from the other two categories of illegitimate offspring.

Differences between the children begotten within consensual domestic unions and extraresidential unions are almost equally important. The child's father exercises full rights and discharges full responsibilities of paternity within the consensual domestic union, so long as this union continues. The child's father has neither full rights nor full responsibilities of paternity in the extraresidential relation. Often a man may evade his paternal responsibilities for the offspring of his broken extraresidential unions. Likewise, a man may evade his obligations towards the issue of broken consensual unions. Obviously such evasion is easier where the rates of mobility are high, the density of population is great, and anonymity is general. Evasion is more difficult and less likely in settled rural communities where mobility is low, the population is small, and individuals have numerous kin. Thus, offspring of the same type of union occupy very different positions according to the social context. An extraresidential union in Carriacou, Latante, and rural Jamaica is likely to be more durable than a consensual domestic union in Grenville or Kingston, and the security of mother and children will differ accordingly. In consequence, we must not treat illegitimates as socially equivalent in these several samples. It would also be erroneous to treat the illegitimate offspring of any single mating form as equivalent without further information on the character of the mating system in the samples under study. In short, the significance of birth status varies in relation to the coresidence or separation of parents and their children, the data on which are presented in Tables 17, 18, and 19. For example,

12. 2 per cent of all dependents in rural Jamaica are illegitimate offspring living with both parents. In Grenville and Carriacou only 0. 4 per cent and 1. 3 per cent of the total dependents are in this position.

It is even more obvious from this analysis that legitimate and illegitimate issue are differentiated structurally. For this reason, Dr. R. T. Smith's definition of conjugal relations in terms of co-habitation, and his equation of marriage and consensual cohabitation are quite inadmissible.[7] It would be nice if we could agree with Dr. Smith that "We need not concern ourselves with this problem" of the distinction between extraresidential and domestic unions, but un-fortunately, unless we did, our analysis could not fail to mislead.[8] It is just as erroneous to treat marriage and consensual cohabita-tion as equivalent in West Indian society as to ignore the extra-residential union as a recognized conjugal form. We have seen how marriage marks the maturity of couples and their unions at Latante and in rural Jamaica, how it is obligatory for all men in Carriacou, and how unstable it is in Grenville and Kingston. We have seen how rigorously Carriacou society forbids consensual cohabitation, and how much value is attached to the well-regulated system of extra-residential mating, which is the sole alternative to marriage there. We have seen how stable are the consensual domestic unions of Latante and rural Jamaica, and how they follow extraresidential mating and precede marriage. We have also seen that adults of senior years will leave their consensual partners if the union does not develop into marriage at the proper time. We cannot agree that there is ". . . absolutely no change in the social position of the man after he is married. "[9] To do so would be to ignore the place of marriage in the individual life cycle, its regulatory position in the mating systems of Carriacou, Latante, and rural Jamaica, and its great instability in Kingston and Grenville.

The differences between consensual cohabitation and marriage in Jamaica are clearly stated by Miss Edith Clarke, who has also distinguished their structural implications.[10] Unfortunately, like Dr. R. T. Smith, Miss Clarke ignores the structurally significant extraresidential form of union. Unlike Dr. Smith, she analyzes the varieties of domestic group by reference to the conjugal status of the principals, and presents a classification of these units which highlights the incidence of fragmented elementary families and the replication of fragments at successive generations. Dr. Smith, on the other hand, by defining households and conjugal relations recip-rocally, considers the family fragments produced by extraresi-dential mating which he ignores as extensions of domestic elementary families which illustrate male marginality, matrifocality, and the developmental cycle of household groups.

Of course, elementary family units are a common basis of household organization; they also develop over time; children grow, some leave the home, some remain childless within it, others bear or bring children into the home. These grandchildren are members of fragmented elementary families whenever the extraresidential union is involved. These scattered elementary families may form separate domestic units later, as Dr. Smith recognizes. Often they do not, and in either case they form no part of the developmental cycle of those elementary families into which the extraresidential mates were born.

This conceptual confusion is only possible because extraresidential mating is excluded from the category of conjugal relations on this basis. We are left with two sets of parents, the first who cohabit and bear children normally, the second consisting of young females who produce them by a series of independent conceptions which represent a normal phase in the development of the families to which these females belong. Needless to say, Dr. Smith evades the question of whether broken domestic unions, legal or other, interrupt or form part of the normal cycle of elementary family and household development. Likewise, he ignores the prevalence of collateral kinship as a basis for domestic placement, or its role in the constitution and development of household units. He does not distinguish households which consist only of a parent and children as a phase of the developing elementary family form; he ignores all single-person units, and assumes that three-generation groups under female heads are residues of those which formerly contained the mates and issue of their present heads. He dismisses cohabiting childless couples and units whose principals are single siblings as not being "real" households, just as he dismisses fertile and durable extraresidential unions as not "real" conjugal relationships. [11]

Dr. Smith's analysis does not deal adequately with his own Guianese data, and certainly does not hold for our samples in its following generalized form.

There are really three phases in the development cycle of the household. In the first phase, young men and women are forming relationships with a series of lovers, and becoming parents without living with a spouse. This is really a latent phase, for it is only when they enter phase two and begin to live together, that the life of a new household group can be seen to begin. The second phase involves the isolation of a nuclear family in its own house. In the third phase, the household has become matrifocal and it usually includes the members of a three-generation matri-line: mother, daughters and maybe sons, and daughters' children. At this stage it may also incorporate other categories of kin, more particularly the mother's sisters or sisters' children. Clearly Phase 1 and Phase 3 of this cycle overlap in time. In some cases the second phase may be bypassed completely, and in others it may be extended either way so that Phases 1 and 3 disappear completely. In the villages under discussion all three phases normally exist as a part of the system. . . .

In spite of variations, the general type of family structure I have outlined for the Guianese villages seems to be fairly widespread in the Caribbean, and something very like it is found in other parts of the world. [12]

Table 20 compares the incidence of structurally distinct types of household groups in these five samples. It will be seen that there is considerable variation in the frequency of alternative forms. In Grenville and Kingston, units based on single parents and their children, on single persons, on siblings, and on childless couples are more frequent than elsewhere. In all, these four structural categories include 40.2 per cent, 45.9 per cent, 52.7 per cent, 66.5 per cent, and 66.9 per cent of the households studied in Carriacou, Latante, rural Jamaica, Grenville, and Kingston, respectively. Table 21 shows what proportions of the total sample are pure structural forms. Table 22 gives an effective classification of units whose principals are cohabiting couples, by reference to their marital status, generations of lineal descendants, and presence or absence of accretions. It will be perfectly clear from these figures that a substantial proportion of these sample households have never at any stage contained or developed from units which contained nuclear families. Our data show that elementary families have an incidence varying from 17.7 per cent at Grenville to 28.5 per cent at Latante. In Carriacou, units with a depth of three or more lineal generations are 36.2 per cent of the total sample; in Latante and rural Jamaica these units are 25.6 per cent and 19.3 per cent, respectively; in Grenville and Kingston they are 15.8 per cent and 11.7 per cent. By no means can such units be regarded as typical. Moreover, these aggregates include some which have never at any time contained an elementary family, some with male heads, and some which are residues of units whose normal development was interrupted by the separation of the cohabiting principals. It is clear that the variety of domestic groups in these samples cannot be explained in terms of domestic elementary families and their development. Neither can the "grandmother family" be regarded as typical nor can the prevalence of collateral kinship be ignored.

We have already shown that the alternative mating forms which

regulate the allocation of parental roles also regulate the constitution and growth of domestic units. They do so in various ways;
by permitting mates to live together or to live apart with their own
kin; by bringing into being new households based on cohabitation,
whether childless or not; and by bringing into households new members whose parents do not live together. In this system, the extraresidential mating form permits persons to live alone or with their
siblings, their children or their grandchildren, while maintaining
conjugal relations. The same mating form also entails the domestic
isolation of some mothers and their children, as well as the domestic association of single mothers and their own mothers, or
single mothers and their collateral kin. These latter associations
may occur in homes with male heads, as well as in those without.
They may be interrupted when the woman resumes consensual
cohabitation or marries, as well as by the widowhood or death of
the household principal with whom she lives. The entire complex
of domestic relations, the range and variety of domestic forms,
the patterns of isolation and association, all are regulated by the
system of mating alternatives and its associated parental roles.

TABLE 1

COMPARATIVE SUMMARY OF SAMPLE POPULATIONS

| | Carriacou | | | Latante | | | Grenville | | | Kingston | | | Rural Jamaica | | |
|---|---|---|---|---|---|---|---|---|---|---|---|---|---|---|---|
| | Male | Female | Total | Male | Female | Total | Male | Female | Total | Male | Female | Total | Male | Female | Total |
| TOTAL PERSONS | 421 | 619 | 1,040 | 237 | 253 | 490 | 162 | 218 | 380 | 566 | 774 | 1,340 | 2,167 | 2,159 | 4,326 |
| Total under the age of 14 | 216 | 226 | 442 | 105 | 89 | 194 | 50 | 74 | 124 | 222 | 216 | 438 | 947 | 896 | 1,843 |
| Percentage aged 0-14 | 20.8 | 21.8 | 42.6 | 22.4 | 18.2 | 40.6 | 15.8 | 19.4 | 35.2 | 16.6 | 16.1 | 32.7 | 21.9 | 20.5 | 42.4 |
| Percentage aged 15+ | 19.6 | 37.8 | 57.4 | 26.8 | 32.6 | 59.4 | 26.9 | 37.9 | 64.8 | 25.7 | 41.6 | 67.3 | 28.2 | 29.4 | 57.6 |
| TOTAL PER CENT | 40.4 | 59.6 | 100.0 | 49.2 | 50.8 | 100.0 | 42.7 | 57.3 | 100.0 | 42.3 | 57.7 | 100.0 | 50.1 | 49.9 | 100.0 |
| Sex ratios of total population over 14 years | 1 : 2.00 | | | 1 : 1.24 | | | 1 : 1.35 | | | 1 : 1.62 | | | 1 : 1.04 | | |
| Sex ratios of adults aged 15-54 years | 1 : 1.6 | | | 1 : 1.20 | | | 1 : 1.19 | | | 1 : 1.46 | | | 1 : 1.01 | | |

TABLE 2

PERCENTAGE DISTRIBUTION OF HOUSEHOLD HEADSHIP WITHIN THE SAMPLE BY AGE AND SEX CATEGORIES

| Age | Carriacou | | | Latante | | | Grenville | | | Kingston | | | Rural Jamaica | | |
|---|---|---|---|---|---|---|---|---|---|---|---|---|---|---|---|
| | Male | Female | Total | Male | Female | Total | Male | Female | Total | Male | Female | Total | Male | Female | Total |
| 15-24 | 0.45 | 0.45 | 0.9 | 1.0 | 1.0 | 2.0 | 6.5 | 3.5 | 10.0 | 3.5 | 4.3 | 7.8 | 2.9 | 0.7 | 3.6 |
| 25-39 | 8.95 | 4.45 | 13.4 | 19.5 | 7.9 | 27.4 | 13.3 | 13.3 | 26.6 | 27.0 | 18.3 | 45.3 | 22.7 | 7.4 | 30.1 |
| 40-54 | 16.4 | 16.2 | 32.6 | 18.6 | 12.8 | 31.4 | 19.2 | 14.2 | 33.4 | 14.8 | 17.4 | 32.2 | 27.4 | 10.6 | 38.0 |
| 55-69 | 9.8 | 27.7 | 37.5 | 14.6 | 11.8 | 26.4 | 5.1 | 10.7 | 15.8 | 4.5 | 6.9 | 11.4 | 13.1 | 7.3 | 20.4 |
| 70+ | 5.8 | 9.8 | 15.6 | 4.9 | 7.9 | 12.8 | 3.5 | 10.7 | 14.2 | 1.0 | 2.3 | 3.3 | 3.8 | 4.1 | 7.9 |
| TOTAL PER CENT | 41.4 | 58.6 | 100.0 | 58.6 | 41.4 | 100.0 | 47.6 | 52.4 | 100.0 | 50.8 | 49.2 | 100.0 | 69.9 | 30.1 | 100.0 |
| TOTAL NUMBER | 93 | 131 | 224 | 60 | 42 | 102 | 54 | 59 | 113 | 216 | 209 | 425 | 702 | 305 | 1,007 |
| Single person households | 7 | 20 | 27 | 4 | 8 | 12 | 5 | 12 | 17 | 29 | 46 | 75 | 120 | 47 | 167 |
| Single person units as percentage of total households | 2.9 | 8.5 | 11.4 | 3.9 | 7.9 | 11.8 | 4.4 | 10.7 | 15.1 | 6.8 | 10.8 | 17.6 | 11.9 | 4.6 | 16.5 |
| Percentage of average household population including single person units | 5.7 | 3.9 | 4.6 | 5.36 | 3.76 | 4.8 | 3.84 | 2.83 | 3.38 | 3.43 | 2.86 | 3.16 | 4.42 | 3.92 | 4.3 |

## TABLE 3

### PERCENTAGE DISTRIBUTION OF HOUSEHOLDS CLASSIFIED BY SEX OF HEAD AND GENERATION DEPTH

| Generations in Home | Carriacou | | | Latante | | | Grenville | | | Kingston | | | Rural Jamaica | | |
|---|---|---|---|---|---|---|---|---|---|---|---|---|---|---|---|
| | Male | Female | All | Male | Female | All | Male | Female | All | Male | Female | All | Male | Female | All |
| 1 | 11.0 | 16.0 | 14.0 | 18.0 | 21.0 | 20.0 | 37.0 | 27.0 | 32.0 | 40.3 | 34.4 | 37.7 | 29.8 | 21.3 | 27.3 |
| 2 | 58.0 | 30.0 | 42.0 | 55.0 | 33.0 | 46.0 | 50.0 | 44.0 | 47.0 | 50.0 | 45.9 | 47.7 | 48.2 | 34.4 | 44.1 |
| 3 | 30.0 | 50.0 | 42.0 | 25.0 | 41.0 | 31.0 | 13.0 | 24.0 | 18.0 | 9.2 | 18.2 | 13.6 | 20.5 | 40.1 | 26.4 |
| 4 | 1.0 | 4.0 | 2.0 | 2.0 | 5.0 | 3.0 | 0.0 | 5.0 | 3.0 | 0.5 | 1.5 | 1.0 | 1.5 | 4.2 | 2.2 |
| TOTAL | 100.0 | 100.0 | 100.0 | 100.0 | 100.0 | 100.0 | 100.0 | 100.0 | 100.0 | 100.0 | 100.0 | 100.0 | 100.0 | 100.0 | 100.0 |

## TABLE 4

### PERCENTAGE DISTRIBUTION OF SAMPLE POPULATION CLASSIFIED BY SEX OF HOUSEHOLD HEAD AND GENERATION DISTANCE FROM HOUSEHOLD HEAD

| Genealogical Generations | Carriacou | | | Latante | | | Grenville | | | Kingston | | | Rural Jamaica | | |
|---|---|---|---|---|---|---|---|---|---|---|---|---|---|---|---|
| | Male | Female | Total | Male | Female | Total | Male | Female | Total | Male | Female | Total | Male | Female | Total |
| +2 | 0.0 | 0.0 | 0.0 | 0.0 | 0.0 | 0.0 | 0.0 | 0.3 | 0.3 | 0.0 | 0.2 | 0.2 | 0.1 | 0.0 | 0.1 |
| +1 | 0.3 | 0.2 | 0.5 | 0.0 | 0.2 | 0.2 | 0.3 | 0.0 | 0.3 | 0.8 | 0.5 | 1.3 | 0.8 | 0.4 | 1.2 |
| 0* | 17.3 | 13.7 | 31.0 | 23.5 | 10.0 | 33.5 | 27.6 | 18.9 | 46.5 | 31.9 | 21.1 | 53.0 | 30.8 | 8.7 | 39.5 |
| -1 | 27.2 | 19.3 | 46.5 | 37.8 | 14.1 | 51.9 | 24.2 | 18.4 | 42.6 | 20.1 | 18.0 | 38.1 | 34.3 | 11.4 | 45.7 |
| -2 | 5.9 | 14.9 | 20.8 | 6.3 | 7.1 | 13.4 | 2.4 | 7.6 | 10.0 | 2.4 | 4.9 | 7.3 | 5.9 | 6.2 | 12.1 |
| -3 | 0.2 | 1.0 | 1.2 | 0.2 | 0.8 | 1.0 | 0.0 | 0.3 | 0.3 | 0.0 | 0.1 | 0.1 | 0.4 | 1.0 | 1.4 |
| TOTAL PER CENT | 50.9 | 49.1 | 100.0 | 67.8 | 32.2 | 100.0 | 54.5 | 45.5 | 100.0 | 55.2 | 44.8 | 100.0 | 72.3 | 27.7 | 100.0 |
| TOTAL PERSONS | 530 | 510 | 1,040 | 332 | 158 | 490 | 207 | 173 | 380 | 741 | 599 | 1,340 | 3,104 | 1,194 | 4,298 |

*Household head's generation.

## TABLE 5

PERCENTAGE DISTRIBUTION OF SAMPLE POPULATION OVER 15 YEARS OF AGE, BY SEX, MATING, AND PARENTAL STATUS

| | Carriacou | | | Latante | | | Grenville | | | Kingston | | | Rural Jamaica | | |
|---|---|---|---|---|---|---|---|---|---|---|---|---|---|---|---|
| | Male | Female | Both | Male | Female | Both | Male | Female | Both | Male | Female | Both | Male | Female | Both |
| Childless single persons | 31.7 | 30.0 | 30.7 | 43.9 | 31.7 | 37.2 | 31.5 | 20.2 | 24.9 | 4.1 | 4.3 | 4.2 | 26.0 | 16.7 | 21.3 |
| Single, parental status n/k* | 13.2 | 7.1 | 9.0 | 0.0 | 0.0 | 0.0 | 0.0 | 0.0 | 0.0 | 37.9 | 32.6 | 34.1 | 12.9 | 5.5 | 9.1 |
| Single parents | 7.3 | 16.6 | 13.5 | 6.8 | 15.8 | 11.8 | 13.7 | 21.0 | 17.9 | 1.4 | 16.9 | 11.1 | 10.8 | 24.2 | 17.7 |
| Total single persons | 52.2 | 53.7 | 53.2 | 50.7 | 47.5 | 49.0 | 45.2 | 41.2 | 42.8 | 43.4 | 53.8 | 49.4 | 49.7 | 46.4 | 48.1 |
| Consensually wed | 2.9 | 1.8 | 2.2 | 12.1 | 10.4 | 11.2 | 11.8 | 12.5 | 12.2 | 28.4 | 17.8 | 21.4 | 19.7 | 18.6 | 19.3 |
| Consensually wed, separated | 0.5 | 0.5 | 0.5 | 0.0 | 0.6 | 0.3 | 0.9 | 9.1 | 5.7 | 0.0 | 0.0 | 0.0 | 1.0 | 1.7 | 1.3 |
| Total consensually wed | 3.4 | 2.3 | 2.7 | 12.1 | 11.0 | 11.5 | 12.7 | 21.6 | 17.9 | 28.4 | 17.8 | 21.4 | 20.7 | 20.3 | 20.6 |
| Married, spouse present | 40.0 | 20.9 | 27.4 | 30.3 | 24.4 | 27.0 | 25.5 | 20.2 | 22.2 | 27.3 | 16.9 | 20.3 | 26.8 | 25.5 | 26.1 |
| Married, spouse absent | 1.0 | 8.1 | 5.7 | 4.6 | 6.1 | 5.4 | 13.7 | 7.8 | 10.2 | 0.6 | 8.7 | 5.8 | 1.3 | 2.1 | 1.7 |
| Total married | 41.0 | 29.0 | 33.1 | 34.9 | 30.5 | 32.4 | 39.2 | 28.0 | 32.4 | 27.9 | 25.6 | 26.1 | 28.1 | 27.6 | 27.8 |
| Widowed | 3.4 | 15.0 | 11.0 | 2.3 | 11.0 | 7.1 | 2.9 | 9.8 | 6.9 | 0.3 | 2.8 | 3.1 | 1.5 | 5.7 | 3.5 |
| TOTAL PER CENT | 100.0 | 100.0 | 100.0 | 100.0 | 100.0 | 100.0 | 100.0 | 100.0 | 100.0 | 100.0 | 100.0 | 100.0 | 100.0 | 100.0 | 100.0 |
| TOTAL PERSONS | 205 | 393 | 598 | 132 | 164 | 296 | 102 | 144 | 246 | 344 | 558 | 902 | 1,209 | 1,264 | 2,473 |
| Per cent of total population single, now mating | 6.9 | 7.2 | 7.1 | 18.2 | 19.5 | 19.0 | 18.8 | 21.0 | 19.5 | 2.2 | 8.7 | 5.0 | 12.3 | 15.3 | 13.9 |

*n/k = Not known.

## TABLE 6

ADULTS BETWEEN THE AGES OF 15 AND 24 AS PERCENTAGE OF TOTAL ADULT POPULATIONS OF THESE SAMPLES CLASSIFIED BY SEX, MATING, AND PARENTAL STATUS

| | Carriacou | | | Latante | | | Grenville | | | Kingston | | | Rural Jamaica | | |
|---|---|---|---|---|---|---|---|---|---|---|---|---|---|---|---|
| | Male | Female | Both | Male | Female | Both | Male | Female | Both | Male | Female | Both | Male | Female | Both |
| Childless single persons | 30.2 | 22.1 | 24.9 | 37.1 | 25.2 | 30.4 | 23.6 | 13.2 | 17.5 | 0.9 | 0.0 | 0.3 | 23.8 | 14.7 | 19.2 |
| Single, parental status n/k* | 4.9 | 0.0 | 1.7 | 0.0 | 0.0 | 0.0 | 0.0 | 0.0 | 0.0 | 22.9 | 18.6 | 20.5 | 3.4 | 0.2 | 1.7 |
| Single parents | 1.5 | 2.8 | 2.3 | 1.5 | 8.0 | 5.1 | 6.8 | 6.2 | 6.5 | 0.3 | 3.4 | 2.2 | 0.7 | 6.8 | 3.8 |
| Total single | 36.6 | 24.9 | 28.9 | 38.6 | 33.2 | 35.5 | 30.4 | 19.4 | 24.0 | 24.1 | 22.0 | 23.0 | 27.9 | 21.7 | 24.7 |
| Total cohabiting | 0.9 | 2.1 | 1.7 | 1.5 | 2.7 | 2.3 | 4.9 | 7.0 | 6.1 | 4.4 | 7.2 | 6.0 | 1.5 | 7.3 | 4.5 |
| TOTAL PER CENT | 37.5 | 27.0 | 30.6 | 40.1 | 35.9 | 37.8 | 35.3 | 26.4 | 30.1 | 28.5 | 29.2 | 29.0 | 29.4 | 29.0 | 29.2 |
| TOTAL PERSONS | 77 | 106 | 183 | 53 | 59 | 112 | 36 | 38 | 74 | 356 | 366 | 722 | 356 | 366 | 722 |
| Persons under 24, single, mating now, as percentage of total population | 2.0 | 2.5 | 2.3 | 10.6 | 13.4 | 11.5 | 13.7 | 10.4 | 11.8 | 0.3 | 2.3 | 1.4 | 4.2 | 8.7 | 6.5 |

*n/k = Not known.

## TABLE 7

PERCENTAGE DISTRIBUTION OF HOUSEHOLD HEADS CLASSIFIED BY SEX, MATING, AND PARENTAL STATUS

| | Carriacou | | | Latante | | | Grenville | | | Kingston | | | Rural Jamaica | | |
|---|---|---|---|---|---|---|---|---|---|---|---|---|---|---|---|
| | Male | Female | Both | Male | Female | Both | Male | Female | Both | Male | Female | Both | Male | Female | Both |
| Childless single persons | 0.0 | 6.2 | 3.6 | 0.0 | 14.3 | 6.8 | 3.7 | 10.2 | 7.1 | 5.1 | 9.6 | 7.3 | 2.5 | 5.2 | 3.3 |
| Single, parental status n/k* | 2.1 | 13.0 | 8.5 | 0.0 | 0.0 | 0.0 | 0.0 | 0.0 | 0.0 | 15.8 | 27.7 | 21.6 | 8.2 | 11.2 | 9.1 |
| Single parents | 2.1 | 19.0 | 12.0 | 3.4 | 23.9 | 11.6 | 11.1 | 28.8 | 20.3 | 0.9 | 29.2 | 14.8 | 11.6 | 47.9 | 22.5 |
| Total single persons | 4.2 | 38.2 | 24.1 | 3.4 | 38.2 | 18.4 | 14.8 | 39.0 | 27.4 | 21.8 | 66.5 | 43.7 | 22.3 | 64.3 | 34.9 |
| Consensually wed now | 4.3 | 0.0 | 1.8 | 18.3 | 4.5 | 12.7 | 11.1 | 10.2 | 10.7 | 35.6 | 9.1 | 22.6 | 27.9 | 5.8 | 21.3 |
| Consensually wed, separated | 1.1 | 1.5 | 1.3 | 0.0 | 0.0 | 0.0 | 0.0 | 20.3 | 10.6 | 0.0 | 0.0 | 0.0 | 1.6 | 4.9 | 2.6 |
| Total consensually wed | 5.4 | 1.5 | 3.1 | 18.3 | 4.5 | 12.7 | 11.1 | 30.5 | 21.3 | 35.6 | 9.1 | 22.6 | 29.5 | 10.7 | 23.9 |
| Married, spouse present | 80.8 | 0.8 | 33.9 | 65.0 | 0.0 | 38.1 | 46.3 | 0.0 | 22.1 | 41.2 | 1.4 | 21.6 | 44.0 | 1.6 | 31.1 |
| Married, spouse absent | 2.1 | 14.5 | 9.4 | 8.3 | 16.9 | 11.6 | 22.2 | 8.5 | 15.1 | 0.9 | 17.2 | 9.0 | 2.1 | 5.9 | 3.3 |
| Total married | 82.9 | 15.3 | 43.3 | 73.3 | 16.9 | 49.7 | 68.5 | 8.5 | 37.2 | 42.1 | 18.6 | 30.6 | 46.1 | 7.5 | 34.4 |
| Widowed persons | 7.5 | 45.0 | 29.5 | 5.0 | 40.4 | 19.2 | 5.6 | 22.0 | 14.1 | 0.5 | 5.8 | 3.1 | 2.1 | 17.5 | 6.8 |
| TOTAL | 100.0 | 100.0 | 100.0 | 100.0 | 100.0 | 100.0 | 100.0 | 100.0 | 100.0 | 100.0 | 100.0 | 100.0 | 100.0 | 100.0 | 100.0 |
| Percentage of single persons now mating | 0.0 | 1.53 | 0.9 | 0.0 | 11.9 | 1.9 | 9.2 | 20.2 | 14.1 | 0.5 | 3.3 | 1.9 | 7.5 | 14.4 | 9.6 |

*n/k = Not known.

## TABLE 8

CURRENTLY MARRIED ADULT MEMBERS OF THE SAMPLE HOUSEHOLDS AS PERCENTAGE OF TOTAL NUMBER OF ADULT MEMBERS IN THEIR RESPECTIVE AGE AND SEX GROUPS

| | Carriacou | | | Latante | | | Grenville | | | Kingston | | | Rural Jamaica | | |
|---|---|---|---|---|---|---|---|---|---|---|---|---|---|---|---|
| | Male | Female | Both | Male | Female | Both | Male | Female | Both | Male | Female | Both | Male | Female | Both |
| 15-24 | 1.3 | 6.1 | 4.4 | 0.0 | 1.7 | 0.9 | 1.4 | 15.8 | 14.8 | 3.1 | 8.6 | 6.5 | 0.6 | 5.5 | 3.1 |
| 25-39 | 39.1 | 42.7 | 40.8 | 29.7 | 36.4 | 33.3 | 30.3 | 36.7 | 34.2 | 31.1 | 28.5 | 29.2 | 23.8 | 37.1 | 30.6 |
| 40-54 | 83.0 | 43.8 | 57.0 | 77.4 | 62.3 | 68.5 | 41.5 | 23.3 | 31.6 | 45.8 | 36.4 | 40.0 | 48.2 | 40.8 | 44.6 |
| 55-69 | 78.5 | 25.6 | 35.7 | 73.3 | 26.3 | 47.0 | 57.1 | 20.0 | 31.8 | 50.0 | 37.6 | 41.3 | 53.5 | 34.9 | 44.0 |
| 70+ | 69.0 | 14.3 | 31.7 | 60.0 | 20.0 | 33.3 | 0.0 | 0.0 | 0.0 | 60.0 | 40.0 | 45.0 | 46.0 | 13.6 | 25.9 |
| Percentage of total currently married | 40.0 | 27.2 | 31.6 | 31.9 | 26.8 | 29.0 | 27.5 | 23.8 | 25.3 | 27.9 | 25.6 | 26.1 | 27.8 | 27.1 | 27.3 |

## TABLE 9

ALL ADULTS WHO HAVE EVER MARRIED AS PERCENTAGE OF TOTAL POPULATION IN THEIR RESPECTIVE AGE AND SEX CATEGORIES

| | Carriacou | | | Latante | | | Grenville | | | Kingston | | | Rural Jamaica | | |
|---|---|---|---|---|---|---|---|---|---|---|---|---|---|---|---|
| | Male | Female | Both | Male | Female | Both | Male | Female | Both | Male | Female | Both | Male | Female | Both |
| 15-24 | 1.3 | 6.1 | 4.4 | 0.0 | 1.7 | 0.9 | 1.4 | 15.8 | 14.8 | 3.1 | 8.6 | 6.5 | 0.6 | 6.0 | 3.3 |
| 25-39 | 39.1 | 42.7 | 40.8 | 37.8 | 47.7 | 43.2 | 43.3 | 42.8 | 43.0 | 31.1 | 30.4 | 29.2 | 24.1 | 40.0 | 31.6 |
| 40-54 | 88.0 | 54.7 | 66.7 | 77.4 | 75.0 | 75.9 | 62.3 | 36.7 | 48.0 | 45.8 | 39.9 | 42.1 | 50.2 | 49.6 | 50.0 |
| 55-69 | 87.4 | 75.5 | 76.0 | 86.6 | 73.7 | 79.3 | 85.7 | 60.0 | 67.0 | 53.3 | 48.0 | 50.2 | 59.0 | 47.2 | 52.7 |
| 70+ | 100.0 | 71.3 | 80.3 | 100.0 | 80.0 | 86.5 | 80.0 | 58.3 | 63.6 | 60.0 | 53.3 | 55.0 | 62.0 | 46.6 | 51.8 |
| Percentage of total ever married | 44.4 | 44.0 | 44.1 | 37.2 | 41.5 | 39.5 | 42.1 | 37.8 | 39.3 | 28.2 | 28.4 | 28.2 | 29.6 | 33.3 | 31.3 |

## TABLE 10

### PERCENTAGE FREQUENCY OF DIFFERENT CATEGORIES OF KIN AMONG DEPENDENT MEMBERS OF THE HOUSEHOLD SAMPLES

| | Carriacou | | | Latante | | | Grenville | | | Kingston | | | Rural Jamaica | | |
|---|---|---|---|---|---|---|---|---|---|---|---|---|---|---|---|
| | Male HH* | Female HH | All | Male HH | Female HH | All | Male HH | Female HH | All | Male HH | Female HH | All | Male HH | Female HH | All |
| Spouses and mates | 18.8 | 0.8 | 10.4 | 18.2 | 1.7 | 14.0 | 26.0 | 4.3 | 16.8 | 31.3 | 5.6 | 20.3 | 21.3 | 2.78 | 16.05 |
| HH's children | 56.8 | 38.5 | 48.4 | 59.9 | 48.2 | 56.6 | 48.9 | 51.7 | 50.1 | 43.4 | 49.9 | 46.8 | 51.2 | 46.9 | 50.0 |
| HH's grandchildren | 9.4 | 36.1 | 21.7 | 8.4 | 24.1 | 13.15 | 2.6 | 21.0 | 10.5 | 4.6 | 15.7 | 9.3 | 7.75 | 26.9 | 12.93 |
| HH's great-grandchildren | 0.2 | 1.3 | 0.7 | 0.4 | 3.5 | 1.25 | 0.0 | 0.9 | 0.4 | 0.0 | 0.3 | 0.1 | 0.4 | 4.38 | 1.49 |
| Total lineal issue of HH | 66.4 | 75.9 | 70.8 | 68.7 | 75.8 | 71.0 | 51.5 | 73.6 | 61.0 | 48.0 | 66.0 | 56.2 | 59.35 | 78.18 | 64.42 |
| HH's mate's issue | 5.0 | 0.8 | 3.1 | 3.0 | 1.7 | 2.5 | 7.9 | 2.7 | 5.7 | 5.2 | 0.6 | 3.1 | 6.42 | 0.55 | 4.78 |
| HH's mate's kin | 8.0 | 0.3 | 4.5 | 4.4 | 2.6 | 3.5 | 2.7 | 0.0 | 1.1 | 6.1 | 0.2 | 3.6 | 3.55 | 0.22 | 2.7 |
| Total kin of HH's mates | 13.0 | 1.1 | 7.6 | 7.4 | 4.3 | 6.0 | 10.6 | 2.7 | 6.8 | 11.3 | 0.8 | 6.7 | 9.97 | 0.77 | 7.48 |
| HH's siblings and their issue | 0.7 | 15.8 | 7.7 | 2.2 | 10.4 | 4.5 | 6.6 | 8.8 | 7.3 | 3.8 | 14.9 | 8.4 | 2.76 | 9.18 | 4.72 |
| HH's parents | 0.0 | 0.3 | 0.1 | 0.0 | 0.9 | 0.25 | 0.0 | 0.0 | 0.0 | 0.8 | 1.5 | 1.1 | 0.93 | 1.46 | 1.1 |
| HH's matrikin | 0.2 | 2.2 | 1.1 | 1.5 | 0.9 | 1.25 | 0.0 | 0.9 | 0.4 | 0.4 | 2.4 | 1.2 | 0.44 | 0.44 | 0.42 |
| HH's patrikin | 0.0 | 0.0 | 0.0 | 0.0 | 2.6 | 0.75 | 0.0 | 0.9 | 0.4 | 0.0 | 0.0 | 0.0 | 0.28 | 0.45 | 0.33 |
| HH's kin, relation n/k* | 0.0 | 0.0 | 0.0 | 0.0 | 0.0 | 0.0 | 0.0 | 0.0 | 0.0 | 0.0 | 0.0 | 0.0 | 0.04 | 0.0 | 0.02 |
| Total parents and collateral kin of HH | 0.9 | 18.3 | 8.9 | 3.7 | 14.8 | 6.75 | 6.6 | 10.6 | 8.1 | 5.0 | 18.8 | 10.7 | 4.45 | 11.53 | 6.59 |
| Junior affines | 0.0 | 2.5 | 1.2 | 1.2 | 3.4 | 1.75 | 0.0 | 0.0 | 0.0 | 0.0 | 1.3 | 0.5 | 0.68 | 2.47 | 1.18 |
| Adopted persons | 0.9 | 1.2 | 1.0 | 0.4 | 0.0 | 0.25 | 2.0 | 6.1 | 3.8 | 0.8 | 2.2 | 1.3 | 1.51 | 2.81 | 1.9 |
| Employees | 0.0 | 0.0 | 0.0 | 0.0 | 0.0 | 0.0 | 3.3 | 0.0 | 1.9 | 1.6 | 0.2 | 1.0 | 1.33 | 0.45 | 1.07 |
| Unrelated persons | 0.0 | 0.2 | 0.1 | 0.4 | 0.0 | 0.25 | 0.0 | 2.7 | 1.6 | 2.0 | 5.1 | 3.3 | 1.41 | 1.01 | 1.31 |
| Total miscellaneous persons | 0.9 | 3.9 | 2.3 | 2.0 | 3.4 | 2.25 | 5.3 | 8.8 | 7.3 | 4.4 | 8.8 | 6.1 | 4.93 | 6.74 | 5.46 |
| TOTAL PER CENT | 100.0 | 100.0 | 100.0 | 100.0 | 100.0 | 100.0 | 100.0 | 100.0 | 100.0 | 100.0 | 100.0 | 100.0 | 100.0 | 100.0 | 100.0 |
| TOTAL PERSONS | 437 | 739 | 816 | 272 | 116 | 388 | 153 | 114 | 267 | 525 | 389 | 914 | 2,402 | 889 | 3,291 |

*HH = Household head; n/k = Not known.

TABLE 11

PERCENTAGE COMPOSITION OF SAMPLE HOUSEHOLDS CLASSIFIED BY SEX OF HEAD AND RELATIONSHIP CATEGORY

| | Carriacou | | | Latante | | | Grenville | | | Kingston | | | Rural Jamaica | | |
| | Male HH* | Female HH | All | Male HH | Female HH | All | Male HH | Female HH | All | Male HH | Female HH | All | Male HH | Female HH | All |
|---|---|---|---|---|---|---|---|---|---|---|---|---|---|---|---|
| Household head | 17.5 | 25.7 | 21.4 | 18.2 | 26.4 | 20.9 | 26.1 | 34.1 | 29.8 | 29.2 | 34.9 | 31.7 | 22.6 | 25.6 | 23.4 |
| Mates and spouses of HH | 15.5 | 0.6 | 8.1 | 15.3 | 1.3 | 10.8 | 19.3 | 2.9 | 11.9 | 22.4 | 3.7 | 14.1 | 16.4 | 2.0 | 12.4 |
| Issue of HH only | 2.3 | 54.6 | 28.1 | 3.9 | 53.3 | 19.7 | 1.0 | 48.1 | 22.3 | 1.4 | 41.6 | 19.3 | 2.1 | 55.8 | 17.0 |
| Issue of HH and mate | 52.4 | 1.8 | 27.6 | 52.4 | 1.3 | 36.1 | 37.2 | 0.6 | 20.6 | 32.9 | 1.3 | 18.9 | 43.8 | 2.5 | 32.6 |
| Issue of mate only | 4.2 | 0.6 | 2.4 | 2.4 | 1.3 | 2.0 | 5.8 | 1.7 | 3.9 | 3.5 | 0.3 | 2.1 | 4.9 | 0.4 | 3.6 |
| Kin of mate only | 6.5 | 0.2 | 3.5 | 3.3 | 1.9 | 2.8 | 1.9 | 0.0 | 1.0 | 4.3 | 0.2 | 2.5 | 2.8 | 0.1 | 2.1 |
| Kin of HH only | 0.8 | 13.7 | 7.1 | 3.0 | 12.6 | 6.1 | 4.8 | 6.9 | 5.8 | 3.4 | 12.4 | 7.2 | 3.7 | 8.7 | 5.1 |
| Junior affines of HH | 0.0 | 1.8 | 0.9 | 0.9 | 1.9 | 1.2 | 0.0 | 0.0 | 0.0 | 0.0 | 0.8 | 0.4 | 0.4 | 1.8 | 0.7 |
| Adopted persons | 0.8 | 0.8 | 0.8 | 0.3 | 0.0 | 0.2 | 1.5 | 4.0 | 2.6 | 0.5 | 1.3 | 0.9 | 1.2 | 2.0 | 1.3 |
| Nonkin | 0.0 | 0.2 | 0.1 | 0.3 | 0.0 | 0.2 | 2.4 | 1.7 | 2.1 | 2.4 | 3.5 | 2.9 | 2.1 | 1.1 | 1.8 |
| TOTAL PER CENT | 100.0 | 100.0 | 100.0 | 100.0 | 100.0 | 100.0 | 100.0 | 100.0 | 100.0 | 100.0 | 100.0 | 100.0 | 100.0 | 100.0 | 100.0 |
| TOTAL NUMBER | 530 | 510 | 1,040 | 332 | 158 | 490 | 207 | 173 | 380 | 741 | 599 | 1,340 | 3,104 | 1,194 | 4,298 |

*HH = Household head.

## TABLE 12

PERCENTAGE DISTRIBUTION OF POPULATION OF SAMPLE HOUSEHOLDS BY SEX OF HOUSEHOLD HEAD AND RELATIONSHIP CATEGORY

| | Carriacou | | | Latante | | | Grenville | | | Kingston | | | Rural Jamaica | | |
|---|---|---|---|---|---|---|---|---|---|---|---|---|---|---|---|
| | Male HH* | Female HH | Total | Male HH | Female HH | Total | Male HH | Female HH | Total | Male HH | Female HH | Total | Male HH | Female HH | Total |
| Household head | 8.8 | 12.6 | 21.4 | 12.3 | 8.6 | 20.9 | 14.3 | 15.5 | 29.8 | 16.1 | 15.6 | 31.7 | 16.3 | 7.1 | 23.4 |
| Mates and spouses of HH | 7.8 | 0.3 | 8.1 | 10.4 | 0.4 | 10.8 | 10.6 | 1.3 | 11.9 | 12.5 | 1.6 | 14.1 | 11.8 | 0.6 | 12.4 |
| Issue of HH only | 1.2 | 26.9 | 28.1 | 2.6 | 17.1 | 19.7 | 0.5 | 21.8 | 22.3 | 0.7 | 18.6 | 19.3 | 1.5 | 15.5 | 17.0 |
| Issue of HH and mate | 26.7 | 0.9 | 27.6 | 35.7 | 0.4 | 36.1 | 20.3 | 0.3 | 20.6 | 18.3 | 0.6 | 18.9 | 31.8 | 0.8 | 32.6 |
| Issue of mate only | 2.3 | 0.1 | 2.4 | 1.6 | 0.4 | 2.0 | 3.1 | 0.8 | 3.9 | 1.9 | 0.2 | 2.1 | 3.5 | 0.1 | 3.6 |
| Kin of mate only | 3.4 | 0.1 | 3.5 | 2.2 | 0.6 | 2.8 | 1.0 | 0.0 | 1.0 | 2.4 | 0.1 | 2.5 | 2.1 | 0.0 | 2.1 |
| Kin of HH only | 0.3 | 6.8 | 7.1 | 2.0 | 4.1 | 6.1 | 2.6 | 3.2 | 5.8 | 1.7 | 5.5 | 7.2 | 2.7 | 2.4 | 5.1 |
| Junior affines of HH | 0.0 | 0.9 | 0.9 | 0.6 | 0.6 | 1.2 | 0.0 | 0.0 | 0.0 | 0.0 | 0.4 | 0.4 | 0.2 | 0.5 | 0.7 |
| Adopted persons | 0.4 | 0.4 | 0.8 | 0.2 | 0.0 | 0.2 | 0.8 | 1.8 | 2.6 | 0.3 | 0.6 | 0.9 | 0.9 | 0.4 | 1.3 |
| Nonkin | 0.0 | 0.1 | 0.1 | 0.2 | 0.0 | 0.2 | 1.3 | 0.8 | 2.1 | 1.3 | 1.6 | 2.9 | 1.5 | 0.3 | 1.8 |
| TOTAL PER CENT | 50.9 | 49.1 | 100.0 | 67.8 | 32.2 | 100.0 | 54.5 | 45.5 | 100.0 | 55.2 | 44.8 | 100.0 | 72.3 | 27.7 | 100.0 |
| TOTAL NUMBER | 530 | 510 | 1,040 | 332 | 158 | 490 | 207 | 173 | 380 | 741 | 599 | 1,340 | 3,104 | 1,194 | 4,298 |

*HH = Household head.

# TABLE 13

RESIDENT COLLATERALS OF HOUSEHOLD PRINCIPALS, CLASSIFIED BY CATEGORIES OF KINSHIP, SEX AND POSITION OF LINKED HOUSEHOLD PRINCIPAL, AND ILLEGITIMACY

| | Carriacou Principal | | Latante Principal | | Grenville Principal | | | Kingston Principal | | | Rural Jamaica Principal | | |
|---|---|---|---|---|---|---|---|---|---|---|---|---|---|
| | Mate of Male HH* | Female HH | Mate of Male HH | Female HH | Male HH | Mate of Male HH | Female HH | Male HH | Mate of Male HH | Female HH | Male HH | Mate of Male HH | Female HH |
| Full siblings | 2 | 3 | 1 | 4 | 0 | 0 | 4 | 3 | 4 | 21 | 9 | 22 | 19 |
| Illegitimates | 0 | 0 | 0 | 2 | 0 | 0 | 1 | 0 | 1 | 3 | 0 | 1 | 3 |
| Issue of full siblings | 13 | 51 | 6 | 8 | 2 | 2 | 2 | 1 | 12 | 17 | 50 | 48 | 33 |
| Illegitimates | 10 | 28 | 5 | 4 | 0 | 2 | 2 | 0 | 10 | 14 | 32 | 27 | 19 |
| Patrilateral kin | 3 | 5 | 3 | 3 | 1 | 1 | 1 | 14 | 10 | 24 | 15 | 11 | 25 |
| Illegitimates | 3 | 3 | 3 | 2 | 1 | 1 | 1 | 12 | 6 | 14 | 11 | 9 | 14 |
| Matrilateral kin | 7 | 9 | 1 | 1 | 0 | 0 | 5 | 3 | 0 | 4 | 2 | 6 | 7 |
| Illegitimates | 5 | 8 | 1 | 1 | 0 | 0 | 4 | 3 | 0 | 2 | 0 | 3 | 1 |
| TOTAL COLLATERALS | 25 | 68 | 11 | 16 | 3 | 3 | 12 | 21 | 26 | 66 | 76 | 87 | 84 |
| TOTAL ILLEGITIMATES | 18 | 39 | 9 | 9 | 1 | 3 | 8 | 15 | 17 | 33 | 43 | 40 | 37 |

*HH = Household head.

ALL RESIDENT COLLATERALS OF HOUSEHOLD PRINCIPALS, OTHER THAN FULL SIBLINGS, CLASSIFIED BY GENERATION REMOVE FROM THE LINKED PRINCIPAL, THE LATTER'S SEX AND POSITION IN THE HOUSEHOLD, AND THE SEX OF THE COLLATERAL'S PARENT THROUGH WHOM RELATIONSHIP IS TRACED

| | Carriacou Principal | | Latante Principal | | Grenville Principal | | Kingston Principal | | Rural Jamaica Principal | | |
|---|---|---|---|---|---|---|---|---|---|---|---|
| | Mate of Male HH* | Female HH | Mate of Male HH | Female HH | Mate of Male HH | Female HH | Mate of Male HH | Female HH | Male HH | Mate of Male HH | Female HH |
| Generation 0† | 3 | 4 | 0 | 1 | 3 | 1 | 8 | 11 | 6 | 7 | 17 |
| Linked through mother | 3 | 2 | 0 | 1 | 3 | 1 | 7 | 8 | 5 | 6 | 14 |
| Generation -1 | 14 | 38 | 8 | 6 | 0 | 4 | 7 | 32 | 49 | 37 | 32 |
| Linked through mother | 11 | 28 | 5 | 6 | 0 | 3 | 6 | 28 | 25 | 19 | 16 |
| Generation -2 | 6 | 18 | 1 | 5 | 0 | 2 | 6 | 2 | 11 | 18 | 13 |
| Linked through mother | 6 | 15 | 1 | 5 | 0 | 2 | 5 | 2 | 6 | 18 | 10 |
| Generation -3 | 0 | 5 | 0 | 0 | 0 | 0 | 0 | 0 | 0 | 3 | 2 |
| Linked through mother | 0 | 4 | 0 | 0 | 0 | 0 | 0 | 0 | 0 | 3 | 0 |
| TOTAL COLLATERALS | 23 | 65 | 9 | 12 | 3 | 7 | 21 | 45 | 66 | 65 | 64 |
| TOTAL LINKED THROUGH MOTHER | 20 | 49 | 6 | 12 | 3 | 6 | 18 | 38 | 36 | 46 | 40 |

*HH = Household head.
†Same genealogical generation as household head.

TABLE 15

PERCENTAGE FREQUENCIES OF DIFFERENT CATEGORIES OF RESIDENT LINEAL ISSUE OF HOUSEHOLD HEADS CLASSIFIED BY DESCENT, AND SEX OF HOUSEHOLD HEAD

| | Carriacou | | | Latante | | | Grenville | | | Kingston | | | Rural Jamaica | | |
|---|---|---|---|---|---|---|---|---|---|---|---|---|---|---|---|
| | Male HH | Female HH | All | Male HH | Female HH | All | Male HH | Female HH | All | Male HH | Female HH | All | Male HH | Female HH | All |
| Own issue | 85.8 | 50.6 | 68.3 | 87.0 | 63.6 | 79.5 | 95.0 | 70.6 | 82.3 | 91.0 | 75.5 | 83.0 | 86.3 | 60.0 | 77.6 |
| Son's issue | 4.5 | 14.6 | 9.5 | 2.3 | 7.9 | 4.0 | 1.2 | 8.2 | 4.8 | 6.3 | 3.1 | 4.7 | 3.7 | 8.7 | 5.3 |
| Daughter's issue | 9.7 | 34.8 | 22.2 | 10.7 | 28.5 | 16.5 | 3.8 | 21.2 | 12.9 | 2.7 | 21.4 | 12.3 | 10.0 | 31.3 | 17.1 |
| TOTAL | 100.0 | 100.0 | 100.0 | 100.0 | 100.0 | 100.0 | 100.0 | 100.0 | 100.0 | 100.0 | 100.0 | 100.0 | 100.0 | 100.0 | 100.0 |

*HH = Household head.

TABLE 16

PERCENTAGE DISTRIBUTION OF RESIDENT LINEAL ISSUE OF HOUSEHOLD HEADS CLASSIFIED BY DESCENT CATEGORY, SEX OF HOUSEHOLD HEAD, AND BIRTH STATUS

| | | Carriacou | | | Latante | | | Grenville | | | Kingston | | | Rural Jamaica | | |
| | | Male HH* | Female HH | All | Male HH | Female HH | All | Male HH | Female HH | All | Male HH | Female HH | All | Male HH | Female HH | All |
|---|---|---|---|---|---|---|---|---|---|---|---|---|---|---|---|---|
| Own issue | L† | 75.5 | 19.5 | 47.6 | 70.0 | 19.3 | 53.7 | 87.0 | 8.2 | 46.7 | 72.2 | 28.4 | 47.0 | 55.6 | 14.1 | 42.0 |
| | U† | 4.4 | 11.6 | 7.9 | 12.8 | 30.7 | 18.5 | 4.2 | 49.3 | 27.0 | 17.6 | 36.2 | 30.0 | 25.7 | 35.6 | 28.5 |
| | N/K† | 5.9 | 19.5 | 12.8 | 4.2 | 13.6 | 7.3 | 3.8 | 13.1 | 8.6 | 1.2 | 10.9 | 6.0 | 5.0 | 11.3 | 7.1 |
| Son's issue | L | 3.4 | 6.5 | 4.8 | 0.0 | 0.0 | 0.0 | 0.0 | 0.0 | 0.0 | 5.5 | 0.4 | 2.9 | 1.2 | 0.0 | 1.0 |
| | U | 1.1 | 8.1 | 4.7 | 2.3 | 7.9 | 4.0 | 1.2 | 8.2 | 4.8 | 0.8 | 2.7 | 1.8 | 2.1 | 6.4 | 3.5 |
| | N/K | 0.0 | 0.0 | 0.0 | 0.0 | 0.0 | 0.0 | 0.0 | 0.0 | 0.0 | 0.0 | 0.0 | 0.0 | 0.4 | 2.3 | 0.8 |
| Daughter's issue | L | 4.9 | 10.4 | 7.6 | 0.0 | 3.4 | 1.1 | 3.8 | 1.2 | 2.4 | 0.0 | 5.8 | 2.9 | 0.5 | 3.3 | 1.4 |
| | U | 4.8 | 23.7 | 14.3 | 10.2 | 26.1 | 15.0 | 0.0 | 15.0 | 8.1 | 2.7 | 14.6 | 9.0 | 8.8 | 25.7 | 14.5 |
| | N/K | 0.0 | 0.7 | 0.3 | 0.5 | 0.0 | 0.4 | 0.0 | 4.8 | 2.4 | 0.0 | 0.8 | 0.4 | 0.7 | 2.3 | 1.2 |
| Total | L | 83.8 | 36.4 | 60.0 | 70.0 | 22.7 | 54.7 | 90.8 | 9.4 | 49.1 | 77.7 | 34.6 | 52.8 | 57.3 | 17.4 | 44.4 |
| | U | 10.3 | 43.3 | 26.9 | 25.3 | 63.7 | 37.6 | 5.4 | 72.7 | 39.9 | 21.1 | 53.7 | 40.8 | 36.6 | 66.7 | 46.5 |
| | N/K | 5.9 | 20.3 | 13.1 | 4.7 | 13.6 | 7.7 | 3.8 | 17.9 | 11.0 | 1.2 | 11.7 | 6.4 | 6.1 | 15.9 | 9.1 |
| TOTAL PER CENT | | 100.0 | 100.0 | 100.0 | 100.0 | 100.0 | 100.0 | 100.0 | 100.0 | 100.0 | 100.0 | 100.0 | 100.0 | 100.0 | 100.0 | 100.0 |
| TOTAL LINEAL ISSUE | | 290 | 288 | 578 | 187 | 88 | 275 | 79 | 84 | 163 | 254 | 257 | 511 | 1,424 | 696 | 2,120 |
| Lineal issue as percentage of resident dependents | | 66.4 | 75.9 | 70.8 | 68.7 | 76.8 | 72.4 | 51.5 | 73.4 | 62.0 | 48.0 | 66.0 | 56.0 | 59.35 | 70.18 | 64.42 |

*HH = Household head.
†L = Lawful, i.e., legitimate; U = Unlawful, i.e., illegitimate; N/K = Birth status not known.

PERCENTAGE DISTRIBUTION OF DEPENDENTS CLASSIFIED BY SEX OF HOUSEHOLD HEAD AND PRESENCE OR ABSENCE OF THEIR PARENTS FROM THE HOME, TOGETHER WITH PERCENTAGE OF LEGITIMATE DEPENDENTS IN EACH CATEGORY

| | Carriacou | | | Latante | | | Grenville | | | Kingston | | | Rural Jamaica | | |
|---|---|---|---|---|---|---|---|---|---|---|---|---|---|---|---|
| | Male HH* | Female HH | Total | Male HH | Female HH | Total | Male HH | Female HH | Total | Male HH | Female HH | Total | Male HH | Female HH | Total |
| Both parents present | 32.4 | 1.9 | 34.3 | 43.0 | 1.5 | 44.5 | 31.2 | 0.4 | 31.6 | 30.2 | 1.7 | 31.9 | 40.5 | 2.3 | 42.8 |
| Legitimate, both parents present | 31.1 | 1.9 | 33.0 | 39.0 | 0.0 | 39.0 | 30.8 | 0.4 | 31.2 | 24.1 | 0.5 | 24.6 | 29.9 | 0.7 | 30.6 |
| Both parents absent | 11.7 | 18.0 | 29.7 | 10.2 | 12.5 | 22.7 | 10.4 | 16.3 | 26.7 | 11.4 | 16.1 | 27.5 | 13.8 | 9.7 | 23.5 |
| Legitimate, both parents absent | 04.6 | 05.2 | 09.8 | 01.8 | 02.1 | 03.9 | 01.4 | 01.8 | 03.2 | 04.0 | 03.1 | 07.1 | 00.1 | 0.0 | 00.1 |
| Fathers only present | 2.1 | 0.3 | 2.4 | 4.8 | 0.0 | 4.8 | 3.2 | 0.9 | 4.1 | 1.9 | 0.4 | 2.3 | 5.4 | 0.5 | 5.9 |
| Legitimate, with fathers only | 0.4 | 0.0 | 0.4 | 1.5 | 0.0 | 1.5 | 1.8 | 0.0 | 1.8 | 0.2 | 0.0 | 0.2 | 1.0 | 0.0 | 1.0 |
| Mothers only present | 2.4 | 21.0 | 23.4 | 6.4 | 13.9 | 20.3 | 6.4 | 29.8 | 36.2 | 5.3 | 28.1 | 33.4 | 8.2 | 16.7 | 24.9 |
| Legitimate, with mothers only | 0.3 | 06.1 | 06.4 | 0.0 | 03.9 | 03.9 | 1.4 | 04.2 | 05.6 | 0.0 | 09.9 | 09.9 | 0.3 | 02.9 | 03.2 |
| With widowed fathers | 0.9 | 0.0 | 0.9 | 2.3 | 0.0 | 2.3 | 0.0 | 0.0 | 0.0 | 0.5 | 0.0 | 0.5 | 0.6 | 0.0 | 0.6 |
| Legitimate, with widowed fathers | 0.9 | 0.0 | 0.9 | 1.4 | 0.0 | 1.4 | 0.0 | 0.0 | 0.0 | 0.5 | 0.0 | 0.5 | 0.6 | 0.0 | 0.6 |
| With widowed mothers | 0.0 | 9.3 | 9.3 | 0.0 | 5.4 | 5.4 | 0.0 | 1.4 | 1.4 | 0.2 | 4.2 | 4.4 | 0.4 | 1.9 | 2.3 |
| Legitimate, with widowed mothers | 0.0 | 9.3 | 9.3 | 0.0 | 4.6 | 4.6 | 0.0 | 1.4 | 1.4 | 0.0 | 3.5 | 3.5 | 0.4 | 1.7 | 2.1 |
| TOTAL PER CENT OF ALL AGES | 49.5 | 50.5 | 100.0 | 66.7 | 33.3 | 100.0 | 51.2 | 48.8 | 100.0 | 49.5 | 50.5 | 100.0 | 68.9 | 31.1 | 100.0 |
| TOTAL PER CENT OF LEGITIMATES | 37.3 | 22.5 | 59.8 | 43.7 | 10.6 | 54.3 | 35.4 | 07.8 | 43.2 | 23.8 | 17.0 | 45.8 | 32.3 | 05.3 | 37.6 |
| TOTAL NUMBER OF ALL AGES | 352 | 359 | 711 | 220 | 110 | 330 | 113 | 108 | 221 | 349 | 359 | 708 | 1,853 | 838 | 2,691 |
| TOTAL NUMBER OF LEGITIMATES | 265 | 160 | 425 | 144 | 35 | 179 | 78 | 17 | 95 | 198 | 121 | 319 | 863 | 147 | 1,010 |
| Total dependents under 24 | 331 | 291 | 622 | 207 | 93 | 300 | 103 | 88 | 191 | 332 | 298 | 630 | 1,720 | 713 | 2,433 |
| Percentage of dependents | 46.8 | 40.9 | 87.7 | 62.6 | 28.4 | 91.0 | 45.4 | 39.8 | 85.2 | 46.9 | 42.1 | 89.0 | 63.9 | 27.1 | 91.0 |
| Percentage of legitimates | 35.4 | 16.4 | 51.8 | 41.5 | 07.5 | 49.0 | 33.2 | 04.5 | 37.7 | 27.4 | 14.1 | 41.5 | 30.6 | 04.3 | 34.9 |

*HH = Household head.

## TABLE 18

PERCENTAGE DISTRIBUTION OF DEPENDENTS UNDER 24 YEARS OF AGE WHO LIVE IN THE SAMPLE HOUSEHOLDS WITH ONE OF THEIR PARENTS, BY BIRTH STATUS AND PARENT WITH WHOM THEY LIVE

| | Carriacou | | | Latante | | | Grenville | | | Kingston | | | Rural Jamaica | | |
|---|---|---|---|---|---|---|---|---|---|---|---|---|---|---|---|
| | Total | L* | U* | Total | L | U | Total | L | U | Total | L | U | Total | L | U |
| With father only | 1.6 | 1.1 | 0.5 | 19.9 | 6.6 | 13.3 | 5.2 | 1.3 | 3.9 | 6.2 | 2.3 | 3.9 | 16.3 | 4.6 | 11.7 |
| With father and his kin | 5.4 | 1.6 | 3.8 | 1.1 | 0.0 | 1.1 | 2.6 | 0.0 | 2.6 | 1.6 | 0.0 | 1.6 | 4.4 | 0.0 | 4.4 |
| Total with father | 7.0 | 2.7 | 4.3 | 21.0 | 6.6 | 14.4 | 7.8 | 1.3 | 6.5 | 7.8 | 2.3 | 5.5 | 20.7 | 4.6 | 16.1 |
| With mother only | 42.7 | 26.2 | 16.5 | 50.4 | 18.6 | 31.8 | 71.4 | 7.8 | 63.6 | 72.0 | 29.3 | 42.7 | 47.0 | 11.1 | 35.9 |
| With mother and her kin | 50.3 | 7.1 | 43.2 | 28.6 | 1.1 | 27.5 | 20.8 | 5.2 | 15.6 | 20.2 | 4.6 | 15.6 | 32.3 | 0.7 | 31.6 |
| Total with mother | 93.0 | 33.3 | 59.7 | 79.0 | 19.7 | 59.3 | 92.2 | 13.0 | 79.2 | 92.2 | 33.9 | 58.3 | 79.3 | 11.8 | 67.5 |
| TOTAL PER CENT | 100.0 | 36.0 | 64.0 | 100.0 | 26.3 | 73.7 | 100.0 | 14.3 | 85.7 | 100.0 | 36.2 | 63.8 | 100.0 | 16.4 | 83.6 |
| TOTAL PERSONS | 183 | 66 | 117 | 91 | 24 | 67 | 77 | 11 | 66 | 257 | 88 | 169 | 759† | 125 | 633 |

*L = Lawful, i.e., legitimate; U = Unlawful, i.e., illegitimate.
†Persons of undetermined birth status are excluded from the classification as "legitimate" or "illegitimate", but are included in the total.

## TABLE 19

PERCENTAGE DISTRIBUTION OF DEPENDENTS UNDER 24 YEARS OF AGE WHO LIVE IN THE SAMPLE HOUSEHOLDS APART FROM BOTH THEIR PARENTS, BY CATEGORY OF KIN WITH WHOM THEY LIVE AND THEIR OWN BIRTH STATUS

| | Carriacou | | | Latante | | | Grenville | | | Kingston | | | Rural Jamaica | | |
|---|---|---|---|---|---|---|---|---|---|---|---|---|---|---|---|
| | Total | L* | U* | Total | L | U | Total | L | U | Total | L | U | Total | L | U |
| With matrikin | 63.0 | 22.7 | 40.3 | 67.0 | 16.2 | 50.8 | 54.5 | 9.2 | 45.3 | 56.8 | 16.3 | 40.5 | 51.3 | 0.2 | 37.8 |
| With patrikin | 30.6 | 11.1 | 19.5 | 26.9 | 0.0 | 26.9 | 16.0 | 0.0 | 16.0 | 21.6 | 11.9 | 9.7 | 26.8 | 0.6 | 23.4 |
| With unrelated persons | 6.4 | 1.1 | 5.3 | 6.1 | 3.1 | 3.0 | 29.5 | 0.0 | 6.6 | 21.6 | 0.0 | 2.6 | 21.9 | 0.0 | 1.2 |
| TOTAL PER CENT | 100.0 | 34.9 | 65.1 | 100.0 | 19.3 | 80.7 | 100.0 | 9.2 | 67.9 | 100.0 | 28.2 | 52.8 | 100.0 | 0.8 | 62.4 |
| TOTAL PERSONS | 187 | 65 | 122 | 67 | 13 | 54 | 44† | 3 | 30 | 153† | 41 | 81 | 499† | 4 | 312 |

*L = Lawful, i.e., legitimate; U = Unlawful, i.e., illegitimate.
†Persons of undetermined birth status are excluded from the classification as "legitimate" or "illegitimate", but are included in the total.

TABLE 20

PERCENTAGE DISTRIBUTION OF HOUSEHOLDS CLASSIFIED BY SEX OF HEAD AND MORPHOLOGICAL TYPE

| Morphological Type | Carriacou | | | Latante | | | Grenville | | | Kingston | | | Rural Jamaica | | |
|---|---|---|---|---|---|---|---|---|---|---|---|---|---|---|---|
| | Male HH* | Female HH | Total | Male HH | Female HH | Total | Male HH | Female HH | Total | Male HH | Female HH | Total | Male HH | Female HH | Total |
| 1. Single persons | 3.1 | 16.6 | 19.7 | 3.8 | 9.9 | 13.7 | 4.3 | 13.4 | 17.7 | 9.1 | 16.0 | 25.1 | 14.8 | 6.6 | 21.4 |
| 2. Siblings | 0.0 | 1.8 | 1.8 | 0.0 | 1.9 | 1.9 | 3.6 | 3.6 | 7.2 | 1.2 | 3.7 | 4.9 | 0.7 | 1.5 | 2.2 |
| 3. HH and children | 0.4 | 11.6 | 12.0 | 2.9 | 10.8 | 13.7 | 2.6 | 16.9 | 19.5 | 1.0 | 15.4 | 16.4 | 2.6 | 8.0 | 10.6 |
| 4. Childless couples | 6.3 | 0.4 | 6.7 | 15.6 | 1.0 | 16.6 | 18.5 | 3.6 | 22.1 | 16.8 | 3.7 | 20.5 | 16.8 | 1.7 | 18.5 |
| 5. Couples and children | 24.2 | 0.4 | 24.6 | 27.5 | 1.0 | 28.5 | 16.8 | 0.9 | 17.7 | 20.2 | 1.2 | 21.4 | 27.4 | 0.6 | 28.0 |
| 6. HH and grandchildren only | 0.0 | 6.2 | 6.2 | 0.0 | 5.9 | 5.9 | 0.9 | 2.6 | 3.5 | 0.3 | 1.8 | 2.1 | 0.7 | 3.4 | 4.1 |
| 7. Couples and grand-children | 3.1 | 0.0 | 3.1 | 0.0 | 0.0 | 0.0 | 0.0 | 0.0 | 0.0 | 0.8 | 0.0 | 0.8 | 0.8 | 0.0 | 0.8 |
| 8. HH, children, and grandchildren | 0.7 | 19.0 | 19.7 | 1.9 | 9.0 | 10.9 | 0.9 | 8.8 | 9.7 | 0.7 | 6.6 | 7.3 | 1.0 | 7.1 | 8.1 |
| 9. Couples, children, and grandchildren | 3.2 | 0.4 | 3.6 | 5.9 | 0.0 | 5.9 | 0.0 | 0.0 | 0.0 | 0.7 | 0.3 | 1.0 | 4.7 | 0.2 | 4.9 |
| 10. HH and issue to 4th generation | 0.0 | 2.2 | 2.2 | 0.0 | 1.9 | 1.9 | 0.0 | 2.6 | 2.6 | 0.0 | 0.5 | 0.5 | 0.0 | 1.0 | 1.0 |
| 11. Couples and issue to 4th generation | 0.4 | 0.0 | 0.4 | 1.0 | 0.0 | 1.0 | 0.0 | 0.0 | 0.0 | 0.0 | 0.0 | 0.0 | 0.4 | 0.0 | 0.4 |
| TOTAL PER CENT | 41.4 | 58.6 | 100.0 | 58.6 | 41.4 | 100.0 | 47.6 | 52.4 | 100.0 | 50.8 | 49.2 | 100.0 | 69.9 | 30.1 | 100.0 |
| TOTAL NUMBER | 93 | 131 | 224 | 60 | 42 | 102 | 54 | 59 | 113 | 216 | 209 | 425 | 702 | 305 | 1,007 |

*HH = Household head.

TABLE 21

PERCENTAGE INCIDENCE OF MORPHOLOGICAL TYPES WITH AND WITHOUT ACCRETIONS AMONG HOUSEHOLDS CLASSIFIED BY SEX OF HEAD

| | Carriacou | | | Latante | | | Grenville | | | Kingston | | | Rural Jamaica | | |
| | Male HH* | Female HH | Both | Male HH | Female HH | Both | Male HH | Female HH | Both | Male HH | Female HH | Both | Male HH | Female HH | Both |
|---|---|---|---|---|---|---|---|---|---|---|---|---|---|---|---|
| Pure forms | 65.7 | 68.0 | 66.9 | 68.5 | 74.0 | 70.7 | 66.7 | 79.5 | 73.5 | 66.5 | 72.5 | 69.5 | 62.0 | 74.0 | 65.5 |
| Pure forms and accretions | 34.3 | 32.0 | 33.1 | 31.5 | 26.0 | 29.3 | 33.4 | 20.5 | 26.5 | 33.5 | 27.5 | 30.5 | 38.0 | 26.0 | 34.5 |
| TOTAL | 100.0 | 100.0 | 100.0 | 100.0 | 100.0 | 100.0 | 100.0 | 100.0 | 100.0 | 100.0 | 100.0 | 100.0 | 100.0 | 100.0 | 100.0 |

*HH = Household head.

TABLE 22

PERCENTAGE DISTRIBUTION OF COHABITING HOUSEHOLD PRINCIPALS BY MARITAL BASIS OF THE CONJUGAL UNION AND CONSTITUTION OF THE DOMESTIC FAMILY

| | Carriacou | | | Latante | | | Grenville | | | Kingston | | | Rural Jamaica | | |
| | Wed | Unwed | Total | Wed | Unwed | Total | Wed | Unwed | Total | Wed | Unwed | Total | Wed | Unwed | Total |
|---|---|---|---|---|---|---|---|---|---|---|---|---|---|---|---|
| Childless couples only | 2.3 | 1.2 | 3.5 | 1.9 | 11.4 | 13.3 | 11.1 | 20.0 | 31.1 | 8.8 | 20.8 | 29.6 | 5.3 | 8.4 | 13.7 |
| Childless couples and others | 10.5 | 3.5 | 14.0 | 13.3 | 5.6 | 18.9 | 11.1 | 13.3 | 24.4 | 5.5 | 12.6 | 18.1 | 10.8 | 10.8 | 21.6 |
| Total childless couples | 12.8 | 4.7 | 17.5 | 15.2 | 17.0 | 32.2 | 22.2 | 33.3 | 55.5 | 14.3 | 33.4 | 47.7 | 16.1 | 19.2 | 35.3 |
| Couples and children only | 43.0 | 1.2 | 44.2 | 31.8 | 5.6 | 37.4 | 24.7 | 8.7 | 33.4 | 21.1 | 9.2 | 30.3 | 21.1 | 10.5 | 31.6 |
| Couples, children, and others | 17.4 | 2.3 | 19.7 | 13.3 | 3.8 | 17.1 | 11.1 | 0.0 | 11.1 | 11.0 | 8.8 | 19.8 | 11.1 | 10.3 | 21.4 |
| Total couples and children | 60.4 | 3.5 | 63.9 | 45.1 | 9.4 | 54.5 | 35.8 | 8.7 | 44.5 | 32.1 | 18.0 | 50.1 | 32.2 | 20.8 | 53.0 |
| Couples and grandchildren | 8.1 | 0.0 | 8.1 | 0.0 | 0.0 | 0.0 | 0.0 | 0.0 | 0.0 | 0.0 | 0.0 | 0.0 | 1.4 | 0.2 | 1.6 |
| Couples, children, and grandchildren | 9.3 | 0.0 | 9.3 | 11.4 | 0.0 | 11.4 | 0.0 | 0.0 | 0.0 | 1.1 | 0.0 | 1.1 | 8.3 | 1.0 | 9.3 |
| Couples and issue to 4th generation | 1.2 | 0.0 | 1.2 | 1.9 | 0.0 | 1.9 | 0.0 | 0.0 | 0.0 | 0.0 | 1.1 | 1.1 | 0.8 | 0.0 | 0.8 |
| Total couples and issue of 3rd or 4th generation | 18.6 | 0.0 | 18.6 | 13.3 | 0.0 | 13.3 | 0.0 | 0.0 | 0.0 | 1.1 | 1.1 | 2.2 | 10.5 | 1.2 | 11.7 |
| TOTAL PER CENT | 91.8 | 8.2 | 100.0 | 73.6 | 26.4 | 100.0 | 58.0 | 42.0 | 100.0 | 47.5 | 52.5 | 100.0 | 58.8 | 41.2 | 100.0 |
| TOTAL PERSONS | 79 | 7 | 86 | 39 | 14 | 53 | 26 | 19 | 45 | 87 | 95 | 182 | 313 | 217 | 530 |

# 8. Conclusion

In the preceding chapter we compared the five household samples, and we examined the applicability of various hypotheses to them. We found that explanations of similarities or difference in terms of demographic or ecological factors were inadequate. We also found that the frequency and structural significance of the elementary family and the "grandmother family" in these societies have been grossly overrated while the significance of collateral kinship has been missed. Neither the elementary nor the "grandmother" family is modal in our samples; and there are several types of domestic unit which cannot be derived developmentally from either of these. In short, domestic groupings cannot be explained in terms of themselves; nor are their varieties and frequencies reducible to such factors as demography, rural-urban differences, or the like.

In comparing these samples, we found that the family organizations of Latante and rural Jamaica were strikingly similar, that Kingston and Grenville were also alike, and that Carriacou was unique in the series. In some respects Latante and rural Jamaica had more in common with Carriacou than with either Grenville or Kingston. In other respects, Carriacou had more in common with Kingston and Grenville than these latter had with the Grenadian and Jamaican peasant samples. In addition we were able to discover regularities within each of these three types of family organization. We also found some regularities common to them all. Our first task, therefore, is to determine whether and in what ways these three differing types of family organization represent varieties of a common system or distinct varieties of system. We have also to determine the principles which regulate the operation and form of each system, to discover their interrelation and bases, and to define their significance for the general sociology of family and kinship systems. We may then try to indicate the courses by which these three varieties of family organization may have developed.

In this discussion, we shall have to step outside the narrow frame of Caribbean society for occasional comparison. Kinship systems being world-wide phenomena, subject, like others, to the rule of internal consistency, even a brief comparison of Caribbean family systems with certain others should illuminate both.

## Unity and Variety

Even at the most superficial level, the five populations we have been studying exhibit several common features in their family organization. Their household heads are of either sex; their members are differentiated by birth status; they practice alternative forms of mating; they differentiate parental roles in correspondence with these alternative mating forms. Their domestic units vary widely in size and constitution. Many adults live entirely by themselves; many women live with their children only, or with their children and grandchildren; materterine kinship provides an important basis for the domestic placement of the illegitimate offspring of kinswomen. Males generally head units based on their cohabitation, and many of these units include the kin as well as the children of their mates by former unions. Cohabitation is governed by neolocal rules of residence. Few households include the head's children and the latter's mates. In very few households do we find parents living as their children's dependents. In no home do we find an individual living with two mates or spouses. These societies all share a formal commitment to monogamy; and although they have all modified monogamy profoundly, polygyny is excluded from them. Marriage generally occurs in or near middle age, and female widowhood is quite common. In all our samples there are substantial numbers of single women of mature age, most of whom are mothers and household heads also. In all our samples legitimate offspring tend to live with both parents in homes of which their fathers are head, and the majority of the children living apart from their fathers or apart from both parents are illegitimate. Children who do not live with either of their parents are generally found living with their mother's kin, especially their mother's mother or collateral kinswomen. Domestic groups consisting of a woman, her daughter and daughter's children are twice as frequent as those of similar structure which do not contain the daughter. We find very few groups which consist of a woman, her son or sons, and their children; hardly any of this structure in which the senior parent is a man. Groups consisting of two or more siblings, their

resident mates and issue are almost entirely absent from these
samples.

The five samples show differences at two levels, in their structure and in the frequencies of particular elements. Structural differences express themselves in differing frequencies also; but
frequency differences do not always represent or entail differences
of structure. We have already shown that demographic differences
are not structural determinants. Differing frequencies in the residential distribution of children of differing birth status express the
operation of structural principles, but do not determine them. We
have seen that the proportions of illegitimate issue who live with
both parents in their fathers' homes vary with the frequency and
stability of consensual cohabitation in the populations studied. In
short, the comparison of sample frequencies can rule out inadequate hypotheses; but in constructing new ones, those data which
describe the distribution of dynamic elements have priority over
others which merely express the effects of these factors. Needless
to say, hypotheses differ in value according to the economy and necessity by which they relate all the formative factors to all the
observed effects within a single system. Bearing these points in
mind, I shall only mention the structurally decisive differences
between these samples now, and leave their differing effects for
analysis later.

The basic differences between the family systems of Carriacou,
of rural Jamaica and Latante, and of Grenville and Kingston, are
to be found in their organization of mating and parenthood. There
is an obvious interdependence of mating and parenthood. Parental
roles are defined differently in differing modes of mating relation.
These differences in mating relations distinguish differing types of
union; hence, different types of union are structural determinants of
family organization, since they involve differing forms of parenthood.

All three familial systems under discussion include marriage and
extraresidential mating forms. In the Latante-rural Jamaica system, and in the Grenville-Kingston system consensual cohabitation
is also important; but this is disapproved in Carriacou. In consequence, Carriacou family structure is based on a dual mating system with four varieties of parenthood. The other mating systems
contain three alternative forms and six varieties of parenthood.
The parental varieties found in Carriacou distinguish the roles
of married and extraresidential fathers and married and single
mothers. These varieties are present in the other systems also;

but in addition those systems contain role definitions for couples cohabiting consensually. I shall examine the position of these consensual couples later.

The Carriacou mating system defines the extraresidential union and marriage as alternatives for females only. Marriage is obligatory for men, and the extraresidential relation is normally complementary for married men. Thus, married men simultaneously discharge differing parental roles for their married and extraresidential families. Single women can only play the mother's role as this is defined within the extraresidential union. Married women can only play the mother's role as this is defined within the identical forms of cohabitation and marriage. Children born before a woman's marriage are therefore socially equivalent to those born afterwards, and her husband is obliged to accommodate them in his home. Alternatively, the bride may leave such children with her kin.

Monogamy is a basic commitment of Carriacou society; but the Carriacou folk have modified monogamy in such a way that men have plural mates, who are separated domestically. Women may only have one mate at a time. They will either live with him in marriage or mate extraresidentially. The system of mating relations in Carriacou is thus quite simple; but it comes as close to polygyny as is possible without a formal commitment to such a system. Carriacou monogamy is defined by the following elements: (1) All men must marry. (2) Marriage is indissoluble. (3) It is the only permitted form of cohabitation. (4) Women may not mate with two men simultaneously. (5) A man may not live with two mates under a single roof. This highly ingenious redefinition of monogamy is distinctive of Carriacou.

The basic difference between the parental roles of Carriacou fathers and mothers in differing forms of union consists in the allocation of primary responsibilities for the issue of wives to their husbands, while single mothers are primarily responsible for the offspring of extraresidential unions. With responsibility goes authority over and custody of the child. Legitimate issue remain under the father's control, while illegitimates remain under the mother's.

This family system depends for its integration on the fact that most men will play both sets of paternal roles simultaneously. It is therefore patrifocal. The patrifocality or matrifocality of a family structure cannot be defined by reference to the domestic organization only, since, as we have already seen, the family structure includes relations between households as well as within them and is not limited to the level of domestic family relations alone. The marginality of the male extraresidential mate in Carriacou at the domestic level is a structural axiom of this patrifocal mating system. Carriacou folk are well aware of this. They symbolize and express these structural necessities in terms of patrilineal descent. Carriacou patriliny entails exogamy within a span of four agnatic generations, and is ritualized by an elaborate ancestor cult. Lineages are known as "bloods." Since a child takes its "blood" from the father, "the woman cannot transmit the blood." I have discussed these facets of Carriacou kinship more fully elsewhere. [1] I mention them here to show how Carriacou folk have systematized and elaborated their social organization in ways which serve to sanction their mating system; Carriacou patrilineages are also comparatively relevant, since they differ sharply from the bilateral kinship organization of our other samples.

In Latante and rural Jamaica on the one hand, and in Grenville and Kingston on the other, the systems of mating relations include three alternative forms, namely, marriage, extraresidential mating, and consensual cohabitation. Two of these forms are also found in Carriacou. The presence of a third alternative, however, serves to distinguish these systems from Carriacou. Moreover, the relation of this third alternative to the other two distinguishes these systems from one another and produces other differences in their family structure. We shall consider this point later. For the moment it is sufficient to distinguish between the Carriacou system and others which have three mating forms.

The coexistence of three mating alternatives entails six coexistent varieties of parenthood. The four which characterize marriage and extraresidential mating are in theory similar to those already described for Carriacou. The other two varieties are associated with consensual cohabitation. In this form of union, a man has primary responsibility for the elementary family and often for his mate's kin and her issue by former unions. However, the indeterminate status of these domestic unions is expressed by lack of legal or religious sanction and by the structural alternative of marriage. It is true that the populations under study do not formally dissolve their marriages by divorce; they merely separate with an informality similar to that of consensually cohabiting mates. However, bigamy, or the remarriage of an undivorced person, is a rare crime in these societies, whereas consensual partners often marry one another or someone else. In short, given the lack of divorce, marriage may not be indissoluble although it is unrepeatable for unwidowed persons. Consensual cohabitation may develop into marriage; it may also break down; its principals may either be separated from their spouses and unable to marry, or they may be single persons who later marry someone else.

The structural indeterminacy of consensual cohabitation is expressed in various ways. In popular speech and in the literature it is referred to as "keeping," without further qualification; as "common-law marriage," when it is neither common law nor marriage; and as "concubinage," without specifying whether either or both concubines are slaves. At law, consensually cohabiting couples are described as "paramours"; statisticians describe them as "consorts." Various analysts have distinguished between the casual and faithful varieties of concubinage, and some between purposive and other forms. [2] Dom Basil Matthews describes it as "the nonlegal union" in contraposition to marriage, when it is of course by no means the only form of nonlegal union. [3] This variety of terms merely illustrates the ambiguous position of consensual cohabitation in these mating and family systems. This ambiguity is perhaps the most important feature of consensual cohabitation and the basis of its pivotal position in those systems which include it.

Consensual cohabitations may dissolve or develop into marriage. Until a couple marries, the future of their union remains uncertain. So does its status; and so does the definition and future performance of mating and parental roles. Consensual couples are well aware of this ambiguity and uncertainty in their relation. The irregular distribution of headship within these unions expresses this neatly; so does the high incidence of childlessness among these couples. So long as the union endures, the mates may share responsibilities for their offspring equally. If the male is household head, he is primarily responsible for the units' economy. Often this is not the case. Always there is the possibility that the union may break down, in which case custom and law leave the children in the woman's care and redefine the couple's parental roles exactly like those of separated extraresidential mates.

While an extraresidential union persists, the male has to fulfill his parental roles in order to maintain his relation with his mate. When this relation breaks down, the male's principal motive for fulfilling these obligations is removed, unless, as happens in Carriacou, the ideology and ritual of lineage compel his observance. In the consensual domestic union, male responsibilities and control remain uncertain until marriage or dissolution occurs. To retain their children and their mate, men in these unions may therefore have to marry. To ensure continued support of their children beyond the legal limit of thirteen years common to Grenadian and Jamaican bastardy laws alike, the woman is strongly motivated to transform her union into marriage; and she will be in her thirties when this need develops. Perhaps the only point on which all consensual couples may agree is that their union cannot continue indefinitely in its current form. This instability and ambiguity give consensual cohabitation its peculiarly dynamic character. Within this union parenthood is also unstable. The parental roles of consensual cohabitation must either develop into those of marriage or into the variety characteristic of broken extraresidential mating. Indefinite persistence of a consensual union in its current form is only possible within certain conditions.

Mating systems which include consensual cohabitation will vary, therefore, according to its structural position within them. If this form of union is to have a constant structural position, it must be set between extraresidential mating and marriage, as a transitional form. Otherwise it becomes an indefinite alternative to either. Yet if its structural position is fixed and constant it can neither follow marriage nor precede extraresidential relations.

We have seen that, in rural Jamaica and Latante, consensual cohabitation has this intermediate place in a regulated succession of mating forms; and that its place within this unfolding series defines its relations with the two other forms of union in constant terms. Grenville and Kingston have no such serial arrangement of mating forms. Consensual cohabitation accordingly lacks any constant structural position in Grenville and Kingston, nor has it any necessary or normal course of development. In consequence, its instability is enhanced, and it transmits this enhanced instability to the rest of the system. In societies with these three mating forms, consensual cohabitation depends for its stability on a fixed place in an irreversible series of mating forms. For various reasons such a series can only have one form, with marriage as the final mode of mating and extraresidential unions as the initial form. Accordingly, consensual cohabitation has a natural place as the intermediate and transitional form of such series. Where this order obtains, as in Latante and rural Jamaica, consensual cohabitations are highly stable, and their stability derives from their position within this developing series. Being inherently dynamic, this form of union can only enjoy stability if it forms one stage in a necessary and irreversible course of development. In Kingston and Grenville, which lack this mating organization, there is no fixed course by which consensual domestic unions develop, and in consequence their instability is great. The number of childless couples engaged in this form of cohabitation indicates the instability of the union in these urban contexts, especially in its definition and allocation of parental roles.

I have argued that the similarities and differences of the family structure in Carriacou, Latante-rural Jamaica, and Grenville-Kingston are all due to the similarities and differences of their mating systems. On this basis all five samples are varieties of a common system, which includes marriage and extraresidential mating. The two rural and two urban family structures are sub-varieties of this general system, distinguished from Carriacou by the inclusion of consensual cohabitation as a third alternative mating form. These rural and urban systems are distinguished from one another by the position which consensual cohabitation occupies in each. We must now test this hypothesis.

Concurrence of marriage and extraresidential mating distinguishes children by birth status, and parents by responsibilities for the domestic care of children born in different sorts of union. Men house their own legitimate offspring, and also some illegitimate offspring of their resident mates by former unions, as well as some of their mates' kin. The offspring of extraresidential matings remain in their mothers' care. In consequence, we shall expect to find that domestic groups have heads of either sex, that most male heads are cohabiting, and that most female heads are not, although the majority of the latter will be single mothers. We shall also expect to find a number of households containing single women and their children, or consisting of women, their daughters or junior kinswomen, and the children of these. In societies which practice marriage and extraresidential mating only, we will expect to find that the two modal forms of domestic unit are those containing elementary families under male heads, and others which contain women and their children, or women, their children, and their grandchildren. This is exactly what we find in Carriacou, where 36.2 per cent of our households have a depth of three or more generations, and of these 28.8 per cent have female heads. Another 12 per cent of this sample contain single parents and their children, those with female heads being 11.6 per cent. One quarter of these homes contain elementary families under male heads (see Table 20). Since the mating organization of Carriacou is simpler than in the four other samples, its domestic organization is simpler also, and the proportion of units having a depth of three lineal generations under female heads will be higher there than elsewhere.

One of the puzzling features already mentioned may now be dealt with. In all our samples, the incidence of domestic groups con-

taining members of three lineally successive generations is always
at least twice as great as that of units having a similar depth without the intermediate generation. If our hypothesis is valid, it should
resolve this puzzle. In fact the explanation of this distribution is
to be found in the conditions of extraresidential mating. Under this
form of union, children remain with their mothers and are often
placed in the homes of their mothers' parents, especially their
mothers' mothers. It is therefore easy to understand how extraresidential mating produces this type of domestic group; it does
so by its definition of parenthood. Similarly, it maximizes the
incidence of these three-generation units inclusive of daughters,
and minimizes the incidence of those which lack daughters, by the
nature of its prerequisites.

An extraresidential union is a publicly recognized relation between a man and a woman, under which the man has exclusive
rights of sexual access to the woman. This male exclusiveness is
the *sine qua non* of determinate paternity. The man may have two or
more extraresidential mates; he may also be married, as is usually
the case in Carriacou. The woman who mates extraresidentially
must remain faithful to her partner so long as the relation endures.
The only way in which single women can guarantee their own faith-
fulness to their absent mates is to live in the homes of their senior
kin, whether their mothers or senior collaterals.

These senior kin certify the relation in various ways; they give
it formal recognition on behalf of the woman's kin. Their presence
enhances its stability by supervision of the woman. They themselves
are essential witnesses in the event of paternity disputes. In consequence, young women who mate extraresidentially prefer to remain
with their senior kin, especially with their mothers or kinswomen.
But if and when the young woman decides to leave the home of her
kin, she is expected to take the children with her. This expectation
is governed by the assumption that young women will continue to
live in their guardians' homes until they enter cohabitation, and that
the cohabiting male is responsible for accommodating the woman's
children by her former mates, as well as those which she bears for
him. In such a system, therefore, the young woman may not need
to keep children of her early unions in the home of her guardian
once she enters cohabitation. The guardian may naturally object
to her cohabitation with men who reject these responsibilities.

In Carriacou we have seen that cohabitation normally involves
marriage, and women far outnumber men. For this reason, single
mothers are less easily able to enter domestic unions in Carriacou
than, for instance, in rural Jamaica and Latante. In consequence,

the relative incidence of domestic units—under single heads—which contain three lineally successive generations in Carriacou is more than three times as great as that of units which lack the intermediate generation. In rural Jamaica and Latante it is only twice as great. In Grenville and Kingston the relative incidence of these alternative forms is very similar to that in Carriacou; but the reason for this is not that Grenville and Kingston lack consensual cohabitation; it is rather due to the instability of these unions themselves. We have already seen that consensual domestic unions are unstable in Grenville and Kingston because they are not firmly tied to alternative mating modes in a single developmental series.

The dual mating organization of Carriacou involves a simpler complex of parental and domestic alternatives than do the three-form systems of the other samples. Most Carriacou children are legitimates who live with both their parents. The illegitimate offspring of extraresidential mating are housed in the homes of their mothers, maternal grandparents and especially grandmothers, mothers' mates, or materterine kin. Thus the four parental varieties of Carriacou are found together with four substitute forms of parenthood.

Table 18 shows that, of the Carriacou children who live with one parent apart from the other, only 7 per cent live with their fathers or fathers' kin. Table 12 shows that the collateral kin of male household heads are excluded from their homes. Such collateral kin are more frequent in all four populations which practice consensual cohabitation. In Latante and rural Jamaica, 21 per cent and 20. 7 per cent of those children who live with one parent apart from the other are to be found with their fathers and fathers' kin; in Grenville and Kingston, which have unstable mating systems, the proportion is 7. 8 per cent in both cases. Although these Grenville and Kingston ratios are close to that of Carriacou, their bases are quite different.

In Carriacou only 42. 7 per cent of the children who live with one parent apart from the other live with their mothers only, apart from the mothers' mates or kin. In rural Jamaica and Latante, 47 per cent and 50. 4 per cent of these children live with their mothers only. In Kingston and Grenville, the ratios are 72 per cent and 71. 4 per cent. In Carriacou as many descendents of the head live in homes with female heads as live in homes with male heads and their mates; in Grenville and Kingston, this is also the position; in Latante and rural Jamaica, resident issue of male heads and their mates outnumber those of female heads by two to one. Moreover, in Carriacou, one half the resident issue of female household heads are grandchildren or great-grandchildren. In Latante and rural Jamaica these remoter issue are 36. 4 per cent and 40 per cent of the resident descendents of female heads. In Grenville and Kingston they are, respectively, 29 per cent and 24. 5 per cent. Clearly the differing distributions of children in these samples illustrate their differences in mating organization and reflect differing systems of parenthood.

In Carriacou, only 11. 6 per cent of the sample households contain single women and their children. In Latante and rural Jamaica such units had an incidence of 10. 8 per cent and 8 per cent, respectively, and there were also several households based on single fathers and their children—units without parallel in Carriacou. In Grenville and Kingston we find some households consisting of single fathers and children, and those based on single women and children have an incidence of 16. 9 per cent and 15. 4 per cent, respectively. It is clear that these parallels and differences in the incidence of domestic forms are linked with differences and parallels in the mating organizations of these samples.

The reason for such linkage is clear. Only in stable domestic unions, legal or other, are mating and parental relations contained within a single domestic unit. Unstable domestic unions scatter the components of elementary families when their mating relations are dissolved. Extraresidential unions involve a scattering of family components as part of the mating relation itself. Consequently the dual mating system of Carriacou and the unstable three-form systems of Grenville and Kingston have similar proportions of scattered elementary families within them. Stable three-form mating systems have a larger proportion of domestic elementary families.

Nonetheless, there are important differences in the constitutions of the dual and unstable three-form systems of mating and in the domestic organizations associated with them. These differences center on the presence or absence of consensual cohabitation and reflect its place in the more complex system. Where this mating form is absent, single mothers generally live with their senior kinswomen in units three generations deep. They do so since the only alternative accommodation open to them is to live alone. In such a system their fathers and paternal kin cannot easily accommodate them in their homes. Neither can they cohabit consensually. In the unstable three-form system, such cohabitation is easily contracted and dissolved, and the domestic association of young mothers and their senior kin is only one of an increased number of alternatives. In consequence, in these conditions we find a reduced incidence of "grandmother families," a relative in-

crease in the significance of collateral kinship for domestic placement, more emphasis on paternal ties at the domestic level, and
larger numbers of women living alone, or with their children, or
with consensual mates.

An adult who lives alone may remain celibate or may mate extraresidentially. He or she may even have more than one partner. In
these societies, men are permitted to have two or more extraresidential mates; women are not. However, single women who
live alone or with young dependents may try to maintain mating
relations with two or more men simultaneously. Such behavior
is possible in dense urban areas or in plantation populations; it
is very difficult to maintain in the static peasant areas. Consequently we find few single women living alone in these rural districts.

Of course, the proportions of women who live alone or with their
senior kin or with their mates are interdependent; consequently, the
number of women living alone will vary inversely with the numbers
who live with their mates or kin. In Carriacou, Grenville, and
Kingston, 28. 2 per cent, 30. 3 per cent, and 31. 4 per cent of our
sample households contain single women, with or without their
children. In Latante and rural Jamaica such units represent 20. 7
per cent and 14. 6 per cent of all households, respectively. In Carriacou 31. 3 per cent of the households sampled are units based on
couples with or without their children; in Grenville and Kingston
such units have an incidence of 39. 8 per cent and 41. 9 per cent,
respectively. In Latante and rural Jamaica, their frequency is
45. 1 per cent and 46. 5 per cent. In Carriacou, households with
a depth of three lineal generations are 36. 2 per cent of the sample;
in Grenville and Kingston their frequency is 15. 8 per cent and 11. 7
per cent, respectively; in Latante and rural Jamaica their ratios
are 24. 6 per cent and 19. 3 per cent. These ratios vary systematically, in accordance with differences or similarities of mating
systems.

The single woman who tries to mate with two or more men simultaneously mates with neither but behaves promiscuously. The
man with plural mates in this system may or may not be equally
promiscuous. Male promiscuity varies with the character of the
mating relations which a man maintains simultaneously; there is
nothing promiscuous about the simultaneous marriage and extraresidential mating of Carriacou men. A man may also have stable
relations with two extraresidential mates; more often, such plural
unions are unstable and may even be casual. Single men are better
able to indulge in such behavior than are those who have resident

mates. Among cohabiting males, moreover, married men are freer to have "affairs" and extraresidential mates than are those who cohabit consensually. The insecurity of consensual domestic unions maximizes the disruptive effect of liaisons by either party. Women seek to assert headship as well as dominance in unions of this sort, since their partner's dependence reduces his opportunities for philandering.

The point to note is that the coexistence of two or more mating forms permits or enjoins a plurality of mates. In Carriacou, this is limited to men and is expected of them. In Latante and rural Jamaica, the single and the married man may have plural mates, but promiscuity is ruled out for both sexes. In Kingston and Grenville the instability and formlessness of mating organization permits and encourages the promiscuity of single adults living in their own homes. This in turn increases the breakdown rates of domestic unions, legal or other. Moreover, the facility with which all forms of union may be broken, and the ease with which extraresidential or consensual domestic unions may be established, militates against finality for any individual relation and either mating form.

I have shown how an analysis of the mating organization explains the family system of each sample, and how their similarities and differences alike are reducible to similarities and differences in mating structure. As illustrations and tests of this hypothesis, I have considered the form and incidence of differing types of domestic groups, the placement of children and grandchildren, and the distribution of parental roles. These three complexes together subsume almost all aspects or features of domestic organization other than the mating relations to which I have related them. I have shown that all are based on these systems of mating and parenthood. This being the case, it is useful to consider briefly the general implications of this analysis.

## Mating and Family Forms

All the societies we have been studying have a formal commitment to monogamy, a ban on polygyny, a plurality of mating forms and of elementary and domestic family organization alike. Of these five populations, only Carriacou has a lineage system. The remainder have bilateral kinship systems with strong emphases on materterine and uterine ties at the domestic level. Carriacou is also unique in the simplicity of its mating and family organization.

Our preceding analysis has shown that the characteristic features of these samples are products of their mating systems. In all cases these mating systems involve severe modifications of monogamy, while formally avoiding polygyny. It is therefore useful to examine the implications of polygyny for a bilateral kinship system and so to define the basic assumptions of monogamy in kinship systems of this type.

As an instance of a polygynous society based on bilateral kinship, we may take the Hausa of Northern Nigeria, with whom I am familiar. [4] The Hausa are Mohammedan grain farmers, living in a series of large states. They have a well-developed economy and a pattern of compact settlement. Each state has a large town as its capital, but most of the people live in villages of one to five thousand persons. In 1804 the Hausa were conquered by the Fulani, who linked these various states into an Empire, of which they are the ruling class. Stratification extends throughout the entire range of male Hausa society; it does not regulate relations between women. The great majority of the Hausa are commoners *(talakawa)* of low status, and many of these people are the descendants of slaves. Slavery was prohibited by the British when they occupied Nigeria in 1900.

Hausa practice polygyny and define all unmarried adults as prostitutes *(karuwai)*. Girls marry at thirteen or fourteen shortly after the menarche. Old women must also be married to fit them for Paradise *(Lahira)*. Illegitimacy is virtually unknown under these conditions. Marriage is virilocal and often patrilocal. There are no households with female heads. There is no mating relation which extends across the boundaries of a domestic unit, with one exception. This exception is the extraresidential form of marriage known as *auren daukisandanka*. In this form, the spouses live apart, and the woman is either an old person who has married for conventional reasons or a widow with several children and charge of her late husband's home and property. Such marriages have an incidence of less than 5 per cent.

Hausa domestic organization is based on the polygynous family. Between one fifth and one quarter of Hausa households are extended families which consist of a man, his sons and their wives, or of brothers, their wives and families. Agnatic kinship provides the basis for this domestic organization, and daughters leave their parents' homes for their husbands', on marriage. In a sample containing 87 compounds and 783 individuals, 373 of whom were males, there were 148 sons and sons' sons, and 107 collateral agnatic kinsmen of the male household heads. Of the 410 females, 276 were wives, 15 were female kin of the wives, and only one was a materterine kinswoman of the household head. [5] In Hausa household organization, maternal kinship has no place. There are no "grandmother families," no resident illegitimate offspring of daughters, almost no single-person units, and a limited range of domestic forms. Hausa practice adoption, primarily of agnatic kin. Hausa marriage is simple in its essentials. The two major differences are those between the marriages of kin and nonkin on the one hand, and the degree of wife seclusion or purdah which obtains, on the other. Marriage is extremely brittle, and on average a woman marries three or four times between the menarche and the menopause. Between marriages a period of enforced celibacy known as *iddah* serves to prevent paternity disputes. Despite the emphasis on agnatic ties at the level of domestic organization, the Hausa kinship system is fully bilateral. The primacy of patrilineal kinship in domestic organization is a simple consequence of the system of domestic polygyny, with its virilocal basis.

Until recently, Hausa mating included the practice of concubinage and of exchange marriage *(auren mutsaya)*. Both these forms are now extremely rare. The concubine was always a female slave of her master. She remained in his compound under the jurisdiction of his senior wife, and her offspring were legitimate and inherited equally with their father's other issue. One king of Zaria, Mamman Sani, was the son of a concubine. On her master's death, the concubine was free, and could remarry. *Auren mutsaya*, or exchange marriage, was limited to slaves, of whom there were very many in Hausaland until 1920.[6] Hausa enforced the marriage of their converted slaves. All slave offspring were reared as Mohammedans, and these *dimajai* (children of slaves) could not be alienated. To establish slave marriages, the owners arranged exchanges between the members of slave families, or between slaves of different owners. In the latter case, a slave couple may have lacked a common *domus*, unless their owners agreed to permit this or arranged the exchange of equivalent slaves. A slave marriage could be annulled or dissolved by the owner but not by the slave. The children of a female slave were the property of her owner; however, the Mohammedan horror of illegitimacy made slave marriages obligatory. Under these circumstances, slave offspring had two sets of kin; their biological parents and parents' families, and the family of their mother's owner. They addressed these two unrelated family lines, the one slave, the other free, by identical kinship terms, and modeled their behavior accordingly. These dual parental roles exactly expressed the position and character of slave marriages.

Despite very wide variations in status, the Hausa commoners and ruling class have an identical mating and domestic organization. To be sure, aristocrats impose a strict purdah *(auren kulle)* on their wives, while lower-status persons, such as butchers, do not. To be sure, wives may initiate divorce more easily when their husbands are commoners than when they are aristocrats. These differences involve neither the form of mating relations nor the domestic organization. Far more important is the fact that the ruling classes have a patrilineal descent system, that these lineages are nonexogamous, and that cousin marriage is practiced widely among aristocrats and commoners alike. Even slave marriage and domestic organization tended to observe the common Hausa forms.

Status differences in Hausa society are perhaps as marked as those in the British Caribbean. Both societies have had similar histories as slave states. Among Hausa of high and low status alike there is a simple uniformity of domestic and mating organization despite differing emphases on bilateral or agnatic kinship beyond the domestic level; but in the marriages of free persons and slaves, there were important differences which also differentiated free and slave household organization.

Within Hausa homes, relations are highly formal. Men remain in the forecourt when they are at home and have little to do with the domestic round. They avoid their children in public. Teknonymy emphasizes this; there is a lifelong taboo on direct contact between parents and their first child. The last-born, who is known as *auta*, is defined as the favorite, with whom his father may play. The chief wife regulates the internal arrangements of the household and distributes duties within it. Children inherit their father's status. Since most fathers have low status, most children inherit low status. However, these households are patrifocal and the men are by no means marginal.

In sum, the similar domestic organization of commoners and aristocrats is linked with similar mating forms. Despite the bilateral kinship system of Hausa commoners, agnatic ties provide the basis of family structure. These ties are necessary concomitants of virilocal polygyny. Conversely, the differences between free and slave families in this society expressed differences in their mating systems. With the abolition of slavery, these familial differences have tended to disappear as the ex-slaves adopted the mating practice of free persons. The intensity of their adoption accounts for the spread of purdah marriage in Hausa society over recent years.

As among the Hausa, so too in the British Caribbean, we find patrilineal and bilateral kinship systems having a common basis in mating organization; but the patrilineal society of Carriacou has a special variant of the general West Indian mating system as its basis. The Carriacou mating peculiarities likewise differentiate Carriacou domestic organization.

We may now contrast a monogamous society whose kinship system is bilateral with the Hausa and the West Indians. America and Britain provide instances of the type, differentiated principally in their levels of conjugal stability and effective kinship range. In such societies, marriage is neolocal and until recently was lifelong. Household groups are based on elementary families; adults may refrain from marriage, but may neither bear children outside of marriage nor have two or more mates simultaneously. The basic assumptions of this system are a lifelong and exclusive monogamy and a neolocal distribution of domestic elementary families. The recent spread of divorce and birth control has increased the instability of this family structure.

The emphasis on neolocal establishment of new elementary families is necessary for, and inevitable in, these bilateral kinship systems. Were it otherwise, there would be a corresponding shift towards uterine or patrilineal alternatives. Emphasis on lifelong monogamy is equally essential, since without it the dissolution and fragmentation of elementary families will create anomalous domestic forms and emphasize one set of parental ties while devaluing the other. Such developments either would be incompatible with the kinship system or would lead to its change. In short, the stability of this type of family structure depends on the prevalence of lifelong monogamy and exclusive domestic family units. Its basic taboos are against illegitimate children and extraresidential mating. Until the recent spread of birth control, these two elements were closely associated.

The history of this system in Western Europe is quite well known. For centuries cohabitation had a purely consensual basis. The Church had a hard fight to eliminate these consensual unions and to establish marriage as the sole form of cohabitation.[7] On the eve of its success came the industrial revolution and the eviction of peasants from country to town. Disraeli, Dickens, Mayhew, and many others have left graphic accounts of these social changes and of the conditions which they created. Even so, illegitimacy remained rare among the new urban proletariat. In the England of 1865 illegitimates represented 6.5 per cent of all births.[8] At that time 64 per cent of Grenadian births were illegitimate, but only 45 per cent of those in Carriacou.

We have to ask how was it that marriage displaced consensual cohabitation in Europe and failed to do so in the British West Indies? How is it that the West Indians, who have formally adopted monogamy and bilateral kinship from Western Europe, practice neither in its pure form? How is it that West Indian and British domestic organization differ so remarkably?

Perhaps the Church's success in enforcing marriage in Europe contains the answer. For more than a century many have tried to promote marriage in the British West Indies; but the illegitimacy rates have remained steady where they have not increased. It seems clear that the Church's success in Europe and its failure in the British West Indies are alike due to the nature of the problems it tackled. Its principal problem in Europe was to persuade governments to accept and support its authority in celebrating and regulating marriage. It had no such problem in the British West Indies after the abolition of slavery in 1838. In Europe, however, the population had for centuries practiced lifelong monogamy; their kinship system was bilateral, and cohabitation had a neolocal base. All that the Church did was to formalize this system by ritual and to strengthen the sanctions against adultery or separation of spouses.

The persistence of high illegitimacy rates, unstable unions, and anomalous forms of domestic groups in the West Indies are all due to the same conditions. These conditions had their historical origin in slavery, especially in the mating organization of slaves. West Indian slaves were not allowed to marry but they were free to cohabit consensually or to mate extraresidentially, as they pleased, except that slaves having different owners could scarcely establish a common home. Many old accounts of West Indian slavery describe these conditions. [9] Slave children were the property of their mother's owner. Slaves could contract or dissolve unions informally, at will. Occasional references indicate that slave headmen often had two or more mates, living with one and visiting the others. In Carriacou, however, there was a notable difference. In 1833 this tiny island had a slave population of approximately 3,300, the great majority of whom belonged to a single owner. This owner sought to replace the system of day work which was general on West Indian plantations by a system of task work. He first encouraged his slaves to accept daily tasks, after completion of which their time was their own, and later introduced a weekly task which the slaves completed in two or three days, after which they worked on their own provision grounds. Carriacou slaves were then encouraged to marry, the wives and children being redeemed by their husbands, who remained slaves in order to enjoy their rights to food, clothing, housing, and especially the provision grounds.

4637820679018

715

Even before the Emancipation, many slave women and their children had been freed in this way.[10] It is thus not surprising that the Carriacou illegitimacy rate in 1865 was lower than that of Grenada and has continued to remain so. With freedom, Carriacou men began to emigrate, and consensual unions were replaced by marriage. Even so, the extraresidential mating relation persisted.

In Jamaica and, as far as our data permit judgment, in Grenada also, Emancipation was followed by two major developments. Many slaves withdrew from their former plantations or so redefined their position vis-à-vis their former masters as to form a free peasantry. In Jamaica, perhaps one half of the slave population remained on the plantations as a landless labor force, tenanting gardens from their former owners. The other half moved off to the hills, squatting or establishing settlements under missionary leadership; and within these free villages, the majority of the senior population adopted marriage.[11] Their juniors, however, did not, and by 1861 the missionary impetus had spent itself without displacing the traditional mating forms.[12] The plains folk on the sugar plantations or in the towns had also been subject to missionary teaching; many of them had also married; but the proportion who did so was far lower in the old plantation areas than in the free villages under missionary control. In fact the economic conditions of the plains folk were if anything worse after Emancipation than before, and by 1861 they had become almost unbearable.[13]

In both the hill and the plains populations of Jamaica, and in other West Indian societies, Emancipation merely permitted the adoption of a new mating form; it could not abolish the old mating system; nor could the new form introduced into this traditional dual system displace either of its original forms. Only in Carriacou where consensual cohabitation had already begun to give way to marriage under slavery and where the heavy male emigration immediately after 1838 further strengthened marriage, did the new form absorb and replace one of the old. In the other areas its institutionalization varied widely. In some it was adopted by senior folk whose matings were already stable; these stable matings were previously for the most part consensual domestic unions. In such communities marriage thus became the final form into which mating relations developed during middle age. The consensual cohabitation which preceded it was thus given transitional place in this development from extraresidential mating into marriage. Latante and the rural peasantry of Jamaica provide contemporary instances of this system. Late marriage remains as typical of these populations as early marriage is typical of the West Indian elites.

In the plantation areas and townships, the change-over was less impressive. The adoption of marriage by some ex-slaves distinguished these married persons from others as social climbers. True, marriage was adopted by persons of differing age; but this age-scatter denied it a fixed place in the individual life cycle. Moreover, its adoption into the traditional dual system only enhanced the inherent instabilities of this system by undermining such finality as consensual domestic unions may have hitherto had. To be sure, these plains folk partially adopted marriage; but they rejected divorce wholesale, and dissolved their marriages informally and resumed extraresidential or consensual domestic unions as they pleased. Grenville and Kingston provide us with contemporary instances of this type of system.

This account of these historical developments is in part speculation, but not entirely. It is based on a fair familiarity with the societies under discussion and with their documented histories. However, we need not rest the case on historical sequence. There are basic structural reasons for the differentiation of mating systems among the ex-slave populations we have been studying.

The basis of this differentiation is the coexistence of extraresidential and consensual domestic unions under slavery. Carriacou owes its high male marriage rate to its high male emigration rate. Given the large female surplus and the prevalence of extraresidential mating, the alternative to a complete replacement of consensual domestic unions by marriage in Carriacou was chaos in family relations. No society with such sex disbalances could maintain or regulate family relations without having at least one obligatory and indissoluble mating relation.

In Latante and rural Jamaica also, extraresidential mating relations continue, side by side with consensual cohabitation and marriage. A stable extraresidential relation becomes a consensual domestic union; a stable domestic union becomes a marriage. These unions are stable, as our previous analysis has shown. Marriage is thus the final form of mating, and occurs late in life. It is typically preceded by consensual cohabitation, and it is to this intermediate position that unions of the latter sort owe their stability. In such a system, marriage rates can only increase by reducing the frequencies of other forms of union which are necessary precedents to marriage. Yet if marriage displaced either of these alternative forms, a different system would result. This seems to have happened in Carriacou, where the alternative mating forms have become complementary for married men. Thus the institutionalization and redefinition of marriage in Carriacou proceeded together, and this redefinition adjusted marriage to the extraresidential form of mating. Marriage was defined as a lifelong union, exclusive for females but not for their husbands, whose plural mating was governed by the principle of dispersal.

In comparing the history of marriage in the West Indies and Europe, we have to ask why the West Indians rejected the idea of lifelong exclusive unions while the Europeans accepted it. We have seen that the Europeans already had unions of this type, and knew no other. Such unions were assumed by their social organization, and others were incompatible with it. Despite the serious disbalances inherent in any rigid system of monogamy, the populations of Northwestern Europe had maintained such a system since the time of Tacitus and before. In the West Indies, on the other hand, the slave mating system encouraged alternative forms of union, neither of which were obligatory or stable. The fragmentation of elementary families was endemic in this slave society and so formed an integral part of the family structure based on alternative mating forms. Diverse definitions of parenthood were thus parts of this system, together with diverse domestic forms. In these conditions, stable conjugal unions and family relations alike were those which had in fact persisted over time; there was no structural basis for assuming their continuity, neither were they subject to regulation other than that imposed on the system itself by the need of self-consistency. In consequence, when marriage was introduced, there were only two alternatives: either it would be redefined and identified with one of the previous forms or it would be institutionalized as a third variety. The structurally impossible development was the elimination of traditional forms by marriage. This did not occur.

It could not and did not occur because lifelong exclusive monogamy, neolocal elementary families, and a balanced bilateral kinship system are interdependent assumptions of such a system. A population engaged in lifelong consensual cohabitation could easily convert this into marriage without changing its family structure. This happened in Northwestern Europe. The West Indians, however, already had a family system based on extraresidential mating and consensual domestic unions. Neither of these was inherently stable, nor could either become so as long as competition with the alternative mating form persisted. Nor could either of these mating alternatives be eliminated, since their residential bases were complementary; and the family organization assumed the operation of both and domestic relations were governed by them. The simple generality of extraresidential mating within these slave societies invalidated the essential assumptions of bilateral monogamous family organization. It did so by maximizing the instability of all forms of mating, by contradicting the monogamous assumption of neolocal exclusive elementary families, by making effective paternal roles contingent on the duration of mating relations, and by its integration with certain forms of domestic grouping which included single women and their offspring. Above all, such mating created a distinct variety of parenthood and distinguished the issue of these unions from the issue of consensual cohabitation; there were thus two classes of illegitimates, two sets of sex-parental roles, two forms of mating, and several varieties of domestic grouping adjusted to these. The preconditions of a monogamous bilateral kinship system were lacking utterly. There is therefore no difficulty in understanding why marriage did not become universal among West Indians.

In Carriacou, marriage was absorbed into the traditional family structure, by incorporating consensual cohabitation and being redefined as a relation exclusive for females but permissive for males. Married men maintained extraresidential relations, and Carriacou society modified marriage to permit plural mating by males. In Latante and rural Jamaica, marriage was institutionalized as the third and final form of mating, the consequence and not the basis of a stable relation. The stability was demonstrated by duration; but the simple adoption of marriage as a final mating form established a sequence which also enhanced the stability of all alternatives. In Grenville and Kingston marriage lacked both finality and fixed position in such a series. In consequence, it had no set relation to the other two forms of mating, and has acquired much of their instability. We can now understand why early marriage in Carriacou is concurrent with extraresidential mating, and why it comes late in the life cycle elsewhere. Given the initial complex of family forms, adoption of early marriage in Carriacou was only possible if such marriages did not exclude men from extradomestic matings. Since extraresidential mating and its allied family forms were an integral part of this family structure, marriage was thus integrated with them by modifications which defined these mating forms as complementary for males but exclusive alternatives for females. In Latante and elsewhere also, the adoption of early marriage on a lifelong basis was incompatible with the current family structure based on coexistent alternatives of mating, parenthood, and domestic grouping. Conversely, the institutionalization of marriage late in life was easily accommodated to this family structure, since it assumed the practice of extraresidential mating earlier, together with the varieties of parenthood and family forms.

In consequence of these alternative developments we find several varieties of family structure in West Indian society. However, all these varieties are based on the coexistence of alternative mating forms, and all include marriage and the extraresidential relation. In most cases, consensual cohabitation is also prevalent. In consequence of their numerous common elements, these family systems represent varieties of a single structural type. The basic type has several distinctive elements, namely, a plurality of parental and mating forms; an inherent diversity and instability of domestic organization; an emphasis on collateral kinship in the domestic system; and a formal commitment to monogamy, which is modified in various ways consistent with the alternative forms of mating.

Anthropology should recognize that marriage does not exhaust mating; that elementary families may be dispersed as systematically as they are nucleated; and that some societies may base their family structure on alternative sets of mating relations and of parental roles. The tendency to assume uniformity in mating relations, domestic organization, and elementary family forms has bedeviled the study of West Indian family relations. Certain elements in this assumption are largely ethnocentric; among these we may include the definition of conjugal ties in terms of coresidence; the Ga of Ghana, the Kagoro and Kadara of Northern Nigeria, the Hausa who marry by *auren daukisandanka,* and the West Indians who mate extraresidentially have conjugal unions which are just as real as their domestic ones. The important distinction between conjugal and casual relations is their public recognition, and the regulation of mating and parenthood within them. Unless these types of relation are defined and analyzed explicitly, there is virtually no chance of understanding complex family structures in which all are part.

# Appendix:
# Composition of Households

# Explanation of Symbols

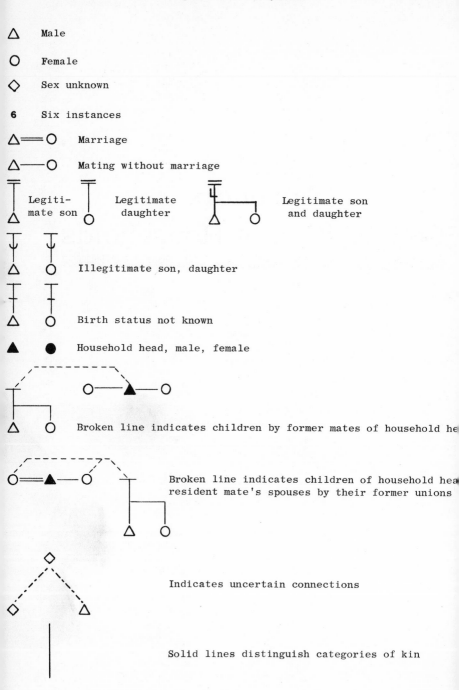

△   Male

O   Female

◇   Sex unknown

**6**   Six instances

△══O   Marriage

△──O   Mating without marriage

Legitimate son   Legitimate daughter   Legitimate son and daughter

Illegitimate son, daughter

Birth status not known

▲   ●   Household head, male, female

Broken line indicates children by former mates of household head

Broken line indicates children of household head, resident mate's spouses by their former unions

Indicates uncertain connections

Solid lines distinguish categories of kin

## Explanation of Diagram Numbers Referring
## to Categories of Kin

1. Household heads, their spouses, mates, and joint issue and kin, including affines.
2. Kin and issue of household head only (= 2a + 2b + 2c + 2d).
    2a. Household head's issue by separate matings, and their affinal kin.
    2b. Household head's full siblings, their issue and affinal kin.
    2c. Household head's mother and matrikin.
    2d. Household head's father and patrikin.
3. Kin and issue of household head's mates only (= 3a + 3b + 3c + 3d).
    3a. Mates' issue by separate matings, and their affinal kin.
    3b. Mates' full siblings, their issue, and affinal kin.
    3c. Mates' father and patrikin.
    3d. Mates' mother and matrikin.
4. Adoptions and nonkin.

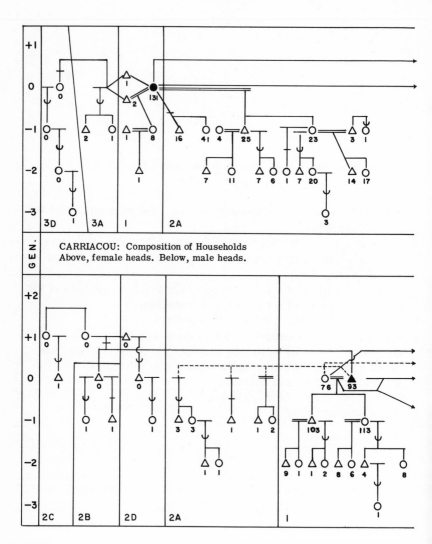

CARRIACOU: Composition of Households
Above, female heads. Below, male heads.

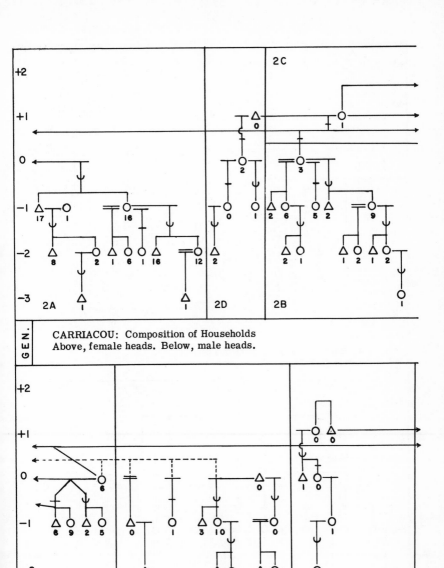

CARRIACOU: Composition of Households
Above, female heads. Below, male heads.

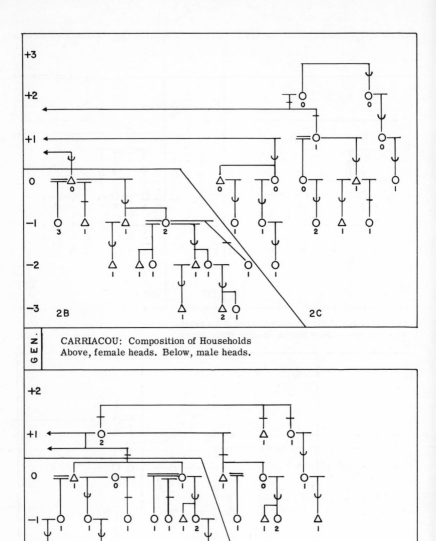

CARRIACOU: Composition of Households
Above, female heads. Below, male heads.

CARRIACOU

| Generations | HH,* mates, joint kin and issue | HH's kin and issue only | HH's mate's kin and issue only | Adoptions and nonkin | Total | Kin and Issue of HH Only | | | | Issue and Kin of Mates Only | | | |
|---|---|---|---|---|---|---|---|---|---|---|---|---|---|
| | | | | | | Issue and their affines | Full siblings, their issue and affines | Mother and matri-kin | Father and patri-kin | Issue and their affines | Full siblings, their issue and affines | Father and patri-kin | Mother and matri-kin |
| Generations | 1 | 2 | 3 | 4 | Total | 2a | 2b | 2c | 2d | 3a | 3b | 3c | 3d |
| Composition of Households with Female Heads | | | | | | | | | | | | | |
| +1 | 0 | 2 | 0 | 0 | 2 | 0 | 0 | 2 | 0 | 0 | 0 | 0 | 0 |
| 0 | 134 | 7 | 0 | 1 | 142 | 0 | 3 | 2 | 2 | 0 | 0 | 0 | 0 |
| -1 | 9 | 185 | 3 | 4 | 201 | 147 | 31 | 6 | 1 | 3 | 0 | 0 | 0 |
| -2 | 1 | 153 | 0 | 0 | 154 | 135 | 15 | 1 | 2 | 0 | 0 | 0 | 0 |
| -3 | 0 | 10 | 1 | 0 | 11 | 5 | 5 | 0 | 0 | 0 | 0 | 0 | 1 |
| TOTAL | 144 | 357 | 4 | 5 | 510 | 287 | 54 | 11 | 5 | 3 | 0 | 0 | 1 |
| Composition of Households with Male Heads | | | | | | | | | | | | | |
| +1 | 0 | 0 | 4 | 0 | 4 | 0 | 0 | 0 | 0 | 0 | 0 | 0 | 4 |
| 0 | 175 | 1 | 5 | 0 | 181 | 0 | 0 | 1 | 0 | 0 | 2 | 1 | 2 |
| -1 | 238 | 13 | 28 | 4 | 283 | 10 | 2 | 0 | 1 | 14 | 8 | 1 | 5 |
| -2 | 39 | 2 | 20 | 0 | 61 | 2 | 0 | 0 | 0 | 14 | 5 | 1 | 0 |
| -3 | 1 | 0 | 0 | 0 | 1 | 0 | 0 | 0 | 0 | 0 | 0 | 0 | 0 |
| TOTAL | 453 | 16 | 57 | 4 | 530 | 12 | 2 | 1 | 1 | 28 | 15 | 3 | 11 |

*HH = Household head.

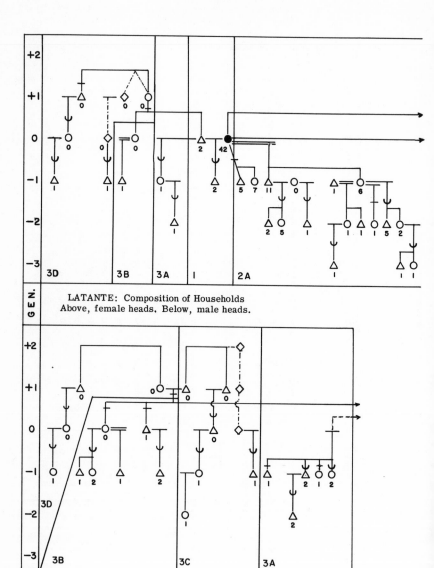

LATANTE: Composition of Households
Above, female heads. Below, male heads.

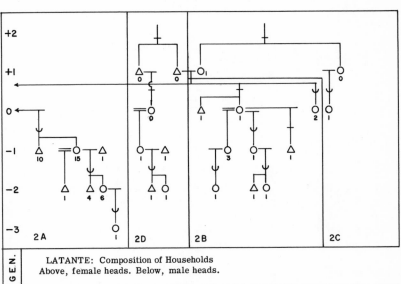

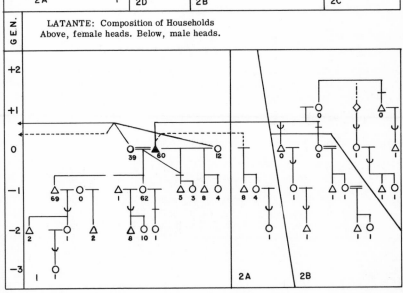

LATANTE: Composition of Households
Above, female heads. Below, male heads.

LATANTE

## Composition of Households with Female Heads

| Genera-tions | HH,* mates, joint kin and issue (1) | HH's kin and issue only (2) | HH's mate's kin and issue only (3) | Adop-tions and nonkin (4) | Total | Kin and Issue of HH Only | | | | Issue and Kin of Mates Only | | | |
|---|---|---|---|---|---|---|---|---|---|---|---|---|---|
| | | | | | | Issue and their affines (2a) | Full siblings, their issue and affines (2b) | Mother and matri-kin (2c) | Father and patri-kin (2d) | Issue and their affines (3a) | Full siblings, their issue and affines (3b) | Father and patri-kin (3c) | Mother and matri-kin (3d) |
| +1 | 0 | 1 | 0 | 0 | 1 | 0 | 0 | 1 | 0 | 0 | 0 | 0 | 0 |
| 0 | 44 | 5 | 0 | 0 | 49 | 0 | 4 | 1 | 0 | 0 | 0 | 0 | 0 |
| -1 | 2 | 63 | 4 | 0 | 69 | 56 | 5 | 0 | 2 | 1 | 1 | 0 | 2 |
| -2 | 0 | 34 | 1 | 0 | 35 | 29 | 3 | 0 | 2 | 1 | 0 | 0 | 0 |
| -3 | 0 | 4 | 0 | 0 | 4 | 4 | 0 | 0 | 0 | 0 | 0 | 0 | 0 |
| TOTAL | 46 | 107 | 5 | 0 | 158 | 89 | 12 | 2 | 4 | 2 | 1 | 0 | 2 |

## Composition of Households with Male Heads

| Genera-tions | HH,* mates, joint kin and issue (1) | HH's kin and issue only (2) | HH's mate's kin and issue only (3) | Adop-tions and nonkin (4) | Total | Kin and Issue of HH Only | | | | Issue and Kin of Mates Only | | | |
|---|---|---|---|---|---|---|---|---|---|---|---|---|---|
| | | | | | | Issue and their affines (2a) | Full siblings, their issue and affines (2b) | Mother and matri-kin (2c) | Father and patri-kin (2d) | Issue and their affines (3a) | Full siblings, their issue and affines (3b) | Father and patri-kin (3c) | Mother and matri-kin (3d) |
| +1 | 0 | 0 | 0 | 0 | 0 | 0 | 0 | 0 | 0 | 0 | 0 | 0 | 0 |
| 0 | 111 | 2 | 1 | 1 | 115 | 0 | 0 | 2 | 0 | 0 | 1 | 0 | 0 |
| -1 | 152 | 17 | 15 | 1 | 185 | 12 | 3 | 2 | 0 | 6 | 6 | 2 | 1 |
| -2 | 24 | 4 | 3 | 0 | 31 | 1 | 3 | 0 | 0 | 2 | 0 | 1 | 0 |
| -3 | 1 | 0 | 0 | 0 | 1 | 0 | 0 | 0 | 0 | 0 | 0 | 0 | 0 |
| TOTAL | 288 | 23 | 19 | 2 | 332 | 13 | 6 | 4 | 0 | 8 | 7 | 3 | 1 |

*HH = Household head.

GRENVILLE

| Generations | HH,* mates, joint kin and issue | HH's kin and issue only | HH's mate's kin and issue only | Adoptions and nonkin | Total | Kin and Issue of HH Only | | | | Issue and Kin of Mates Only | | | |
|---|---|---|---|---|---|---|---|---|---|---|---|---|---|
| | | | | | | Issue and their affines | Full siblings, their issue and affines | Mother and matri-kin | Father and patri-kin | Issue and their affines | Full siblings, their issue and affines | Father and patri-kin | Mother and matri-kin |
| Generations | 1 | 2 | 3 | 4 | Total | 2a | 2b | 2c | 2d | 3a | 3b | 3c | 3d |

Composition of Households with Female Heads

| Generations | 1 | 2 | 3 | 4 | Total | 2a | 2b | 2c | 2d | 3a | 3b | 3c | 3d |
|---|---|---|---|---|---|---|---|---|---|---|---|---|---|
| +2 | 0 | 1 | 0 | 0 | 1 | 0 | 0 | 1 | 0 | 0 | 0 | 0 | 0 |
| +1 | 0 | 0 | 0 | 0 | 0 | 0 | 0 | 0 | 0 | 0 | 0 | 0 | 0 |
| 0 | 64 | 5 | 0 | 3 | 72 | 0 | 4 | 1 | 0 | 0 | 0 | 0 | 0 |
| -1 | 1 | 62 | 1 | 6 | 70 | 58 | 0 | 3 | 1.75 | 1 | 0 | 0 | 0 |
| -2 | 0 | 26 | 2 | 1 | 29 | 24 | 1 | 1 | 0 | 2 | 0 | 0 | 0 |
| -3 | 0 | 1 | 0 | 0 | 1 | 1 | 0 | 0 | 0 | 0 | 0 | 0 | 0 |
| TOTAL | 65 | 95 | 3 | 10 | 173 | 83 | 5 | 6 | 1.75 | 3 | 0 | 0 | 0 |

Composition of Households with Male Heads

| Generations | 1 | 2 | 3 | 4 | Total | 2a | 2b | 2c | 2d | 3a | 3b | 3c | 3d |
|---|---|---|---|---|---|---|---|---|---|---|---|---|---|
| +1 | 0 | 0 | 1 | 0 | 1 | 0 | 0 | 0 | 0 | 0 | 0 | 1 | 0 |
| 0 | 94 | 7 | 0 | 4 | 105 | 0 | 4 | 0 | 0 | 0 | 0 | 0 | 0 |
| -1 | 73 | 5 | 10 | 4 | 92 | 2 | 3 | 3 | 0 | 8 | 2 | 0 | 0 |
| -2 | 4 | 0 | 5 | 0 | 9 | 0 | 0 | 0 | 0 | 5 | 0 | 0 | 0 |
| TOTAL | 171 | 12 | 16 | 8 | 207 | 2 | 7 | 3 | 0 | 13 | 2 | 1 | 0 |

*HH = Household head.

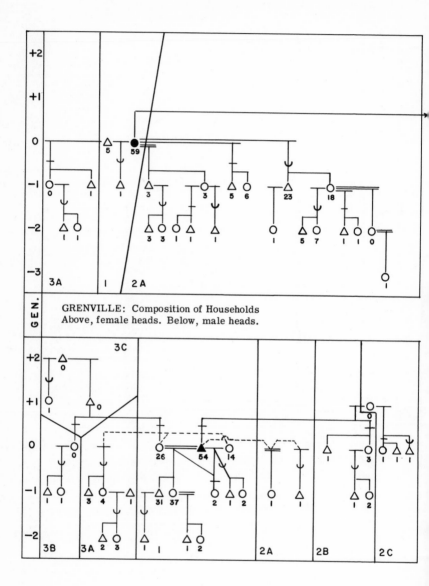

GRENVILLE: Composition of Households
Above, female heads. Below, male heads.

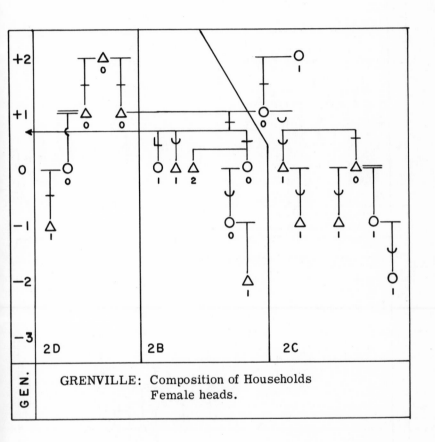

GRENVILLE: Composition of Households
Female heads.

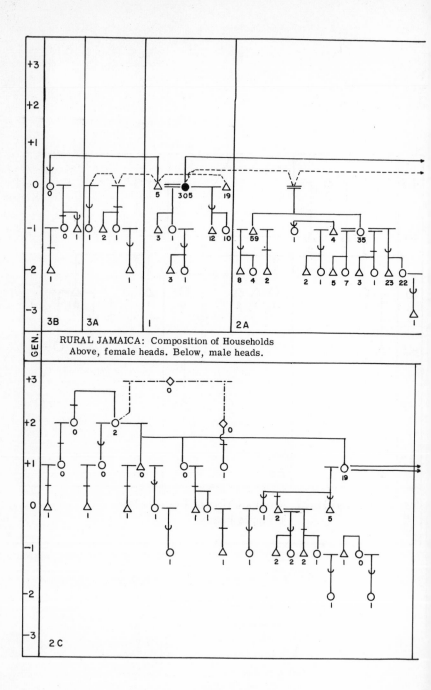

RURAL JAMAICA: Composition of Households
Above, female heads. Below, male heads.

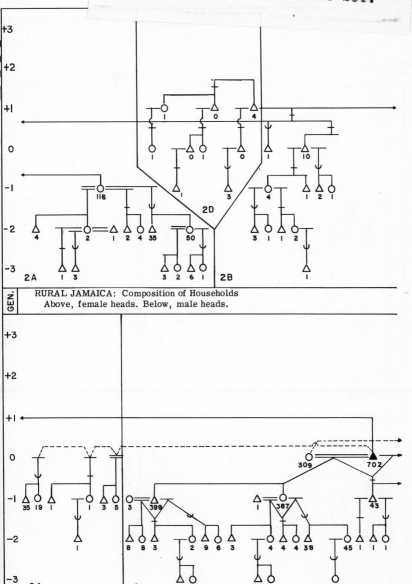

RURAL JAMAICA: Composition of Households
Above, female heads. Below, male heads.

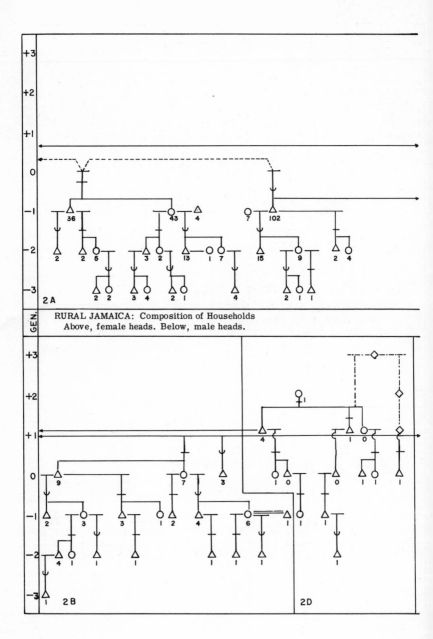

RURAL JAMAICA: Composition of Households
Above, female heads. Below, male heads.

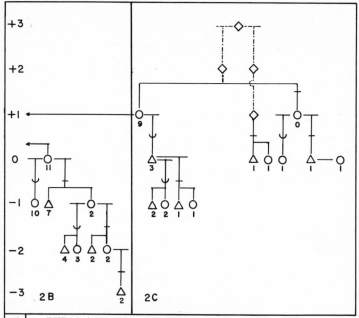

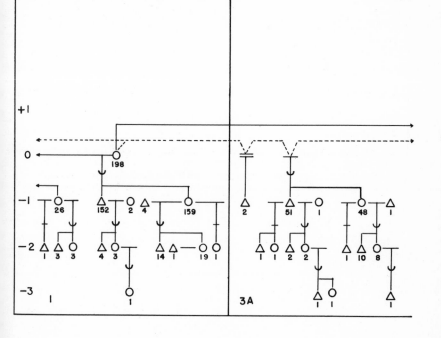

RURAL JAMAICA: Composition of Households
Above, female heads. Below, male heads.

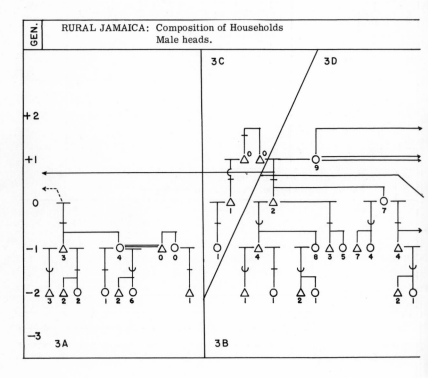

RURAL JAMAICA: Composition of Households
Male heads.

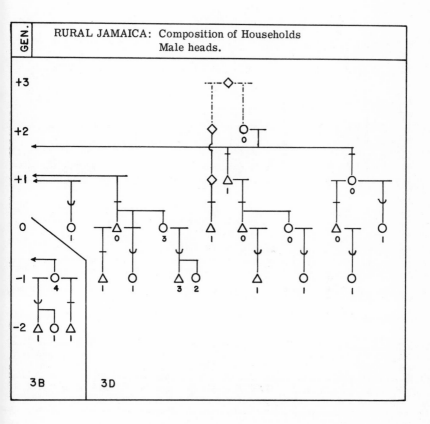

RURAL JAMAICA: Composition of Households
Male heads.

RURAL JAMAICA

| Generations | HH,* mates, joint kin and issue | HH's kin and issue only | HH's mate's kin and issue only | Adoptions and nonkin | Total | Kin and Issue of HH Only | | | | Issue and Kin of Mates Only | | | |
|---|---|---|---|---|---|---|---|---|---|---|---|---|---|
| | | | | | | Issue and their affines | Full siblings, their issue and affines | Mother and matrikin | Father and patrikin | Issue and their affines | Full siblings, their issue and affines | Father and patrikin | Mother and matrikin |
| | 1 | 2 | 3 | 4 | Total | 2a | 2b | 2c | 2d | 3a | 3b | 3c | 3d |
| Generations | | | | | | | | | | | | | |
| **Composition of Households with Female Heads** | | | | | | | | | | | | | |
| +1 | 0 | 14 | 0 | 0 | 14 | 0 | 0 | 9 | 5 | 0 | 0 | 0 | 0 |
| 0 | 329 | 32 | 0 | 13 | 374 | 0 | 22 | 8 | 2 | 0 | 0 | 0 | 0 |
| -1 | 26 | 444 | 5 | 24 | 499 | 407 | 27 | 6 | 4 | 4 | 1 | 0 | 0 |
| -2 | 4 | 259 | 2 | 0 | 265 | 241 | 18 | 0 | 0 | 1 | 1 | 0 | 0 |
| -3 | 0 | 42 | 0 | 0 | 42 | 39 | 3 | 0 | 0 | 0 | 0 | 0 | 0 |
| TOTAL | 359 | 791 | 7 | 37 | 1,194 | 687 | 70 | 23 | 11 | 5 | 2 | 0 | 0 |
| **Composition of Households with Male Heads** | | | | | | | | | | | | | |
| +2 | 0 | 3 | 0 | 0 | 3 | 0 | 0 | 2 | 1 | 0 | 0 | 0 | 0 |
| +1 | 0 | 25 | 10 | 0 | 35 | 0 | 0 | 20 | 5 | 0 | 0 | 0 | 10 |
| 0 | 1,209 | 37 | 16 | 61 | 1,323 | 0 | 19 | 14 | 4 | 0 | 9 | 1 | 6 |
| -1 | 1,176 | 99 | 160 | 40 | 1,475 | 64 | 22 | 11 | 2 | 110 | 39 | 1 | 10 |
| -2 | 186 | 14 | 53 | 1 | 254 | 1 | 10 | 2 | 1 | 42 | 11 | 0 | 0 |
| -3 | 10 | 1 | 3 | 0 | 14 | 0 | 1 | 0 | 0 | 3 | 0 | 0 | 0 |
| TOTAL | 2,581 | 179 | 242 | 102 | 3,104 | 65 | 52 | 49 | 13 | 155 | 59 | 2 | 26 |

*HH = Household head.

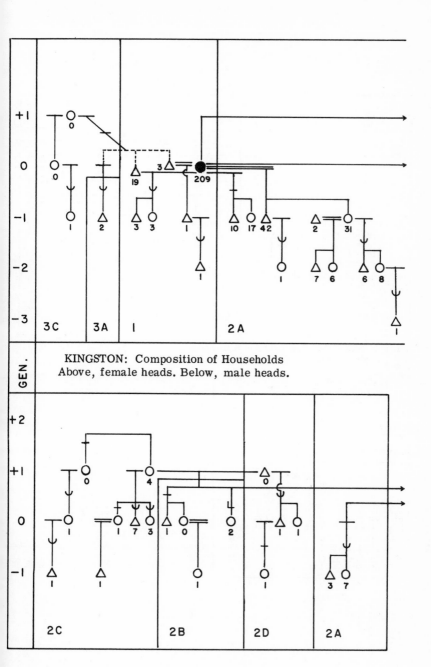

KINGSTON: Composition of Households
Above, female heads. Below, male heads.

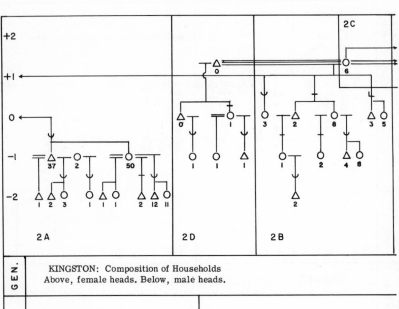

KINGSTON: Composition of Households
Above, female heads. Below, male heads.

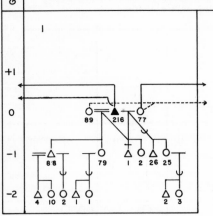

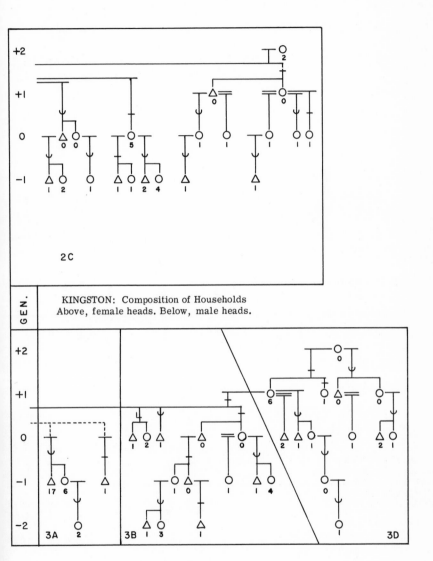

KINGSTON: Composition of Households
Above, female heads. Below, male heads.

KINGSTON

| Generations | HH,* mates, joint kin and issue | HH's kin and issue only | HH's mate's kin and issue only | Adoptions and nonkin | Total | Kin and Issue of HH Only | | | | Issue and Kin of Mates Only | | | |
| | | | | | | Issue and their affines | Full siblings, their issue and affines | Mother and matri-kin | Father and patri-kin | Issue and their affines | Full siblings, their issue and affines | Father and patri-kin | Mother and matri-kin |
| | 1 | 2 | 3 | 4 | Total | 2a | 2b | 2c | 2d | 3a | 3b | 3c | 3d |

Composition of Households with Female Heads

| Generations | 1 | 2 | 3 | 4 | Total | 2a | 2b | 2c | 2d | 3a | 3b | 3c | 3d |
|---|---|---|---|---|---|---|---|---|---|---|---|---|---|
| +2 | 0 | 2 | 0 | 0 | 2 | 0 | 0 | 2 | 0 | 0 | 0 | 0 | 0 |
| +1 | 0 | 6 | 0 | 0 | 6 | 0 | 0 | 6 | 0 | 0 | 0 | 0 | 0 |
| 0 | 231 | 32 | 0 | 20 | 283 | 0 | 21 | 10 | 1 | 0 | 0 | 0 | 0 |
| -1 | 7 | 223 | 3 | 8 | 241 | 191 | 15 | 14 | 3 | 2 | 0 | 0 | 1 |
| -2 | 1 | 64 | 0 | 1 | 66 | 62 | 2 | 0 | 0 | 0 | 0 | 0 | 0 |
| -3 | 0 | 1 | 0 | 0 | 1 | 1 | 0 | 0 | 0 | 0 | 0 | 0 | 0 |
| TOTAL | 239 | 328 | 3 | 29 | 599 | 254 | 38 | 32 | 4 | 2 | 0 | 0 | 1 |

Composition of Households with Male Heads

| Generations | 1 | 2 | 3 | 4 | Total | 2a | 2b | 2c | 2d | 3a | 3b | 3c | 3d |
|---|---|---|---|---|---|---|---|---|---|---|---|---|---|
| +1 | 0 | 4 | 7 | 0 | 11 | 0 | 0 | 4 | 0 | 0 | 0 | 0 | 7 |
| 0 | 382 | 17 | 12 | 18 | 429 | 0 | 3 | 12 | 2 | 0 | 4 | 0 | 8 |
| -1 | 221 | 14 | 31 | 3 | 269 | 10 | 1 | 2 | 1 | 24 | 7 | 0 | 0 |
| -2 | 23 | 0 | 8 | 1 | 32 | 0 | 0 | 0 | 0 | 2 | 5 | 0 | 1 |
| TOTAL | 626 | 35 | 58 | 22 | 741 | 10 | 4 | 18 | 3 | 26 | 16 | 0 | 16 |

*HH = Household head.

Adoptions and Nonkin

**CARRIACOU**
female heads

*Birth Status Not Known*
Adoptions: female, three
Boarders: male, one
*Illegitimate*
Adoptions: male, one

male heads

*Birth Status Not Known*
Adoptions: male, one; female, two; total, three
*Illegitimate*
Adoptions: male, one

**LATANTE**
female heads

Adoptions and nonkin: none

male heads

*Birth Status Not Known*
Adoptions: male, one
*Legitimate*
Adoptions: female, one

**GRENVILLE**
female heads

*Birth Status Not Known*
Adoptions: male, one; female, six; total, seven
Boarders: male, one
Unrelated: male, one
*Illegitimate*
Unrelated: female, one

## GRENVILLE
male heads

*Birth Status Not Known*
Employees and issue: female, four
*Illegitimate*
Employees and issue: female, one

## RURAL JAMAICA
female heads

*Birth Status Not Known*
Adoptions: male, twelve; female, twelve; total, twenty-four
Employees: male, two; female, two; total, four
Unrelated: male, six; female, three; total, nine

male heads

*Birth Status Not Known*
Adoptions: male, seventeen; female, twenty; total, thirty-seven
Employees and issue: male, thirteen; female, seventeen; total, thirty
Unrelated and issue: male, twenty-one; female, ten; total, thirty-one
*Illegitimate*
Adoptions: male, one
Employees and issue: male, one; female, one; total, two
Unrelated and issue: male, two; female, one; total, three

## KINGSTON
female heads

*Birth Status Not Known*
Adoptions and issue: male, one; female, two; total, three
Unrelated and issue: male, one; female, one; total, two
*Illegitimate*
Adoptions and issue: male, three; female, two; total, five
Boarders: male, three; female, four; total, seven
Employees: female, one
Unrelated and issue: female, eleven

male heads

*Birth Status Not Known*
Adoptions and issue: female, two

KINGSTON
   male heads

*Birth Status Not Known*

Employees: male, one; female, seven; total, eight

Boarders: male, four; female, two; total, six

Unrelated: male, three; female, one; total, four

*Legitimate*

Adoptions and issue: male, one; female, one; total, two

# Notes

▨▨▨▨▨▨

Chapter 1

1. For field techniques and training methods, see M. G. Smith and G. J. Kruijer, *A Sociological Manual for Extension Workers in the Caribbean,* Caribbean Affairs Series (Trinidad: University College of the West Indies, 1957), pp. 152-57, 172-75.

2. Director of Statistics, Jamaica, letter to writer, Nov. 15, 1957.

3. M. G. Smith, *Labour Supply in Rural Jamaica* (Kingston, Jamaica: Government Printer, 1956).

4. Director of Statistics, letter, Nov. 15, 1957.

5. Edith Clarke, *My Mother Who Fathered Me* (London: Allen and Unwin, 1957). See also George Cumper, "The Jamaican Family: Village and Estate," *Social and Economic Studies,* (Mona, Jamaica: University College of the West Indies, Institute of Social and Economic Research, 1958), VII, 2.

6. See Fernando Henriques, "West Indian Family Organization," *Caribbean Quarterly,* II, No. 1 (1952), 16-24; M. J. Herskovits, *The Myth of the Negro Past* (New York: Harper and Bros., 1941); Dom Basil Matthews, *The Crisis in the West Indian Family* (Trinidad: Port of Spain, Extra-Mural Department, University College of the West Indies, 1953). T. S. Simey, *Welfare and Planning in the West Indies* (London: Oxford University Press, 1946); R. T. Smith, "The Family in the Caribbean," *Caribbean Studies: A Symposium,* ed. Vera Rubin (Jamaica: Institute of Social and Economic Research, University College of the West Indies, 1957), pp. 67 ff. (Reprinted, Seattle: University of Washington Press, 1960.)

7. R. T. Smith, *The Negro Family in British Guiana* (London: Routledge and Kegan Paul, 1956). Edith Clarke, *My Mother Who Fathered Me.*

8. R. T. Smith, *The Negro Family in British Guiana,* pp. 108-22, especially 108-13.

9. *Ibid.*, pp. 221-24 ff.

10. R. T. Smith, "The Family in the Caribbean," pp. 67-75.

11. Royal Anthropological Institute, *Notes and Queries in Anthropology*, 6th edition (London: Routledge and Kegan Paul, 1951), pp. 70-71. Presumably the third class of compound family may include those based on the remarriage of divorced parents.

12. See Report of Royal Commission on the West Indies, 1938; Dom Basil Matthews, *The Crisis in the West Indian Family*, and T. S. Simey, *Welfare and Planning in the West Indies;* Mary Proudfoot, *Britain and the United States in the Caribbean* (London: Faber and Faber, 1954).

13. See works by M. J. Herskovits, T. S. Simey, Fernando Henriques, and Dom Basil Matthews already cited. Also Fernando Henriques, *Family and Colour in Jamaica* (London: Eyre and Spottiswoode, 1953), and in this context, E. Franklin Frazier, *The Negro Family in the U. S. A.* (Chicago: University of Chicago Press, 1939).

14. Edith Clarke, *My Mother Who Fathered Me*, pp. 30-31, 113-40.

Chapter 2

1. *West Indian Census 1946* (Kingston: Government Printer), Part H, p. 1, Table 1; Part G, p. 49, Table 43.

2. *West Indian Census 1946*, Part B, p. 26, Table 39.

3. I am grateful to Mr. F. A. Phillips, then District Officer of Carriacou, for providing me with assistant teachers for this survey, and for many other facilities.

4. M. G. Smith, "The Transformation of Land Rights by Transmission in Carriacou," *Social and Economic Studies*, V, No. 2 (Mona, Jamaica: Institute of Social and Economic Research, University College of the West Indies, 1956), 116, Table 2.

5. I. Schapera, "Marriage of Near Kin among the Tswana," *Africa*, XXVII, No. 2 (1957), 154, and n. 2.

6. R. T. Smith, *The Negro Family in British Guiana* (London: Routledge and Kegan Paul, 1956), pp. 108-15, 221-24. "The Family in the Caribbean," in *Caribbean Studies: A Symposium*, ed. Vera Rubin (Jamaica: Institute of Social and Economic Research, University College of the West Indies, 1957). (Reprinted, Seattle: University of Washington Press, 1960.)

Chapter 3

1. *Grenada Handbook and Directory, 1946* (Grenada: Government Offices), p. 392.

2. *Ibid.*, pp. 107-9.

## Chapter 4
1. These status judgments are based on my detailed analysis of social stratification in Grenada which will be published in due course.

## Chapter 5
1. M. G. Smith, *Labour Supply in Rural Jamaica* (Kingston, Jamaica: Government Printer, 1956), p. 31, Table 6. For other aspects of this study, see M. G. Smith, "Community Organization in Rural Jamaica, " *Social and Economic Studies*, V, 3 (Mona, Jamaica: Institute of Social and Economic Research, University College of the West Indies, 1956); and M. G. Smith and G. J. Kruijer, *A Sociological Manual for Extension Workers in the Caribbean*, (Caribbean Affairs Series [Trinidad: Extra-Mural Department, University College of the West Indies, 1957]), pp. 13-113, especially pp. 84-95.

## Chapter 6
1. See W. F. Maunder, "The New Jamaican Emigration, " *Social and Economic Studies*, IV, No. 1 (Mona, Jamaica: Institute of Social and Economic Research, University College of the West Indies); also Clarence Senior and D. R. Manley, *A Report on Jamaican Migration to Great Britain* (Kingston: Government Printer, 1955); also G. W. Roberts and D. O. Mills, "A Study of External Migration Affecting Jamaica, 1953-1955." Supplement to *Social and Economic Studies*, VII, No. 2 (Mona, Jamaica: Institute of Social and Economic Research, University College of the West Indies, 1958).
2. Edith Clarke, *My Mother Who Fathered Me* (London: Allen and Unwin, 1957); also M. G. Smith and G. J. Kruijer, *A Sociological Manual for Extension Workers in the Caribbean*, (Caribbean Affairs Series [Trinidad: Extra-Mural Department, University College of the West Indies, 1957]).
3. *Report on a Sample Survey of the Population of Jamaica, October-November, 1953* (Kingston, Jamaica: Government Printer, Department of Statistics, 1957). See Tables 14 and 18, pp. 31-32, 40.

## Chapter 7
1. Edith Clarke, *My Mother Who Fathered Me* (London: Allen and Unwin, 1957), pp. 22-28.
2. See Yehudi Cohen, "Structure and Function: Family Organi-

zation and Socialization in a Jamaican Community," *American Anthropologist*, Vol. LVIII, No. 4 (1956); Fernando Henriques, "West Indian Family Organization," *Caribbean Quarterly*, II, No. 1 (1952), 16-24; Henriques, *Family and Colour in Jamaica* (London: Eyre and Spottiswoode, 1953); M. J. Herskovits, *The Myth of the Negro Past* (Harper and Bros., New York, 1941); Mary Proudfoot, *Britain and the United States in the Caribbean* (London: Faber and Faber, 1954); T. S. Simey, *Welfare and Planning in the West Indies* (London: Oxford University Press, 1946): Dom Basil Matthews, *The Crisis in the West Indian Family* (Port of Spain, Trinidad: University College of the West Indies, Extra-Mural Department, 1953).

3. Franklin Frazier, *The Negro Family in the U. S. A.* (Chicago: University of Chicago Press, 1939).

4. R. T. Smith, *The Negro Family in British Guiana* (London: Routledge and Kegan Paul, 1956); Smith, "The Family in the Caribbean," in *Caribbean Studies: A Symposium*, ed. Vera Rubin (Jamaica: Institute of Social and Economic Research, University College of the West Indies, 1957). Reprinted, Seattle: University of Washington Press, 1960.

5. M. G. Smith, "The Hausa System of Social Status," *Africa*, Vol. XXIX, No. 3 (1959).

6. Edith Clarke, *My Mother Who Fathered Me;* also G. E. Cumper, "The Jamaican Family: Village and Estate." *Social and Economic Studies*, Vol. VII, No. 1 (Mona, Jamaica: Institute of Social and Economic Research, University College of the West Indies, 1958).

7. R. T. Smith, *The Negro Family in British Guiana* (London: Routledge and Kegan Paul, 1956). "Common residence is a basic criterion of an effective conjugal tie" (p. 110). "There is no difference in the customary rights and duties of the couple towards one another, whether they are married or not. . . . There is of course absolutely no change in the social position of the man after he is married, nor is there any real change in the rights, duties and obligations involved in the relationship of the conjugal pair" (pp. 178-79). "A common-law marriage does not exist, according to our definition, unless the couple actually live together. . . . Where a woman lives with her parents and has several children for a man with whom she has never lived, she is not in a common-law union, though she may have a quite definite semi-conjugal relationship with the man" (pp. 184-85). It is worth pointing out that women and their issue born of extraresidential unions represent 25 per cent, 20. 2 per cent, and 21 per cent of the total dependent population of units whose female heads include the children's maternal grandmothers, in the samples studied by Dr. Smith at August Town, Perseverance,

and Better Hope in British Guiana. See Table IXa, p. 101.

8. *Ibid.*, p. 185.

9. *Ibid.*, p. 179.

10. Edith Clarke, *My Mother Who Fathered Me,* pp. 29, 73-122.

11. R. T. Smith, *The Negro Family in British Guiana.* "The couple may have had children in common already, in which case the formation of a household group had in some senses been anticipated with the birth of their first child. On the other hand, they may have no children when they set up house, but the assumption is that they will have children eventually, and, from an analytical point of view, one might say that a household group in the real sense of the term has not come into being until this condition has been met. In practice, we find very few couples living together without children, unless the children have grown up and dispersed, and a couple who do not produce offspring of their own often adopt children" (p. 108). "There is a tendency for children to be born whilst she is still in her parents' home and before she has established a real conjugal relationship, and this must be regarded as an important feature of the system" (p. 109).

Regarding the treatment of single-person households, see p. 97: "For all three villages certain cases have been excluded, including those where a man or woman lives completely alone."

As regards the developmental cycle, see pp. 111-12: "It is in the stage of the early development of the household group that we get the greatest incidence of occurrence of the nuclear family as the dwelling group. . . . Nearly every household group goes through the stage of being a nuclear family group at some time during its existence. . . ."

Also p. 257: "We have shown quite conclusively that the normal type of domestic unit in British Guiana comes into being as a result of a man and a woman entering a conjugal union of some kind, and that the elementary or nuclear family is the normal type of co-residential unit, particularly at that stage of development where the children are young. The variations from this norm arise as a result of the strength of the mother-child relationship and the relative weakness of the conjugal bond, and they generally result in the emergence of the typically solitary unit of a woman with her daughters and their children."

In our samples, rather more than a third and often nearly one half of those children who do not live with both parents or with their fathers live away from their mothers also. See Table 17.

12. R. T. Smith, "The Family in the Caribbean," pp. 70-71.

Chapter 8

1. M. G. Smith, Kinship and Community in Carriacou. Unpublished MS.

2. T. S. Simey, *Welfare and Planning in the West Indies* (London: Oxford University Press, 1946); Fernando Henriques, *Family and Colour in Jamaica* (London: Eyre and Spottiswoode), 1953, pp. 104-5; Edith Clarke, *My Mother Who Fathered Me* (London: Allen and Unwin, 1957). R. T. Smith, *The Negro Family in British Guiana* (London: Routledge and Kegan Paul, 1956), pp. 97 *et passim*.

3. Dom Basil Matthews, *The Crisis in the West Indian Family* (Port of Spain, Trinidad: University College of the West Indies, Extra-Mural Department, 1953).

4. M. G. Smith, *The Economy of Hausa Communities of Zaria* (London: H. M. Stationery Office, 1955); M. F. Smith, *Baba of Karo: A Woman of the Muslim Hausa* (London: Faber and Faber, 1955). For a summary account of Hausa society, see the Introduction to *Baba of Karo;* for details of Hausa domestic and mating organization, see *Economy of Hausa Communities*, pp. 19-40, 61-64.

5. M. G. Smith, *The Economy of Hausa Communities of Zaria*, p. 25, Table 8.

6. See M. F. Smith, *Baba of Karo*, for an account of Hausa slave settlements. For a comparison of Hausa and West Indian slavery, see M. G. Smith, "Slavery and Emancipation in Two Societies," *Social and Economic Studies,* Vol. III, Nos. 3, 4 (Mona, Jamaica: Institute of Social and Economic Research, College of the West Indies, 1954).

7. Rattray Taylor, *Sex in History* (London: Thames and Hudson, 1953).

8. *St. George's Chronicle*, May 16, 1868. St. George's, Grenada, British West Indies.

9. See for example Rev. R. Bicknell, *The West Indies as They Are* (London; 1825); Mrs. Carmichael, *Domestic Manners and Social Conditions of the White, Coloured and Negro Populations of the West Indies* (2 vols., London: 1833); M. G. Lewis, *Journal of a Residence among the Negroes of the West Indies* (London: 1845); J. Stewart, *A New View of Jamaica* (Edinburgh: 1823). For a summary account of West Indian slave society, see M. G. Smith, "Some Aspects of Social Structure in the British Caribbean about 1820, " *Social and Economic Studies*, I, No. 4 (Mona, Jamaica: Institute of Social and Economic Research, University College of the West Indies, 1953) 55-80.

10. *St. George's Chronicle*, August 24, 1833, p. 273.

11. For an account of these developments in Jamaica, see M.

G. Smith, "Slavery and Emancipation in Two Societies."

12. Philip D. Curtin, *The Two Jamaicas* (Cambridge, Mass.: Harvard University Press, 1955).

13. W. G. Sewell, *The Ordeal of Free Labour in the British West Indies* (New York: Harpers, 1861): E. B. Underhill, *The West Indies* (London: Jackson, Walford and Hodder, 1862); A. V. Long, *Jamaica and the New Order, 1827-1847* (Mona, Jamaica: Institute for Social and Economic Research, University College of the West Indies, 1956): see Appendix D, p. 99, for records of marriages in three parishes.

# Bibliography

Bicknell, Rev. R. *The West Indies as They Are*. London, 1825.

Carmichael, Mrs. *Domestic Manners and Social Conditions of the White, Coloured and Negro Populations of the West Indies*. London, 1833.

Clarke, Edith. *My Mother Who Fathered Me*. London: Allen and Unwin, 1957.

Cohen, Yehudi. "Structure and Function: Family Organization and Socialization in a Jamaican Community," *American Anthropologist,* Vol. LVIII, No. 4 (1956).

Cumper, George E. "The Jamaican Family: Village and Estate," *Social and Economic Studies,* Vol. VII, No. 2. Mona, Jamaica: Institute of Social and Economic Research, University College of the West Indies, 1958.

Curtin, Philip D. *The Two Jamaicas*. Cambridge, Mass.: Harvard University Press, 1955.

Frazier, E. Franklin. *The Negro Family in the U.S.A.* Chicago: University of Chicago Press, 1939.

*Grenada Handbook and Directory, 1946.* Grenada: Government Offices, 1946.

Henriques, Fernando. "West Indian Family Organization," *Caribbean Quarterly,* II, No. 1 (1952), 16-24.

————. *Family and Colour in Jamaica*. London: Eyre and Spottiswoode, 1953.

Herskovits, M. J. *The Myth of the Negro Past*. New York: Harper and Bros., 1941.

Lewis, M. G. *Journal of a Residence among the Negroes of the West Indies.* London: 1845.

Long, A. V. *Jamaica and the New Order, 1827-1847.* Mona, Jamaica: University College of the West Indies, 1956.

Matthews, Dom Basil. *The Crisis in the West Indian Family.* Trinidad: Extra-Mural Department, University College of the West Indies, 1953.

Maunder, W. F. "The New Jamaican Emigration," *Social and Economic Studies,* Vol. VI, No. 1. Mona, Jamaica: University College of the West Indies, 1955.

*Notes and Queries in Anthropology.* (6th ed.) Royal Anthropological Institute. London: Routledge and Kegan Paul, Ltd., 1951.

Proudfoot, Mary. *Britain and the United States in the Caribbean.* London: Faber and Faber, 1954.

*Report on a Sample Survey of the Population of Jamaica, October-November, 1953.* Department of Statistics. Mona, Jamaica: Government Printer, 1957.

Roberts, G. W., and D. O. Mills. "A Study of External Migration Affecting Jamaica, 1953-1955," Supplement to *Social and Economic Studies,* Vol. VII, No. 2. Mona, Jamaica: Institute of Social and Economic Research, University College of the West Indies, 1958.

*St. George's Chronicle.* (August 24, 1833), p. 273.

Schapera, I. "Marriage of Near Kin among the Tswana," *Africa,* Vol. XXVII, No. 2 (1957).

Senior, Clarence and D. R. Manley. *A Report on Jamaican Migration to Great Britain.* Kingston: Government Printer, 1955.

Sewell, W. G. *The Ordeal of Free Labour in the British West Indies.* New York: Harper and Bros., 1861.

Simey, T. S. *Welfare and Planning in the West Indies.* Oxford: Clarendon Press, 1946.

Smith, M. F. *Baba of Karo: A Woman of the Muslim Hausa.* London: Faber and Faber, 1955.

Smith, M. G. "Some Aspects of Social Structure in the British Caribbean about 1820," *Social and Economic Studies,* Vol. I, No. 4. Mona, Jamaica: Institute of Social and Economic Research, University College of the West Indies, 1953.

————. "Slavery and Emancipation in Two Societies," *Social and Economic Studies,* Vol. III, No. 3. Mona, Jamaica: Institute of Social and Economic Research, University College of the West Indies, 1954.

————. *The Economy of Hausa Communities of Zaria.* London: H. M. Stationery Office, 1955.

————. "Community Organization in Rural Jamaica," *Social and Economic Studies,* Vol. V, No. 3. Mona, Jamaica: Institute of Social and Economic Research, University College of the West Indies, 1956.

————. *Labour Supply in Rural Jamaica.* Kingston, Jamaica: Government Printer, 1956.

————. "The Transformation of Land Rights by Transmission in Carricou," *Social and Economic Studies,* V, No. 2. Mona, Jamaica: Institute of Social and Economic Research, University College of the West Indies, 1956.

————. "The Hausa System of Social Status," *Africa,* Vol. XXIX, No. 3 (1959).

————. Kinship and Community in Carricou. Unpublished MS.

————, and G. J. Kruijer. *A Sociological Manual for Extension Workers in the Caribbean.* (Caribbean Affairs Series.) Trinidad: Extra-Mural Department, University College of the West Indies, 1957.

Smith, R. T. *The Negro Family in British Guiana.* London: Routledge and Kegan Paul, Ltd., 1956.

————. "The Family in the Caribbean," in *Caribbean Studies: A Symposium,* ed. Vera Rubin. Mona, Jamaica: Institute of Social and Economic Research, University College of the West Indies, 1957. Reprinted, Seattle: University of Washington Press (1960).

Stewart, J. *A New View of Jamaica.* Edinburgh, 1823.

Taylor, Rattray. *Sex in History.* London: Thames and Hudson, 1953.

Underhill, E. B. *The West Indies.* London: Jackson, Walford and Hodder, 1862.

*West Indian Census 1946.* Kingston, Jamaica: Government Printer, 1946.

# Index

307